# Race for Education

D0088300

Following the end of apartheid in 1994, the ANC government placed education at the centre of its plans to build a nonracial and more equitable society. Yet, by the 2010s a wave of student protests voiced demands for decolonised and affordable education. By following families and schools in Durban for nearly a decade, Mark Hunter sheds new light on South Africa's political transition and the global phenomenon of education marketisation. He rejects simple descriptions of the country's move from 'race to class apartheid' and reveals how 'white' phenotypic traits like skin colour retain value in the schooling system even as the multiracial middle class embraces prestigious linguistic and embodied practices the book calls 'white tone'. By illuminating the actions and choices of both white and black parents, Hunter provides a unique view on race, class, and gender in a country emerging from a notorious system of institutionalised racism.

MARK HUNTER is Associate Professor of Human Geography at the University of Toronto Scarborough. His research methods combine ethnographic, historical, and geographical techniques and his first book, *Love in the Time of AIDS: Inequality, Gender, and Rights in South Africa*, won the 2010 Amaury Talbot Prize and the 2010 C. Wright Mills Award.

# THE INTERNATIONAL AFRICAN LIBRARY

*General Editors*

LESLIE BANK, *Human Sciences Research Council, South Africa*
HARRI ENGLUND, *University of Cambridge*
ADELINE MASQUELIER, *Tulane University, Louisiana*
BENJAMIN SOARES, *University of Florida, Gainesville*

The International African Library is a major monograph series from the International African Institute. Theoretically informed ethnographies, and studies of social relations 'on the ground' which are sensitive to local cultural forms, have long been central to the Institute's publications programme. The IAL maintains this strength and extends it into new areas of contemporary concern, both practical and intellectual. It includes works focused on the linkages between local, national and global levels of society; writings on political economy and power; studies at the interface of the socio-cultural and the environmental; analyses of the roles of religion, cosmology and ritual in social organisation; and historical studies, especially those of a social, cultural or interdisciplinary character.

*For a list of titles published in the series, please see the end of the book.*

# Race for Education

*Gender, White Tone, and Schooling in South Africa*

Mark Hunter

*University of Toronto*

International African Institute, London

*and*

CAMBRIDGE
UNIVERSITY PRESS

# CAMBRIDGE
## UNIVERSITY PRESS

University Printing House, Cambridge CB2 8BS, United Kingdom

One Liberty Plaza, 20th Floor, New York, NY 10006, USA

477 Williamstown Road, Port Melbourne, VIC 3207, Australia

314-321, 3rd Floor, Plot 3, Splendor Forum, Jasola District Centre, New Delhi - 110025, India

79 Anson Road, #06-04/06, Singapore 079906

Cambridge University Press is part of the University of Cambridge.

It furthers the University's mission by disseminating knowledge in the pursuit of education, learning and research at the highest international levels of excellence.

www.cambridge.org
Information on this title: www.cambridge.org/9781108727631
DOI: 10.1017/9781108635189

© Mark Hunter 2019

This publication is in copyright. Subject to statutory exception and to the provisions of relevant collective licensing agreements, no reproduction of any part may take place without the written permission of Cambridge University Press.

First published 2019

*A catalogue record for this publication is available from the British Library*

*Library of Congress Cataloging in Publication data*
Names: Hunter, Mark, 1971- author.
Title: Race for education : gender, white tone, and schooling in
    South Africa / Mark Hunter.
Description: Cambridge ; New York, NY : Cambridge University Press, 2019. |
    Series: International African library ; 60 | Includes bibliographical
    references and index.
Identifiers: LCCN 2018040448 | ISBN 9781108480529 (hardback : alk. paper)
    | ISBN 9781108727631 (pbk. : alk. paper)
Subjects: LCSH: Discrimination in education–South Africa. | Education–South
    Africa–History. | Educational equalization–South Africa.
Classification: LCC LC212.3.S6 H86 2019 | DDC 379.2/6096–dc23
LC record available at https://lccn.loc.gov/2018040448

ISBN  978-1-108-48052-9  Hardback
ISBN  978-1-108-72763-1  Paperback

Cambridge University Press has no responsibility for the persistence or accuracy of URLs for external or third-party internet websites referred to in this publication, and does not guarantee that any content on such websites is, or will remain, accurate or appropriate.

For Atiqa and Leila, again

# Contents

# Figures

# Maps

# Tables

# Preface and acknowledgements

*Race for Education* is based in Durban, a city in which I feel very much at home, although the book is influenced by politics that cross many settings. In 2009 when I began research, the media was full of stories criticising South Africa's dismal school-leaving ('matric') pass rate. In 2015, focus dramatically shifted, however, when #RhodesMustFall and #FeesMustFall activists based at universities forcefully demanded affordable and decolonised education. Months later, 13-year-old Zulaikha Patel became a global icon of defiance when she challenged a formerly white school by refusing to cut her Afro-textured hair. As I wrapped up the book in 2017, the government announced a policy of free higher education for the poor – even though primary and secondary schools charged ever-rising fees.

My other lives in Canada and Morocco convinced me that forces shaping South Africa were not exceptional. At the University of Toronto's Scarborough campus, where I have taught for the past 12 years, student numbers have doubled, with many learners being children of first-generation immigrants to Canada. Faculty and students work hard, but rising fees mean that the majority of learners leave with large debts. Some graduates find high-paying jobs, whereas 'qualification inflation' devalues the degree for many others. Meanwhile, in 2015, aspects of Canada's colonial structuring of education were exposed when the Truth and Reconciliation Commission's report described the government's past policy of using residential schools to forcefully assimilate indigenous peoples as 'cultural genocide'.

The third place where I stay every year, Morocco, is a country where youth unemployment robs young people of a future, and where there has been a rapid rise of prestigious private French, and now increasingly English, schools for a middle class willing to pay to avoid public schooling.

Thus, if my privileged movements are in any way representative, the questions this book considers – an increased amount of education in the context of marketised systems and racially toned hierarchies of prestige – apply across the globe.

In researching these themes in South Africa, I need to start by thanking all the teachers and families who spoke with me, without whom there would be no book. I also owe a great debt to research assistants Sibongile Buthelezi, Lindiwe Cele, Margaret du Plessis, and Byron Louw. Michela du Sart and Jordan Raghunandan drew the maps, and Beyhan Farhadi assisted with the referencing.

In Durban, Jeff Guy's 2014 death was such a sad loss. His passion for painstaking empirical work and the region's history was unparalleled; he had an unconditional intolerance for the high-output, low-research trend in modern academia. In Durban circles, I have also long benefited from the support of David Szanton and former PhD supervisor Gillian Hart; from Glen Robbins' generosity in sharing ideas and sources; from overlapping curiosities with economist Dori Posel; and from friendships with Bill Freund and Vishnu Padayachee (since my master's degree days in Durban).

Extremely helpful readers of part or all of an early version of this book were Mike Ekers, Kira Erwin, Bill Freund, Atiqa Hachimi, Gillian Hart, Bridget Kenny, Tania Li, Thembisa Waetjen, and two anonymous readers for the press. Graduate students from my class on race and class put forward helpful suggestions, and I learned much from the collegiality of friends at Toronto's vibrant and critical Geography Departments. I am lucky to share the thriving Scarborough Department with Ahmed Allahwala, Glenn Brauen, Michelle Buckley, Sue Bunce, Mike Ekers, Steven Farber, Thembela Kepe, Ken MacDonald, John Miron, Sharlene Mollett, Rajyashree Reddy, and Andre Sorensen. Generous funding was provided by the Social Science and Humanities Research Council.

Many South Africanists not already mentioned have invited me to present my work, commented on drafts, offered friendship, or simply talked about their own or their children's experiences of schooling. I would like to thank Richard Ballard, Debby Bonnin, Keith Breckenridge, Catherine Burns, Sharad Chari, Owen Crankshaw, Julia de Kadt, Edith Dempster, Sarah Emily Duff, Sibusisiwe Nombuso Dlamini, Marijka du Doit, Kira Erwin, Aslam Fataar, Andy Gibbs, Tim Gibbs, Meghan Healy-Clancy, Vashna Jagarnath, Peter Kallaway, Jill Kelly, Grace Khunou, Daniel Magaziner, Monique Marks, Achille Mbembe, Thenjiwe Meyiwa, Bheki ka Mncube, David Moore, Elena Moore, Rob Morrell, Nicoli Nattrass, Sarah Nuttall, Julie Parle, Sue Parnell, Richard Pithouse, Deborah Posel, Ben Roberts, Jenny Robinson, Melanie Samson, Dianne Scott, Jeremy Seekings, Nafisa Essop Sheik, Stephen Sparks, Cathy Sutherland, Lynn Thomas, Chris Webb, Samantha Willan, and Jochen Zeller.

I thank the Department of Education and DataFirst for providing access to schooling data. Archivists to acknowledge particularly are Neli Summers at Killie Campbell Africana Library, Zeeneth Ishmail at

Independent Newspapers, Rishi Singh and Unnay Narrine at the Durban Archives, and Eshara Singh at Bessie Head Library.

At the International African Institute, Stephanie Kitchen has been the consummate professional, a strong and wise supporter of African scholarship. Harri Englund provided helpful and positive feedback. At Cambridge University Press, I am grateful for the skilled presence of Maria Marsh, Cassi Roberts, and Abigail Walkington. Judith Forshaw copyedited the book with patience and great expertise. Based in Toronto, Celia Braves is a justly celebrated indexer. I thank artist Lexi Bella as well as Zulaikha Patel and her mother for permission to use the front cover image.

My wife, Atiqa Hachimi, an Arabic sociolinguist, has long educated me about language, a big theme in this book, and we also co-wrote an article on telephone call centres. Atiqa is my best friend and number one supporter, and her love took me through the tough times of research and writing. At the centre of my world too, and an accomplice in this journey through schooling, is Leila, our now ten-year-old daughter. In fact, since I started research on this book, she has studied in eight different schools in Canada, Morocco, and South Africa, always embracing them with a passion to learn and to make new friends. Leila, you know this: we love you and are proud of you.

# 1    Introduction

One typically humid day in 2013, two friends, Wandile and David, sit together chatting in a primary school in Durban's Bluff suburb. This scene would have been unheard of four decades earlier because laws would have forced Wandile to attend an 'African' school and David a 'white' school.

An air of anticipation surrounds the two learners because they are in the final year of the school. Wandile's and David's families, both middle class, have recently sent off applications to a prestigious senior primary school located in the city's Berea suburb.

Yet David is called for an interview; Wandile is not. When it becomes clear that this pattern is repeated across the classroom, black parents begin to talk. Wandile's mother, Mrs Ngcobo, phones the school to complain. 'I said it straight that I have a feeling that you prefer whites,' she recalls, 'I think that is why they all of a sudden became soft and . . . it got me an interview and got me a space.' However, concerned about possible recriminations against her child, she eventually enrols her son into a private school in Berea.

From a different perspective, a similar story played out at a Bluff preschool attended by my then two-year-old daughter in 2010. Its parents had voted in the early 1990s to desegregate the school, and more than a dozen minibus taxis now brought black learners with the financial means from distant apartheid townships. The school's principal was angry, however, that one Berea school was aggressively 'poaching' white students from the Bluff. 'He fishes for white children,' she said of the male principal. 'He comes to the Bluff to wine and dine preschool principals to encourage them to direct whites to his primary school.' Whereas in 2003 this 'poaching' Berea school had twice as many black African as white students, by 2010 it had four times as many white students.[1]

These two vignettes help explain why education became so central to young people's growing impatience with life after apartheid. In its 1994 election manifesto, Nelson Mandela's African National Congress (ANC) pledged to make education a priority in building a

1

nonracial society. It would introduce a single free schooling system to replace the racially divided apartheid system and a new curriculum to promote humane ideals.[2]

However, in 2015, thousands of students took to the streets in what Achille Mbembe termed the country's 'Fanonian moment' – referring to Frantz Fanon's famous teachings on colonial racism.[3] The #Rhodes-MustFall and #FeesMustFall movements demanded free higher education, the decolonisation of curricula, and the removal of symbols of colonialism beginning with the statue of famous colonialist Cecil John Rhodes from the University of Cape Town. Protests were led by the 'born free' generation (those born after the fall of apartheid), 'increasingly disillusioned by and ... push[ing] back against the notion of the Rainbow Nation'.[4] Meanwhile, black high-school students remonstrated against teachers' censuring of Afro-textured hair and derision of African languages.[5]

Yet if the racist actions of the two Berea schools with which I opened fit squarely with students' recent dissent, we must also note some puzzles. While both schools showed bias towards enrolling white students, they did recruit some better-off black students and also attracted a considerable number of Afrikaans-speaking learners who left Afrikaans schools that had much whiter student bodies. Moreover, the principal of the English-medium school my daughter attended remembers being shocked when parents in one of the city's most politically conservative suburbs voted so strongly in favour of desegregation. How do we understand the importance of race to educational events but also its explanatory limits?

### Follow the children

This book adds to existing research exposing continued inequalities in South Africa's education facilities and exam results. However, it rethinks South Africa's political transition by revealing how the prestige of whiteness, or what it calls 'white tone', became reformulated in the everyday workings of a marketised education system. It shows how 'white' phenotypic traits retain value in society even if some better-off 'black' people can now buy prestigious cultural dispositions.

This approach allows it to shed new light on questions that refuse to go away in South Africa: does society remain fundamentally structured by race, or is the country moving towards a kind of class apartheid? South Africa has long been a laboratory for these discussions because of its sizeable mining and manufacturing economy and extreme system of institutionalised racial segregation. The 'race–class debate' that simmered in the 1970s and 1980s questioned whether apartheid was driven by racist ideologies or by capitalists' need for cheap labour. Some scholars sought to theorise how race and class 'articulated' with each other, but limited empirical work undergirded this approach, especially in relation to education and gender.[6] Labour, and particularly male labour, has been the traditional home of race–class debates around the world.[7]

In the political realm, South Africa's race–class debates fed into the 'two-stage theory': the belief that the anti-apartheid movement should achieve first national liberation then socialism. The first stage, Nelson Mandela's dramatic move from prisoner to president and the ending of minority white rule in 1994, was decisive. The second demanded an improvement in the economic lives of the black majority.

In the post-apartheid period, like magnets that could not be switched off, race and class continued to pull explanations towards one of two poles. Some on the left argued that privilege had merely become deracialised. Neoliberal policies, it was said, drove a shift from race to 'class apartheid'.[8] Others, however, insisted that the emphasis on reconciliation and nation building meant that racial fault lines – for instance on land ownership – were never adequately addressed.

This book refuses to separate race and class and also insists on the necessity of foregrounding gender. It builds on David Goldberg's analysis of 'racial neoliberalism' that locates South Africa, once again, as a paradigmatic case.[9] Crucially, this approach conceives of race as *formative* of what came to be called neoliberalism – broadly, the belief that the market and not the state should play the fundamental role in driving the economy. This contrasts with David Harvey's influential analysis of neoliberalism as a class project, as well as Wendy Brown's recent account of neoliberalism as a governing rationality 'extending a specific formulation of economic values ... to every dimension of human life'.[10]

*Race for Education* considers these questions through a gendered and schooling-focused window. It takes a journey through macho rugby matches, single-sex schooling culture, and family obligations now labelled as the 'black tax'. If political economists like to 'follow the money' to understand the economic structure of society, this ethnography 'follows the children' to show the 'routine and insidious' actions at work.[11] I show how schooling *marketisation* – a concept I prefer to 'neoliberalism' – does not flatten racialised meanings and practices but is reworking them. By marketisation, I follow Tikly and Mabogoane's description: children's increased daily movement for schools, public schools' charging of fees, schools' increased competition for desirable students, and the moderate growth in private schools.[12] Today, public schools can charge fees of up to 50,000 rand a year (US$4,500 or £3,500), and one Johannesburg study found that only 18 per cent of schoolchildren attend their local school.[13]

## The arguments

This book rejects the view that apartheid simply transmuted into 'class apartheid' or 'racial neoliberalism' by describing and analysing changing spatio-temporal processes in the city of Durban. The arc of the study begins in the 1950s, when apartheid's social engineers established one of the most – perhaps *the* most – racially and spatially planned education systems in the world. The vision of apartheid planners was of local schools for local populations in racially (but, for whites, also class) defined suburbs. I follow scholars in labelling this period of segregation one of *racial modernism*.[14]

However, in the 1970s, class divisions increased in society, and, from 1976, white private schools began to admit a tiny number of black students. I use the term *marketised assimilation* to draw attention to what I consider to be the first period of schooling desegregation (roughly from 1976 to the late 1990s). During this time, a limited number of better-off black children with an 'ability to be assimilated' (in the words of one school) were admitted into white (and later Coloured and Indian) schools. Contrary to the belief that the ending of apartheid represented a rupture from what came before it, I stress continuities between early desegregation from the 1970s and the desegregation of white public schools in the 1990s.

This analysis of the initial desegregation period allows me to show that, from the late 1990s and 2000s, competition among schools and among parents intensified and resulted in what I call the *racialised market*. Cultural signals of whiteness – a school's victory on the rugby field, its rejection of 'black hair', its success at imparting a 'white accent' – became key grounds on which formerly white schools fought to retain prestige, justify high fees, and equip learners for the labour market.

Thus, this book shows that marketisation does not just advantage better-off families; it reconstitutes and works through racialised and gendered differences. A central aim of this book is to show how the marketised schooling system feeds from and reconstitutes the valuing of certain phenotypic traits and racial-cultural attributes.

The title of this book, *Race for Education*, signals its attention to race, specifically the question of why race has not diminished in significance when the South African constitution actively promotes nonracialism. Of course, nonracialism is itself a contested term, some people equating it to colour-blindness, others seeing its realisation in multiculturalism (hence the *Rainbow* Nation), and others viewing it as inseparable from anti-racism.[15]

While this book considers the remaking of 'race', it is, of course, by no means a comprehensive account. For instance, I don't consider how apartheid's four racial categories are kept alive in laws that seek to redress past injustices.[16] I don't unpack race's deployment in the public sphere, for instance when one government minister denounced Mmusi Maimane, the first black leader of the Democratic Alliance party, as 'using a black face to protect the interests of the white minority'.[17] Acts of racial violence in society are also not studied. In 2016, a Facebook post by white realtor Penny Sparrow went viral when she compared black South African beachgoers to 'monkeys'; later that year a video circulated showing two white farmers pushing a black man into a coffin and threatening to bury him alive.[18] My primary focus is on the hidden logics at work in the education system.

A second meaning of the 'race for education' is the '*rush* for education'. A different shade of the following question resonates in many settings across the world: what does mass education mean when large numbers of people are struggling to find work? In South Africa, a huge rise in post-primary education from the 1970s was accompanied not by economic growth (as predicted by theorists of 'human capital') but by unemployment: the current jobless rate remains above 40 per cent.[19] Public education is a vital road to social equity but its benefits are limited if some learners buy their way into the best schools and go on to secure scarce work.

Focusing on another implied meaning of the term 'race' – *movement* – also helps us consider in new light another key paradox: why have government interventions to redistribute educational expenditure not, apparently, improved the quality of the education system? While the enrolment rate for grades 1–7 increased to an impressive 98 per cent, the government itself noted in 2011 that: 'Apart from a small minority of black children who attend former white schools and a small minority of schools performing well in largely black areas, the quality of public education remains poor.'[20] In spite of education spending being around 6 per cent of gross domestic product (GDP), South African schools were ranked bottom in maths and science tests out of 50 countries, and the country remains one of the (or perhaps *the*) most unequal in the world.[21]

By following the movement of children, I show a musical chairs-like process, whereby better-off children tend to travel to more prestigious schools and leave empty desks that need to be filled by other learners. Despite, and indeed because of, the state's efforts to create free schools for the poor, families' resources are drawn up the system – ending up ironically in formerly white schools in particular. Thus, post-apartheid reforms have led to the partial deracialisation of privilege but not to a fundamental reduction in inequality and not to the fundamental 'de-whitening' of the grammar of privilege. In short, the state's redirection of money towards poorer schools has been simply too little.

This study, as should now be clear, considers *material* and *symbolic* inequalities in relation to one another. And no book pioneered this approach better in the colonial world than Frantz Fanon's *The Wretched of the Earth*.[22] Written in 1961, the study is a damning critique not only of colonialism but of the 'national bourgeoisies' who overthrew colonial rule but upheld capitalism through preserving the prestige of whiteness.

Fanon's writings on the experiences of racism and the failings of postcolonial elites gained huge popularity in South Africa in the 2010s. But the details of how exactly whiteness is entrenched in the country's political economy has received less attention. *Race for Education* traces how racialised principles such as branding have infiltrated the very heart of public services and can be used to justify the 'poaching' of certain students. It shows how shack dwellers, whose numbers have grown after apartheid, are excluded from the best schools because they are both poor *and* black.

As well as families (introduced later) and schools, a third related institution this book considers – again from both material and symbolic perspectives – is the labour market. In 1994, whites formed only 11 per cent of the population but their average wages were more than five times higher than those of black Africans.[23] Today, unemployment rates are 40 per cent and 8 per cent among black Africans and whites respectively.[24] Yet it is also significant that numerically more black African than white people now work in high-skilled, high-income jobs.[25]

If the middle class is now predominantly black, this does not mean that race is no longer important in the world of work. Factory jobs have given way to service work, and many employers see English – especially 'white English' attained at a formerly white school – as both a 'skill' and a quality useful in screening multiple applicants. A school's former racial classification therefore indicates not just its facilities and exam results but its ability to bestow dispositions valued by employers.

Durban, the country's third largest city, is known for its subtropical climate, large port, beaches that attract tourists all year round, and, until quite recently, its large industrial economy. From 2009 to 2017 I collected archival documents, made ethnographic observations, undertook more than 500 interviews, and collected and analysed quantitative data on schools and residential areas. I studied schools in three areas of the city and families in the first two. To the south of the city is the township of **Umlazi**, built in the 1960s for black isiZulu-speaking Africans removed from central urban areas; Umlazi contains 84 public schools. The second research area is the 'rough and tough' **Bluff**, a formerly white suburb built for English and Afrikaans speakers close to the southern industrial basin; this contains ten public schools. And the third is the **upper-Berea ridge**, the heartland of 'traditional' white schools that modelled themselves on British private schools; this area is historically English-speaking and contains ten public schools. I pay

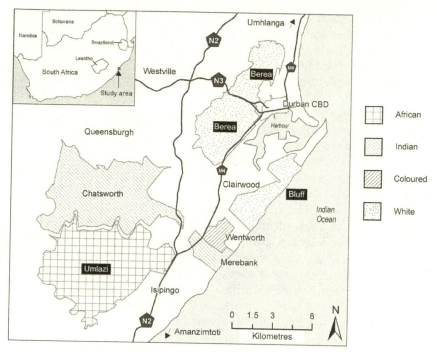

Map 1.1 Durban's racial zoned residential areas in the apartheid period.

specific attention to black children leaving Umlazi for outside schools and white Bluff residents moving into Berea's schools (see Map 1.1).

### Thinking through race, class, and gender to understand schooling

This section starts with some general points and vignettes that illuminate the need to study the interaction of raced, classed, and gendered processes; makes some introductory arguments about schooling and the limits of qualifications; and then moves on to define the book's key term: 'white tone'.

Let us begin with the observation that analyses of post-apartheid South Africa too often separate the outcomes of class formation from the processes of class making. Regularly, for instance, commentators hold up the rapid growth of the 'black middle class' as evidence that class is now more important than race as an axis of inequality in society.

There are, of course, very good reasons to emphasise the deracialisation of privilege – the shift from race to class – after apartheid ended. In 1990, the year when white public schools first voted to open their doors to black children, funding for white learners was on average four times higher than for black African children (the ratio was nearly *18* times more in 1969–70).[26] However, today in Durban more black than white children attend formerly white schools. These institutions use their high fees to employ on average nine extra ('governing body') teachers in addition to the teachers funded by the state on the basis of student enrolment numbers. This creation of new class-based exclusions is fore-grounded in landmark books titled *Elusive Equity* and *Changing Class*.[27]

But how do we explain schools' 'poaching' of white students? Is this evidence of a stubborn 'apartheid mindset', or something more? Addressing this question requires attention to whiteness, or what I call 'white tone'. This has gendered and classed components.

Revealing the significance of gender, formerly white boys' schools can now throw huge sums of money at sports scholarships or bursaries to attract desirable learners: compared with girls' schools, fees at boys' schools were 37 per cent higher in 2007 and 50 per cent higher in 2012.[28] Scholarships almost always promote 'white sports', but these do not benefit only white-identified people: Khule Nkosi, a star black rugby player from a small town in the KwaZulu-Natal Province, was given a package worth R100,000 a year to study at one formerly white school.

Schools' competition on and off the sports field also helps explain why many young white people have done quite well after apartheid ended: in Durban, the proportion of whites in high-skilled higher-income jobs increased from 60 per cent to 78 per cent from 2005 to 2014.[29] As well as offering generous sports bursaries, some prestigious Berea schools broke with the past by recruiting 'rough and tough' white students from the Bluff in order to give the school a whiter 'demographic'. Tellingly, one working-class father's first reaction to his son's 'traditional' Berea school was that it was a 'Harry Potter school' (that is, a school modelled on British private schools).

### Symbolic power and schooling

The examples flagged above reveal that schools are not just institutions that bestow credentials or qualifications (terms used interchangeably in this book to denote the passing of examinations). Schools are also symbolic organisations: a learner benefits from and adds to a school's 'name'. In *The State Nobility*, Pierre Bourdieu details how elite French higher education institutions both compete for prestige and provide graduating students with dispositions and status that benefit them in the labour market.[30] This two-way process upholds what he calls 'symbolic power' – a concept that has similarities to what Antonio Gramsci calls 'hegemony'.[31]

We consider differences in theoretical approaches later, but for now a working definition of symbolic power is that it 'actualizes and officializes visions of the world' and is 'an invisible power which can be exercised only with ... complicity'.[32]

This attention to cultural/symbolic hierarchies helps decentre South Africa's much-studied annual matriculation ('matric') school-leaving certificate, which is taken at the end of grade 12 (the term 'matric' is still widely used, although the qualification is now called the National Senior Certificate). I show throughout the book how young people's schooling greatly affects their chances of attaining credentials. However, it is important to note that, until relatively recently (as was common in most of the industrial world), even privileged white students were not expected to pass the matriculation exam, let alone attend university; of the 860,000 white children in the schooling system in 1970, only 36,000 were in standard 10 (grade 12).[33]

Moreover, as unequal as schooling was, black people succeeded over time in gaining additional schooling qualifications. From 1967 to 1988, the number of black African children in standard 10 grew from 2,075 to over 190,000.[34] After apartheid, this expansion accelerated: more than 400,000 learners now pass the grade 12 matriculation exam every year, and the number of black university students increased from fewer than 100,000 in 1989 to nearly 700,000 in 2013.[35] Put simply, South Africa's post-1994 education system did partially open the 'doors of learning', to use the famous words of the liberation movement's Freedom Charter written in 1955.

Yet it should be remembered that the full sentence of the 1955 Freedom Charter was in fact that the 'doors of learning *and culture*' should be opened (my italics). As more people gained qualifications, and at higher levels, a matriculation pass certificate, a qualification that would have placed a person among the elite a few generations ago, became devalued to the extent that it might not even get a person an interview today. This phenomenon is sometimes put in terms of education being a 'positional good', or, in Max Weber's terms, as qualifications being akin to 'patents'.[36] Learners seek ever more qualifications to get ahead of the pack – an undergraduate degree after matriculation pass, master's after undergraduate degree, etc. A lot of ink has been spilled debating whether this credential inflation stimulates economic growth, or whether employers use educational qualifications mainly to screen numerous candidates.[37]

But, to return to questions of race, the point I wish to stress is that qualification inflation makes it more important for schools to provide distinction in other ways. What residents of Umlazi Township call 'multiracial schools' – formerly white, Indian, and Coloured schools – have not only better facilities but home-language English teachers.[38] And at the pinnacle of South Africa's public schooling system have long been, and remain, schools established for whites, which amount to only 7 per cent of the country's schools.[39] Most parents in a township will identify these schools as providing learners with what sociolinguists term 'white South African English', which retains high prestige in society.[40] Whereas the apartheid government succeeded in radically promoting the status of Afrikaans, English is by far the most prestigious of the country's now 11 official languages despite it being only the fifth most spoken home language (after IsiZulu, IsiXhosa, Afrikaans, and Setswana).[41]

### White tone

I develop the concept of 'white tone' in this book to provide an educational lens onto the making of racial-cultural hierarchies. The association between whiteness and positive characteristics – including civilisation, freedom, and modernity – was first highlighted by black writers including W. E. B. Du Bois, Frantz Fanon, and Steve Biko.[42] Although produced in complex ways, the prestige of whiteness has its roots in the slave trade (spanning the Indian and especially the Atlantic oceans) and European colonialism (spanning most of the world).[43] From the sixteenth century, European powers established social and geographical hierarchies based on perceived phenotypic differences including skin colour, facial features, and hair texture. Non-Europeans were positioned as inherently inferior but, increasingly over time, capable of being 'civilised'.[44]

David Goldberg defines whiteness as 'the relative privilege, profit, and power of those occupying the structural social positions of whites in a hierarchically ordered racial society'.[45] Integral to this definition is that whiteness is not identical to white people. Like the now more widely accepted term 'masculinities', the concept of whiteness aims to account for multiple 'configurations of practice' that are simultaneously embodied and institutionalised.[46] A large volume of scholarship denaturalises whiteness, for instance by showing how immigrant groups such as the Irish became 'whiter' over time.[47]

Education is intricately woven into the history of whiteness. Schools were 'one of Britain's most successful exports to the Empire', and elite institutions modelled on British private schools can be found scattered across Africa, the Caribbean, and Asia.[48] In the African continent, hundreds of churches and schools were built by foreign missionaries. These, in the words of Steve Biko, equated 'all that was valuable with whiteness'.[49]

Yet schooling is also entangled with movements for racial liberation. In the American South, W. E. B. Du Bois documents black leaders' fight to establish schools, noting that in the early nineteenth century it could be unlawful to teach a free person of colour to read and write.[50] In the 1950s and 1960s, many leaders of newly independent countries had been educated at mission schools; they helped to establish tens of thousands of new schools in postcolonial settings.

Where does apartheid schooling fit into this dynamic? In brief, the implementation from 1948 of apartheid – Afrikaans for 'apartness' – went firmly against the post-war trend of decolonisation. Apartheid's architects were also unable to rely for authority on racial science that had become tainted by Nazi genocide and the destructive recent world war. As Paul Gilroy notes, it is possible to see apartheid as coinciding with (and to some extent representing) a shift in race thinking, 'from biology to culture, from species to ethnos'.[51]

This 'biology to culture' shift is not a clear one, as Gilroy himself recognises. But it is certainly true that the 1953 Bantu Education Act aggressively took forward one strand of racial thinking developed in the colonial era: 'Bantu' children should be taught in African languages and allowed to develop along their own lines. Central to this strategy was the state's closing down or taking over of mission schools. This patchy system of schools had produced English-speaking leaders who included lawyers Nelson Mandela and Oliver Tambo. Mission schools assimilated black students, so it was thought, too quickly into dangerous aspects of (white) civilisation.

In simple terms, apartheid's racially divided education system created not just vast chasms in schools' facilities, class sizes, and exam results. It ensured that African and white schools in particular had very different tones: African schools were expected to have a practical and tribal tone; white schools had a more scholarly and universal tone. I use the word 'tone' in part because it surfaces frequently in schooling discussions themselves, particularly when social boundaries are being asserted.[52] Peter Randall, author of a pioneering study of elite South African white schools, describes it as 'that marvellous Victorian word, typically vague' and shows how elite South African schools, mostly built for boys, fashioned a distinctive class tone in their assemblies, classrooms, and playgrounds.[53] Tone also has long-standing racial inferences. In nineteenth-century Trinidad, the principal of Queen's Royal College, a school with alumni who include C. L. R. James, argued that the 'tone' of the institution would be lowered by non-white students gaining scholarships to attend.[54]

Specifically, I use 'white tone' in three interrelated ways. First, I use it to underline how in the post-apartheid period some formerly white schools came, over time, to see their whiteness as a branding tool to attract richer white and black fee-paying parents. White tone therefore goes beyond viewing a school's 'poaching' of white students as driven by a backward-looking instinct, and it shows that schools' current attention to learners' hair, uniform, and language is not underpinned by a paradigm of 'assimilation' alone.[55]

Second, I use white tone to refer to the role schools, especially formerly white schools, play in bestowing prestigious linguistic and embodied practices shaped by racial-cultural hierarchies. At its loosest, 'white tone' serves as a metaphor for the way in which elite schools deracialised privilege without overturning the prestige of whiteness. This approach forces us to revisit apartheid's cultural histories, including the development of hierarchies within 'white' and 'black' society. And it shines a spotlight on experiences whereby some people in society are in tune with spaces of power, while others are marginalised.

Third, white tone speaks to the ways in which, for historically subordinated groups, whiteness can index both a form of oppression and a route to status and power. Examining racism in the US, W. E. B. Du Bois used the term 'double consciousness' to refer to how black people had to '[look] at one's self through the eyes of others'.[56] Frantz Fanon wrote about whiteness as a dehumanising force that resulted in colonised subjects being 'dominated but not domesticated'.[57]

We shall see that, in South Africa at the beginning of the twentieth century, isiZulu speakers viewed schools as offering opportunities but also representing a 'thing of the whites'. We shall also spend some time tracing the rise of excellent township schools that came to challenge a single hierarchy of prestige at the top of which are 'white' schools. Whiteness, in short, is always shaped by subordinate as well as dominant groups, and in a postcolonial society is always vulnerable to being cast as oppressive; in the world of work, as we shall see, it tends to hold more sway in private than in public institutions.

By now it is clear that white tone is slippery to define and is not a notion that can be applied in all settings or at all times. Like musical tone, people can interpret it differently depending on time and place. Human subjectivity is formed by myriad social-discursive processes, and cultural practices can never be neatly ordered into hierarchies. Some readers might consider that I am mistaking 'white tone' for a post-apartheid 'middle-class tone'; there are many overlaps between the two. I am also primarily concerned with the consolidation of prestige in English schools, rather than, for instance, with tracking how Afrikaans schools use their language policy to exclude black students. While the latter is important and widely discussed, Afrikaans has lost its protected status, and between 2002 and 2016 the number of Afrikaans-only schools dropped from 1,814 to 1,234.[58]

Consider, for a vivid illustration of white tone's linguistic dimensions – a major theme in this book – the words of Melo Magolego. He is referring to 'model C' schools, which were one of four types of desegregating white schools initiated in the early 1990s. Over time, the name came to refer to all formerly white English-medium schools. Magolego writes:

The accent with which one speaks English is no trifling matter in SA. A model-C accent speaks of a schooled experience. It speaks of a familiarity with white culture. It speaks of an acquaintance with certain cultural symbols. A model-C accent speaks of the ease with which an investment bank would hire you to join their corporate finance team (all in the name of culture fit) ... That is to say, a model-C accent is a passport asserting you [are] one of the coconut bourgeoisie. On the other hand when someone speaks with a vernacular accent they are often seen as being in a rude state of refinement. A vernacular accent is the voice of unreason ... A vernacular accent is associated with those guys that burn things. Those guys that cannot articulate their concerns but have to resort to violence. Those guys who cannot enunciate English to some snobbish satisfaction.[59]

## The geographical schooling market

In June 1976, schoolchildren living in Johannesburg's Soweto Township took to the streets to march against the state's imposition of Afrikaans as a medium of instruction. When police bullets mowed down hundreds of young people, the brutality of the apartheid regime was relayed around the globe. In the wake of the Soweto Uprising, researchers – many also activists – developed a rich corpus of work showing schooling's connections to segregation, urban politics, labour, and political struggle.[60] Other important studies came to foreground gender, transnational connections, Islamic schooling, and art education.[61]

In 1994, the ANC-led government inherited a country deeply divided in the realms of work, education, housing, health, and much more. Questions linger about why the oldest liberation movement in the continent, elected into power with more than 60 per cent of the vote, did not implement a more radical programme of state-led redistribution. The collapse of the communist bloc, compromises made during the negotiated settlement, and capital's success in wooing a black bourgeoisie are all offered as explanations.[62] Others point to the expansion in social grants, now 17 million in number for a population of 55 million, as evidence of South Africa's broadly social democratic path.[63] What is clear, however, is that education marketisation was consistent with the generally market-friendly thrust of post-apartheid policy, even if it emerged as something of an 'unintended experiment'.[64]

We need to recognise, too, that free-market ideologies have infiltrated most education systems around the globe over the last 30 years. 'School choice policies are sweeping the globe,' says David Plank and Gary Sykes. 'In countries on every continent, governments have decided that giving parents more choices among schools is an appropriate policy response to local educational problems.'[65] President Trump's appointment of businesswoman-politician Betsy DeVos as the US Secretary of Education in February 2017 fitted squarely with these trends. The now very large academic literature on schooling marketisation shows how middle-class parents make considerable investments, monetary or otherwise, to send their children to the best schools.[66]

Schooling marketisation in South Africa, I will argue, has roots going back to the 1970s. Nevertheless, as many accounts describe very well, a key moment came in the early 1990s. Shortly after Nelson Mandela was released from prison in 1990, the National Party government devolved power to whites-only schools and encouraged them to charge fees and admit better-off black students. In 1992, leaders of the ANC, then a liberation movement negotiating democracy, labelled this the 'privatisation of education'.[67] However, when it was elected to power in 1994, the ANC came to believe, in part persuaded by foreign consultants, that allowing affluent schools to charge fees would prevent the mass exodus of white children to private schools and free up state resources for poorer schools. Moreover, the apartheid government's devolution of powers to schools struck a chord with the liberation movement's long-standing struggle for 'people's education'.[68]

As such, the post-apartheid government tinkered with an already marketised system rather than ending it. The 1996 South African Schools Act mandated that learners – once *admitted* into a school – could attain fee exemptions if they could not afford to pay the fees. It also barred racial and other forms of discrimination by schools. Provinces have some policy leeway, but most followed what educators in Durban call 'soft zoning'. This means that schools are required to give preference to local families but can also admit learners who live outside these areas.

While the middle class, including many ANC politicians, now choose expensive schools for their children, the government did significantly extend free education for the poor. During the apartheid era, black parents, unlike most whites, were forced to pay school fees and other costs. In the democratic era, the simple fact that core state funding became dependent on a school's number of learners rather than their 'race' redistributed resources to poorer schools. In addition, the state categorised each school into one of five quintiles based on its surrounding socio-economic profile and used this information to provide extra educational resources to poorer schools. Most significantly, in 2007 the state abolished fees in the poorest schools, and, by 2016, 65 per cent of South African learners attended these 'no-fee' schools.[69]

Thus, unlike many Western countries where 'quasi-markets' increased competition within a publicly funded system, South Africa's public education system includes both free and very expensive schools. This public–private mix is in fact common in the Global South, partly because private education has increased significantly.[70] As such, inequalities in school funding and facilities remain striking. In KwaZulu-Natal in 2009, the poorest 'no-fee' category of school received only R635 (US$57) more

Figure 1.1 Durban High School, Berea. Opened in 1866, and moved to the Berea in 1895, this formerly white boys' school is Durban's oldest school. Photograph: Hugh Bland.

state funding per pupil per year than the richest category of school.[71] Yet the fees collected at richer schools amounted to R10,000–30,000 (US $900–2,700) a year per learner (Figure 1.1 shows a formerly white school).

Rural–urban divides remain particularly wide. In the KwaZulu-Natal Province, in which Durban is located, nine of the 12 school districts are predominantly rural.[72] Rural learners, many now accessing 'no-fee' schools, are often burdened with long walks to school or depend on a patchy scholar transportation service (the state's only official transportation for schooling); when children arrive, the school might not even have basic sanitation facilities.[73] Code-switching (i.e. switching between English and isiZulu) is common even in classes where English is the medium of instruction.[74] These are some of the reasons why better-off rural parents, including teachers themselves, seek to move their children into urban schools.

Urban areas, the focus of this book, foster a vibrant schooling market because transport arteries connect rich and poor areas. Umlazi Township has more than 400,000 residents and its average per capita income is only R1,900 a month (around US$170).[75] Schools are typically able to charge fees of only R200 a year, and most learners live in shack settlements or 'matchbox' township houses. While many parents are unemployed, those with the means might try to send their children to a racially mixed school located in a formerly white, Indian, or Coloured area (Figure 1.2 shows a township school).

In the most privileged, formerly white, schools, children are taught by native English speakers and can access excellent facilities that include computer labs and swimming pools. Monthly per capita incomes in a

Figure 1.2 Menzi High School, Umlazi. The school premises are only a little longer than Durban High School's swimming pool! When Menzi opened in 1967 it was the only day (non-boarding) high school in KwaZulu-Natal for black Africans. Photograph: Mark Hunter.

formerly white suburb are likely to be over R10,000. The school fees can be over R20,000 a year (see Table A1.1 in Appendix 1). We will dissect further the schooling system in this book, but for now I introduce briefly the other main protagonists: families.

## Beneath the 'black tax': gender and the family

Future historians will consider the 2015 #RhodesMustFall student protests as a key moment in South Africa's democracy. When they do, they might notice that it was around this time that the term 'black tax' exploded in social media, in newspapers, and on the radio. The term refers to the pressure young black wage earners face to support poorer family members and implies that white workers do not have the same level of familial responsibility. Numerous newspaper stories tell how the black tax 'cripples our youth's aspirations', leaves some 'a few pay cheques away from poverty', and leads black people to 'work twice as hard as whites'. By 2015, at a #FeesMustFall rally outside the ANC's headquarters, students were voicing the anti-apartheid slogan '*Amandla ngawethu*' ('Power to the people') and then following it with 'Away with black tax, away.'[76]

This book does not seek to explain how and where the 'black tax' term became deployed. The term's rise is certainly consistent with the growth of the black middle class and the sense that the government's attention to racial reconciliation came at the expense of redressing past injustices.

However, the 'black tax' opens up important questions this book does consider. How are families shifting in size, location, and structure, and how is this inflected by the country's racial history? Compared with black earners, do white learners benefit more from families and support them less? Which family members pay the most attention to children's schooling? Even if feminist scholars have long decentred the naturalness of the mother–child bond, researchers have given relatively little attention to the ways in which schooling creates gendered obligations and how these change over time.[77] There are also critical blind spots surrounding the study of the ways in which race interacts with families and schooling markets.[78]

I draw on a wealth of South African scholarship on changing forms of households to show the importance of understanding *connections among* and *differences within* households/families.[79] Since the nineteenth century, the migrant labour system has separated thousands of black African men from their families and apartheid policies removed more than 3.5 million black people from 'white' areas.[80] Apartheid, at times, promoted modern nuclear families, especially in urban townships. However, after a period of rising unemployment and falling marriage rates, only 30 per cent of black African children today live with their father, compared with 83 per cent of white children.[81]

While I demonstrate that white families are generally able to send their children to excellent schools, I show that the family is not a static entity. White children from the working-class Bluff suburb often live with their parents for many years after they finish schooling. Many ageing parents also move back in with their children, both to save money and to help with raising grandchildren, including ferrying them to and from school. The fundamental imperative is for kin to organise themselves in a way that preserves past social mobility: that is, to prevent downward intergenerational social mobility.

In Umlazi Township, I show mothers' long-standing sacrifices to enable their children to attend school. African women were disadvantaged in terms of housing, inheritance, and work, and saw schooling as a means to a better future. Very often, mothers' efforts were tied to the hope that their children would support parents and other family members. Intergenerational and intragenerational social mobility are thus intertwined – and the glue that connects them is family obligations, now articulated by some as the 'black tax'.

The rise of the term 'black tax' shows vividly how political consciousness can derive from family life. However, I also demonstrate how in Umlazi Township stark social divisions can be normalised within a single household. For instance, one child might attend a free school and another a school that costs R30,000 a year. The faces of class inequalities are not just millionaire businessmen and politicians but brothers, sisters, and cousins.

More generally, the fact that many South Africans are accessing more qualifications in no-fee schools helps explain why protests against inequalities in the basic education system are still rare (in contrast to those at fee-charging higher education institutions). Respondents in one national survey consistently ranked education second in terms of their satisfaction with government performance.[82] In the conclusion, I draw on the work of Antonio Gramsci to understand why the basic education system remains so uneven and how white tone retains authority in society.

## Studying the schooling system

I grew up in the UK and first lived in South Africa in 1988 for a 'gap year' between secondary school and university. My 'project', as it was called, was teaching at a Catholic mission school for physically handicapped children in the 'homeland' of Transkei. Sometimes the students, out of earshot of the nuns, sang with unforgettable beauty the words '*Oliver Tambo thetha noBotha akhulule uMandela*' – a struggle song telling President Botha to release the imprisoned leader Nelson Mandela, who had been raised not far from the school.

To work at this mission school, it wasn't necessary to be a Christian. How, then, was I, a 17-year-old with three A-levels, qualified to teach children as old as 21? The answer speaks to key themes in this book. First, I am white; thus, it was assumed, I was a legitimate purveyor to black children of modern Western culture. Second, I am a native English speaker, whereas other teachers spoke isiXhosa at home. Third – and here I think local specificities played out – I held a driving licence. I could transport the learners to the hospital and to their rural homes, and, from the perspective of the nuns, undertake everyday errands (one American sister frequently summoned my co-volunteer and me from our small flat by shouting 'British boys!').

The year changed my life. At university, I swapped studying physics for studying politics and development, and I spent a lot of time working with the tail end of the anti-apartheid movement. During the last 30 years, with several exceptions, I have been fortunate to study, work, live, and research in South Africa for all or part of every year.

I began research on schooling in Durban in 2009 while finishing my first book on the history of the HIV/AIDS pandemic. When living in the early 2000s in a shack settlement in an area north of Durban, I was struck by the confidence, invariably articulated in English, of the few children who attended formerly white or Indian schools. Wishing to conduct research in a city with a large number of schools (including one for my young daughter to attend), my wife and I rented for five months in 2009 one of the many furnished apartments meant for vacationers on Durban's Bluff, which is the first stop from Durban along KwaZulu-Natal's south coast. I began to conduct open-ended interviews with local schools and tried to connect this to family politics with which I had some familiarity because of my HIV/AIDS research.

I interviewed, sometimes several times, members of more than 200 families. I also conducted 90 interviews with school staff, usually principals or deputy principals. I give particular attention to admissions and funding, and do not consider curriculum changes or other aspects of day-to-day teaching.[83] When the politics of language developed as a key theme, I also interviewed around 40 workers and managers at telephone call centres and attended a private call centre training course for a week. Archival work included exploring records on the establishment and running of schools, plans for the construction of the apartheid city, civil court cases on issues from bridewealth to child maintenance, and old magazines, newspapers, and newsletters.

Ethnographic research included getting to know families over five years. On a day-to-day basis in Umlazi, I worked with Lwandle, a female research assistant in her thirties. Most interviews in Umlazi were conducted by me in isiZulu accompanied (and sometimes aided) by Lwandle, transcribed in isiZulu by another research assistant, and translated by me, occasionally with the help of the transcriber. I worked with a retired female resident from the Bluff to establish contacts in the area, although I undertook most interviews in English on my own. Around half of the interviews, as well as all of the Household and Schooling Survey (see below), were conducted during a nine-month sabbatical stay in 2012 and 2013. Subsequent annual research trips of two to five months (up to 2017) allowed me to follow developments in families and schools.

My daughter (Leila) has attended Durban schools for nearly two and a half years in total on the Bluff and in Berea. As parents, my wife and I wanted to do the best for our daughter – as such, our own actions are complicit in moulding class, race, and gender structures. As a white foreigner, I felt that schools particularly welcomed my interest in admitting my daughter because doing so would enhance their own prestige. However, the need to study race in practice is evidenced by the fact that I was never quite sure how our olive-skinned daughter (with a Moroccan-born mother and white British-born father) was viewed: did her Canadian accent trump her skin colour? How important was it that her white father rather than her mother (who was sometimes viewed as 'Coloured' in South Africa) dropped her off every day? Or was race unimportant, and the most important issue for the school was the fact that we paid our fees up front?

This book demonstrates how education is entangled with processes of *racialism*: how people come to be regarded as, and sometimes identify as, separate 'races'.[84] And it shows how these 'races' can be institutionalised and organised in a *racist* hierarchy: with consequences for where people live, where they go to school, and ultimately whether they experience what Ruth Gilmore calls 'premature death'.[85] I emphasise the importance of gendered social relations to the construction of race and class, although I recognise that gender identities and binaries are not specifically problematised in this book (I do use non-binary singular pronouns when appropriate, for instance saying 'they chose a school' rather than 'he or she chose a school').

While it is easy to agree on the 'constructiveness' of race, not everyone approves of using the same racial terms. To understand South Africa's schooling system, I continue to use apartheid's four racial categories of 'African', 'white', 'Indian', and 'Coloured', or derivate terms such as 'formerly white schools'. All are based on the fantasies of racial classifiers: for instance, 'Coloured' is sometimes oversimplified as 'mixed race' when it is in fact a state-imposed category bringing together those 'loosely bound together for historical reasons such as slavery, creolisation and a combination of oppressive and selective preferential treatment under apartheid'.[86]

When I use census or other data to illustrate racial patterns, for the sake of consistency I use contemporary racial categories rather than those used in the past ('black Africans' or 'Africans', for instance, were previously 'Natives', then 'Bantu', and 'whites' were previously 'Europeans'). To improve the book's readability, I try to avoid, where possible, putting terms such as 'white' or 'African' in scare quotes, or using terms such as 'white-identified'. However, the use of terminology such as white learners or black learners does not indicate that racial meanings are fixed, as the book shows throughout.

With the rise of the Black Consciousness Movement in the late 1960s and 1970s, the term 'Black' became a political category used by all people of colour. I use it in this way where its meaning is clear (and I capitalise it when discussing Black Consciousness, but not elsewhere). I also use 'black' or 'black African' at times when discussing residents of Umlazi, because black is a term residents use when self-identifying along racial lines. Although the boundaries of languages are themselves socially produced, I prefer the terms 'Afrikaans speakers' and 'isiZulu speakers' (rather than 'Afrikaners' and 'Zulus') because they better imply that identities are fashioned in practice.

### Durban/eThekwini and limits of the study

EThekwini municipality, still commonly called Durban, was created in 2000 when the boundaries of the old 'white' Durban city were extended to incorporate black townships and proximate rural areas. The latest (2011) census found the racial breakdown of eThekwini to be as follows: 74 per cent African, 17 per cent Indian, 6.5 per cent white, and 2.5 per cent Coloured (nationwide, the census recorded the following racial breakdown: 79 per cent African, 9 per cent Coloured, 9 per cent white, and 1.4 per cent Indian).[87] The trend in recent decades is for Durban's

black African population to increase significantly and its white population to shrink (in contrast, the absolute – but not relative – white populations of Johannesburg and especially Cape Town are growing).

Of course, considering only one city does raise questions about the
wider conclusions that can be drawn from this study. Durban was
established as 'an offshoot of the British settlement at the Cape' and
had a reputation as the 'last outpost of the British empire'.[88] But South
African cities as a whole, and not just Durban, are marked by the strong
influence of British culture in architecture, schools, and workplaces.

South and central Durban, the area I concentrate on, form what
Taylor calls a 'competition space': that is, an area of strong competition
among schools.[89] A good network of road and rail connections links
schools and parents in the area spanning Berea to Umlazi Township.
To some extent, Durban's western and northern suburbs (e.g. Westville,
Kloof, Hillcrest, and Umhlanga) have similarities with US-style 'edge
cities', and uphold privilege because they are affluent white enclaves.
However, as I discuss later, black people make up a much larger proportion of the middle class in South Africa than they do in the US.[90] Suffice
it to say that south-central Durban is a region where a large amount of
travelling for school takes place, but one that I do not believe tells an
exceptional story in South Africa.

A further limitation I need to flag is that I seemingly jump over the
former Coloured area of Wentworth and the Indian townships of
Chatsworth and Merebank in focusing on Umlazi, the Bluff, and
Berea. Durban remains home to many of the country's 'Indian' population, a fact rooted in the colonial government's importation of indentured labour to staff the region's sugar cane plantations. A large number
of Indian students now attend formerly white schools, and formerly
Indian schools are affordable options for black Africans living in the
city. While I do consider Indian students and workers at times, it needs
to be noted that this book is not an attempt to write a comprehensive
history of schooling in the city, or even in south and central Durban.[91]
Instead, its key themes of political economy and symbolic politics draw it
to the top and the bottom of the urban educational market – that is,
formerly African and formerly white schools and residential areas. The
study draws on a 'relational' understanding of space whereby places are
conceived as interconnected rather than bounded.[92]

I give more attention to parents than to students but did sometimes
talk with learners who were present at interviews or who had recently
completed schooling and had become parents. I justify focusing on
parents because early decisions on preschools and primary schools set
children on radically different paths. At the same time, I recognise that
children, particularly older children, do have an influence on the schools
they attend.

Historians tend to give the name of interviewees and the dates of interviews, whereas my study (and institutional ethics protocol) followed the anthropological tradition, which emphasises anonymity. Thus, the names of all persons interviewed (and my research assistants) are changed, and, in a few cases, small details are altered to prevent identification. When I use pseudonyms, I try to reflect the feel of interactions by using titles such as 'Mrs', as well as first and surnames, roughly as they were used at the time. I give the real names of some schools whose histories are widely known and to those I mention in passing. However, I hide the names of schools that I use as particular (often controversial) examples. Almost all white secondary schools were established as single-sex institutions and I give particular emphasis to boys' schools. However, I also compare these with girls' schools that desegregated more evenly and whose fees are much lower.

While I integrate discussions about qualitative research in the text and footnotes, Appendix 1 provides a 'Note on quantitative and survey data'. In brief, my research assistants and I conducted a Household and Schooling Survey comprised of 231 households. I also draw on what I call 'Durban Schooling Data', a data set I developed based on information provided by the Department of Education on 441 Durban schools. A final point to note is that South Africa's currency, the rand, fluctuated in value greatly during the course of this research (one US dollar being worth between 6 and 16 rand). When I undertake conversions in this book I use a value of US$1 to R11 (which is roughly equivalent to £1 to R14).

### The book's structure

The book's early chapters are cultural and social histories of south and central Durban, showing how schooling helped produce the apartheid city. While one motive for these chapters is to provide context to Durban, a second aim is to underscore how apartheid segregation subsequently became the terrain on which a marketised system developed. This argument needs to be subdivided, and I do so using the three broad periods introduced earlier: *racial modernism*, *marketised assimilation*, and *racialised market*. Of course, any attempt to squeeze complex historical patterns into different periods will always be partial (that is, considered through certain lenses) and inexact (that is, using artificial breaks in time to emphasise analytical points). I summarise these periods in Table 1.1.

Part I ('Racial modernism – 1950s and 1960s') centres on the making of apartheid's racialised schooling systems. At this time, children were schooled in racially defined – but, for white society, also class-defined – residential zones. Chapter 2 explores the expansion of white secondary

Table 1.1 *Summary of different educational periods and themes considered in this book*

| | Schools | Families | Labour market |
|---|---|---|---|
| **Pre-apartheid (1910–48)** | Black Africans educated mainly in state-aided mission schools. White education expands quickly to bring together Afrikaans and English speakers in the post-1910 Union of South Africa. | Many black African families divided by migrant labour. Many white families generously housed, including by the state. | Mission schools foster a small but influential professional African class. The best jobs reserved for whites. |
| **Racial modernism (1948–late 1970s)** | Mission schools for Africans closed or taken over by the state; Bantu education promotes African languages in primary schools that are built rapidly. Peak of racial funding gap: white learners funded 18 times higher than black African learners in 1969. | Black families moved from cities to townships and rural areas. Mothers place a great emphasis on schooling. White suburbs develop with distinct class-based differences. | Black Africans typically employed in booming factories as labourers or semi-skilled workers. Schooling helps divide whites into professional/business and technical work, although all work is well paid. |
| **Marketised assimilation (late 1970s–late 1990s)** | The 1976 Soweto Uprising sparks a new era of social protests. Secondary schools for Africans built rapidly, a few becoming excellent. White private schools desegregate slowly by selecting better-off black students; segregation begins to erode slowly in urban spaces. From 1991, white public schools desegregate and charge fees. | Inequalities in townships become manifest in private housing and shack settlements. Marriage rates begin to decline. | Black Africans, increasingly women, move into supervisory, professional, and service work. Unemployment rises. |

Table 1.1 (*cont.*)

| | Schools | Families | Labour market |
|---|---|---|---|
| **Racialised market** (2000s–) | New private schools established by corporations. | Urban areas desegregate. Both black and white families have complex multigenerational forms. The rise of the term 'black tax' captures the obligations black wage earners have to their families. | Service work continues to increase in importance compared with manufacturing work. The prestige of 'white tone', especially 'white English', is important to finding work. Unemployment rises to over 40 per cent. |
| | Competition among public schools intensifies: formerly white schools compete on the basis of their 'white tone'. | | |
| | Fees among top schools rise rapidly, but schools in poor areas become 'no-fee' schools. | | |

schooling and how this patterned spatial hierarchies within white society. The chapter also considers the advancement of Afrikaans speakers through separate Afrikaans-medium schools. Chapter 3 turns to Umlazi Township and focuses on the expansion of primary schools in the 1960s, and the particularly active role that mothers, disadvantaged by race, gender, and class, played in the schooling of their children.

In Part II ('Marketised assimilation – late 1970s–1990s'), Chapter 4 details rising differentiation in black and white society and shows how the desegregation of private schools took place when black students were expected to 'fit in' to the dominant white schooling culture. Better-off black children moved into white schools, and white parents generally remained committed to local schooling.

In Part III ('Schooling and work after apartheid'), I show that where a person goes to school helps determine if and where they work. Chapter 5 shows that, for Umlazi residents, attending 'multiracial' schools with native English teachers is critical to finding any work in a service-centred economy.

Part IV ('Racialised market – 2000s onwards') focuses on schoolchildren's movement. I use the term *racialised market* to show how cultural signals of whiteness are formative of the schooling market. Chapter 6 considers the growing competition among schools. In Chapter 7, I contemplate the new family forms on the Bluff, including extended white families, and the decline of live-in domestic workers. In Chapter 8, centring on Umlazi, I look at children travelling to the best township schools and outside multiracial schools, and how the expense of the latter requires a learner to be '*fundisa*-ed' ('sponsored', or literally 'caused to learn').

In the conclusion to the book, Chapter 9, ('Hegemony on a school bus'), I summarise the material and symbolic forces driving schooling inequalities and pay specific attention to the politics of language.

*Part I*

# Racial modernism – 1950s and 1960s

# 2  'Larney' and 'rough and tough' schools
## The making of white Durban

Durban's 'traditional' schools – or, as some called them, 'larney' (fancy) schools – are situated on the Berea ridge, a residential area rising 500 feet from the city centre, with commanding views of the Indian Ocean, harbour, and the Bluff headland.[1] In 1958, despite the ascent of Afrikaner nationalists into political power, it was still said of Durban High School, the city's oldest school, that one would find its English-speaking old boys 'entrenched everywhere that counts – in politics, industry, banking, the arts, diplomacy, the learned professions'.[2] As in other colonial settings, South Africa's top schools looked up to British private schools, from which many of their first teachers had been recruited.

In addition to Berea schools, this chapter foregrounds a new breed of working-class English- and Afrikaans-medium schools as well as their south Durban suburbs. Rob Donkin, in his autobiography *A Bluff Scruff Miracle*, describes the pride Bluff residents feel for their white working-class suburb: 'One needed to earn the right to be known as "rough and tough Bluff scruff",' he says. 'It was a title to be proud of and was a sought-after and feared reputation, especially by the "town clowns".'[3]

While the origin of the idiom 'rough and tough and from the Bluff' is difficult to determine, some people link it to the hierarchical organisation of schools in the city. A former school principal, Mr Smit, who grew up on the Bluff in the 1950s referred to the building of three new high schools on the Bluff when explaining the phrase. Reflecting a view I heard from others of his generation, he said, 'You had these elites and, ja, they looked down on the people of the Bluff ... The old traditional schools, I think they will look down, you know, on the others.' The dividing of suburbs by class created a strong sense of local community, and marriage between Afrikaans and English speakers in working-class areas such as the Bluff became relatively common.

Little has been written about hierarchies among white schools and white suburbs, a major theme in this chapter. However, these were central to the period of racial modernism instigated by the election of the apartheid government, which this chapter also introduces. The rapid expansion of white education in class-defined suburbs in the 1950s and

Table 2.1 *Summary of hierarchies among Durban's schools*

| Dominant schooling type | Subordinate schooling type | How hierarchy was instituted |
| --- | --- | --- |
| Berea's traditional schools | Schools in working-class/ lower-middle-class south Durban | The former followed an academic curriculum and showcased the national sport of rugby; the latter's curriculum stressed practical skills, and students often preferred soccer to rugby. |
| English schools | Afrikaans schools | Highly contested under apartheid, but English was more dominant (especially in Natal) in business and professional jobs. |
| Boys' schools | Girls' schools | The former benefited from the power of old boys' networks, and masculinities that position men as leaders in society. |
| White schools | Black schools | The former benefited from massive funding advantages. Schooling for black Africans expanded at the primary-school level, and for Indians at all levels. |

1960s necessitated an end to the intermingling of poorer whites and black people in cities. Segregated schooling worked to normalise the assigning of a 'race' to every South African and thus hardened borders between groups who came to be called 'white', 'African', 'Indian', and 'Coloured'.

These differences in whiteness, and among white people, were also formative of the reform period from the 1970s, as we shall see later in this book. Moreover, the trajectory of public schooling desegregation from the 1990s rested on two key aspects of racial modernism: the spatiality of schooling hierarchies and the gendered cultural signifiers of class, including sports. By the 2000s, some schools were throwing thousands of rand at rugby scholarships to promote their whiteness, and soccer lost its appeal. Eventually, many white Bluffites 'up-classed' by sending their children to Berea's schools – ones that historically had shunned learners from working-class areas.

This chapter begins by showing how the 1950 Group Areas Act removed black residents from 'white' areas and redrew the city's schooling geography. To highlight the significant differences among white areas it focuses on the Berea and the more working-class Bluff areas. The next section outlines the work and training advantages provided to white people, including Afrikaans speakers, and the 'insider and outsider' status of Indian workers. Finally, we look briefly at differences between boys' and girls' schools. Table 2.1 summarises the schooling and spatial hierarchies discussed in this chapter.

## Schooling and the making of the apartheid city

The global rise of publicly funded schools is entwined with the establishment of nation states both in the West and in its colonies. The particular influence of English-language education is rooted in the British Empire's control over nearly one-quarter of the world's population in the early twentieth century.

On the southern tip of Africa – a continent imperialist Cecil John Rhodes famously wanted to connect from 'Cape to Cairo' – Britain granted dominion status to South Africa in 1910. This followed Britain's military defeat of Afrikaners/Boers, a group predominantly of Dutch descent, in the 1899–1902 Anglo-Boer War. The formation of the Union of South Africa necessitated the amalgamation of the British colonies of Natal and the Cape and two former Boer republics.

A single public education system was vital to bringing together English- and Dutch/Afrikaans-speaking whites in the new nation; public expenditure on schools increased fivefold in the country's first 20 years.[4] The top schools fashioned an Anglophone elite, but education also aimed to uplift a group of 'poor whites', mostly Afrikaans speakers, whose existence was 'anomalous and unacceptable' to white society.[5]

After 1948, the apartheid government continued its support for white schooling but positioned race at the centre of a more ambitious plan for social order. Following its surprise election victory, the National Party, led by D. F. Malan, passed a slew of new legislation. The 1950 Population Registration Act created a register of every South African's 'race'; the 1949 Prohibition of Mixed Marriages Act and 1950 Immorality Amendment Act outlawed sexual intimacy and marriages between white people and people of other races; the 1952 Black (Natives) Laws Amendment Act extended urban influx (pass law) controls to African women; and, as we will see in Chapter 3, the 1953 Bantu Education Act instituted an inferior public education system for African people.

It was the 1950 Group Areas Act, however, that transformed the racial cartography of South African cities. Urbanisation up to this point was often unplanned, as signified by the growth of racially mixed areas. In Durban, the Act resulted in the removal of an estimated 75,000 Indians and 81,000 Africans; this was more than 50 per cent of the city's total number of Indians and 60 per cent of Africans.[6] New black townships such as Umlazi were built on the edges of all cities. Whites, who made up 19 per cent of the country's population in 1960, remained largely unaffected by removals, or became beneficiaries of cheaper land.[7]

Intensified racial segregation had another profound legacy: it helped make apartheid's four racial categories ordinary and lived – in intimate interactions, identities, acts of oppression, and forms of resistance. The

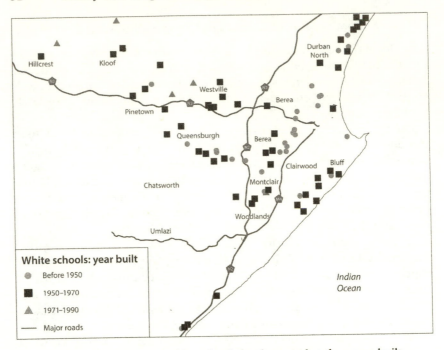

Map 2.1 Durban's white schools by the year that they were built.
*Source:* Adapted from Simon Haw, *Taking Stock: the Natal Education Department looks back* (Pietermaritzburg: Natal Education Department, 1995), pp. 106–7. Other sources suggest that there are some minor errors in this list, but it remains a useful and broadly accurate reference point.

houses and schools built for 'whites', 'Indians', 'Coloureds', and 'Africans' gave these categories a solidity that persists to this day.

As such, urban schooling was not just cast in the mould of apartheid but *formative* of apartheid. For those classified as white, the removal of black residents – together with suburbanisation and the expansion of secondary education – stretched the schooling system outwards spatially. Finances came pouring in to the white education system: from 1950 to 1970, funding per white student increased by a factor of two and a half on the back of an economy that 'never had it so good'.[8] During this time, 50 new primary and secondary schools were built in new or growing white suburbs, including on the Bluff, Woodlands, and Montclair (to the south of the central business district (CBD)); Westville and Kloof (to the west); and Durban North (to the north). Indeed, by dating the establishment of white schools, we can track the growth of Durban's familiar inverted T shape serviced by the N3 (east–west) and M4 and N2 (north–south) highways (see Map 2.1).

Durban's southern suburbs, a major area of white schooling expansion, saw substantial Group Areas Act removals, second in the city only to Cato Manor/Umkhumbane located west of Berea. Since the beginning of the twentieth century, thousands of 'Indian' market farmers, most of them descendants of indentured sugar-cane labourers, had rented or bought land in south Durban. Many lived in wood and iron structures and grew fruits and vegetables for the city. Around 400 Indian people lived in a 90-year-old fishing village at the Fynnlands part of the Bluff, and a 'Zanzibari' community, discussed below, lived off Bluff Road.[9] Significant clusters of 'African' shack dwellers resided in Bayhead near the port and Happy Valley to the south.[10]

Yet mixed-race spaces were anathema to the Group Areas Act – live-in servants notwithstanding. The northern part of the Bluff was zoned as white, Merebank and Chatsworth townships were built for Indians, and Wentworth township was built for Coloureds. The biggest area to resist removals in south Durban was the predominantly Indian business area of Clairwood, inland from the Bluff's western ridge (see Figure 2.1).[11]

The Bluff's coming of age as a white suburb was therefore grounded in twin forces of destruction and construction: the removal of black residents and the building of new institutions for whites, including schools. In 1965, the *Bluff Ratepayer* commented after the opening of two English secondary schools and a co-educational Afrikaans high school: '[O]ne of the very few ways in which the Bluff holds its own, or is even in advance of other areas, is in the wealth of educational facilities which we possess.'[12] Secondary schooling was relatively new for working-class whites and helped cement whiteness's association with civilisation and intelligence.

Moreover, when you needed a 'race' to attend a school, what could be more innocent than identifying along racial lines? At Epsom, a school in the lower Berea with a reputation for admitting children who were considered on the borderline between being white and Coloured, backlogs in classification in the early 1960s led to the 'tragedy' of some children having 'no race' and thus no clear path through schooling.[13] Yet, as this example suggests, urban apartheid did not fall into place easily, and I further illuminate this point through two examples: the difference between the upper and lower parts of Berea, and the centrality of class to racial classification.

## The Group Area Act's spatial limitations: the upper and lower Berea

For Durbanites, the Berea ridge evokes an image of cool sea breezes and large family houses (Figure 2.2). However, the lower areas of the ridge, stretching from the Greyville racecourse to Umbilo's factories, long housed poorer white as well as Indian, Coloured, and African residents.[14] Some

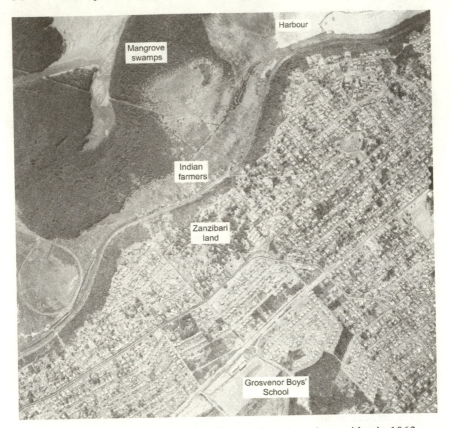

Figure 2.1   The Bluff's racially mixed northern inner ridge in 1963.
This photograph was taken at the time of Group Areas Act removals.
A strip of Indian houses can be seen on farmland to the north of the
railway track. The recently removed Zanzibari community lived just east
of the railway tracks. At the bottom centre of the picture is the new
Grosvenor Park Boys' School built for whites.
*Source:* eThekwini Municipality.

Indians, who outnumbered whites in the city, had the means to buy
property on the Berea. While opposition among whites to this Indian
'penetration' had a long history, the 1950 Group Areas Act mandated the
removal of all Indian renters and property owners in areas such as Berea.[15]
Also facing removals were black Africans living in municipal hostels and
family accommodation close to the central business district.

   Yet, in the lower Berea and CBD, a significant number of Indian
businesses and residences did manage to survive apartheid removals. Over
1,300 Indian businesses, owned primarily by Muslim traders, many with
ancestors from Gujarat, were located in or near Grey Street, just inland

Figure 2.2 Durban's southern Berea ridge rising up from the harbour.
The upper Berea has a long reputation as a more middle-class and white
area than the lower Berea suburbs.
Photograph: Mark Hunter.

from the 'white' CBD.[16] While this Indian business district, and the
surrounding residential areas, faced constant restrictions and threats of
removal, residents protested determinedly. State entities were also hesitant
to raze institutions that might promote ethnic and racial identities. At
nearby Greyville, a cluster of 13 black education institutions remained
standing, including Orient Islamic School, Sastri College, and M. L.
Sultan Technical College.[17] The state's inability to sever connections
between race, class, and place had important consequences, as we shall see.

**Race, class, and classification**

The notion of 'race' that justifies so much violence in the world is, in
historical terms, a mutable one: at various times it has been used to refer
to root, pedigree, culture, ethnicity, nation, and phenotypic differences.[18]
Thus, convinced of their own superiority, nineteenth-century English
speakers could deride the backwardness of the Boer/Afrikaner 'race'.[19]

In the apartheid period, however, race became the basis of a massive
system of classification and segregation. What were some of the principles by which 'race' attained authority so soon after the horrors of
Nazi eugenics? To recognise a person as white, Natal's educational
ordinance had historically used descent as a criterion (i.e. purity of blood
for three generations).[20] In contrast, the 1950 Population Registration
Act called on a person's 'habits, education and speech and deportment
and demeanour'.[21] This 'common-sense' definition sped up the

classification process and allayed fears among white families that they might have black ancestors.[22]

In practice, classifiers combined phenotypic traits such as skin colour, facial features, and hair texture with cultural codings of race. Social class became especially important in determining boundaries between whites and Coloureds, and between Africans and Coloureds: groups who were not always definitively categorised through visual markers. Class could be indicated by a person's place of residence, dress, accent, and even sports played. Deborah Posel documents how one race classification board in Johannesburg noted that 'a soccer player is native [the precursor of "African"], a rugby player is a Coloured'.[23]

Connecting race to culture gave racial classification a fuzziness, a lack of precision, that continued throughout apartheid and beyond, as we shall see. It made whiteness never fixed but always shot through with class in particular, and it made schools important nodes in the regulation of race. As Posel shows, white schooling communities could exclude children who looked or acted 'Coloured' (i.e. broadly mixed race) even if their parents were classified as 'white'.[24]

At the same time, the fuzziness of race meant that a child's schooling could be used as evidence that they should be reclassified 'up' the racial hierarchy. The 'Zanzibaris' were a group descended from freed slaves who settled on Bluff land purchased by the Grey Street Mosque Trust. When this Muslim community faced removal in the early 1960s, the Native Affairs Department first classified its members as 'natives'. However, representatives from the Grey Street Mosque and the city's Native Administration Department argued that the community's children attended Indian schools, were Muslim, and should therefore live in an Indian area.[25] The Zanzibaris were eventually classified as 'Other Asiatics' and moved to the Bayview section of the new 'Indian' township of Chatsworth. The Zanzibari land came to house a residence for elderly white people called 'Peacehaven'.

White schools' extensive powers over admissions, and therefore the racial ordering of society, need to be flagged at this point. Whereas the Pretoria government took control over African, Coloured, and Indian schooling, it left the administration of white schools to the four provinces. Natal Province oversaw 360 white schools but its jurisdiction stretched more than 500 kilometres, making it obligatory that certain powers be devolved to individual schools.[26] Thus, South Africa never developed city-based local education authorities that administered admissions like those formed in Britain.

With power over who they admitted, schools were in a position to make life-changing judgements about an applicant's race and class. Because upper-class schools were generally located some distance from black and working-class white residents, one easy way for schools to exclude questionable applicants was to insist that they attend their own local schools. A former teacher from a top Berea boys' school described an informal system of zoning whereby the school used Mansfield, a working-class white school located down the Berea ridge close to the black education complex, as a buffer to keep out undesirable students who did not live close to the elite school. 'Every day we used to thank the Lord for Mansfield,' he told me.

This former teacher, now in his seventies, also suggested that admissions processes could utilise pseudoscientific measures of race, such as the infamous 'pencil test' that assessed a person's race from their hair texture:

You see, Mansfield, in the days of apartheid or what have you, a lot of the kids that went there were Coloured. They wouldn't have them here [the prestigious Berea school]. I mean one of the tests they did – I mean it was bloody Germany all over again. The kid would apply here and the Head would say, yes OK, and then he wasn't sure if he might be Coloured or something. Because if he was Coloured, *well*, he could have slightly frizzy hair, although if he had more predominantly the white genes then he probably had smooth hair. But one of the tricks is they ... put a pencil in the guy's hair – and if it doesn't fall out then you don't accept him. I mean really, you know. And, of course, the Coloureds, a lot of them did go into Mansfield or what have you.

As a white-classified school, it seems very unlikely that Mansfield believed it was admitting 'a lot of' Coloureds. One former Mansfield student whom I asked about this comment said that perhaps the former teacher meant Portuguese students. While the extent that the pencil test was used in white schools is hard to determine, the practice follows logically from the fact that white schools administered admissions and excluded children who were not thought to be white.

What is clear is that Mansfield's reputation for admitting working-class whites and perhaps even Coloureds evoked ideas that 'poor whites' existed 'on the borders of respectability, of colour, of whiteness'.[27] One University of Natal report written in the 1970s also described Mansfield School (along with Greyville racecourse and the Botanic Gardens) as a 'buffer' that divided white residential areas from the predominantly Indian educational complex.[28] Moreover, the sentiment that working-class whites needed racial upliftment is evidenced in a newspaper article that celebrated the 'missionary work' of teachers leaving Durban High School to head lesser-status white schools.[29] Missionaries were, of course, the quintessential bringers of civilisation to black society.

If a person's social class affected their racial classification in the early apartheid period, by the late 1960s this was changing. A major success of the apartheid state was its institutionalisation of race in identity cards and segregated 'group areas'. Children mostly attended their local school in racially zoned suburbs and racial classification itself shifted to being a 'purely administrative and bureaucratic matter' when children's race followed that of their parents.[30] As Keith Breckenridge writes, this system of racial descent was 'invented' in that it rested on the arbitrary foundations of mass classification in the 1950s and 1960s (i.e. through 'common-sense' definitions).[31]

A second factor stabilising racial identities was rising white living standards. In the 1960s, the wage differential between skilled (white) and unskilled (black) work was four to six times what it was in Europe and the United States.[32] If even working-class children attended affluent white schools and had their clothes washed by a black maid, how could they be seen as somehow black? Indeed, as race separation intensified, it is noticeable that derogatory terms directed towards working-class whites such as 'Scumbilo' (addressed to those from the working-class Umbilo area) and the 'rough and tough Bluff' did not explicitly evoke race. At the same time, residues of past meanings lingered. One white Durbanite told me that poor whites could continue to be referred to as 'white Kaffirs' (Kaffir is a highly derogatory racist term used for black Africans).[33]

Below, I continue to highlight differences in whiteness and among white-classified people by contrasting elite 'traditional' schools located on the Berea with more working-class schools located in south Durban, specifically the Bluff.

## Berea elites and traditional schools

After the British proclaimed Natal a colony in 1843, the Berea ridge became a favoured place for settlement (Figure 2.3). When British writer Anthony Trollope visited Durban in 1877, a city then of around 4,000, he noted that the views from the Berea ridge 'would be very precious to many an opulent suburb in England'.[34] As a settler community whose ideas of whiteness were always in the process of being made, great attention was placed on decorum; as Trollope notes, 'a colonial town is ashamed of itself if it has not its garden, its hospital, its public library, and its two or three churches, even in its early days'.[35]

Durban's population swelled in the twentieth century, and a house's height on the Berea slopes became a good predictor of its price.[36] Anthropologist Eleanor Preston-Whyte described the upper parts of Berea's Morningside area in the early 1960s as 'remarkably homogeneous': overwhelmingly white and English speaking, with men working as professionals and in businesses – and their wives occupying their time with '[b]ridge, sport and charity work'.[37] The term 'Berea style' is testimony to how Berea became synonymous with cultural prestige. The style signalled elegance and class, such as its Edwardian white iron balconies that afforded residents a cool sea breeze to offset the humid subtropical climate.

Figure 2.3 Victorian family scene on the Berea ridge with the Bluff headland visible in the background.
*Source:* Campbell Collection (digital image repaired with permission).

All of Durban's early prestigious schools were located on the Berea ridge. Durban High School, which opened in the city centre in 1866, relocated to the Musgrave suburb in 1895. Durban Girls' High School opened in 1882, Durban Preparatory High School was set up in 1910 to channel students into Durban High School, Glenwood High School moved to Berea in 1934, and the private Durban Girls' College opened in 1877. These establishments had close ties to Natal's earliest schools built in the colonial capital of Pietermaritzburg and its nearby Midlands region.

Further afield, in the older Cape colony, elite English schools were built from the 1840s. In Johannesburg, a city developed only after the discovery of gold in 1886, imperial leader Lord Milner established so-called 'Milner schools' to anglicise this Afrikaner heartland.

So influential were South Africa's top schools, including those on the Berea, that it was said in 1993 that only 23 'historic' white schools – overwhelmingly English-medium – produced 'the lion's share of our political and social leadership'.[38] In turn, South Africa's prestigious schools formed part of a network of elite Anglophile institutions that dotted British colonies from the Caribbean to India.

Peter Randall shows how South Africa's elite schools modelled themselves on English private schools, with their 'boarding, house system, prefect system, "school spirit" and compulsory games'.[39] 'Along with the model,' writes Randall, went 'a vision of Englishness compounded of playing the game, midnight feasts in the dormitories . . . and the sporting life of the English landed gentry'.[40] In this hierarchical school system, prefects enjoyed considerable powers, and the practice of 'fagging' ensured that younger students undertook tasks for their seniors. Single-sex institutions reflected and perpetuated the view that upper-class men should be educated to lead, and women schooled to become respectable wives.

In Britain, the gulf between government and private (ironically called public) schools continues to this day. But in South Africa private and top-tier government schools shared many features. One 1974 study of 'white South African elites' found that seven of the country's top 12 schools were in fact government schools, with Durban High School producing the most influential leaders in the country.[41] By promoting discipline and leadership skills, including through 'cadet' military training, which included using live ammunition, government schools sought to produce brave gentlemen acting in the service of the British Empire.[42] British troops defeated the Zulu Kingdom after a series of bloody battles in 1879 but the threat of African society continued to loom large.

Again with a legacy that continues to this day, school sports had a central place within the British private school model. Rugby, with its scrums, tackles, and teamwork, anchored a heteronormative masculinity within schools that valued discipline and physical prowess. Robert Morrell's study of settler masculinity in colonial Natal shows that, for the Natal gentry, 'soccer became emblematic of threatening, socially integrative forces within society. As it [the Natal gentry] forged its class identity so it took to itself the rugby code as an additional, racially exclusive, identifying feature.'[43] Cricket, another British sport played in elite schools, made gentlemen – but rugby made soldiers.

Certain English schools were therefore labelled 'traditional' not just because they were old. They played sports together and showed fidelity to the English private school model, and their powerful old boys (and to a lesser extent old girls) became interlocked in networks of power – albeit increasingly overlapping with the growing Afrikaner business and political establishment. 'Traditional' or 'great' were not terms ever associated with schools built for children destined for the lower ranks of farming, the trades, commerce, or industry, however old the schools might have been. These included, in the lower Berea area, Clarence Primary School and Mansfield Primary School, which were opened in 1905 and 1911 respectively. South of the Berea area, Hillary Primary (built in 1889) and Seaview Primary (opened in 1904) were located near the Old Main Line, which from the late nineteenth century had connected Durban to the capital Pietermaritzburg by rail.

For a final window onto 'traditional' schools' sense of superiority let us return to the 1960s and the issue of 'zoning': that is, admitting learners who lived locally. In the booming post-war period, admissions were largely uncontentious because children attended their local school: this was the rationale behind the expansion of schools shown in Map 2.1.

In the early 1960s, however, Natal Education Department (NED) made a controversial attempt to enforce zoning in central parts of the city. A 1966 survey of central Durban's schools found that considerable money was wasted subsidising school transport because one out of every four children travelled further than they would if they attended their nearest school.[44] In the face of this challenge to their autonomy, old boys from Durban High and Glenwood High defended the schools' favouring of the children of old boys.[45] Their attitude reflected English society's siege-like mentality when Afrikaans speakers ('the Nats') ascended to positions of power after the National Party's election victory and threatened the (implicitly neutral) English school tradition.[46]

Eventually, the NED and Berea schools reached a compromise: a zoning system that allocated points based on children's place of residence and on whether they had ties to the school through either their siblings' or father's schooling. The NED labelled zoning as 'preferential admissions' or 'restrictive admissions' and allowed schools the freedom to take out-of-area students when they were not full. As we shall see later, similar compromises over zoning – this time between the white and black middle class – were reached in the post-apartheid period.

To summarise, if a little crudely, the configuration of practices associated with whiteness became embroiled with the bricks and mortar of elite schools, with the upper-middle-class suburbs in which they were located, with the sports they played, and with the links between them and Britain. As we shall see below, the NED believed that new working-class schools should aspire to this cultural world, even if they channelled lower-class whites into industrial and trade work.

## The rough and tough Bluff suburb

At the turn of the century, 'to live on Durban's Bluff was to be a pioneer of hardy stock. There were no amenities, no roads'.[47] White residents lived on farms, in residential houses on the inner of two ridges stretching south to north from Wentworth to Fynnlands station, or at the Catholic mission. Only in 1932 did Durban city incorporate the area now called south Durban in order to facilitate the expansion of industry and white housing.

The Bluff's first schools were primary schools, namely Van Riebeeck Park (1920) and Fynnlands (1936). While local governments supported white housing from the 1920s, it was in the post-war period that south Durban's suburbs mushroomed, including the Bluff, Woodlands, Montclair, and Yellowwood Park (next to and a step up from Woodlands and Montclair).[48] Many of south Durban's white residents, including a large number of European immigrants, worked at local factories in Jacobs, Mobeni, and Prospecton; at one of two local oil refineries; at the airport; and at the port – the country's busiest by far.[49]

Figure 2.4  A railway house, renovated and extended, in the Fynnlands part of the Bluff. Liquid bulk storage and the Bluff headland can be seen in the background. Photograph: Mark Hunter.

However, no employer promoted the white working class more than the state-owned South African Railways and Harbours Administration. Van Tonder's semi-autobiographical book *Roepman* ('call man') describes the modest conditions of Afrikaans speakers in the Bluff's 'railway camps' linked to the port. He remembers shunters, drivers, and ticket examiners living in cramped conditions, with sometimes 'ten people ... in a three-bedroomed house'.[50]

At the same time, the Bluff and other parts of south Durban gained reputations not just as working-class areas but also as 'open suburbs of Durban for young families with growing children'.[51] Upper-middle-class suburbs such as Westville and Durban North grew rapidly and their excellent schools in particular decentred Berea's image as the heartland of upper-crust society. On the Bluff, privately owned accommodation constituted a bedrock of middle-class houses that raised the area's reputation (later, rental railway houses were themselves sold off) (Figure 2.4). A smaller number of affluent families lived on Marine Drive in houses that overlooked the Indian Ocean and shelved steeply down to the beaches. This blurring of class distinctions is why I talk of the area at times as a working-class/lower-middle-class suburb.

*Schooling culture on the Bluff and in south Durban*

Schools everywhere in the world are complex and varied institutions where young people's sexual, political, and gendered identities are constantly in flux. The 1966 Grosvenor Boys' magazine is 28 pages long and has sections dedicated to poetry, a young Christian association, science club, a speech and drama festival, and debating, as well as numerous pages devoted to sports. It reported that the library had 3,700 books; that the gardens were beautiful; and that students won awards for science projects.[52]

However, for the purposes of this book's themes, let us return to the Bluff's position in the country's schooling hierarchy. New secondary schools built for working-class white children conferred qualifications (in Weber's words, 'educational patents') that justified whites' appointment into positions above black South Africans. The curriculum provided a view of white society as superior. 'Cadet' training, which increasingly fell under the auspices of the South African Defence Force, prepared young men for compulsory military service.[53]

Within the logic of white schooling hierarchies, the Bluff's English schools were presented as requiring academic and, even more importantly, cultural upliftment. Grosvenor Boys' High's first principal, who had taught at Berea's Durban High School and played rugby for Natal, was seen as 'the right man to set Grosvenor Boys' High on its feet, especially on the rugby field'.[54] As the president of the Surf Lifesaving Association of South Africa said in an address to the Bluff's Grosvenor Boys' School: '[The] "moral" training and "development of character" cannot be fully achieved without participation in sports.'[55]

While the city's top schools channelled graduates into high-status work, the expectation in the 1960s was that most male Bluffites would find skilled working-class or junior professional jobs. Natal's Director of Education chose New Forest School in Woodlands, south Durban, to discuss new practical options in the curriculum. At the end of standard 6 (grade 8), he said, all pupils would take science, practical maths, and social studies, with boys channelled into handicrafts and geometrical drawing and girls ushered into home crafts, health education, office routines, and typing.[56] Philip Roberts studied at New Forest in the late 1960s and told me: 'I would say more than half left in standard 8 those days to do a trade.' Some established their own small plumbing, building, or other businesses.

The sense of social distance between working-class Bluffites and 'larney' people can been seen in the account of one resident who attended an Afrikaans school on the Bluff and recalled looking for professional work in Berea in the 1970s:

MR LOUW: When I went for my first interview, there was a kid ... and he actually wore a school tie to the interview. And he said to me, 'Where did you go to school?' And I said, 'Dirkie Uys,' and he said, 'Where is that?'

AUTHOR:    Which interview was that?
MR LOUW:  I wanted to sign up for articles at an auditing firm and the guy sat
                    next to me and he said, 'It's an old school tie type of job.'

However, as Mr Louw's attendance at this interview suggests, bright
learners at working-class schools were not completely shut off from
professional jobs. Of the 1965 matriculants at the Bluff's Grosvenor
High, 11 planned to attend university out of a starting cohort of around
150.[57] Within the walls of white schools, differentiation took place by
means of separate streams or tracks, sometimes organised using IQ tests.
The introduction in the 1960s of ordinary-level exams (separated from
advanced-level) was a deliberate strategy to give less academic students
a way to stay longer at school (after 1973 these became standard and
higher grades).[58]

Philip Roberts, the former Woodlands schoolboy quoted above, was in
the school's top stream. After he passed his matriculation exam, he found
a job as a cashier in a bank and then worked his way up to become a bank
manager. The white schooling system also allowed the top-tracked students to transfer into more prestigious schools with stronger academic
reputations. One former student of south Durban's New Forest School
noted that some of the top students of the 8A class would transfer to
Berea's Durban High School and Glenwood, where they would study
standards 9 and 10 (grades 11 and 12). The movement of a pupil did not
seem to be seen, as it later would, as poaching, but rather as a sort of
endorsement of the quality of the lesser-ranked school.

### Working-class sports

If rugby was thought to have unmatched potential to uplift white boys,
working-class communities carved out a distinct sporting counterculture.
The Natal Education Department discouraged soccer in white schools
especially in the 1950s and 1960s, when many schools were 'finding their
feet'; indeed, a soccer association for high schools was only established in
1986.[59] However, learners at working-class schools often preferred
soccer to rugby, playing the former after school and at weekends. Mr
Morris, a former professional soccer player who studied at an English-
medium south Durban school, told me: 'Rugby was very dominant in
our schools in those days and the principals used to in fact try to shun us
away from soccer, so much so that if you were caught trying to go to
soccer when you should have been playing school rugby, you would get
into trouble. I mean serious trouble.'

Another male former south Durban student, who wore a Liverpool FC
shirt when we met, explained how soccer was promoted at local club
level, rather than under the disapproving authority of schools. This

soccer culture, and its sense of being a counterculture – including through racially mixed soccer teams – is the subject of the film *Soccer: south of the Umbilo* (2010), written and directed by John Barker, the son of former national soccer team coach Clive Barker (the Umbilo River marks the beginning of south Durban).[60] The film shows how the south Durban region produced both Barker and Gordon Igesund (national team coach from 1994 to 1997 and 2012 to 2014 respectively).

I gained further insights one day when I was invited by an organiser to a reunion at a sports club in Montclair, just inland from the Bluff. Around a hundred men, most of whom had known one another since the 1960s, stood chatting with beers in hand. A few wives sat unobtrusively at one side of the hall. The men I chatted with recalled their pride in the working-class culture of this area, some contrasting it to the 'larney' central parts of town. One man in his sixties told me: 'We didn't talk about university in our house ... it was "Go and earn a wage, son."'

After a lot of beer had been consumed, the evening climaxed with a boisterous quiz about old soccer moments in south Durban – passionate descriptions of famous players, tackles, and goals scored and saved – followed by the old soccer team posing for a group photograph. I left the reception with my own Polaroid photograph, given to me on the insistence of a man with whom I had talked and who posed next to me for the picture. We chatted in part about similarities between South Africa and the UK; I had played club soccer (football, as we called it) while attending school in England in the 1970s and 1980s, whereas rugby union was mainly played at private schools. At the gathering, I didn't see any black former soccer players in attendance, nor Afrikaans speakers – the latter, as we shall see below, advanced largely by circumventing rather than challenging the power of English speakers.

## The advancement of Afrikaans speakers

In Durban in the 1950s, only 15 per cent of whites were Afrikaans speakers. Nationally, in contrast, 58 per cent of whites spoke Afrikaans as a home language, many concentrated in the Orange Free State and Transvaal provinces, and the western parts of the Cape.[61] The particular dependence of Durban's Afrikaans speakers on railway work meant that they tended to be concentrated geographically near railway infrastructure, namely in the Bluff, Seaview, Hilary, Bellair, and Queensburgh.

The upward mobility of Afrikaans speakers in South Africa is a remarkable story of ethno-national advancement. The 1910 Union of South Africa established English and Dutch as the two official languages (Afrikaans substituting for Dutch in 1914), but English remained dominant in spheres of power.[62] Although some Dutch/Afrikaans speakers were affluent farmers and professionals, thousands of 'poor whites' moved from rural areas to cities ill equipped with skills or capital. In 1918, a group of intellectuals founded the Broederbond, a secret cultural organisation that came to play a central role in Afrikaner nationalism and eventually in implementing apartheid.[63] Afrikaner nationalists evoked past injustices, notably the British concentration camps in the Anglo-Boer War, and erased awkward truths to strengthen their unity. These included Afrikaans' roots as a creolised version of Dutch, first written in Arabic and spoken by slaves and other immigrants (many Muslim) and indigenous persons including Khoikhoi in the Cape (Afrikaans remains spoken more by black than by white families, including 'Coloureds' in the Cape).[64]

Afrikaans-speaking children had historically been accommodated in parallel-medium schools where English-speaking culture prevailed (parallel medium meant separate Afrikaans- and English-medium classes in the same school). One former employee described the Anglophile Natal Education Department as following a 'deliberate policy of cultural imperialism'.[65] Gathering steam from the 1930s, Afrikaner nationalists demanded separate schools, and they had their first victory in Durban when Port Natal School was opened in 1941 in south Berea. Following the National Party's triumph in the 1948 election, this move accelerated: two Afrikaans primary schools and one secondary school were opened on the Bluff, and additional co-educational Afrikaans schools were opened in Queensburgh, Durban North, Amanzimtoti, and Pinetown.

When I visited the Bluff's Afrikaans secondary school, built in 1961, the principal walked me down a corridor and pointed to pictures of past principals adorning the walls. He told me that all but one head had left for promotion in the education bureaucracy. A prominent picture was of the founding headmaster, Philip Nel, who was placed in charge of Indian education in 1964 and then served as the director of the white NED from 1967 to 1977.

As indicated by the zoning controversy, however, Afrikaans-speaking administrators preferred compromise to conflict in dealing with English schools that, after all, were responsible for most of the province's educational accolades. Indeed, separate schools – along with the raising of Afrikaans' status nationally – were successful in propelling Afrikaans speakers from blue- to white-collar and government jobs such as teaching, the police force, and the army (a Special Forces training unit occupied the northern tip of the Bluff). Around 70 per cent of high-school teachers in the 1970s graduated from Afrikaans-medium schools.[66] Moreover, Mr Van Rooyen, a former teacher who matriculated from Port Natal School in 1958, described the effects of state-backed *volkskapitalisme* ('people's capitalism'), which aimed to create an Afrikaner capitalist class, as follows:[67]

[When I was young] there were only two [children of] professional people in the school. There was ... the manager of the bank they called Volkskas and the chap in charge of the insurance company, Sanlam. Only two. The rest were working on the railways, or in the army ... And eventually more and more [parents] became business people.

Although in Afrikaner folklore the English were imperialists, Grundlingh documents the Afrikaans speakers' quick embrace of Western consumer items, including cars, in the booming 1960s.[68]

The rising confidence of Afrikaans speakers played out elsewhere in the cultural realm, including on rugby pitches around the country. From the early twentieth century, Afrikaans speakers came to venerate rugby for its 'ruggedness, endurance, forcefulness and determination'.[69] With the backing of both English and Afrikaans speakers, rugby became a symbol of the strength of the white settler nation and its attachment to – but also its independence from – the colonial power of Britain. Rugby prowess won respect for Afrikaans schools when some were skilled enough to play prestigious English schools, such as those in Berea, that controlled what amounted to the A league (south Durban English schools typically played in a lower-status group of schools). One teacher at Port Natal School, the first Afrikaans school in Durban, described to me the time when his school beat Durban High School, as 'one of the highlights of my career'. On the Bluff, the much-anticipated rugby match between the local Afrikaans and English boys' schools, dubbed the 'Boer War' in reference to the 1899–1902 war, represented a moment of competition as well as a shared passion. It symbolised bloody past conflicts, but also that social mobility anchored in schooling could smooth over differences among whites.

Nationally, white South Africans had every reason to unite. After police gunned down 60 people in Sharpeville in 1960, an uncertain political climate ensued. The country, a republic after 1961, became increasingly ostracised from the international community. These political tensions, along with labour shortages, did not halt the state's implementation of the Bantu Education Act. But they did encourage state officials to see Indian and Coloured workers as providing a buffer between white and African society, and this had important educational implications, which I review briefly below.

## Indian workers and schooling

Bantu Education's core belief, considered in more detail later, is captured in the much-quoted statement by then Minister Hendrik Verwoerd (president from 1958 to 1966): 'There is no place for him [Africans] in the European community above the level of certain forms of labour.'[70] Indeed, until the 1970s, almost all schools built for black Africans were primary schools. While Africans were thought of as suited for 'routine repetitive work', Durban's large Indian population were thought to be capable of filling jobs requiring 'initiative and quick thinking'.[71] Anti-Indian sentiment was particularly strong in Durban, but in a structural sense Indian workers were both 'insiders and outsiders' under apartheid, in Bill Freund's words.[72]

After the Second World War, industry had transformed from 'small-scale craft workshops to large-scale factory production'.[73] A more stratified division of labour created a demand for semi-skilled machine operators, technicians, and supervisors. The shortage of white labour, only partly mitigated by immigration, put constant pressure on the system of racial job reservations.

This tension played out in the state's approach to Indian schooling. In 1969, Philip Nel, a key official in Indian and white schooling, as noted above, visited an Indian school on Natal's south coast. One student, Vishnu Padayachee, who went on to become a distinguished professor of development economics at the University of Witwatersrand, remembers Nel lambasting his teacher for spending too much time teaching science to students who wouldn't need those skills.[74] As a former principal of the Bluff's working-class Dirkie Uys Afrikaans High School, Nel must have sensed the difficulties of maintaining race-based job reservations when academic subjects were open to non-whites.

Yet Indian communities and industrialists put great pressure on the state to invest in Indian secondary schools.[75] Until the 1950s, Indian educational institutions had depended heavily on the support of local businesses, communities, and religious organisations as well as trans-oceanic links to India itself. Few learners progressed past primary school. However, between 1955 and 1965, the number of Indian high-school pupils, many pushed into new townships, increased from 3,024 to 13,000.[76] A small university for Indians was established on Salisbury Island off the Bluff in 1961 and enrolments swelled after it moved to Westville in 1971. By this period, Indians were overwhelmingly home-language English speakers, or, as sociolinguists say, 'Indian South African English' speakers.[77]

Whereas administering the 'Bantu' required the expertise of anthropologists, somewhat similar educational frameworks were applied to Indian and white learners. 'Differentiated' secondary education, explored through visits to Europe, became a key focus of Philip Nel's tenure in charge of both Indian and white education.[78] Clairwood School for Indians was opened in 1956 and combined academic subjects with workshops for motor mechanics, woodwork, fitting and turning, plumbing, welding, panel beating, and spray painting.[79] Speaking at Clairwood as the head of Indian education in 1964, Mr Nel said:

During the past two decades there has been a phenomenal expansion in secondary education in various parts of the world ... pupils entering secondary schools differ in age, aptitude, ability, and physical stamina ... The ideal secondary school should obviously offer a wide range of differentiated courses.[80]

In the workplace, however, Indian workers faced constant discrimination. Mr Reddy grew up in Cato Manor and remembers his family being removed to the new Indian township of Merebank. His father worked in a shoe factory, a common job for Indian men at this time. In his interview, he recalled the painful bias that directly affected his work path:

I worked for C. G. Smith [a chemicals company] and they had white guys coming in straight out of school and being sponsored to go to university or Technikon, etc. And I approached management to say that I would also like that benefit ... I said, 'But those guys are new and I have been here five years. They just walk in and you are able to send them, so why can't you do that for me?' And I was told in no uncertain terms that if I bring something up again like that I will lose my job. No. It was very blatant and they were not ashamed to say you are different ... I mean I worked for nearly 37, 38 years and for all that time I have always had a white person coming in, you have been told teach him the job, and a month or so after he is in the job an announcement is made that he is my boss. It happened often and I think it's one of the most frustrating things that I have had to deal with in my working life. And you know his shortfalls and you know his weaknesses. Yet he is your boss.

## Gender, white families, and schooling

A final form of educational differentiation occurred along gender lines. Robert Morrell's study of colonial Natal brings to life the world of old Natal families and old Durban families (who came to be known as ONFs and ODFs). He described middle-class women as having a strong sense of independence, even in the nineteenth century.[81] By the mid-twentieth century, headmistress Dorothy D. E. Langley (daughter of former Durban High School principal Aubrey Langley, famed for bringing rugby to the school), told the Johannesburg High School Old Girls' Club in 1954 that: 'Women surely appreciate the knowledge that they can be economically secure ... Without being feminists, we watch and appraise the work of women in welfare, municipal and political arenas.'[82]

Jobs reserved for whites created a demand for educated white women, and the number of white female matriculants tripled from 1960 to 1990.[83] One government official urged students at Durban Girls' High School to meet the shortage of white (male) labour while counselling them to not neglect their roles as mothers and wives.[84] However, it remained the case even in the mid-1980s that only a small proportion of white women who passed the school leaving examination enrolled in tertiary education courses.[85] Overwhelmingly, men took up elite professional, political, and business positions in South African society.[86]

As in the case of boys' schools, the location (and thus status) of a girls' school affected not only the amount of polish it gave girls as potential wives but also the type of employment into which it channelled them. Berea's popular Durban Girls' High School celebrated old girls moving into jobs that included commerce, teaching, and nursing, with some top students entering university.[87] In contrast, at Grosvenor Girls' School on the Bluff, girls were schooled in shorthand and typing, with many leaving school for work at age 16.[88] Girls' schools shared with boys' schools an attention to neat school uniforms and hair, but they placed much less emphasis on the sports they played such as hockey and swimming.

In the home, black female domestic workers increasingly replaced black male workers in the post-war period.[89] When servants relieved much of the drudgery of housework and childcare, white women had more time for paid work and children's schooling. Mothers wrote most of the letters to the Natal Education Department in the 1960s requesting places for their children in boarding establishments attached to some of the best schools. Complaints about men's indifference to their children were common in correspondence. Mrs Fuller, a mother of two living on Wentworth Road near the Wentworth railway depot on the Bluff, wrote to the department in 1963 about her concerns. Her eldest child had found work in the railways, but her youngest child, aged 15, was still at school. Her husband was pressuring the youngest to find work on the railways and leave school too, but the mother wanted help in continuing the child's education through a hostel or boarding school:[90]

[M]y problem though is this. My ex-husband is giving me no support whatsoever towards the boys and has failed to do so for several years. My present husband has taken a real stepfather's attitude towards these: he makes no secret of his actual hate for them, consequently the home is a desperately unhappy place for them.

Men, in the few instances when they did write to the Department of Education, had a firmer and more demanding tone. Mr Riddle wanted to admit his son to a prestigious Berea boys' school and gave the following reasons: 'I would very much like him to enter a school where besides passing the usual exams they will also make a gentleman out of him.'[91]

However, to say that schooling was largely a female domain is not to say that men did not have close relations with their children; it is just that earning the household salary was seen as the man's most important role. Von Tonder's account portrays his Bluff father as a distant disciplinarian who worked long hours, with his mother being responsible for the daily care of the children.

A relevant question, itself inherently gendered, is whether young people tended to choose marriage partners on the basis of home language (English or Afrikaans) or their shared work and residential location. This is difficult to quantify, but there are many mixed Afrikaans–English couples on the Bluff. It appears to have been much more likely that a working-class English speaker would marry a working-class Afrikaans speaker (who spoke English as a second language) than someone from an upper-class Berea family. In almost all the cases I have encountered, children of mixed-language couples studied at English-medium schools.

Indeed, throughout the apartheid era and beyond, white Bluffites celebrated the suburb's sense of community. Implicit in their identification as 'ratepayers' was residents' resentment at the city's superior treatment of more 'larney' areas. When a Bluff councillor advocated for his constituents, a fellow councillor asked sarcastically: 'And where is the Bluff?'[92] Environmental pollution provided another area of cooperation, Stephen Sparks showing how a white 'civic culture' developed to reduce pollution from South Africa's first oil refinery, built in Wentworth in the 1950s.[93]

Moreover, in everyday life, leisure and shopping spaces played an important part in bringing residents together. In 1962, for instance, residents could visit the Bluff drive-in cinema to see *The Gene Krupa Story* about the legendary US jazz drummer.[94] One resident remembered:

You had things like movies happening and local discos ... Friday nights were movies in the hall ... And the drive-in was the other place we used to meet. If we didn't go to the Bluff drive-in, we went to Umbilo or Durban drive-in.

As well as soccer and rugby, the Bluff's proximity to the beach gave it an appeal not enjoyed by other working-class suburbs. And the large winter swells that directly hit the shores gave surfers a way to distinguish themselves from the 'town clowns' enjoying the city's more protected beaches.

## Conclusions

The unprecedented prosperity of white South Africans in the 1960s was underpinned by a large expansion of schooling, especially at the secondary-school level. Race had fuzzy boundaries in the early apartheid period, being especially related to social class. However, segregated schooling became a key means through which '[t]he racial becomes the spatial. The social construction of race becomes one with the physical occupation of space. The racialized becomes the segregated, and racial meanings become inscribed upon space.'[95]

The privileged position of white schools should not, however, occlude differences among them. The National Party's efforts to improve the status of Afrikaans in comparison to English stole the headlines. But elite English-speaking schools, centred on the Berea ridge, remained at the top of the schooling hierarchy in Durban – as similar schools did across South Africa, and, indeed, across the British Empire. A particular configuration of whiteness was tied to the upper Berea's lifestyle: old boys' networks, rugby, cricket, and businesses and professional work. Berea's suburbs, including Musgrave, Morningside, and Essenwood, looked down literally and metaphorically on the rest of the city.

Over the harbour on the 'rough and tough' Bluff, differences existed among Afrikaans and English speakers but a strong sense of local white community developed. Typical work taken by Bluff school leavers was in the trades or in lower-middle-class professions. Among the English in particular, soccer was widely played after school and at the weekends.

Thus, education did not simply unfold in pre-existing racially imprinted areas; it helped to make a raced and classed city. Whiteness – or white tone – was not neatly legislated but made in mundane acts including those shaped by schooling. We will see how this planned schooling system became more marketised in the 1970s and 1980s and how working-class jobs no longer automatically guaranteed middle-class life-styles. Ultimately, this led to quite different schooling trajectories among young white people. Before considering this, we need to explore the making of Durban's largest township, Umlazi.

# 3    Umlazi Township and the gendered 'bond of education'

Umlazi Township was built for black 'Africans' removed from central parts of Durban. Located 20 kilometres south of the city, Umlazi's first houses were completed in 1962; only a decade later it had a population of between 200,000 and 250,000 people.[1] Townships were not new to South Africa. But the 1950 Group Areas Act resulted in the massive building or extension of these settlements on the outskirts of every city.

In one of Umlazi's small 'matchbox' houses lives Precious Mhlongo, a short, grey-haired woman in her eighties. One of her eyes is partially closed, half-conscious of the world, the other alert. She can often be seen, back arched, stick in hand, navigating the insufferably steep driveway of her home. There are very few flat areas in this hastily built settlement.

Mrs Mhlongo grew up in the 1930s in one of Natal's rural 'reserves' – rural areas designed to separate black Africans from white society. Schooling was not part of her life until she was nine years old. Not only were schools few and far between, but her father's reluctance to educate her was a common sentiment among older men at this time.[2] Mrs Mhlongo explained why:

They said that girls should marry and not study ... they said that I am going to be *isigebengu, ihumusha, isifebe* [roughly: scoundrel, prostitute, loose woman] ... they said that education is a thing of the white people ... my mother liked education but my father didn't.

After her father's death, Mrs Mhlongo's mother, a strong Christian, sent her to school for six years, helped by her working son (Mrs Mhlongo's brother). Several years later, Mrs Mhlongo married a young man from the area who worked in Durban. Reliant on the money he sent home, she oversaw the day-to-day running of their rural *umuzi* (homestead), raised their children, and grew maize, beans, and a few other crops able to survive the depleted rural soil.

Over time, however, her husband's contributions dwindled, his visits became less frequent, and they grew apart, eventually separating permanently. Finding herself single in her late twenties, Mrs Mhlongo's primary-school English helped her to find work as a domestic worker in a small town on Natal's south coast. When her employers relocated, she moved with them to Durban. Several years later she rented a room in a house in Umlazi Township – a quite common, though unlawful, living arrangement. Then, in the early 1970s, she acquired the four-room house we were sitting in, registering it in her adult son's name.

Over the last 40 years, Mrs Mhlongo has lived in this same Umlazi Township house with her children, grandchildren, and great-grandchildren, always encouraging them to study. Her children attended some of the best secondary schools in Umlazi. When schooling desegregation began in the 1990s, some of her grandchildren were enrolled in formerly white schools; recently, she looked after her granddaughter's son so that he could attend a nearby formerly Coloured school. In turn, her children's and grandchildren's sense of obligation is reflected in the improvements they made to the house when they found work – backyard rooms, a new refrigerator, a television, and the last time I saw her, in 2017, a new bed. Sometimes, however, she questioned out loud whether her family members were doing enough to support her.

Chapter 2 compared the 'larney' Berea and 'rough and tough' Bluff to reveal the formative role of class in the making of Durban's white suburbs. Here, in our second chapter on racial modernism, we consider a township built for 'Africans' and give specific attention to gender. This is not a comprehensive history of Umlazi Township, nor of 'Bantu education', but introduces arguments developed later in the book.

The chapter's first theme is the extraordinary role 'African' women have played in promoting their children's schooling in South Africa. Although many men are committed to schooling, and have long been so, a striking feature of Umlazi Township today, so taken for granted that it is hardly commented upon, is that women, be they grandmothers like Mrs Mhlongo in their eighties or unmarried young women in their twenties, play a central role in promoting schooling. Born in the 1930s, Mrs Mhlongo's generation was the last to be cast as *izifebe* (loose women/prostitutes) for being overeducated and the first to see their grandchildren attend 'multiracial' schools outside the township.

I situate mothers' attention to schooling in relation to the multiple forms of oppression that women face. Successive governments from the colonial period onwards conceived of African women not only as inferior to whites but as obedient daughters and wives. When women worked, their employers paid them less than the typical wages paid to men. For a domestic worker such as Mrs Mhlongo, with almost no prospect of occupational advancement, her children's schooling provided some hope of long-term assistance, even the bettering of her life. It follows that the moral obligations educated and employed children have to support family members – what in recent years has been labelled the 'black tax' – has deep gendered as well as racial roots.

Before the apartheid era, mission schools provided almost all formal education for black Africans. The 1953 Bantu Education Act brought schooling under the remit of the state, expanded primary education to feed booming industries, and altered the basis on which racial hierarchies became instituted – a second theme this chapter particularly emphasises. As we saw, apartheid's racial classifiers melded phenotypic differences with 'common-sense' understandings of race. Thus, a person's higher social class indicated a certain proximity to whiteness. But this racial-cultural hierarchy, as policed as it was by the state, could spell danger. If black South Africans who attended mission schools, such as Nelson Mandela, could speak fluent English, attain academic credentials, and aspire to professional work, what were the grounds for denying them political rights?

Bantu education resulted in the closure of most mission schools and initiated the era of mass primary-school education that directed learners into the lowest-paid and lowest-status work. It aimed to channel African aspirations along 'tribal' lines and, to a degree, away from the English language and a 'bookish' approach to school. The tone of a Bantu education school should not be English, academic, and aspirational – aspects coded as 'European' or 'white' – but ethnic and practical. Thus, scores of new primary schools were established in areas to which Africans were moved. These included urban townships such as Umlazi and rural 'reserves' that formed the basis of what became semi-autonomous 'Bantustans' or 'homelands'. Educators were required to teach in the medium of African languages.

As we shall see in Chapter 4, apartheid's racial modernism unravelled under its own contradictions. Political protests, employers' demands for a more skilled workforce, the rise of English-medium secondary schools, the failure of homelands to legitimise apartheid, and the desegregation of private white schools were to shake the foundations of apartheid from the 1970s. In Umlazi, a market in schooling began to develop alongside the growth of secondary schools, the best of which modelled themselves on mission schools. But the education system to this day remains shaped – in terms of facilities, geographies, and cultural dispositions (or symbolic power) – by this period of racial modernism. We begin this chapter, as Mrs Mhlongo began her life, in rural South Africa. We then move to Umlazi Township and foreground mothers' attention to housing and schooling.

## Gender, 'white' schooling, and the institutionalisation of 'tradition'

To ask why Mrs. Mhlongo's father might oppose his daughter's schooling is to recognise that the moral economy of rural life was profoundly gendered. We are situated at this point in rural parts of Natal and Zululand (annexed to Natal in 1897) on the south-eastern tip of the continent. What follows is a somewhat broad-brush introduction to this world.

Precolonial society in southern Africa was never static but it is possible to reconstruct some key features. The primary physical institutions were *imizi* (homesteads; singular: *umuzi*) in which family members raised livestock and cultivated crops. An *umuzi* was founded after marriage and therefore after the giving of *ilobolo* cattle (bridewealth) from a groom's father (an *umnumzana* or head of *umuzi*) to a bride's father.[3] Marriage and *ilobolo* had enormous significance not just to the couple themselves but to relations between *umuzi* and *umuzi* and brother and sister. Indeed, central to Shaka's forging of the mighty Zulu kingdom in the early nineteenth century was his power to permit marriage only after a young man completed military service.

This rural way of life became connected, emotionally and economically, with urban workplaces and white-owned farms brought by colonialism and capitalism. Following the discovery of diamonds and gold in the 1850s and 1880s, African men's circular rural–urban movement became the defining labour pattern in southern Africa.[4] After 1910, when the four colonies became provinces to form the Union of South Africa, a national framework of laws intensified segregation. The 1913 Land Act granted Africans only 8 per cent of the country's land, extended to 13 per cent in 1932. Men were forced into wage labour because productive land was now scarcer and they had to pay taxes. In cities, African men were required to carry 'passes' to justify being away from rural areas.

In sum, whereas elders had educated young people for generations about the moral duties of rural life, this world became entangled with new movements and commodities brought by settler rule. But it was mission schools that introduced a radical new idea of education.

As part of their global civilising mission, churches in Natal and Zululand came to form 'one of the world's densest concentrations of missionary talent and denominational diversity'.[5] Missionaries established almost all of the first schools for Africans but they struggled at first to recruit converts. They brought new ideals, seeing their role not just as imparting formal knowledge but also as introducing modern clothes, hairstyles, and ideas of cleanliness.[6] Yet converting heathens to Christians required a certain understanding as well as preservation of aspects of African society, for instance in order to publish bibles in African languages. This reflected a basic dilemma that criss-crossed Asia, Africa, and the Caribbean: to what extent should indigenous groups or former slaves be assimilated into 'white' culture?

The principal response in Natal was not assimilation but 'indirect rule' or the 'Shepstone system' (named after Natal's Secretary of Native Affairs, Theophilus Shepstone).[7] Forged from the mid-nineteenth century through improvisations and contestations, the state devolved day-to-day powers to male *amakhosi* ('chiefs') who were paid a salary to rule over their subjects in 'locations'/'reserves'. Chiefs were rarely obedient servants of colonialism but neither could they survive if they actively opposed settler rule. Overseen by white officials, male chiefs administered 'customary law', which was one of the two interdependent systems of law in South Africa, the other being Roman-Dutch law.[8]

Some scholars criticise the way in which the concept of 'gender' can be unquestionably applied to understand African society.[9] Age had great importance and *ilobolo* had long been understood as a form of 'child-price' and not simply 'bride-price' (it could be returned if a married woman was infertile).[10] Nevertheless, as Jeff Guy argues, indirect rule rested on male chiefs, fathers, and colonial administrators forming something of an 'accommodation of patriarchs'.[11] Developing this argument for the 1920s and 1930s, Shula Marks describes how Zulu nationalists, state officials, and missionaries came together to promote a conservative gendered version of Zuluness.[12] What came to be called Zulu *amasiko* or 'traditions' therefore represents not customs carried seamlessly forward from the past, but practices forged through changing gendered power dynamics.[13]

As the urban economy grew, men spent years in cities saving up for *ilobolo* (bridewealth) and channelling money back to rural areas *ukwakha umuzi* or 'to build a home'.[14] To ensure women's commitment to rural life, fathers and sons had a stake in mobilising 'traditional' gendered and generational practices, including the powerful concept of *inhlonipho* (or 'respect'). To act with *inhlonipho* was to be bashful and shy and avoid eye contact and certain words and phrases. Not just fathers and uncles but mothers and *amaqhikiza* (older girls) sustained *inhlonipho* by guiding and controlling the chaste behaviour of young women.

Schools, however, seemingly worked against this rural moral economy. They taught in the language of English, encouraged children to look adult teachers in the eye, and gave young people knowledge that could potentially undermine gendered and generational power. Salary-earning professionals such as teachers and clerks showcased the benefits of mission schools but they were small in number. Especially for non-Christians, early schools could be seen as taking time and money away from vital rural tasks, for instance the herding of cattle.

The insulting term *izifebe* mentioned by Mrs Mhlongo, however, demonstrates the particular abuses thrown at African women whose schooling was thought to undermine rural life and its traditions. *Isifebe* (plural: *izifebe*) can be translated as 'prostitute' or more generally a 'loose' or 'immoral' woman.[15] Women I interviewed who grew up in the 1920s and 1930s recalled clearly, and with a hint of both injustice and humour, that *izifebe* was used to castigate over-schooled women; it especially conjured up images of an educated woman abandoning a rural home for the immorality of the city.[16]

Thus, a series of questions and concerns linked to schooling reverberated through society. If a schooled woman abandoned the home, who would look after the rural *umuzi* (homestead)? Might a brother's marriage be delayed if his family received no *ilobolo* from his sister's marriage? Dilemmas divided but also united parents: a mother might wish her daughter to gain education, but, like a father, she might fear that it would lead to her estrangement from the rural home.

Because of the association between schools and European and American missionaries, formal education could be portrayed, as Mrs Mhlongo remembers, as *into yabelungu* (a thing of the whites). The term 'thing of the whites' reflects a certain binary between whiteness/blackness, tradition/modernity, Christian/heathen. In this schema, all schools could be cast as 'white'. But meanings of blackness and whiteness blurred in everyday life.[17] Indeed, schooling manifested profound predicaments, and it is for this reason that I noted fathers' disapproval of 'over-schooled' rather than 'schooled' daughters. Derogatory terms directed at schooled daughters, including *izifebe*, both tempered the pace of and reflected the reality of women's growing urban migration.

Given that the association between schooling and 'loose women' is recent enough to survive in the memory of older people, it is remarkable how quickly young women moved into the schooling system. By the 1950s, South African girls achieved parity with boys in primary schools; by 1980, more African girls than boys were in higher secondary schools.[18] The speed with which girls entered schools was unparalleled across the African continent.

There are complex reasons lying behind South Africa's feminisation of schooling. An overarching change is the remarkable rise of the Christian faith in the twentieth century (today 80 per cent of South Africans identify as Christian). A second is urbanisation, which created a demand for female work. From the early twentieth century, a growing number of people born in rural areas, including women such as Mrs Mhlongo, moved into cities: from 1921 to 1951 the male–female ratio in cities decreased from six to one to two to one.[19] Women undertook formal employment such as domestic work and informal activities such as brewing and selling beer.

Related to the above, declining agricultural capacity in reserves and the increasing mechanisation of white farms (on which many African families lived) drove individuals into cities. Eleanor Preston-Whyte's research in the 1960s suggests that changes to, and the insecurity of, rural family life underscored many of the reasons domestic workers gave for coming to Durban: a family death, a husband's or father's desertion, and illegitimate childbirth.[20]

Over time, working women became associated with the sending back of remittances, and not just the abandonment of rural kin.[21] Anthropologist Mphiwa Mbatha noted in his study published in 1960 that educated daughters' remittances provided more benefit to families than the *ilobolo* (bridewealth) their marriage brought to the homestead.[22]

Thus, young people's lives became positioned within circuits of school, work, and wages rather than principally marriage and childbirth. Indeed, South Africa's fertility rates fell at a rate unmatched anywhere else on the continent; total fertility dropped from seven to six children per woman in the 1960s and to three by 1996.[23] In a rural-centric economy, having a large number of children had ensured a source of agricultural labour and a way to connect families through marriage. However, over time women had fewer children, and those children attended school for longer. Let us now turn to urban areas, to where many women like Mrs Mhlongo moved.

## Modern families and modern schools in Umlazi Township

Before the 1950 Group Areas Act was implemented, all South African cities had racially mixed areas located relatively close to city centres. Umkhumbane/Cato Manor, west of Durban's Berea ridge, was a huge shack settlement that housed mostly black Africans but also Indians and Coloureds. In 1960 its population was estimated at between 60,000 and 120,000 people.[24] Downtown areas could also house black people. In central Durban, several large hostels and company compounds housed single African men, one small hostel housed single African women, and Baumanville location housed several hundred mostly married African couples. In the suburbs, a majority of Durban's domestic workers, who numbered approximately 25,000 around this time, stayed on their employers' properties, some with their children.[25]

As we have seen, the 1950 Group Areas Act resulted in the removal of tens of thousands of Africans to townships or rural 'reserves' (the latter if Africans did not have 'Section 10' urban rights gained from birth or long-term residency in the city). KwaMashu Township, opened in 1958, replaced sugar-cane farms to the north of Durban. The larger Umlazi Township was established on 'reserve' land, of which there was a large

Figure 3.1 A *gogo* (granny) and grandchild outside a 51/9 'matchbox' house in Umlazi Township. These family houses, often built on steep banks, were designed for working men and their families but some legally 'emancipated' women also accessed them. Behind to the left is an extended house. Photograph: Mark Hunter.

amount immediately south of the city. The township's location on Umlazi reserve meant that it was able to contain better than most townships inherent tensions in urban policy. These centred on apartheid ideologues' promise to retribalise Africans in rural reserves and industrialists' demands for labour stabilisation in booming towns.[26]

Umlazi's basic design was very similar to that of other townships built in the apartheid era. It had only a single major entrance and was surrounded by a 'buffer zone' to ensure separation from other racial groups.[27] Influenced by modern British and American planning trends, townships' iconic 'matchbox' houses were built with two bedrooms, a small kitchen, a tiny bathroom, and a small lounge (Figure 3.1). These 'NE 51/9' houses – i.e. designed for non-Europeans in 1951 – had a living space of 51.2 square metres; they were slightly bigger than the NE 51/6 houses, also built in townships, which had a living space of 41 square metres and an outside toilet. Records show that Umlazi's inside toilet model was only chosen because the steep terrain made outside toilets barely if at all cheaper.[28]

Modern leisure facilities constructed on a shoestring budget in the township included a golf course and swimming pools.[29] Built close to the

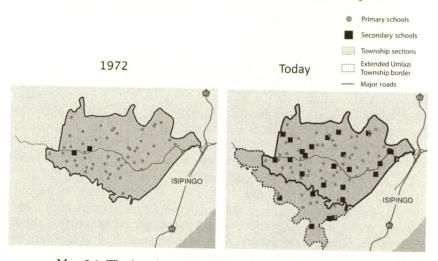

Map 3.1 The location of Umlazi's primary and secondary schools, 1972 and today. *Source*: Plans of the township are taken from T60/2/1692/3 Admn. Van Bantoedorpe, Box 2/1848, Department of Bantu Administration and Development, National Archive Repository, Pretoria; the list of schools built in December 1971 are based on 'Umlazi New Township School Board – school fund deficit balances at 31st December, 1971', File R-02295, Department of Education and Culture, KwaZulu-Natal Archives Repository, Ulundi.

township's entrance, Umlazi's male hostels housed single men in crammed conditions.[30]

Townships' division into discrete 'sections' meant that schools were spatially distributed on a roughly neighbourhood-by-neighbourhood basis. Umlazi was built with 20 sections labelled alphabetically, each one containing around 1,000 houses. These were labelled A to Z (excluding I, O, and X), with the addition of AA, BB, CC, and DD to make the current 27 sections. The urban schooling formula allowed for one lower primary school per 800 families, meaning that, in effect, a section acted as a school's catchment area.[31] Map 3.1 shows how almost all of Umlazi's early schools were built at the primary level.

Yet the funding of these Bantu education primary schools was so poor that, according to one review, '[c]hildren double up at the desks, try to write on their laps'.[32] Many schools, especially at first, used the 'platoon' system that involved doubling up learners in morning and afternoon sessions. Throughout the apartheid period, pupil–teacher ratios remained at between 50:1 and 70:1.[33]

Menzi High was the township's solitary high school at first, but its facilities did not improve on those in primary schools. As depicted in Figure 1.2, the classrooms and courtyard were small and poorly built, and the school's entire premises were in fact only a little larger than the swimming pool built for Durban High School's white pupils. The school inspector wrote in August 1968: 'This new school is short of almost everything. Proper laboratory facilities are a crying necessity. The furniture that was ordered has not come ... There is no money for equipment such as audio-visual aids ... There is a sad lack of maps and other equipment ... The school has no library room. The library books are kept in two wooden cupboards in a classroom.'[34]

The gross underfunding of Bantu education, along with the building of monotonous townships and the employment colour bar, worked to 'compress' the class structure of African society in the early apartheid period.[35] Up until that time, Leo Kuper had talked of a small mission school-educated 'African bourgeoisie' that included a tiny number of doctors, lawyers, and government clerks.[36] In Umlazi, to the extent that social difference was factored in to blueprints, planners built houses on relatively large sites of approximately 3,500 square feet '[to] enable future vehicular access to the houses'.[37] In the main, however, townships were built with labourers and semi-skilled factory workers in mind. Major employers in south Durban included oil refineries and manufacturers of products that included matches, tyres, metal products, soap, chemicals, and plastics.[38]

One consequence of class compression in Umlazi was that differences between neighbourhoods were small, and therefore where you lived did not determine the nature of your local school. This was very different from white Durban, where suburbs and their schools were clearly demarcated by social class: for instance, the 'rough and tough' Bluff and the 'larney' Berea. However, one commonality that cut across the period of racial modernism was that children usually attended their local school.

Some previous studies of townships, including my own, emphasise that family township houses were a material expression of apartheid's patriarchal as well as racialised intervention – a kind of urban version of what Guy called an 'accommodation of patriarchs'.[39] Granting men houses, officials said proudly, would provide them with self-respect that would rescue them and their families from the disorderly 'squalor' of shacks.[40] However, below I emphasise women's efforts to remain living in cities with their children, and use as evidence for this point a series of court cases in which women became 'emancipated' from the control of men. As the story unfolds further in this chapter, we will see how urban-based women encouraged their children to attend schools, which grew rapidly in number.

## Women's legal 'emancipation' and attention to housing

To implement urban apartheid the national government relied on cities and provinces, and each area had its own institutional history and approach to African women.[41] Under the Natal Code of Native Law, first written in 1891, a 'native female' was a 'perpetual minor in law and [with] no independent powers'.[42] This position endured in Natal and KwaZulu because Natal was the only territory in the colonial era that codified customary law (i.e. wrote it into a legal document).

Natal women's disadvantaged legal status left a paper trail when hundreds of urban women applied for 'emancipation' in the 1960s. This status allowed them to escape the control of male guardians and attain the right to head an *umuzi* (household), and therefore acquire greater control over their children (gaining full 'exemption' from customary law was much more difficult). The requirement for emancipation, which women had to demonstrate in Bantu Affairs courts, was that they were of 'good character, education, thrifty habits'.[43]

Notably, of the roughly 250 emancipation cases from the 1960s I examined, virtually all involved mothers applying to access housing in Durban's bourgeoning townships; most were employed as domestic workers, nurses, or teachers and between the ages of 30 and 50.[44] Once women had secured the finances and references to apply for emancipation, their applications appear to have been approved fairly routinely.[45]

Children's education loomed large in women's stories. Nesta Msomi, a widow working as a live-in domestic worker in Durban, attained emancipation in 1966 in order to access an Umlazi house. She had two children: a daughter living with relatives in rural Mtinkulu and a son, Joseph, attending teacher training at the newly built University College of Zululand. She told the court: 'I have very high aspirations in as far as the education of my children is concerned, despite my meagre earnings.' Her employer supportively wrote that she 'has proved herself to be a thoroughly honest and trustworthy servant ... has dedicated herself to her children. It is to provide a home and to foster a family life that she is making this endeavour to obtain accommodation at Umlazi.' A Methodist reverend also wrote to support Mrs Msomi's application.[46]

So long as a woman had at least one dependent child, being unmarried did not exclude her from attaining a township house. Winnifred Mhlongo, educated to standard 6 and the mother of four children born out of wedlock, was forthcoming in her application: 'I no longer have an intention of getting married but desire to devote all of my life to the upbringing of my children, for whom I am the sole support.' The court accepted that she should be emancipated in order to apply for a family house, and noted the evidence of her thrifty habits and her male guardian's support for emancipation (both legal requirements).[47] Through many cases such as these, women's 'emancipation' enabled a cohort of single women to head Umlazi houses – probably not more than one in ten, but a significant minority.[48]

The efforts of this tier of educated, employed women to access township housing must be seen in the context of wider gendered struggles against apartheid regulations. Women played a leading role in opposing removals from Cato Manor and resisting the extension of pass laws to include them. And when women famously shut down the city's beer halls in 1959 they were angry not just at apartheid's forced removal of African people. The municipality's long-standing monopoly over sorghum beer – a major source of funding for 'native administration' – came with invasive police raids to destroy liquor illicitly brewed by women.[49]

Although they were unsuccessful in opposing core elements of apartheid, women took advantage of spaces created when apartheid planners tried to implement their ambitious racial agenda. By the 1950s, the Pretoria government, led by the National Party, was placing enormous pressure on Durban City, run by the United Party, to expedite the removal of tens of thousands of shacks, especially from Cato Manor. Sighart Bourquin, who served as manager of the Native Administration Board before heading the Port Natal Administration Board, wrestled with this daunting task. He agreed that a single woman could access township housing 'if she is living together with her own children who are dependent upon her and for whom she is providing a home'. He also acknowledged that marriage status was an insufficient way of allocating housing, as unmarried couples were often quite 'respectable people who, for some length of time, have lived together as man and wife'.[50]

Another way in which women accessed houses was by getting married quickly ('at the drop of a hat') to gain housing through a husband with Section 10 (urban) rights.[51] A final way for a single woman to access a township house was through its registration by a son. In fact, a township superintendent advised Mrs Mhlongo to register a house under her son's name.

Yet in the late 1960s, apartheid urban regulations tightened and the avenues for single women to attain township houses narrowed considerably. Consistent with the mounting state controls on urban women, including through pass laws, a 1967 circular from the Department of Bantu Administration and Development sought to restrict single women being placed on housing waiting lists.[52] By 1968, Bourquin was replying to letters from women's patrons (usually a domestic worker's madam) with the news that the growing housing backlog meant that the city had to give priority to men.[53] The social justice group Black Sash came to assist a large number of widows who faced eviction on their husband's death, and noted state officials' opposition to the 'racket' of emancipation.[54] As the 1970s progressed, the waiting lists for rental housing grew longer, making it almost impossible for men, and not only women, to access housing in Umlazi. In the 1980s, as we shall see, all new houses were built by private developers.

A final gendered twist that centres on housing began in the 1960s but accelerated in the late 1970s and 1980s. Umlazi's planners had always envisioned that houses would be sold to residents, and this happened steadily from the 1960s onwards, speeding up when the township fell under the control of the KwaZulu homeland in the 1970s (houses in townships located in 'white' areas were not sold off until the 1980s). While individual men, typically an original occupant's brother or son, often made the case that they should inherit and be able to sell a house, other family members, typically women, positioned houses as *ikhaya* – a term for 'rural home' but in this context usually translated into English to mean 'family house'. *Ikhaya* conjures up not just physical structures but members of a family symbolised by non-commodified patterns of land use in rural areas.[55]

Although housing remained a contested terrain, family members' argument that a township house is for their *use* is further evidence of the efforts women made, with and through their children, to make a life based in Umlazi – and we will see now how this interacted with schooling.

## A cultural project: Bantu education in the early apartheid era

The 1953 Bantu Education Act forced the closing, state takeover, or effective privatisation of state-aided mission schools that had provided virtually all education for black Africans. There are several windows through which Bantu education can be considered. The first emphasises the system that followed: mass public primary schooling. As Jonathan Hyslop has shown, Bantu education's significant expansion of primary schools addressed industrialists' demands for basic numeracy and literacy skills and the state's concern at the growth of uneducated urban youth.[56] From 1955 to 1962 student enrolments sky-rocketed by 670,000 children, most of this growth being at *lower* primary schools (today's grades 1–4).[57] In this sense, Bantu education's expansionism in South Africa was consistent with late British colonial policy on 'mass education in Africa'.[58]

Bantu education can also be recognised as just one of many education systems forged in the context of racial orders shaped by slavery and colonialism. In the early decades of the twentieth century, a mobile and connected group of intellectuals debated not only the appropriate education policy in colonial Africa but suitable 'negro education' in the United States and schooling among the 'North American Indian'. The latter was the topic of a 1939 conference co-organised at the University of Toronto by Charles Loram and anthropologist Thomas McIlwraith. Loram, a South African, had administered Natal's 'native' schools before his career took him to an academic post at Yale University.[59] His 1917 book (based on his PhD) *The Education of the South African Native* had argued for the channelling of Natives/Africans into 'adapted' education paths that favoured practical school subjects such as agriculture and crafts.[60]

In circumstances in which indigenous groups greatly outnumbered settlers, as in colonial Africa, this idea of 'adaptive' African education resonated with existing practices of indirect rule that devolved power to chiefs.[61] It sat awkwardly, however, with the mission school system. As noted, mission schools long fostered a small but influential group of English-speaking writers, teachers, lawyers, and political leaders – including Nelson Mandela, whom the state incarcerated in 1964. For their critics, mission schools' 'bookish' bias signalled too rapid African assimilation that could threaten settlers' authority and the stability of African society. Adaptive education, in contrast, would prevent the 'break-down' of tribal culture.

Saul Dubow's work in the late 1980s convincingly showed that 'liberal segregationists' were as much part of the making of apartheid as racist Afrikaner nationalists, and recent research on Bantu education supports this view.[62] Cynthia Kros argued that its chief architect, Werner Eiselen, an anthropologist by training, had a strong commitment to preserving African culture.[63] He was certainly not alone, for a similar view was posited by fellow anthropologist Bronislaw Malinowski, one of the most influential scholars of this era.[64]

To promote African languages, one of Bantu education's most controversial rules was that all primary-school instruction should be in the medium of African languages. Linguistic variation is intrinsic to all societies, and so we need to take a short diversion at this point to note that when we talk of 'languages' we mean institutionalised languages. In nineteenth-century Africa, missionaries authored most of the early African-language dictionaries and therefore helped establish linguistic boundaries.[65] As settlers increased in number, 'tribes', tied into wider language groups, became the basic building block of the colonial government's system of 'indirect rule'. It was on the back of this history that 'Bantu', a linguistically rooted term, came to supersede the term 'native' in the apartheid period.[66]

Bantu culture was therefore envisaged as a base from which African leaders could move forward with some autonomy – and perhaps even, as Healy-Clancy suggests, simulate decolonisation elsewhere.[67] The 1951 Eiselen Commission report, sometimes referred to as the blueprint for Bantu education, argued that there was no point in teaching Africans academic subjects that are never applied in practice and that 'Bantu cultures cannot cope with modern conditions'. However, the report continued: '[T]hey contain in themselves the seeds from which can develop a modern Bantu culture fully able to satisfy the aspirations of the Bantu and to deal with the conditions of the modern world.'[68] In rural areas chiefs exerted influence on local school boards and committees that were given powers to appoint teachers and run schools.[69]

To the extent that subjects such as maths and sciences were taught and Africans advanced into secondary school, homelands came to be viewed as the avenue for African advancement. To create a layer of authority above tribes, the 1959 Promotion of Bantu Self-Government Act paved the way for ten semi-autonomous Bantustans/homelands that were justified by the existence of discreet African languages. At the tertiary level, Fort Hare University, a meeting place for Africans from across the continent until the 1950s, was turned into a university for Xhosa speakers, and two other small ethnic universities were built: one of these was the University College of Zululand, located in what would become the KwaZulu homeland.

The upshot was that Bantu education was part of a system of ethno-racial schooling that came to encompass every single South African. At the top of a hierarchy of prestige were 'white' cultural and linguistic forms, including the two official languages of English and Afrikaans. In Bantu education's schools, which were overwhelmingly primary level, English and Afrikaans persisted only as taught subjects to enable Africans 'to follow oral or written instruction; and to carry on a simple conversation with Europeans about his work and other subjects of common interest'.[70] Eiselen himself admitted that the quality of spoken English declined because of the turn to mother-tongue instruction.[71] The disdain among African intellectuals to Bantu education's tribal turn is captured in the title of the book *Education for Barbarism* written by Isaac Tabata, who himself had attended school at the famous mission institutions of Lovedale and Fort Hare.[72]

Before ending this section on Bantu education, two points need to be noted. First, many educationalists to this day argue that children learn faster when schooled in their home language. In fact, in 1953 – the same year as the Bantu Education Act was passed – the United Nations Educational, Scientific and Cultural Organization (UNESCO) published a report strongly encouraging mother-tongue instruction.[73] The real question, even among Bantu education's opponents, was the timing of the switch from the vernacular to South Africa's official languages of English and Afrikaans (usually the former). When this switch took place late, as in apartheid South Africa, children struggled to cope with all subjects at the secondary-school level.

Second, while mission-schooled nationalist leaders such as Tabata equated Bantu education with 'barbarism', for most parents there was no realistic alternative. A few mission schools became fully private institutions but these were affordable for only a tiny minority (see below). Consequently, parents in rural areas and townships channelled substantial resources into the construction and maintenance of Bantu education schools as well as for fees and books – this was a requirement, unlike in free white schooling.

We can return to Mrs Mhlongo's family for evidence of the high regard that rural communities developed for schooling. One day I accompanied her to the rural home where she grew up. Certificates on the wall celebrated the success of Mrs Mhlongo's nephew (her sister's son), whose earnings helped build up the family house. Prominent was a framed standard 6 continuation certificate from 1962 (needed to attend secondary school) and another for Form 1 (first year of secondary school) from a school some 30 kilometres away.[74] Material items of different eras signalled the benefits of his employment with the state's railway company – a shiny gate, a porch, wooden ceilings, security bars, a recently painted pit latrine toilet, chickens in a newly built pen, and a satellite dish for TV.

### The gendered 'bond of education'

> To remember my mother's insistence on education is to remember that there were sharp divisions within the black community about how to struggle for freedom. For someone like my mother, whose lack of education had limited the job opportunities available to her, education was key.
> Jacob Dlamini, *Native Nostalgia*[75]

Let us now bring together the two preceding themes: mothers' advocacy of schooling and Bantu education's instigation of mass primary schooling. In cities, educated Christian families, encouraged by the church to adopt modern nuclear forms, were among the first groups to embrace townships from the 1920s.[76] Research by Archie Mafeje and Monica Wilson, as well as by Leo Kuper, demonstrates that Christianised urban men long gave prodigious attention to education. In particular, teachers enjoyed very high social status.[77] According to one male school principal writing in *Bona* magazine in 1965, raising and schooling children had intrinsic benefits: 'You should not expect any gain, just parental satisfaction and the fulfillment of duty.'[78]

While many men approved of schooling, I want to stress here the specific educational connections between mothers and children, or what I am calling a feminised 'bond of education'. Before the era of Bantu education, mission schools had educated more men than women at the highest grades: in 1955, men accounted for four out of five students in higher secondary schools.[79] In contrast, Bantu education made it easier and more common for all children (including girls) to be educated, albeit at low levels and in shockingly uneven and racist terms. Not only did schoolgirls progress further but primary-school teacher posts were effectively reserved for women: in the words of Verwoerd, 'to save money in teacher training and salaries, and also because women are generally better than men in handling small children'.[80]

Consider how the cost of government and mission schools differed. A small but significant number of mission schools survived apartheid by converting to fully private institutions, including Natal's Marianhill,

Inkamana, Montebello, and Inanda Seminary (the first two co-educational and the latter two girls' schools, which were seen to be less threatening than boys' schools).[81] One account written in the mid-1960s noted that a mission boarding school might cost R80 a year, whereas township day schools might charge a fraction of that amount: R2 for school fees, R2.45 for texts and exercise books, and R8 for a school uniform (at standard 3).[82] Schooling expenses rose with the level of education, not only because of the cost of books but because only lower primary schools were funded as part of the township housing scheme; higher primary and secondary schools were funded by the Umlazi school board, which relied on parents' support.[83]

Of course, Umlazi Township's residents had varied abilities to afford schooling, and different experiences at schools. Some township women were professionals such as teachers and nurses who had attended secondary school; others were domestic workers with mainly primary schooling; still others would have had no formal education. Some teachers showed great commitment to girls' schooling whereas others discouraged girls from studying 'male' school subjects such as science and maths.[84] All of these circumstances would have affected gendered identities. Put another way, women's 'agency' to encourage children's schooling was not predetermined or discrete from wider relations and practices.

While there are many reasons for mothers' strong support of schooling, however, we can make a cautious comparison between a mother's attention to a child's education and a father's efforts to earmark certain expenses. Migrant men in Lesotho, James Ferguson noted, invested earnings in cattle because this represented a 'stored asset for the future', protected from what they perceived to be women's frivolous expenses.[85] Taking this well-known analysis further, we can contend that mothers, by diverting female and male wages into the domain of education, knew that the future ability of their children to find work was being enhanced year by year. This was an investment in social relations that could not be sold off when times got bad or when relatives made desperate claims. Education was a domain that protected meagre incomes and provided benefits, especially important to women, in the long term.

Indeed, anthropologist Mphiwa Mbatha noted in his 1960 study that when relations between husbands and wives are not good, 'the tendency of the mother to lavish love upon and to cling to her children carries the hope that the child will be grateful for the love and care shown and support her in her old age'.[86] Eleanor Preston-Whyte noted the priority female domestic workers gave to schooling their children. Most of the domestic workers in her study were unmarried but had children whom they looked upon as 'security and comfort' for old age, with daughters remaining especially faithful to them. 'Extremely close bonds were found to exist between mothers and daughters ... The key to success was seen as education ... They envisaged daughters as nurses or teachers and sons as doctors and lawyers.'[87] Researching domestic workers two decades later, Jacklyn Cock similarly argued that 'their hopes for the future focused on their children, and education was seen as the means whereby their children could escape to a better life. Something no one can take away from you.'[88]

Mrs Dlamini, whom I spoke with four times from 2012 to 2016, moved to Umlazi in 1968 as a young nurse with her husband, a builder, who is now deceased. I always struggled to meet with her because of her many church commitments, but when we met our interviews were long. She had questions to ask me just as I had questions to ask her. She was schooling her grandchild in a formerly white school but was in arrears with the fees, and wanted advice on government rules about fee exemptions.

Schooled at the prestigious Loram School in central Durban (closed in the wake of the Group Areas Act), Mrs Dlamini encouraged her children and grandchildren to attend the best available township schools. She made a connection between township wives' vulnerability and the attention they devoted to schooling:

The owner of the house was a man. If there was a problem, a man said, 'This is my house; I'm going to *xosha* [send you out] you if you fail to obey my rules' ... Sometimes you find the man working but not coming back home with the money ... the mother struggles to find something for the children to eat. When children are educated, they will support the mother because they know how she struggled for them to get an education.

Bongiwe Phiri came to the Durban area in 1940 to study at the famous mission school, Adams College, where she completed standard 7. Its alumni include the ANC's first president, John Dube, cabinet minister Nkosazana Dlamini-Zuma, and former head of the KwaZulu homeland Mangosuthu Buthelezi. After leaving school Mrs Phiri worked as a cleaner in various hotels in the city and then married a factory worker, the couple moving into Umlazi Township.

Like many women of her age, she married an older man who lived a shorter life than she did – her husband died in 1979. Her four children all studied at highly regarded schools in Umlazi. Two found professional jobs in nursing and teaching, while another moved overseas to work as a chef. Today, the most visible signs of her educated children's support lie in the elaborate modifications to the house, including new rooms, a tiled roof (replacing asbestos), new doors, burglar bars, and a neat kitchen containing a sparkling new oven. She remembered that when she was young '[m]others liked school more ... they knew that education was the key to success.' She continued: 'Girls don't abandon the home; my daughter who is overseas is sending me money. When a son is married he forgets about looking after his family because he is looking after his wife.'

Mandla Shange was born in 1938 and spent his early years with his grandmother in Bulwer, while his parents lived in Cato Manor. His father worked at a large brick company, and his mother's first work was as a primary-school teacher. She quit this job, however, because of its low salary and became a domestic worker – testimony to the poor pay and conditions in the teaching profession. Although Mrs Shange separated from her husband, she paid for her son, Mandla, to attend boarding school until standard 8, which must have been an enormous strain on her salary. He eventually became a traffic policeman in Durban and purchased a house in Umlazi. When I asked him about whether daughters or sons tended to repay the debt to their parents – the other side of the bond of education – he said that he had provided some financial support to his mother. She had continued as a domestic worker until her death, however, and, he added with a smile, perhaps one encouraged by the presence of a male interviewer, that 'daughters were friends, they supported their mothers … We used to just look for girlfriends!'

What these narratives of 'reliable daughters and unreliable sons' perhaps downplay, however, is that daughters were seen not only as potential sources of earnings but as providers of domestic labour and care. Sons, in contrast, generally contributed less to caring and domestic work but had higher average earnings than daughters. A study of contributions to Umlazi households in the mid-1980s found that 'male workers, who have education levels of more than Standard 9, aged between 31 and 50 years and who are employed as factory workers, will contribute most to the household'.[89]

Turning the clock back to when this group went to school in the 1960s and 1970s, we can see that they would have been on the crest of a countrywide wave of rising levels of schooling. Also relevant to the social mobility of this group, as we will see in more detail later, were significant wage increases, especially in industrial work, following the 'Durban strikes' in 1973 and the subsequent unionisation of the workforce and emphasis on training. Moreover, being born and schooled in a township had intrinsic benefits. Having Section 10 rights to live and work in urban areas meant that, in Hyslop's words, 'any level of urban education was by definition more valuable in the labour market than an equivalent level of rural education'.[90]

One final relationship mediating the bond of education must be stressed: that of domestic workers and their employers. Racial paternalism had long tailored relations between white bosses and black miners and farmers.[91] Acts of racial maternalism, or at times paternalism, could centre on employers' support for their domestic workers' children, sometimes in a small way in the giving of hand-me-down clothes and sometimes more substantially.[92] Mrs Mhlongo's children received help from her white employer, and it was quite common for children of domestic worker to serve 'as the medium to bridge the gap between servant and mistress'.[93] Live-in domestic workers were one group that white families could (literally) not live without.

Indeed, one reason why domestic workers tolerated, and still endure, long hours, poor pay, and sometimes authoritarian and racist working conditions is that the madam of the house might help to better the lives of their children. Former domestic workers with whom I spoke in Umlazi tended to evaluate their working years not so much in terms of the salary that they earned, but whether 'umlungu wami' ('my white person') was good or bad in a maternalistic/paternalistic sense. Did they support my child? Did they leave pots, pans, furniture, and cash when they left the country? Of course, positive recollections of racial dependence must be interpreted in the context of massive unemployment today and the presence of a white interviewer; however, it is clear that white women (and, to a lesser extent, white men) have long shaped the relationship between black domestic workers and their children.

Thobeka (to whom we return later) is in her fifties and lives in a shack in Umlazi. She told me that she had worked as a live-in domestic worker for a white family whose children she helped raise. When 'abelungu bami' (my white people) moved overseas, they gave her money to buy a site and its umjondolo (shack).

AUTHOR:    So, you called your whites 'abelungu bami' [my whites]?
THOBEKA:   [At work] I called them by their names but when I returned I said abelungu bami.
AUTHOR:    Did you like your white people?
THOBEKA:   I liked them because they gave me money [after they had moved overseas] when I was struggling; they sent me R4,000.

This brings me to another reason for noting these racialised forms of patronage: they reverberated through the very practice of me undertaking research in Umlazi. When I was based in Umlazi I tried to disrupt associations of whiteness with power by speaking as much as possible in isiZulu and undertaking everyday acts of inhlonipho ('respect'), such as talking and moving in a deferential way. Even so, as a white employer of a local research assistant I sometimes overheard myself being talked about as 'umlungu wakhe' (her white person), a phraseology that my research assistant, her fiancé, and I turned into something of a joke. In a few instances, a poorer resident with whom I left a business card – as required by my research ethics approval – sent me a text message to ask me for a job. Then, my research assistant was quick to tell them that I was her umlungu. The phrase umlungu wami rolled easily off the tongue, a person's 'possession' of a white person's employment quick to be claimed. The term compared favourably to references of a bad boss as *inja* or dog. I raise these themes, which we will return to later, not just to situate myself as a researcher in Umlazi, but because they demonstrate the pervasiveness of racial forms of patronage in everyday life.

## Conclusions

On paper, women like Mrs Mhlongo should not exist: that is, rural-born women who moved from being seen as *isifebe* for being over-schooled to becoming township house owners and strong champions of schooling. Apartheid dealt a particularly cruel blow to African women already classified in Natal as legal minors. Group Areas legislation brutally cleared the informal urban spaces in which they tended to live, pass law legislation was extended to target women, and the massive township house-building project rested principally on the figure of the 'industrial man'. Thousands of women were dumped back into rural areas, and those in Natal who were 'emancipated' left written records only because of their disadvantaged status. Emancipated women represented a small minority of women in Natal, and were predominantly domestic workers, teachers, and nurses.

To understand why there are quite a lot of women like Mrs Mhlongo in Umlazi today, however, is to read some of the conventional histories against the grain. The racist Bantu Education Act did lead to a massive expansion of primary schooling. This was gendered in the sense that mission schools disproportionately benefited men; Bantu education put a lot more children into classrooms and at a reduced cost. While the state encouraged rural schooling, primary schools in townships such as Umlazi were built quickly, paving the way for the growth of secondary schools in the 1970s. With schools located closer, many mothers came to place great importance on educating children precisely because of the discrimination women faced: in housing, by husbands, in law, and in the labour market.

The landmark 1953 Bantu Education Act has been studied from a number of perspectives: employers' labour requirements, the failures of the patchy mission-school system, the wider programme of racial modernism, transnational debates about assimilation or adaptive education, and much more. It is now clear that the Act cannot be reduced to simplistic racial explanations. Nevertheless, one of Bantu education's chief aims was to change the tone of African schooling: to move from a 'bookish' and academic ('white') tone to an ethnic one that stressed practical work.

But what happened to these relations when the heavy demand for labour ended and unemployment rose? What happened to schooling when secondary schools mushroomed? What happened to bonds of education when marriage rates began to drop? We will address these questions next. And in Chapter 4 I bring together white and black parts of the city in the 1970s and 1980s as we move away from the modernist period to understand the shift towards schooling marketisation.

*Part II*

# Marketised assimilation – late 1970s–1990s

# 4   The routes of schooling desegregation
Protest, co-option, and marketised assimilation

One day in 1992, two primary-school children, one from Umlazi Township's Fakude family and the other from the Bluff's Steyn family, woke up, had breakfast, and put on their uniforms to attend a Bluff English-medium school. Two momentous events preceded this act. First, in February 1990 President F. W. de Klerk shocked the world by releasing Nelson Mandela from prison. Second, eight months later, the Education Minister Piet Clase encouraged white parents to vote, school by school, on whether to desegregate their schools and assume more autonomy, including by charging fees. The scale of 'yes' votes surprised many commentators because the criteria for change – an 80 per cent turnout and 72 per cent of parents voting in favour – was 'almost impossible to achieve', in the words of one newspaper.[1] Why did white parents vote to desegregate their schools? And on what terms did this take place? Let us return to the two families.

In 1985, great turmoil in Umlazi Township followed the state's brutal assassination of lawyer and anti-apartheid activist Victoria Mxenge.[2] However, for the Fakude family, led by a male railway worker and his wife, a nurse, it was also the time when they bought a six-room house in a small, privately built new Umlazi area called Chappies. Named after its developer, Chappies was financed by a company that boasted that 'they never built two houses that are the same STYLE [original capitals] next to each other'.[3] This sense of individuality, the antithesis of the more than 20,000 identical four-room matchbox houses built by apartheid planners, was reinforced by the area's cul-de-sac design that afforded a quiet and private ambience. Chappies' families were led by workers who had moved up the employment ladder, often into semi-skilled, professional, or supervisory work.

Meanwhile, in the white Bluff suburb, also in 1985, Mr and Mrs Steyn rented (and later bought) a house from the same employer, the state-owned South African Railways and Harbours (SAR&H). Mrs Steyn worked as a railway police officer, and her husband worked as a fitter and turner – both solid, working-class white jobs. Built on a steep bank, the railway bungalow with a familiar hipped roof was slightly bigger than the Umlazi house but not remarkably so; it had three bedrooms, a bathroom, and a small sitting room. Mrs Steyn explained to me the importance of railway employment to Afrikaans speakers such as herself: 'The railways would give anybody a job ... Even if you had no qualifications, they would give you a job if you were white. And you also had a house.'[4]

Chapters 2 and 3 considered the period of racial modernism when segregated residential areas and schools divided the population into four races. Planners and administrators in the early apartheid period had what Ivan Evans calls a 'basic hostility to the market'.[5] However, in the 1970s and the 1980s, the state promoted a black business class, encouraged private developers to build houses in townships, permitted some black employees to advance at work, and shifted financial responsibilities onto the shoulders of white parents. Along with these reforms came the state's oppressive crackdown on anti-apartheid activities.

Foregrounding schooling, I use the term 'marketised assimilation' to capture themes that stretch roughly from 1976 to the late 1990s. I follow Tikly and Mabogoane in using 'marketisation' to mean children's increased daily movement for schooling as well as public schools' charging of fees, and schools' increased competition for 'quality' students.[6] I show how growing class inequalities in Umlazi Township enabled a few black parents to send their children to private white schools that began slowly to desegregate after 1976. I also track the rise of a top tier of excellent township secondary schools that selected the brightest students, some of whom travelled from afar. Voluntary fees in white schools and growing class differentiation among parents represented somewhat similar forces in white areas. This reconfiguration of class and race provides the first context to understand why formerly white public schools opened their doors to black students from 1991.

The second theme in this chapter is the cultural or symbolic basis of these changes. Bantu education emphasised a particular tone: tribalism, African languages, and practical subjects. By 'assimilation', however, I mean that black children were expected to 'fit in' with the culture of the English-medium white schools they entered. I show how this was consistent with the enthusiasm many Umlazi residents had for English-medium secondary schools. Moreover, English gained prestige when native Afrikaans speakers such as the Steyns turned to English-medium schooling. And businesses, especially in the growing service sector, demanded more fluency in the English language.

This chapter draws on a *relational* understanding of space that treats places as interconnected rather than separate. It begins with Umlazi Township, moves to the Bluff, and then brings together both places to rethink the early desegregation period. Most studies date the beginning of schooling desegregation to Minister Clase's reforms in the early 1990s. However, I show how interconnected historical processes that began in the 1970s – growing class divisions, greater competition among schools, and the rising prestige of English – profoundly shaped the movement of black learners into previously unenterable schools. By unearthing the deep routes/roots of schooling desegregation we can better understand the current education system: one that successfully nurtures a multiracial English-speaking middle class but effectively excludes millions of South Africans from formal work.

## Class formation and schooling in Umlazi Township

By the late 1970s, the project of racial modernism was in crisis. After a decade of relative political quiet following the imprisonment of Nelson Mandela and other freedom fighters, a new era of activism revealed significant chinks in apartheid's armour. In 1973, a wave of strikes, beginning in Durban's factories, spurred the country's modern trade union movement.[7] The 1976 Soweto Uprising sent a generation of activists into exile. And neighbouring Angola's and Mozambique's independence in 1974 demonstrated the fragility of colonial rule. Whereas the economy had boomed in the 1960s, it entered a downward spiral: between 1973 and 1994, the gross domestic product (GDP) per capita at constant prices fell annually by 0.6 per cent.[8]

The rising tide of political opposition generated an appetite within the National Party to 'create a "moderate" black middle class'.[9] The conditions for upward class mobility – certain types of jobs expanding and certain groups taking up new positions – became especially evident in urban areas. Male supervisors, policemen, and owners of businesses were some of the first groups to buy private houses such as those in Umlazi's Chappies section. In turn, African women increasingly moved into professional work such as nursing and teaching and service work such as sales.[10] The KwaZulu government's modification of customary law in 1981 to 'emancipate' all African women reduced women's dependence on men for housing and loans.[11]

At the same time, rising unemployment and the state's retreat from public housing created new divides. From the late 1970s, shack settlements swelled around KwaZulu's townships and then within the townships themselves.[12] Umlazi-born novelist Sifiso Mzobe writes: 'For every suburb there is a township, so for each section in the township a shanty-town – add a ghetto to a ghetto.'[13] Thus, in contrast to the earlier period marked by 'class compression', class formation (or 'decompression') intensified in the 1970s and 1980s.

A person's schooling helped determine whether they experienced upward class mobility or became part of what was then a relatively new category in South Africa – the unemployed. Blade Nzimande, a Communist Party leader and future minister, wrote his PhD thesis 'Corporate guerrillas' on black class mobility. It was not elite mission schools, he noted, but Bantu education schools, including secondary schools, that were nurturing a black petty bourgeoisie. Some of the new elites were even *izingane zabawashi* ('children of washerwomen').[14] Would this group, Nzimande asked, align itself with the black nationalist movement or the apartheid state? Would race trump class or vice versa?

We now know that black South Africans (however classified) remained largely united in their opposition to apartheid. Those favouring the 'class' side of the race–class debate, however, can argue that their analysis explains the rapid growth of intra-racial class inequalities after 1994. Yet I insist that a fresh look at schooling can provide new insights into these questions. This analysis must be gendered, a point hinted at by Nzimande's discussion of *izingane zabawashi*. And we must give attention to differences among black and white schools, and to the blurred boundaries between complicity and resistance.

### Schooling expansion amid repression and reform

The expansion of secondary schooling in South Africa, propelled by funding changes in 1972, was nothing short of spectacular.[15] In the early 1970s Umlazi Township had only two schools that educated children to senior certificate/matriculation level: Menzi High and Vukuzakhe High. However, in the 1970s and 1980s, almost all of the now 27 high schools were built or converted from existing schools (see Map 3.1). By 1985, more than one in four residents aged 15–29 had attained a senior certificate/matriculation or higher qualification, twice the ratio of over thirties.[16] Just as the building of primary schools in the 1950s and 1960s created a demand for secondary schools, the building of the latter created a demand for higher education. In 1978, an Umlazi councillor stated that 'education is a priority' among residents and proposed that the small golf course, Umlazi's exemplar modernist leisure project, should make way for a branch of the University of Zululand.[17]

Yet education departments prioritised quantity over quality. The widely noted situation today – poorly built secondary schools staffed by underqualified teachers – is in many ways a product of a relatively short period of schooling growth in the late 1970s and 1980s. Many schools were built by one of the ten Bantustans/homelands that gained autonomy over education at this time.[18] In 1972, the KwaZulu Legislative Assembly was established; the homeland gained self-government status in 1977. KwaZulu's charismatic leader Mangosuthu Buthelezi was a strong advocate of education and had some success in attracting funding from business. In 1979, Mangosuthu Technikon opened in Umlazi, supported by the business-led Urban Foundation.[19]

However, KwaZulu's education department summed up the situation of most African schools in the 1980s: they were 'suffering from the shortage of everything except pupils'.[20] Pupil–teacher ratios, which stayed below 30:1 in white schools in the 1980s and shrunk significantly in both Indian and Coloured schools to about the same number, remained above 50:1 in African schools.[21] After noting the addition of 3,500 new teaching posts between 1980 and 1981, the KwaZulu education department said: 'Unfortunately most of the posts created are being filled by unqualified teachers.' Only 7 per cent of teachers in primary schools had passed standard 10 (matriculation) or higher.[22] School inspectors at this time wrote detailed reports about each school they visited, and a whole section of these reports was dedicated to whether teachers were sober or drank alcohol.[23] However, there were some exceptional schools that became schools of choice, and we turn to these now.

### Umlazi's excellent schools

When the annual matriculation results were published in 1991, Natal and KwaZulu schools accounted for ten of the top 20 black African establishments.[24] These can be divided into two types of school. The first, represented by the Catholic schools Inkamana and Montebello, were mission schools that became fully private (i.e. they lost state-aided grants). Mission schools, as noted earlier, had been part of the region for more than a century. They had been the avenue by which a small elite of black South Africans had advanced socially and economically – and for that reason a target of Bantu education.

Umlazi Township's Vukuzakhe and Umlazi Commercial exemplified a less well-known type of school: high-performing government schools. These two schools were not alone in excelling in Umlazi. In 1981, a school inspector recorded that Zwelibanzi School overcame desperately poor resources and that '[t]he discipline of the pupils was remarkable and encouraging'.[25] Commenting on Menzi, Umlazi's first high school, a school inspector noted in 1984: 'The tone of the school is good. Teachers and students revealed the spirit of dedication and determination.'[26]

Before discussing these schools further, I need to clarify that 'excellent' is used here as a relative term for schools recognised in the community for their high standards within a grossly underfunded educational system. Learners shared desks, teachers were badly paid, and facilities were minimal. Moreover, schools' performances waxed and waned over time: some of the excellent schools could slump in performance, whereas other schools improved to become excellent.

Despite these qualifiers, there is general agreement among residents that around seven out of Umlazi's 27 high schools had this high reputation at one point, with some still having this standing to this day. These seven schools – Menzi, Zwelibanzi, Vukuzakhe, Velabahleka, Umlazi Commercial, Ogwini, and Comtech – could boast alumni such as Judge Simon Ndlovu from Menzi and CEO Cyril Gamede, who attended Vukuzakhe. Umlazi Comtech, the newest of these, reflected the sense in 1991 of political change by giving emphasis to training for management positions.[27]

What were the common features of Umlazi's excellent schools that allowed them to become islands of quality in an ocean of poorly performing schools? When I interviewed senior teachers and principals involved with these schools, they talked of being part of a tight-knit group of leaders who overlapped as students or early on in their careers. An important school attended by several current Umlazi principals was Umlazi's Makhumbuza Junior Secondary School, as it was then called. Mr Mshololo, the widely respected principal of Menzi High who died in 2015, passed JC (grade 10) at Makhumbuza and then studied at Adams College, by then a state-run institution, although previously a famous mission school. He told me that Makhumbuza became a feeder school and role model for Menzi: 'So the tone and, yes, the tone set by the then [Menzi] principal I would say his philosophy was comfortable to the philosophy that Makhumbuza had.'

Another graduate of Makhumbuza who went on to become a principal noted: 'It was the best school then. It was some kind of a replica of a mission school. We had 11 periods a day. Four o'clock, last period, we could go home ... all our teachers from grade 1 right up to Menzi were mission school products.'

The last comment points to a second major theme in the history of Umlazi's excellent schools: their explicit attempt to implement a mission school model in an urban setting. Writer Es'kia Mphahlele describes the ambiguous politics of mission schools: 'It was not that they inspired political rebellion ... On the contrary, they preached patience, obedience to authority, and respect for the laws of the country.' Yet, he argues, what was important was that 'they provided a launching pad'.[28] Professor Bernard Magubane, who was schooled in a Durban Catholic school in the 1940s, remembers African teachers, politicised by the formation of the ANC Youth League in 1943, who told students 'that provincial exams would be marked by people who had no way of knowing whether you were black or white'.[29]

Both Mphahlele and Magubane worked as teachers but left the profession disillusioned by the 1953 Bantu Education Act; not only were mission schools closing but the dominant conservative model of professional teachers' organisations became consolidated.[30] However, as Magubane's reference to exams suggests, schools' ability to provide educational credentials continued to position them as powerful forces that could undermine racial hierarchies. Black Consciousness, a movement ascendant in the 1960s and 1970s, itself had strong theological roots that helped connect duty, justice, and black autonomy to the acquisition of knowledge.[31]

Thus, building on the mission-school tradition – idealised, experienced in practice, or experienced by mentors who had studied in mission schools – leaders of excellent township schools put time and effort into creating the best learning environment resources would allow. To provide an alternative study space to overcrowded township houses, the schools sought to recreate the 'total institution' model of boarding mission schools by starting early and finishing late, typically operating from 6.30 a.m. to after 4 p.m. Students' discipline, punctuality, and neatness were closely monitored and indiscretions punished with corporal punishment. Vukuzakhe's principal, Isaac Kubeka, studied at a Presbyterian high school in Polela, Natal, followed by Fort Hare University. Mr Kubeka's attention to discipline bequeathed him the somewhat affectionate nickname of *Nsimbi*, or iron.[32]

Selective admission policies were another common feature of Umlazi's excellent schools. Radical plans to 'open the doors of learning', in the words of the 1955 Freedom Charter, did not prevent excellent schools using primary-school reports and/or entrance exams to select the brightest students. Due to limited school places, selective admissions had a long history; recall the 1962 standard 6 continuation certificate on the wall of the house of Mrs Mhlongo's relative. And Umlazi's families supported selection to 'excellent' schools because competition motivated children to knuckle down in the hope of being admitted. As Mrs Dlamini told me: 'I think everyone knew that if you want to go to Vukuzakhe, you must work hard because Vukuzakhe was catering for brilliant students.'[33]

Therefore, unlike primary schools, which generally admitted students who lived locally, excellent secondary schools could attract learners from afar, including Johannesburg's turbulent townships. Within Durban, the boom in the private 16-seater minibus taxi industry in the 1980s, part of the state's relaxation on black businesses, significantly reduced commuting times. By 1991, Nzimande and Thusi found that 78 per cent of Umlazi's students travelled more than 2 kilometres for schooling, and that 'if, during the early hours of the day, one stands at the entrance to any African township, one will notice the high number of students disembarking from trains, buses or taxis'.[34] And if excellent schools helped drive a schooling market, they also encouraged the mastery of English, to which we turn now.

*'English is your only salvation'*
Among those educated at mission schools, English had long been the language of social advancement and, by association – because early

leaders of the ANC came from a small educated stratum – English was also central to the rise of African nationalism. As Neville Alexander shows, however, English's dominance was not unquestioned within the liberation movement.[35] In the 1940s, Jacob Nhlapo proposed to institutionalise two main languages, Nguni and Sotho, by harmonising the country's African languages, a strategy that influenced Alexander's own language activism. However, the spark that initiated the 1976 Soweto student uprising was the proposal that some lessons be taught in the medium of Afrikaans – 'the language of the oppressor'.

Though a world apart, both anti-apartheid activists and white English-medium schools (considered earlier) therefore shared one thing in common: they viewed the colonial language of English as relatively neutral. For many activists, English was a language functional to liberation. It challenged the state's promotion of Afrikaans as a medium of education and its favouring of 'tribal' African languages in ethnically organised schools. For the latter, English was the grammar of liberalism that could bring reason to the ideological Afrikaner state.

Moreover, when it came to replacing English with African languages in schools, the state's establishment of ethnic homelands partially backfired. Several homelands, including KwaZulu and Transkei, used their new-found autonomy to reject Bantu education's cornerstone policy of using African languages as a medium of schooling throughout primary schools.[36] Indeed, Bantu education officials showed great frustration at homeland leaders who promoted English in 'old-fashioned private high schools'.[37] This was, after all, precisely the mission-school model that Bantu education had sought to end.

Thus, Umlazi's excellent schools, administered by the KwaZulu homeland from the mid-1970s, promoted English as a means to access new work opportunities. One former principal of Zwelibanzi High told me how his school actively recruited teachers who spoke the best English and how he promoted English to students throughout the school day:

I was trying to motivate them, and I even remember that I had an inscription written ... which said, 'English is your only salvation,' because I wanted everybody to realise that if you knew English, you stood a better chance of passing the other subjects as well because they were taught in English, so we needed to have very good English teachers for the others to survive in biology, mathematics, science. We needed to have a very strong team of English teachers.

It is important to be clear, and I will return to this point later, that Umlazi's excellent schools supported multilingualism rather than the slavish promotion of English. Indeed, while in charge of Vukuzakhe School, Mr Kubeka wrote a ground-breaking dissertation on Zulu dialects at the University of Natal.[38] For many influential figures in the region, English and isiZulu were not seen as mutually exclusive, as Bantu education's advocates had hoped. Indeed, the founder of the Inkatha Zulu cultural movement in the 1920s was mission-schooled John Dube, who had been the ANC's first president.[39] The leader of the KwaZulu homeland, Mangosuthu Buthelezi, who rejuvenated the Inkatha cultural movement in the 1970s, studied at the elite mission institutions of Adams and Fort Hare.[40] In practice, teachers in township schools were native isiZulu speakers and so English was often mixed with isiZulu in the classroom.

Of critical importance, too, was the growing significance of English in the world of work. Not only did professional and service work come to play a bigger role in the economy, but the organisation and administration of work became more regulated by formal rules. In factories and mines, the *izinduna* (literally, 'chief's assistants') supervisory system had been based on the personal authority of African supervisors in recruiting and managing workers. However, from the mid-1970s, the trend was towards unions and personnel managers agreeing written rules. For employers, improving skills often meant improving workers' 'attitudes' through better worker–management 'communication'.[41] Similar processes, it must be noted, might have worked to increase the value of Afrikaans elsewhere, such as in the Transvaal or Cape provinces.

### Schooling for liberation

In galvanising worldwide opinion against apartheid, no image was more powerful than Sam Nzima's photograph of Soweto student Mbuyisa Makhubo carrying the limp body of 13-year-old Hector Pieterson, who had been shot by police. The 1976 Soweto student uprising initiated a new era of activism, including demands for 'liberation before education'. However, Umlazi was 'minimally affected' by the uprising in Soweto and other townships; protests were somewhat tempered by Inkatha's power in the region.[42] Indeed, by 1982, KwaZulu officials were claiming that the introduction of the Inkatha youth movement in schools had had a 'salutary effect on discipline'.[43]

Nevertheless, in the 1980s tensions did rise between activists aligned with the ANC and supporters of Inkatha.[44] Mangosuthu Buthelezi, Inkatha's leader, opposed sanctions, independent unions, and anti-apartheid activism. Even though KwaZulu never accepted formal 'independence', as did four other homelands, Buthelezi earned the wrath of the ANC, which had initially viewed him as an ally. School principals walked a fine political line. After activist Mxenge's murder in Umlazi in 1985, residents recall that principal Mr Kubeka's house was petrol-bombed by activists angry that Vukuzakhe had ignored calls to boycott schooling.

Nationwide, the apartheid government declared a state of emergency in 1986 as youth-led revolts, many organised under the banner of the United Democratic Front (UDF), made townships 'ungovernable'.[45] Propelled by the apartheid government's support for Inkatha, known after 1990 as the Inkatha Freedom Party, a chilling period of Inkatha–ANC political violence threatened to derail elections until a last-minute ceasefire in 1994.

While regional differences matter, I want to emphasise here how the schooling system became a continual site of ambiguity and tension for both state institutions and the liberation movement. The state's failure to rehabilitate rural 'tribal' life became exposed when black communities demanded equal schooling and some of the best schools remained located in urban areas.[46]

From the perspective of the liberation movement, education had an ability to both promote individual social mobility and address collective racial injustices. The line between the two was not easy to draw: to what extent was a school graduate who worked as a homeland administrator, policeman, or factory supervisor a collaborator or a pioneer of black advancement? Some of these tensions were reflected when activists referred to the thwarted social mobility of the 'black child'. Notably, the phrase is a singular noun (i.e. not 'black children') and this contrasts with the commonly used collective terms 'people', as in 'people's education', and 'youth', as in the ANC's Youth League. As such, the term 'black child' fused ideas of innocence, individualism, the family, and structural racism – indeed, it re-emerged in speeches in the 2010s as students demanded the decolonisation and decommodification of education.

Suggesting the ambiguous position of education, one former UDF activist told me that sporadic attempts to shut down schools in Umlazi did not extend to a blanket opposition to their activities. Any principal whose school achieved high pass rates was revered in the community.[47] The former activist's main bone of contention was Inkatha's interference with the syllabi. 'I didn't want the school to be closed down, but we wanted the proper subjects at schools,' he told me. He was referring to the 'Ubuntu-botho' (roughly 'humanism') syllabus, introduced in 1979, which glorified the Zulu cultural movement in order to promote loyalty to Inkatha.[48]

Thus, school boycotts and activism that won headlines at the time were interspersed, in some schools, with hard work by teachers and students and new work opportunities for school leavers. Indeed, excellent public schools developed elsewhere. Soweto Township, the site of the famous 1976 uprising, itself has a history of excellent public schools. From the mid-1950s to the mid-1970s, these schools offered, in Clive Glaser's words, 'a vital route to upward mobility'.[49] Even when tumult gripped the education system after 1976, Soweto residents recognised that some schools had better reputations than others.[50] In 1986, after two years of boycotts, the Soweto Parents Crisis Committee called for students to return to school.[51] In Durban's KwaMashu Township, Isibonelo School was said to have 'defied the odds to produce senior government officials, CEO's [sic] and some of the country's football legends of the late 70's and early 80's'.[52] So, although Umlazi is where some of the country's best schools were located, the trends that shaped them were not exceptional.

To summarise: the upshot of the aforementioned changes was that, by the 1980s, many parents from the township, and some from outside, were sending their children not to their nearest secondary school but to a small number of favoured English-intensive schools; one excellent Umlazi school, Vukuzakhe, had boarding facilities to enable the admission of non-local students. As we shall see, a small number of children also travelled to Coloured and Indian public schools and private white schools outside the township. Important aspects of a schooling market – schools picking learners and parents picking schools – existed in Umlazi well before the 1990s. And as we note below, white Durbanites also increased their attention to schooling at this time.

### White education in class-based suburbs: schooling amid anxiety

It was an unwritten rule of apartheid that any improvements for black people would not take place at the expense of whites. Thus, black occupational advancement happened at segregated institutions such as hospitals or schools, or when white workers left certain positions to move up the employment ladder. When the economy was booming in the 1960s, the second mechanism, the 'floating colour bar', meant that 'there was no clash of interest' between the educational and occupational advancement of blacks and whites.[53] Yet when the economy slowed and black South Africans attained more years of schooling, racial job reservations became harder to uphold, especially in companies that had relatively flat employment structures. Educational investments became a means by which many whites tried to immunise themselves from their weakening structural position.

Of course, economic changes and political tumult cut through white South Africa in many different ways. Vincent Crapanzano's ethnography published in 1985 presented students at English universities as unashamedly Eurocentric and generally unreflective about their own lives; for them, whiteness was superior and the norm.[54] In contrast, Nicky Falkof's study of Satanism and family murder in the 1980s provides a vivid account of anxiety among a poorer group of Afrikaans speakers.[55]

In Durban, letters written to newspapers by white residents capture the heightened sense of unease in the city. One disillusioned Durbanite wrote in 1979 that 90 per cent of junior office and sales positions 'are now filled by Indian and Coloured girls ... being paid lower salaries'.[56] In 1979, a 'disgruntled whitey' wrote a letter to the *Natal Mercury* complaining that industry required matriculation passes for most jobs, asking of the government: 'What is their plan for the future of "Whitey"?'[57]

By 1987, the principal of Bluff's Grosvenor Boys' High School was advising that standard 10 was no longer sufficient, and 'school leavers have to achieve some technical skill or trade'.[58] The proportion of whites attending university went up from 7.1 per cent to 28.3 per cent between 1952 and 1985 and was second only to the figures for the United States.[59]

In the cultural sphere, perhaps the most significant change at this time was the unbanning of television in 1976. Television's beaming of images of musical icons and hippy counterculture hindered the state's imposition of a conformist national doctrine. Moreover, images of black middle-class Americans troubled the idea that racial hierarchies were innate. As Jonathan Hyslop wryly notes, 'Bill Cosby had helped to turn the white South African middle class from race warriors to class warriors.'[60]

In this uncertain economic and cultural milieu, preschools became an attractive way to give children a head start. These fee-charging institutions, sometimes called pre-primary or nursery schools, sprouted across all the suburbs of the white city.[61] In the 1970s alone, 34 pre-schools were opened in Natal, almost three times as many as had existed previously.[62]

Another reason why preschools were necessary was because 'the working mother has become a permanent feature of our present day society'.[63] The number of white women in white-collar employment alone increased from 235,000 in 1965 to 401,000 in 1983.[64] In the 1980s, the women's magazine *Femina* – though continuing with long-standing themes of cookery, fashion and beauty, and knitting and crafts – increasingly came to showcase working women and the new options this brought, including to live apart from men.[65]

Spending more money on each child was enabled not just by women working for wages but by reductions in family size (which also reduced school enrolments). A 'so-called privileged white' (man) wrote a letter to the *Mercury* in 1980 saying:

I would have loved to have had more children than the two I am fortunate to have, because I could afford to provide for only two children and pay for two children's education; not like the so-called poor non-whites who have many children and do not worry about them because the newspapers will always bring their plight to the notice of everybody.[66]

The sarcastic label 'so-called privileged white' reflects more than just a 'colour-blind' view of society that denied the existence of white advantage. It shows a growing sense of white racial insecurity that could motivate educational investments among smaller-sized families. One mother who schooled in the Bluff in the early 1980s remembered: 'My whole thing was to have children – lots of them. Now I've got two children. We stopped at two, because we wanted to give them the best.'

Consider, too, for partial insights into dilemmas in white society in the 1980s, two magazines launched in this decade. Started in 1984, the magazine *Careers for You* gives a sense of students' and parents' greater attention to schooling. The magazine offered advice for applicants on writing letters of application and preparing for interviews.[67] At the same time, the rules on racial job reservations still gave employers an incentive to hire white workers, and the magazine was filled with enticing advertisements placed by employers, including for a retail store management trainee and an engineering company apprentice.

Tapping into the growing interest in children and schooling, in 1987 the magazine *The Child* was launched 'for thinking adults involved with children'.[68] Its first edition carried a long article titled 'Education: who should carry the can?' The piece quoted the Free Market Foundation advocating that parents should have greater 'freedom to choose' schools.[69] While never reaching much above 5 per cent of attendees, the number of white children in private schools grew from the mid-1980s and more sharply after 1990.[70]

There is evidence, too, that schooling came to matter more to a person's standard of living. Census data offer evidence of the erosion of the apartheid formula that even working-class suburbs should provide middle-class lifestyles. In 1970, only 21 per cent of Bluff residents with grade 8 (standard 6) education or above had passed the matriculation (grade 12) exam, and Bluff residents were predominantly employed in production-related work; in contrast, in the upper Berea, 34 per cent of those with higher than grade 8 (standard 6) had matriculation or above, and the area had a large number of professional, administrative, managerial, and sales workers.[71] Yet, despite these differences, both Bluff and Berea monthly earnings were concentrated in the R3,000–6,000 bracket in 1970, with the gap only significant in the top two income categories, where a higher proportion of Berea residents earned over R6,000.[72]

However, if we turn to 1991 data, we see a much bigger gap in both education and income between Berea and Bluff households: 72 per cent of Berea residents had passed matriculation compared with 47 per cent of Bluff residents; and nearly 40 per cent of Berea residents compared with only 7 per cent on the Bluff were concentrated in the four top income categories, earning at least R50,000 a year.[73] Firm conclusions are difficult to draw because of the many factors that affect census data. But these findings are consistent with the greater educational 'payoff' provided by work that required more education, such as professional or administrative work, and/or better-off Bluff residents moving into more prestigious suburbs, including Berea.

### No longer a 'Rolls-Royce type of education': white schooling under threat

While parents became more anxious about the future, white schools themselves stood on increasingly shaky ground. The post-war baby boom had ended; from 1960 to 1991 the proportion of residents under five on the Bluff dropped from 10 per cent to 4 per cent, and, in Berea, from 8 per cent to 3 per cent.[74]

In the 1960s, as we saw, the Natal Education Department (NED) had pushed for zoning in Berea: that is, for children to attend schools in a defined catchment area. Yet, by 1974, a NED survey spoke of how the significant number of children travelling into central Durban provided 'support' to the area's schools.[75] In 1967, a city plan for the Bluff recommended opening ten new schools; two decades later the prevailing question was which schools should close.[76]

The redirection of finances towards black schools, which particularly followed the 1981 De Lange Commission's report on education, forced parents to channel more money into white education. In a sharp break from the past, some white schools began to charge parents voluntary fees. Such changes led one politician in 1982 to describe the demise of 'a Rolls-Royce type of education' for whites.[77]

To understand the losers in what was becoming a more marketised system we need to return to the existence of sharp differences between upper-middle-class and more 'rough and tough' white schools. Schools with the lowest status, and therefore the least ability to attract students and collect fees, faced the biggest threat of closure. In 1988, the English-medium Mansfield School, a working-class institution located on the lower Berea, closed its gates after 77 years.[78]

Afrikaans schools were particularly badly hit. Mixed Afrikaans–English parents tended to choose English schools for their children, and the traditional Afrikaans jobs on the railways were eroded by technological developments and the rise of the automobile. The proportion of Afrikaans speakers on the Bluff dropped from 35 per cent in 1970 to 26 per cent in 1991.[79] In 1990, two Afrikaans primary schools on the Bluff were forced to merge, and in total in that year, five Afrikaans-language schools closed in Natal.[80] Countrywide in the 1980s, an icon of Afrikaner power, the Nederduitse Gereformeerde Kerk (NGK or Dutch Reformed Church), faced sinking congregation numbers.[81]

For Mr and Mrs Steyn, introduced earlier, sending their children to English schools was a painful but pragmatic choice. 'As I said to you, I am Afrikaans,' Mrs Steyn told me, 'and I went through a lot of researching and want to do the best for my kids. I am not fluent in English ... I hear it a lot, but I don't speak it ... I know that my kids were going to be clever. I knew they would study further.'

Thus, a series of sea changes swept through white schools and society in the 1970s and 1980s: rising costs, whether for preschools or in voluntary fees, more competition from black workers, and a tighter labour market in a period of recession. For parents, these all manifested the sense that education was an investment with a particular payoff; for schools, there was the gradual realisation that they needed to find ways to fill empty seats in the classroom. One solution was to admit a small number of black students, as we shall see.

## Desegregation: an 'ability to be assimilated'

It is now time to return to two questions. Why did public schooling desegregation receive support from many white schools and parents in the late apartheid period? And what were the main features of the early period of desegregation? Schooling desegregation in fact began in 1976 when private schools, at first Catholic, opened their doors to a small number of black children in the wake of the Soweto Uprising. Convent schools led the 'open school movement' and used the language of being 'open to the people of God' to justify their opposition to racial segregation.[82] In Natal, by 1979 there were 173 black learners in 20 private schools: 100 Coloured, 35 African, 33 Indian, and 5 Chinese.[83]

NED records reveal the middle-class occupations of black parents who applied to private schools in the 1970s and 1980s: applicants included a doctor, teacher, sales manager, nurse, businessman, social worker, and lawyer.[84] Pam Christie noted the 'high number of African professional women, usually nurses and teachers' who placed their children in Catholic private schools, while Blade Nzimande found that one in four of the African personnel practitioners he surveyed sent their children to 'multiracial' private schools.[85] So, from the perspective of Umlazi Township, clearly there was a small class of parents who had the means to pay high fees for private schools.

As we saw in Chapter 2, in the early apartheid period a child's social class – interpreted through 'common-sense' indicators such as dress, demeanour, hair, and accent – could influence whether they were *classified* as white. After this initial period of fluidity, 'race' became entrenched on ID cards and in the everyday spaces in which children lived and schooled. Yet, in deciding which black children would be admitted to white schools, race and class became (re)connected in new ways, albeit with schools continuing to pay attention to phenotypic traits. Signifiers of a child's middle-class status – for instance, their English ability and parents' occupation – gave an applicant a better chance of being accepted. Gender interacted in important ways too. Meghan Healy-Clancy's study of Inanda Seminary shows how girls' mission schools were viewed by the state as less threatening than boys' schools.[86] Consistent with the perceived lesser threat of black girls, NED documents show that females outnumbered males at white private schools by a ratio of 5:1.[87]

Thus, class and gender differences influenced the philosophy of racial assimilation that governed black children's entry into private schools. In the words of one private school principal, schools looked for students who had the 'ability to be assimilated'.[88] In 1979, the Bluff's Catholic Convent School applied to the NED to admit an African girl who 'speaks English fluently as she is at present attending a Nursery school for Coloured children'.[89] An African child should be admitted, another school wrote, because she was 'clean and well-behaved and [can] comply with moral standards'.[90] A Coloured girl applying for Durban's Maris Stella School was said to be 'very fair in complexion'.[91]

The head of an Anglican private school described how spiritual values melded with the political imperative to develop a black middle class:

Church foundations [are] able to use the authority of the Church to challenge segregation; they serve people who have nothing to fear from an enriched middle class; they are repositories of values and a tradition which is readily understood by the Black community; and they are geared to developing leaders in business and the professions.[92]

From 1985, white private schools were joined by Indian and Coloured public schools in desegregating in small numbers, with African students continuing to be screened by tests such as for English competence.[93] Pushing forward desegregation was the United Democratic Front, supported by both black and white activists.

It was in 1990, however, shortly after the release of Nelson Mandela from prison, that desegregation arrived abruptly at the doors of white public schools. Minister Piet Clase set up a procedure whereby parents could vote, school by school, for the status quo or to convert to a model A, B, or C type of school. The difference between the models lay principally in the autonomy a school gained and the proportion of fees it would be responsible for collecting (a model A school became a private school; a model B school remained funded by the government but gained power over admissions; a model C school became a state-aided school responsible for maintenance costs).[94]

To understand the pattern of schooling desegregation, we need to return briefly to regional differences. The Soweto Uprising invigorated sharp educational struggles in the Transvaal Province, and this is where, in 1980, teachers, academics, and activists formed the National

Education Union of South Africa (NEUSA) to advocate for schooling desegregation.[95] In Natal, English speakers had long sought to preserve their privileges by distancing themselves – when occasion demanded it – from what they presented as crude Afrikaner racism.[96] By the beginning of 1992, 136 of Natal's 254 white schools had taken the plunge and voted on desegregation, with 127 voting 'yes'. Elsewhere, schools were slower to trigger ballots, although when they did most parents voted for change; 537 of the 2,111 white schools had voted to desegregate by 1992, although only four were in the Orange Free State.[97]

Like private schools, public schools initially had absolute power over admissions and therefore over the ability to admit 'nice blacks', in the words of one Durban governing body chair.[98] In January 1991, when the first black pupils were admitted into public schools, some black children transferred directly from private schools.[99] Joanne Kuper, now in her fifties and living on the Bluff, pointed to the importance of black children's attendance at the local Catholic private primary school in pioneering the desegregation of public schools. She said, 'The first was the Catholic school up here because it was semi-private, and they got some of the Africans in there, and then it just came normally.'

Durban's white schooling hierarchies introduced in Chapter 2 also allow us to understand how white parents' reasons for desegregating schools varied according to their location. The schools in the most privileged areas of Berea and the outer suburbs of Westville and Durban North were the first to trigger a ballot. They voted overwhelmingly in favour of desegregation. In the upper Berea, the heartland of white schooling, schools had suffered the least from dropping pupil numbers. They felt confident that they could select the right black students by assessing parents' ability to pay fees, using aptitude tests, gauging the students' proficiency in English, and filtering students by age (i.e. excluding students who had repeated schooling years).

There was much more initial opposition to schooling desegregation on the more working-class Bluff. With close links to the Conservative Party, which had split from the National Party in 1982 to oppose reforms to apartheid, right-wing activists founded the Own Schools Association (OSA) to maintain 'white schools for white children'.[100] Letting in a few black students, the OSA warned, was the 'thin edge of the wedge'; once the gates were breached, white schools would be flooded with '*kia* kids', the black children of domestic workers.[101]

Opponents of reform called for 'racial pride and patriotism' and mobilised long-standing resentment towards the hypocrisy of Durban's 'middle-class whites' and 'Big Money Boys'.[102] Unlike wealthy residents, so the argument went, Bluff residents had fewer economic resources to erect a class-based firewall against desegregation. Thus, although 61 schools in Natal voted in 1990 to admit black children in 1991, not a single school in south Durban decided to vote at that time.[103]

Yet because voting did not take place in a single poll but was staggered by school and broadly by suburb, parents on the Bluff began to see that the actual process of schooling desegregation was proceeding slowly and relatively painlessly. Some parents argued that taking proactive control of desegregation would allow them to pre-empt school closures or black students being foisted on them by a future black government.

In 1991, Bluff English schools established a steering committee to encourage parents to vote for desegregation, and when the ballots were counted, the resultant proportion of 'yes' votes at the schools ranged from 75 per cent to 87 per cent.[104] Afrikaans schools followed, although they retained an element of separation by introducing 'parallel' English streams. The pragmatism surrounding schools was seen on the Bluff in 1991, when votes in favour of desegregating schools occurred alongside a 'swing to the right' in local elections to oppose a 'black-dominated city'.[105]

In 1992, the government converted most desegregating white schools to the model C option to push greater financial responsibility onto parents. Most schools had voted for the model B option, which involved a higher level of state subsidy. The subsequent rise in school fees in white schools became a constant topic in Durban's newspapers.[106] Fervent discussions took place over the rights and wrongs of taking parents to court for non-payment of fees and on ways to raise revenue by hiring out facilities and putting up advertising billboards.[107] 'From being the dry and dusty halls of learning we all remember,' the *Natal Mercury* said, 'schools have effectively become business enterprises.'[108] 'Headmasters are wary of Model C education,' the same article continued, 'because they need to be both businessmen and educationalists to survive.'[109] Indeed, given the generous previous funding of white schools, it must have been an enormous shock to find that the non-payment of fees led to a Bluff boy having his books and stationery withheld.[110]

More widely, white families recognised that they had a lot to lose if the country sank into a civil war.[111] The introduction of standard and higher grade exams had led E. G. Malherbe to criticise in 1977 what amounted to grade inflation: 'candidates could obtain the matriculation certificate [for university entry] under conditions which previously would have qualified them for a school-leaving certificate'.[112] In 1990, white schools averaged 96 per cent matriculation pass rates, with black African schools achieving only 37 per cent pass rates.[113] Indeed, by 1993, one editorial opined that matriculation results in white schools had 'reached a point of excellence so suspiciously high' that there was reason to wonder whether the qualification 'is really a passport to life'.[114] The rising matriculation rates in Coloured and, especially, Indian schools, where the pass rate was 95 per cent in 1990, represented both a threat to whites and a potential buffer against the African majority.[115]

*Desegregation through black children's mobility*

There was another reason why parents and teachers felt confident that they could control desegregation. Before schooling desegregation took place, some of its advocates had argued that white schools would desegregate when black parents moved into white suburbs and their children entered local schools.[116] Some white areas 'greyed' illegally in the 1980s, and influx controls and the Group Areas Act were scrapped, respectively, in 1986 and 1991, in effect ending forced residential segregation.[117]

Yet, at first, black families were slow to move onto the Bluff. Moreover, even so-called '*kia* kids' did not swarm into white schools as some feared, because many domestic workers' quarters had been converted into garden cottages or granny flats (as we shall see in Chapter 7). Although some black families did move into white areas and their children attended local white schools, schoolchildren's mobility became the dominant model of schooling desegregation in south Durban; by 2009, only 32 per cent of attendees at one Bluff secondary school lived in the suburb.[118] (Later, we will consider in detail schoolchildren's mobility.)

From the perspective of Umlazi families, schoolchildren's mobility was already a common phenomenon, especially to access excellent township schools. Unlike in white areas, where middle-class parents lived in middle-class suburbs and accessed local middle-class schools, an increasing gap between rich and poor in Umlazi did not map neatly onto class-distinct suburbs and schools. Pockets of middle-class housing within townships tended to be small. Chappies comprised only around 20 homes, and even the building of BB section, which was made up entirely of private houses, did not lead to the ensconcing of middle-class parents who would foster and protect excellent local schools. By the late 1980s and early 1990s, shacks had sprung up on more or less every patch of unoccupied land – on sheer slopes, next to streams, or close to roads where the township's original planners had not built four-room houses. Moreover, an *ikhaya* (family house) was difficult to sell, and so matchbox houses tended to be extended in situ.

In short, Umlazi parents with the means continued to send their children to Umlazi's excellent schools and a few private multiracial schools, as they had increasingly done in the 1970s and 1980s. But now they also chose multiracial public schools.

*Marketised assimilation: the birth of the model C school*

We saw earlier how Bantu education attempted to 'divide and rule' black Africans by forcing them into African-language schools in segregated spaces. Homelands, the pinnacle of this state fantasy, lagged behind white society, so official doctrine went, because black people themselves were less well developed economically and culturally than whites. This ideology allowed opponents of political reforms in suburbs such as the Bluff to position racial integration as the takeover of the First World by the Third World.[119] Yet when schools voted in favour of desegregation, it also signified the acceptance of a small number of children from the Third World to enter the First. To do so, white schools positioned themselves as civilising forces. Thus, as Pam Christie argues, desegregation entailed 'the preservation of the "traditional values and ethos" of white schools, rather than their transformation'.[120]

To preserve their ethos, white public schools, like private schools before them, showed some preference at first for admitting Indian and Coloured pupils. These students, who spoke English at home, were seen as having less distance to travel culturally to white society and did not potentially challenge the culture of a school in the same way as the admittance of African pupils would. Thus, one Bluff primary school introduced a zoning policy that allowed the school to admit children from Indian and Coloured areas of Merebank and Wentworth but not from the more distant Umlazi.[121]

However, when black African students began attending white schools in larger numbers it became apparent that, on the whole, they or their parents did not want to turn white education on its head. With respect to language, English had long been emphasised in Umlazi's best schools, at private former mission schools, and at private white schools. The overriding mode of assimilation helps explain the birth of one of the lasting names from this period, the 'model C school'. This is still widely used to denote formerly white schools.

Introduced as a bland administrative concept, the term 'model C' came to symbolise a school's cultural whiteness, or white tone, including its preservation of white, native English teachers, but not necessarily its admittance of only white learners. It was a subcategory of a 'multiracial school', which is an older term that came to be used for white, Indian, and Coloured schools that admitted black African students. But in contrast to 'multiracial', which explicitly refers to 'race', 'model C' became a colour-blind term that more subtly evokes race. Specifically, it signals how whiteness became anchored not in racial classification but in middle-class English cultural forms. Notably, formerly white Afrikaans-medium schools, which also took on model C status, were generally still spoken of as 'Afrikaans schools'.

Moreover, English model C schools gained prestige when Afrikaans parents such as the Steyns chose them above Afrikaans schools. Indeed, had Durban's white parents prioritised keeping schools white, they could simply have enrolled their children in Afrikaans-medium schools, which few black Durbanites wanted to enter. But most parents did not do this. Although some Afrikaans-speaking parents continued to choose effectively all-white Afrikaans schools (this being a major reason for continued de facto segregation in some parts of the country), Durban's English schools appeared to offer a better future. Thus, if, before the onset of apartheid, 'more well-to-do members of the Afrikaans-speaking community naturally prefer their children to associate with English-speaking children of their own social status', as apartheid came to an end many Afrikaans students in Durban adopted a similarly pragmatic position.[122]

Finally, the fear of swarms of black residents rushing to buy or rent property in white suburbs was not realised in the early years of desegregation.[123] Many family members opposed selling township houses, and the jump in cost to suburban houses was large. Hence, as long as white Bluff residents remained loyal to local schools, as most were at this time, the schools were able to control their assimilation of 'nice blacks'. Poorer, more culturally distant black students were kept out by the high cost of fees and travelling.

## Conclusions

I have argued in this chapter that a number of forces worked to drive and shape schooling desegregation. Inequalities in Umlazi increased significantly. White schools faced a drop in enrolments. I have also shown that there were very few disputes about the basic grammar of desegregation. For isiZulu and Afrikaans speakers, English was clearly the language of social power. It was a language used in the political struggle to overcome apartheid's ethnic vision but it was also a language of co-option. In everyday life, the two were never easy to disentangle: Umlazi's excellent schools, under the control of the Zulu nationalist government, saw themselves as showcasing black achievement and providing leaders for a free South Africa.

We also saw continuities in desegregation from 1976, when private schools first admitted black children, to the 1990s, when the entire public schooling system desegregated. Schools became less concerned with racial purity, symbolised by the 'pencil test' (the pencil falling signalling that a child was white). Class was no longer a tool to decide if someone should be classified as white. By the 1990s, better-off black learners were admitted into 'model C schools' if they had the 'ability to be assimilated'.

As we shall see, however, over time assimilation became an increasingly inadequate concept, on its own, to understand schooling in South Africa. I show in Chapter 6 how this early period of marketised assimilation gave way to heightened competition among formerly white schools and to the era of the *racialised market*. What became more important was the way in which learners could market a school, including by explicitly advertising its 'white tone'. However, first we need to look deeper at parallel changes in the labour market.

*Part III*

# Schooling and work after apartheid

# 5    Schooling and the labour market
## Symbolic power and social networks

> Symbolic power works partly through the control of other people's
> bodies and belief . . . on deep-rooted linguistic and muscular patterns
> of behaviour, either by neutralizing them or by reactivating them to
> function mimetically . . .    Pierre Bourdieu, *The Logic of Practice*, p. 69

In the 1960s white Bluffites had viewed Durban's central business district (CBD), or 'town', as a place to shop, or perhaps visit an elderly
relative staying on the picturesque Victoria Embankment. It was somewhere to escape from south Durban's booming factories, and to be
reminded that apartheid was fulfilling its promise to raise white living
standards. Few whites related to the fear of removals that hung over the
Indian business district, or the humiliation black Africans faced when
they were examined naked inside KwaMuhle Native Administration
Building – their only crime being to seek work in the city.

Today, however, Durban's CBD is a very different place. Street
hawkers, in the hurried atmosphere of the city, sell fruit and vegetables
on the pavements, some in the shadow of the Edwardian City Hall and
other colonial buildings. Minibus taxis lurch towards the pavement,
stopping to drop off and collect passengers. Liberation heroes are celebrated: Prince Alfred Street is now called Florence Nzama Street; Joe
Slovo Street is the new name for Field Street.

Durban is part of the amalgamated KwaZulu-Natal Province; gone
are bumper stickers celebrating Natal as the 'last outpost of the British
Empire'. IsiZulu is the most spoken language on the streets, and
radios are tuned into UKhozi FM, whose headquarters are located in
K. E. Masinga Road, named after the country's first black radio announ-
cer. The nearby beachfront, reachable via taxi even by rural dwellers, is
one of the few spaces in South Africa accessed by the rich and poor,
black and white: where middle-classness is not a prerequisite for leisure.
Yet for Anglophile critics – always quick to draw contrasts with Cape
Town – Durban has become just another untidy African metropolis.

I get a sense of the subtler persistence of English culture, a main theme
in this chapter, when I arrive at an old building with a greying exterior,
take the lift to the sixth floor, and am drawn to an eye-catching sign

showing a smiling white woman talking on the telephone – I have reached the offices of a telephone call centre training company. It is 2010 and this Durban training company has agreed to let me participate in a week-long 'outgoing' training session. Their openness was, I suspect, partly because a foreign white participant would help legitimise the 'international' status of the course.

Sometimes called 'white-collar factories', call centres link groups of telephone operators to customers via modern information technology. Workers can make 'outgoing' calls to sell a product or collect a debt, or answer 'incoming' calls when customers phone a help desk. Most call centres in Durban are based in the CBD or in clusters located north of the city.

Halfway through one morning, the facilitator gains our attention with a request. 'Now in your groups, begin preparing role plays to sell a [mobile/cell phone] contract.' The 'dolphins' – the name given to our group – look at one another. Eyes fall quickly on me as a white native English speaker. I shake my head and say, 'No, no, I'll watch.' Then a woman in her early twenties turns to a person sitting next to her and says comfortably in English, 'Let's do this together.' When it becomes evident that this second woman's English falls short of what is required, a young man takes over from her. But he, too, looks nervous and forgets his lines. Eventually, he is replaced by a confident young woman whose fluency in English suggests that she studied at a formerly white school. Linguist Rajend Mesthrie describes the type of prestigious English bequeathed by this institution as something akin to 'a South African version of Southern British English' (or perhaps 'BBC English').[1]

Nearly all participants on the three-week course are women, and all (except me) would have been classified as 'African' in the apartheid era. The course trainer – a lanky, animated 'Indian' man in his early thirties – was adept at overstatement: anyone, he said, can change their accent and communication style, learn how to sell, and – so he floated with a suggestive air – earn enough to buy a Lamborghini. But generally, those who spoke the most fluent English performed the best in exercises and exuded the most confidence: they initiated and dominated the conversations and communicated with an ease common to speakers with command of a prestigious language and accent.

I introduce call centres here, and return to them later, because their growth reflects a decisive employment shift over recent decades in South Africa and in many other parts of the world: from predominantly male manufacturing work to disproportionately female and English-intensive service work.[2] In Durban, a city that grew on the back of its port and manufacturing industry, the fastest-growing work today is in retail services: this includes community, social, personal, and financial services (thus both the private and public sectors).[3] In 2010, when I participated in the training course, employees at the top end of South Africa's over 1,000 call centres could earn between R5,000 and R10,000 a month; this put them in the upper 3 per cent of Umlazi Township's 20- to 29-year-olds in terms of income.[4] So how does someone find work in one of the few job sectors that grew after apartheid?

The formal requirement for call centre work is typically only a school-leaving matriculation certificate, a credential attained by almost half a million people every year. Nearly two-thirds of call centre employees nationally are women, a common trend in service work.[5] However, crucial to being successful in obtaining call centre work is whether applicants speak with an acceptable English accent – one most readily gained from being schooled at a 'multiracial' school (a formerly white, Indian, or Coloured school) with predominantly native English teachers. For employers, English represents both a 'skill' and a means by which a large pool of applicants can be screened. The training course I attended was in practice a kind of selection process for English fluency, since the names of the top 'performers' were passed on to call centres with which the training company had contacts.

Anticolonial activist-philosopher Frantz Fanon famously warned against a national bourgeoisie becoming a conservative force: 'Dressed like a European, speaking his language, working alongside him.'[6] As we have seen, from the 1970s the apartheid state deliberately promoted black social mobility including by tolerating, and then promoting, schooling desegregation. After apartheid ended in the early 1990s, thousands of black South Africans accessed multiracial schools, the most prestigious of which were white schools. The ANC made some efforts to address cultural inequalities by adding nine African languages to the existing official languages of English and Afrikaans. Yet English became 'first among equals': it was chosen as the language of instruction by the vast majority of secondary schools because of its prestige and, more practically, the lack of textbooks in African languages.[7]

To show connections between cultural dispositions and work I continue to draw on Pierre Bourdieu's concept of *symbolic power*.[8] I show that multiracial schools provide their learners with cultural advantages, and especially confidence in speaking English. Bourdieu also stressed that when school graduates move into positions of power they are able to influence what counts as prestige; there is a 'dialectical [two-way] relation between the school system and the labor market'.[9] Yet, prestige is always contested and changing, especially in a new democracy such as South Africa, and especially when the ruling political party has considerable influence over public-sector employment.

To be clear, while I foreground cultural aspects of schooling, educational qualifications matter when it comes to finding work. A person with tertiary/higher education is more than twice as likely to be in work as someone with only a matriculation exam.[10] However, a significant expansion in schooling has not lessened the country's problems of inequality, unemployment, and low economic growth. As more and more people access qualifications, each one is devalued: in South Africa, the rate of unemployment among people with tertiary education doubled between 1994 and 2014.[11] Postgraduate students can gain 'degrees without freedom', in Jeffrey, Jeffery, and Jeffery's words about India.[12]

In what follows, I demonstrate that for Umlazi-based students their type of schooling is critical to whether they secure *any* work. In contrast, schooling for white Bluff residents largely affects what *kind* of employment a person takes up. I also show in this chapter how residents of Umlazi and the Bluff access very different *social networks*, including ones grounded in schooling, to help them find work.

A final qualifier: it is not easy to draw firm conclusions about young people's particular social trajectories or life chances. While I show that children from better-off families access high-fee schools, I do not look at how they might benefit from better nutrition, the availability of reading material at home, or other advantages.[13] More generally, I followed a relatively small group of young people over a five-year period and draw on a fairly small survey. These limitations notwithstanding, what is clear is that a person's schooling greatly affects whether they find work, and what work. Recognition of the different paths from school to work provides a necessary prelude for the rest of the book, which focuses on how parents choose certain schools, and schools select certain learners.

## Schools and work

Today, it is common to see signs on company gates declaring that '*awukho umsebenzi*' ('there is no work'). To give a sense of the high demand for a job whose only formal requirement is a matriculation pass, I begin with a shocking case. In 2012, *15,000* people applied for 90 positions as a trainee road transport inspector (traffic cop) in KwaZulu-Natal. In a scorching-hot stadium in Pietermaritzburg, the organisers used a fitness test to screen candidates, asking them to complete a 4-kilometre run within 30 minutes. On this fateful afternoon, six people collapsed and died – another slit his own throat when he failed the test.[14]

In the context of chronic unemployment, Figure 5.1 summarises the schooling hierarchy in south and central Durban that helps explain the differing employment prospects of the city's residents. Two decades after apartheid ended, a school's former racial classification still correlates closely with its financial strength and cultural dispositions, such as the accent passed on to learners. For instance, in 2012, formerly white schools had average fees of nearly R10,000, compared with R1,000 in formerly Indian and Coloured schools and R200 in formerly African schools (US$900, US$90, and US$18 respectively).

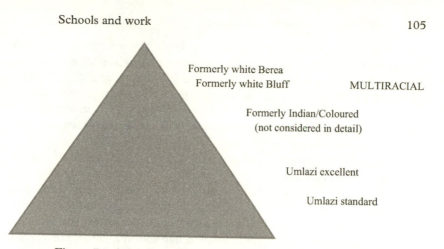

Formerly white Berea
Formerly white Bluff                          MULTIRACIAL

Formerly Indian/Coloured
(not considered in detail)

Umlazi excellent

Umlazi standard

Figure 5.1 Schooling hierarchies in south and central Durban

But divisions within racialised schooling systems are important too. As we saw in Chapter 2, Berea's 'traditional' white schools established themselves at the top of the schooling hierarchy. They outranked newer 'rough and tough' Bluff schools and the excellent Umlazi schools that developed in a sea of poorly performing township schools. Taken together, these inter- and intra-racial schooling divisions create a hierarchy that attracts learners north and west – from Umlazi into multiracial schools and from the Bluff to Berea schools.

The Household and Schooling Survey conducted for this study found that, among Umlazi's school leavers aged 20 to 25 years, 14 out of 64 had attended multiracial secondary schools. Only three who graduated from these schools were unemployed. Seven had entered higher education institutions. Many of the jobs they found were what we might call 'English-intensive': in retail (two women), in insurance (one woman), in car sales (one man), and in the police force (one man and one woman).

In contrast, of the 40 20- to 25-year-olds who attended 'regular' Umlazi secondary schools – that is, not one of the three 'excellent' Umlazi schools – a majority, 24, were unemployed (60 per cent). Only five accessed higher education institutions, two through the distance-learning university UNISA (one man and one woman), and three at Umlazi's Mangosuthu Technikon (two men and one woman). One man was serving time in prison. One woman was repeating matric at a 'finishing school'. If this group finds work, it is in disproportionately casual (i.e. non-permanent) and low-paid work. While one man found work as a bank clerk, lower-status jobs included the following: cleaner (three women), casual casino worker (one man), casual factory worker (one woman), casual hair salon worker (one woman), security guard (man), and self-employed salon owner (woman).

Young people who had attended Umlazi's three schools that were considered 'excellent' at the time of the research had a trajectory somewhere between graduates of multiracial schools and those leaving standard Umlazi schools (for more information on why parents choose 'excellent' schools, see Chapter 6). Notably, half of this group studied further at higher education institutions, a fact that helps explain this group's relatively low unemployment levels.[15]

Turning to the formerly white suburb of the Bluff, three of the ten white school leavers aged 20 to 25 at the time of the survey were not working, although all had attended university.[16] At first glance this level of unemployment appears quite high. However, the follow-up visits found that one man had found work as a financial adviser, another man was working as a teacher, and the woman had found a job as a marketing events coordinator. Other jobs young white people found included marketing and advertising, fabric buyer, insurance, and part-time wildlife guide. Indeed, taking Durban as a whole, the proportion of whites in high-skilled, high-income jobs actually increased from 60 per cent to 78 per cent from 2005 to 2014.[17] As we have seen, higher education is an important path for some school leavers and one with significant benefits, and we consider it first.

## Higher education

Money buys education credentials, and not just the much-vaunted matriculation certificate. Children from better-off families are most likely to access higher education because they attend high-performing (usually urban) schools and their parents can afford to pay tuition fees. Moreover, even when means-tested grants are provided, application processes cost money, and the National Student Financial Aids Scheme (NSFAS) doesn't cover all educational costs. The government's recent promise to introduce free higher education for poor and working-class students will reduce some but not all of these barriers to universities and colleges.

Related to the above, a good predictor of which learners get to access higher education institutions is whether they attended a school built for whites, Indians, Coloureds, or Africans. Those who study at formerly white schools, whether by travelling to or living in an affluent suburb, are most likely to pass the matriculation exam at the advanced level required to access higher education institutions (certificate, diploma, or bachelor level). They are also more likely to pass 'gateway' subjects such as pure maths rather than maths literacy. If we take university matriculation passes in Durban, we see that 58 per cent of students at formerly white schools passed matriculation at the level required to apply (but not necessarily be accepted) for a bachelor's degree course; the figure was only 20 per cent in formerly African schools.[18]

Since 2015, the #RhodesMustFall and #FeesMustFall movements have placed the country's 26 public universities in the spotlight. The most privileged research institutions were built for whites; at the other end of the scale are institutions that include Mangosuthu University (former Technikon) built in Umlazi Township. However, let us consider new private higher education institutions for more insights into the changing benefits that higher education can provide. One of these, Varsity College, was established in Durban in 1991 and is owned by ADvTECH, a leading educational corporation that owns a number of private schools. These private higher education institutions put little or no emphasis on academic research, and hence they do not claim to provide an experience similar to research universities such as the Universities of Cape Town, Witwatersrand, or KwaZulu-Natal. Why have they grown so fast? There are many reasons, but one of them is the rising competition for places at higher education institutions after racial restrictions on these institutions were ended. For some families in Durban, as we shall see, Varsity College represents a middle-class and 'whiter' alternative to the country's traditional universities – an image helped by its white demographics, location in affluent suburbs, small class sizes, excellent educational and sporting facilities, and absence of student protests.

Varsity College is also attractive to students who have the finances but not the necessary grades to enter research-intensive universities. Varsity College's selling point is its strong contacts with local businesses, contacts nurtured by its tailor-made courses in topics that include corporate affairs and communication, event management, public relations, and digital and social media. To aid the development of these niches, ADvTECH moved away from using ready-made courses developed by the University of South Africa (a distance-learning university) to courses designed by its own accreditation institution.

Tina, a white mother from the Bluff, eventually persuaded her ex-husband to provide surety for a loan to send their daughter to Varsity College. She said: 'We are sitting at – it must be about R110,000 now for the two years now so far in capital only ... I am looking at about R300,000 in total [US$27,000], for the four years of studying.' When I first got to know the family, Tina's daughter, Rachel, was enrolled in a bachelor of arts programme in corporate communication. I caught up with Rachel in 2016, and she had left Varsity College and had found work with a high-end call centre, being quickly promoted into human resources. She told me that the private university gave her a foot in the corporate world, and her trajectory supported this view.

Themba, raised in Umlazi and in her early twenties, studied at formerly white schools before attending Varsity College. Although she said that the number of black students at Varsity College was rising, she offered a sharp racial decoding of the institution:

THEMBA: I studied there one year for the BCom law. I saw white people and realised that it is a private institution and is costly; that is why it is only whites ...
AUTHOR: What do white people study?
THEMBA: Most they do a secretary diploma.
AUTHOR: What about the men?
THEMBA: There was doing sport science because ... they can become sport teachers in private school. Most of the girls there were doing secretarial courses because they know once they finish, they will find the job tomorrow.

In Themba's view, therefore, Varsity College channelled white learners into choice courses and cosy white job networks. Themba's belief that white managers had a strong influence over hiring in the business world is borne out by the fact that 59 per cent of senior managerial positions are still held by white people, mostly men.[19] Despite employment equity legislation, the rate of black upward mobility within the private sector is considerably slower than it is in the public sector.[20]

Let us return now to call centres to develop further the argument that 'non-qualification' attributes gained from education are increasingly important, including the symbolic power of English.

## Symbolic power: English and service work

Sociolinguists have studied how call centres can feed off and institutionalise existing language hierarchies; for instance, a worker in India or Pakistan will be asked to practise 'accent neutralisation' to satisfy the Western customers with whom they typically speak.[21] Although call centres in Durban generally service South Africa businesses, the government eyes the huge success of countries such as India that attract business from the English-speaking world.[22] Some call centres in South Africa do now service English-speaking international customers of Amazon, EasyJet, and British Telecom.

Jobs in call centres follow familiar racial hierarchies. People identified as white tend to find work in management positions or as operators at the highest-paying call centres.[23] In Durban, those identified as Indian, all of whom speak English at home, make up the majority of call centre workers. English is only very rarely the home language of black Africans, and this helps explain why this group accounts for only 27 per cent of all call centre workers in South Africa.[24]

In Umlazi I was introduced to call centre employees by someone who had worked in the industry.[25] A disproportionate number – slightly more than half – of the 29 call centre workers we interviewed were educated in formerly white, Indian, or Coloured schools: that is, multiracial schools. Umlazi's several excellent schools, which long emphasised English, were over-represented among those who had attended school locally. Generally, the highest-paid workers were those who had schooled at multiracial schools.

A person's perceived English competence also affects their progression within a single call centre. Twenty-five-year-old Zodwa had attended a formerly white school and spoke fluent 'white' South African English, which she described as having a 'twang'. Zodwa worked for ten months at an 'incoming' call centre where customers phoned in; this work was generally thought to be less stressful than 'outgoing' work such as sales or debt collection.[26] For her, call centre work provided experience and an income that was a stepping stone to better-paid work, including through further studies.[27]

Most of the employees at Zodwa's firm were African and had attended formerly white schools, or, to a lesser extent, formerly Indian schools. The minority of workers who had attended township schools, she said, were often asked to work the unpopular 'graveyard' shift – from 10 p.m. to 7 a.m. The justification for this was that there were more isiZulu callers at night, as informal shops in townships (such as shebeens and spaza shops) stay open late and sell prepaid mobile phone airtime that can generate customer queries.

The lowest-paying call centres in Durban place the least emphasis on English, and a few even promote fraud. One 22-year-old woman, Thuli, was born and educated in Umlazi Township. She worked at the call centre for four months and earned R300 or R400 per week, considerably lower than a typical call centre salary. Specifically, she was paid R50 commission for every person's bank account details she managed to acquire, for instance by telling them that they had won a competition but had to pay a small fee for the prize to be released. The archetypal person who might be persuaded to give their bank details, she said, was an elderly isiZulu-speaking person living in a rural area, someone to whom Thuli would speak in her home language. She clearly did not like committing fraud, and this motivated her to quit.

### English as a screen

In 2010 I visited a call centre that serviced a large South African mobile phone company. The room where a manager and I chatted had a panopticon-like view of the open floor below and the company's mostly black African workforce. He talked me through the five-stage recruitment process his firm followed: perusing a candidate's CV, conducting a telephone interview, administering an in-house assessment and then a scenario test, and finally conducting a face-to-face interview. What is significant about this process is that English does not just represent a necessary 'skill' in order to communicate with customers. It operates at every stage as a screen – a way in which employers filter a large number of applicants in the selection process.

Spoken English is especially important because it indexes a number of social dispositions and attributes: an applicant has a good schooling background, can be assimilated into the dominant business culture, attended a school with computers and other technology, and so on. It should be remembered that there is nothing technologically impossible about call centres employing monolingual isiZulu speakers, just as they are happy to employ monolingual English speakers. IsiZulu is, after all, spoken by 11.6 million South Africans at home, compared with fewer than 5 million who speak English at home.

Discussing an office environment, Themba – who, as we have noted, studied at Varsity College – described the importance of an English accent to finding jobs today. She is adamant that her 'white' English accent served to get her hired in a junior job at a finance company ahead of 25 other hopefuls (all African).

Many people were applying, and there was only one post. The lady who was interviewing me, a manager there, said she was impressed by the way I spoke English. She said, 'You sound like you are coming from overseas,' and I asked why; she said I speak differently. I couldn't say anything to her because I needed the job . . .

Themba explained that her school bestowed not just a prestigious accent but a confident disposition:

The teachers [at black African schools] do not encourage confidence because [learners] do not look at [educators] in the eyes and speak loudly. I notice that when you speak English with a person learning in these schools, they speak with zero tones, and if the white person speaks with them, they laugh a lot, like ha ha yes, ha ha yes. When I speak with the black person who went to the black school, they are not confident and speak with a zero tone; that is how we identify black schools.

Themba was one of the few Umlazi residents with whom I spoke who explicitly brought up racism. Studying at a formerly white school gave Themba a particular expertise in decoding the networks through which, to use an example she gave, white managers preferred to employ white female graduates from Varsity College in secretarial jobs. Her comment above – 'I couldn't say anything' – captures how black people's social mobility can necessitate passing through formerly white institutions, and in doing so they face painful dilemmas. Black schools, she says, are unable to provide the correct 'tone'.

Themba was also one of the few informants (black or white) who directly challenged my authority to undertake research. While not everyone in Umlazi showed enthusiasm for my study, I felt that inter-locutors viewed me as an educated, white, male professor (the four being mutually supporting) researching a subject that was of general public good (or at least not crassly profiting me individually). But Themba showed impatience at my questions, perhaps with my own 'white tone'. She wanted to know why I was asking so much about black schools. Why, though, does Themba emphasise the 'tone' a school bestows?

### 'White English' as a form of prestige

Sociolinguists developed the terms 'White South African English', 'Black South African English', and so on to show the fundamental importance of apartheid's four racial categories to linguistic variety in South Africa. In reality, there has always been diversity within these categories, for instance between a working-class white accent and a more upper-class 'larney' accent. Today, learners at multiracial schools, who might speak Afrikaans, English, or isiZulu at home, contribute to the modification of English when they interact daily in this language.

However, accents are not evaluated equally but can be organised in a hierarchy, one with roots in apartheid's system of racial segregation. In Umlazi, 'white' English is almost unequivocally talked about as 'higher English' ('isiNgisi esiphezulu'). Whereas in the early twentieth century isiZulu speakers could portray any school as a 'thing of the whites', today formerly white schools retain that meaning. Moreover, 'Coloured English' is usually rated as being better in Umlazi than 'Indian English', as the quotes below reveal. Consider these comments from two Umlazi residents, the first a woman in her fifties and the second a woman in her early thirties:

At School A [a formerly Coloured school] they teach proper English if you compare it to Indian schools ... there people get fake English.

There is a difference between the Indians when they are talking and Coloureds. It is like, if you [are] asking the Indian maybe the directions. He says go down there and see the 'Sunday', instead of the 'church'.

There are long-standing interactions between people classified as 'Afri-can', 'Indian', and 'Coloured' that underlie these language hierarchies.[28] My point, though, is that parents see accent as a reason to choose one school above another, and accent remains, for the time being at least, heavily associated with apartheid's racial categories.

It should be noted that Umlazi residents gain English fluency from not just schools but from watching television, listening to radio, chatting with friends, and in other ways. Andile was 17 when I met him at an Umlazi secondary school known for relatively poor matriculation results. He told me, 'We do not talk English in this school like other schools; if we talk in

English they [other students] criticise us and they say we think we are better than them, they say "*siyazitshela*" ("we tell ourselves" or look down on others].' But when I asked him why his English was so good he said, 'I learn from TV ... English movies.' This example of young people 'cultivating agency' is adroitly captured in Aslam Fataar's study of a student who grew up in the Eastern Cape, moved to Cape Town, and worked extraordinarily hard to better his schooling, including his English.[29]

At this point we can turn briefly to the language of Afrikaans. I did not meet a single Umlazi resident who attended an Afrikaans-medium school. For many, the language will forever be the 'language of the oppressor'. Yet, as Mahmood Mamdani notes, in many ways Afrikaans 'represents the most successful decolonising initiative on the African continent'.[30] Promoted by the state and Afrikaans-speaking intellectuals, in less than half a century this creole language took its place next to the colonial language, English.

Today, however, many white Afrikaans-speaking learners in Durban are moving into English-medium schools. In one sense, the drift of Afrikaans speakers from almost all-white schools to multiracial English-medium schools could be read as one from 'race to class': that is, learners are abandoning whiter schools for those that yield more long-term opportunities. But, as captured in the following quote from an Afrikaans-speaking mother, advancing the interests of young white people can also represent a 'stand against the masses' – a clear reference to black people.

You know what makes it [learning in Afrikaans] difficult? When you leave school. You study [at higher education institutions], and your study material is going to be in English. Jobs in Durban – 99 per cent of it – you have got to be English. So it makes it so much easier to bring your child up ... And then when the whole 1994 thing started, we knew that we have to be together. It doesn't matter if it's English, Afrikaans, Italian, or whatever, we have to now stand together against the masses. That's the way I see it. Masses – you know what I am talking about. It's the truth.

It needs to be noted that home-language Afrikaans speakers, who are almost all white in Durban, have always been conversant in English. The question is not whether they are bilingual but how, when, and where they use Afrikaans and English. To advance in relation to the 'masses', Afrikaans speakers with the means are seeing the oldest and most prestigious English schools as important vehicles for social mobility. We will return below to the social networks enabled by these 'traditional' schools, and we do so by situating these within the context of other advantages provided by social networks, beginning in Umlazi Township.

## Who you know ... social networks in Umlazi and the Bluff

Umlazi Township: '*Awukho umsebenzi*' ('There is no work')

The end of institutionalised racial discrimination, together with affirmative action and other black economic empowerment (BEE) policies, increased the size of the black middle class to around 2 to 4 million people, depending on definitions.[31] The ruling ANC's strong grip on the state means that the party operates 'as a massive jobs agency' by 'deploying' favoured cadres in beneficial jobs.[32] Not only can cadres secure lucrative jobs in government but 'tenderpreneurs' can benefit from multimillion-rand tenders. In 2016, the immense web of patronage surrounding President Jacob Zuma was exposed by the Public Protector as 'state capture'. However, outside this realm of elite connections, competition for work is brutal. Umlazi residents I met who were unemployed one year were usually still unemployed the next, or perhaps in some kind of *itoho* (casual work).

So how does a school leaver in Umlazi try to find work or advance their children's prospects? Patronage depends on vertical social hierarchies and race continues to structure these relationships in crucial ways. The importance attached to white patrons is expressed in the term *umlungu wami* (my white), which was used in Umlazi to describe my relationship to my research assistant, as indicated earlier. Moreover, as we shall see, white madams can help a loyal domestic worker with school fees, writing a letter to help the child's admittance to a local school, and helping a son or daughter to find work. The very ambiguity of these intimate acts ensures their persistence: are they moments of solidarity, an investment in a future of nonracialism, or a cynical way in which employers sustain the loyalty of their workers?

A second form of patronage works through local-level political institutions. Umlazi's three layers of overseeing government – the city, provincial, and national – are all controlled by the ANC. In the Umlazi section in which I worked, I heard that the ANC councillor mediated the following work for constituents: HIV coordination, work maintaining toilets, and building for local projects.

Patrons, of course, demand support. In 2012 I gained a sense of the culture of political patronage when I visited an Umlazi councillor's administrative offices. This office had once housed an apartheid township superintendent, and I had been told that there could be found records of the township's history (in fact there were none). As I arrived, two men in dark suits with prominent gun bumps focused their eyes on me. Different factions within the ANC fight, and kill, over the spoils of public office – a shocking 89 people were killed in suspected political attacks in the KwaZulu-Natal Province from 2014 to 2017.[33] Soon after my short visit, I was taken aback by the persistent calls from a volunteer in the office asking me for a 'donation' for a local project (it was unclear what the project involved).

In addition to kickbacks, patrons demand political support at election time. When voter-clients are linked to the state in such a way, so-called 'service delivery protests' reflect not just residents' demand for housing, water, or other services, nor merely disdain for the national government. Residents' anger can reflect a feeling that local promises have been betrayed – or that another patron is more likely to keep their pledges.[34]

A further way of finding work is through advice or contacts offered by family members and friends. The best example of this I came across among our surveyed group – and a throwback to the industrial era in terms of the work being undertaken – was a family where the father (now deceased) had worked at the local Toyota assembly factory. His four sons, aged in their twenties and early thirties, had all found work at this prominent south Durban company. More generally, family members provide knowledge and sometimes contacts at a place of work. Interacting, then, with a 'distributive economy', whereby a small number of wages filter down to poorer family members, is an economy of advice and favours.[35]

Finally, multiracial schools themselves foster a network of friends who are quite likely to be employed. Especially at a time when almost everyone in the city has a mobile phone, news about work opportunities can travel from township to suburb in seconds. However, the advantages provided by schooling networks are somewhat tempered by Umlazi's location 20 kilometres south of the CBD and the large number of jobseekers in the township. Finding work, in short, is hard work.

### Connections benefiting white Bluffites

In contrast to Umlazi, the Bluff is located close to the city centre and port, and therefore to employers that pay relatively high wages. In this formerly white suburb, residents themselves tend to have considerable assets and disposable income – one national estimate is that white people have, on average, 13 times more assets than black African people.[36] In contrast to Umlazi's 'family houses' that primarily have a use value, houses on the Bluff are more likely to be used by smaller numbers of people and can be sold much more easily. Houses, cars, and pensions can generate an income, and also entail work to service them.

We will meet again in Chapter 7 the Mitchell family, whose daughter, Sarah, advertised her child's swimming skills to try to gain admission to a Berea school. Trained as a beautician, Sarah gained experience working for her father's business before she found a job as a junior bookkeeper.

Mrs Mitchell's other daughter, Joanne, got a job with the help of her brother in an architectural firm. Local businesses such as plumbers, electricians, building repairers, and installers of satellite television are another important source of work for young white Bluffites. Julia, a Bluff mother in her forties, describes how her son found electrical work:

Yes. He got the job through a friend who phoned him. And then after that [his employer] went overseas to have an extended working holiday with his wife. And he passed Liam on with the goodwill to GH Electrical, and that is where Liam is working at the moment.

The Crawley family live in a modest house and their son, James, enrolled in Berea's technical school, 'because he is technically minded' – still a common saying on the Bluff. He hoped to obtain formal work but also had a 'backup plan'.

Well, we have got a friend, old Stephen, and he has offered James the opportunity to go and work with him, and he does electrical and all that type of thing. And there is also one of our friends, Henry, also does electrical. So, we have thought about sending him there during the school holidays just to get a little bit of experience in the engineering sector in the work environment.

The continued demand for white workers with trade skills derives, in part, from the fact that white people tend to trust other white people to oversee work inside their homes.

Of course, local networks that assist young white Bluffites do not prevent parents and learners feeling anxious about the future. Young people can sit at home for several years waiting for an opportunity for work, and, in these cases, parents might then compare this with their comfortable lives in the apartheid era. Moreover, class matters: a family with a lower income tends to have fewer material assets, fewer beneficial social contacts, and less ability to finance higher education. But, as we touch on now – and as we will see in more detail later – many Bluff residents over time came to 'jump class' in a sense, by leaving 'rough and tough' Bluff schools for Berea's 'traditional' schools. This served to enhance social networks among learners and parents who were previously divided by language (Afrikaans, English, and isiZulu) and/or the specific emphasis of the curriculum (practical or academic).

## Entering Harry Potter schools: Berea schooling and work

The importance of a secondary school's 'name' is confirmed by a telephone conversation I had with an old boy of a Berea 'traditional' boys' school. When I rang Mr Morris, a recognised expert on the school's history, he started quizzing me: 'What school did I attend?' 'Berkeley,' I replied, having introduced myself by stating my North American affiliation, and knowing that in the United States, 'school' refers to a place of higher education. 'No, what *school?*' he asked again. 'UKZN [University of KwaZulu-Natal, where I had studied for a master's degree],' I replied, unsure. 'No, *school?*' By that time, it dawned on me that he had heard my English accent and was conversant with elite English high schools, with which the top South African schools have strong ties. When I eventually gave him the name of my co-educational comprehensive school in the UK, he said, with some disappointment, that he had never heard of it. School, in other words, for him meant not a person's final school – which would denote their highest qualification – but the *high school*, which signified their character, calibre, and social networks.

The schools with the best 'name' in south and central Durban are 'traditional' schools located in the upper-middle-class Berea suburb. The networks they foster became apparent one Saturday afternoon in May 2012 when two of the city's old rugby rivals played a match beamed live on satellite television. The school hosting the match was known for its generous rugby scholarships and also for maintaining a whiter student body than its rivals. As students cheered loudly from the stands – their attendance was compulsory – I walked with a former teacher around an expensive new stand funded by an old boy. We chatted briefly with the marketing officer, who was on edge because representatives of competitor schools were there, he thought, to poach rugby-playing students.

Being a white man myself, I was not surprised to find that I would be welcomed into this mostly, but by no means exclusively, white male world. My teacher friend and I were greeted as 'sir' by schoolboys. But moving with a firm and friendly handshake from 'old boy' to parent to current pupil, I felt the weight given to networking: the underlying question was not 'How are you?' but 'Who are you?' Business cards were exchanged, promises of contact made (Figure 5.2).

Many of the schoolboys I met that day were from south Durban, including the Bluff. In the 1960s and 1970s, prestigious Berea schools looked down on Bluff residents as 'rough and tough' cousins. Today, one current attendee at a Berea school, Jonathan Venter, grew up on the Bluff and won a sporting scholarship/bursary for hockey and surfing (both traditionally white sports) to attend one of Berea's schools. His father is an engineer in a local factory, and his mother runs a business from home. Jonathan's father explained how two Berea secondary schools tried to lure Jonathan: 'If you have your provincial or [sports] colours, then you automatically are classified for a bursary. [One] school offered David a 100 per cent bursary, but we took 75 per cent from [another].' The family's working-class roots were evident in their surprise when they attended the Berea school for an interview: 'We walked into the very old, traditional school and said, "This looks like Harry Potter's place"

Figure 5.2  Friends watching a schoolboys' rugby match with TV camera in the background. Photograph: Mark Hunter.

[the wizard school Hogwarts, based on a British boarding school and depicted in the children's books by J. K. Rowling].'

While girls' schools are also organised in a hierarchy, boys' schools have larger and richer old boys' networks. They also have deeper ties to the country's top universities. Their social ties are especially useful for accessing Durban's business world. Mrs Venter said that the school helped Jonathan to find work: 'Invariably the directors are from these schools. They ask if Mr So-and-so [teacher] is still there … And [former students] all belong to the Old Boys' Society, which is something the schools don't have here on the Bluff.'

Another Bluff parent put the advantages of traditional schools like this:

The school has such a big old boys' club. I think, at the end of the day, that is what is the big thing. The old boys' club. It's a case of who you know and not what you know. You might go to an employer who sees you are from … the same school, so I will employ you. There was a company of chartered accountants. They are old boys [from one school]. They only take boys [from the school]. Do their training, get their articles, send them overseas for a year or so, and then they must move on and make space for the next crowd … For me it's the … old boys' club.

Black pupils admitted into 'traditional' Berea schools can benefit too. Andile, a former student of the school where the rugby match was held, told me that when he interviewed for a job in a local business, his potential boss immediately recognised the school he had attended. The manager had studied at a rival school, and the pair struck up an immediate rapport over schoolboy rugby. 'Was Mr Jones still involved in rugby?' 'How are the team's recent results?' Andile was offered the job.

### Networked to overseas labour markets

In his 1985 book, Vincent Crapanzano noted that it was common for students at English universities to entertain the possibility of leaving South Africa for Europe – the 'locus of culture'.[37] Today, the demand for teachers and nurses in Western countries is a key driving force behind black workers' emigration.[38] Yet, it is still predominantly white South Africans who have the schooling, finances, networks, and ancestral passports that enable them to move overseas. A 'Bluff Reunited' Facebook group has more than 5,000 members, many living in Australia, the UK, Canada, and elsewhere overseas.[39]

One émigré from the Bluff was Joanne, age 45. Aided by her parents' earlier move, Joanne had emigrated to Toronto in 2010. I caught up with her in 2015 in a suburban estate north of the city. She had found work and was positive about the move; her son was missing beach life but was now attending university.

Rather than white Bluffites seeing emigration as a first choice, however, this example shows how it can take place after much deliberation. Joanne's own parents had moved to Canada in the 1980s, back to South Africa in the 1990s, and then back again to Canada a few years later to be followed by Joanne.

This gradual acceptance of emigration is seen, too, in the Crawley family. The family was close-knit: when I arrived, I always seemed to interrupt them watching a comical YouTube video or engaged in another fun activity. The three-bedroom house was located in a lower-middle-class area of the Bluff and had been bought at a good price: 'It looks small from the outside, and people driving past it thought it was a pokey house and left.' Both parents were employed in lower-middle-class white-collar work in banking and government services.

When I first met the Crawley family in 2012, the daughter, Jane, was attending the local Bluff girls' school. As noted later, compared with boys' schools, Durban's girls' schools desegregated and imposed fees in a more even way and therefore attracted local residents for longer. In 2014, Jane told me that she was not confident that she would do well in her imminent matriculation exams, although her uncle, a retired maths teacher, had been giving her extra lessons. The family had organised a neat binder with information on different options and had visited several possible institutions. One of these was a local private university (a competitor of Varsity College) that offered small classes and niche courses. Jane's mother told me about the visit:

I actually think it was quite offensive ... they said something about, 'Oh it's mostly white people,' or something. But if you think of it, students come here because there are no black people. I actually think it is quite offensive.

The 'actually' in the above comment suggests that the company went too far in its racial branding. However, Mrs Crawley was also uncertain about the local public university's attempt to reframe its identity as an African university.[40]

The University of KwaZulu-Natal had a philosophy at one stage, about five years ago or six years ago, that they were an African university ... And I am not quite that thrilled with that theme, and they were trying to work out what it means as well.

In June 2015, I returned to find that Jane had moved to the UK in the preceding year. She had failed to secure one of the 40 places for graphic design at the Durban University of Technology (300 people had applied). Old girls' school networks, less influential than boys', had not helped her to find work. According to her mother, Sarah, attending a private university would cost 'more than what we paid for our house'. Jane has an ancestral visa through her grandfather and moved in with her mother's sister. When I returned in 2016, they told me that she was working in a supermarket in the UK and was determined not to return home.

One Bluff family for whom moving overseas was, they said, a desirable first option was the Layden family. Angry at affirmative action policies, Mr Layden told me that his two sons were planning to leave for Australia. Yet the conversation revealed that his children had both done quite well jobwise:

MR LAYDEN:    They eventually want to go over there because they are not happy
              here, because there is no future for whites.
AUTHOR:       But Brandon has that job [we discuss his two promotions].
MR LAYDEN:    Ja. He has got that job and he has also got a car now.
AUTHOR:       OK. Why does he think there is no future when he has quite a
              good job?
MR LAYDEN:    Well, with all this load-shedding [electricity cuts to save power]
              and what have you that is going on.

Mr Layden's comments point to how affirmative action policies tend to conflate a wider series of annoyances: from crime to 'load shedding' to black people moving into the neighbourhood. David Goldberg has written that affirmative action has become a 'poster child' for the view that addressing racial injustices amounts to racism itself.[41] While there are many questions to be asked about how employment equity legislation has a bias towards richer students, affirmative action is almost never considered by its critics in light of the advantages provided by configurations of whiteness.

### Contestations over the Rainbow Nation

I want to begin this section by restating the point that South Africans have followed varied, contradictory, paths. While some white parents and learners gravitate towards the security of institutions that exclude black people, others can see advantages in embracing selective aspects of 'Rainbow Nationism'. To understand this dynamic, let us continue with a puzzle that Diane Reay and colleagues sought to unravel in London.[42] Aware of a wealth of literature showing that white middle-class parents choose schools with a whiter and higher-class reputation, the authors asked why then do some middle-class parents choose local comprehensive schools with questionable reputations? Hoping to find a strong culture of civic responsibility, even anti-racism, they instead found that, to the extent that this feeling existed, it was mixed with a sturdy dose of pragmatism. Parents felt that there were positive gains for children in mixing with 'ordinary' people – that is, children of different classes and different ethnicity and race – what the authors call 'a darker shade of pale'.[43] Some parents who themselves had attended private school were resentful that they had missed out on social mixing when they were young.

Something similar happens in certain times and places in South Africa. The stature of Nelson Mandela, the new flag and anthem, the integrated sports teams, and the national television's slogan 'Simunye' ('We are one') all came to represent reconciliation and oneness in the new South Africa. The 'Rainbow Nation' has always been an icon riddled with contradictions but it does have a material grounding in a changing world of prestige.

Mrs Entwistle, in her fifties, joined the governing board of her local Bluff secondary school soon after her son enrolled in the institution. She criticised other white parents who sought out schools with the largest proportion of white children, suggesting that learners in these schools develop an 'attitude' that is detrimental to their long-term prospects:

When you go into work and you have somebody other [a black person] telling you what to do, you are not going to stay long at that work. You are going to have an attitude. So, we have actually always been open about that – we don't mind. We haven't minded from the beginning.

As we will note in more detail later, some schools enhance their 'white tone' by choosing learners with white phenotypic traits or those who excel in 'white sports' such as rugby. But white people are a minority group, and Mrs Entwistle is articulating the fine line that exists between a white person's confidence and their developing an arrogant, even racist, attitude that might harm them in the world of work.

For their part, most Umlazi parents argue that 'multiracial' schools located outside the township lead to work opportunities that value English. However, an important distinction in the labour market must be made between private- and public-sector work. While 'white English' is prized in the private sector, it has less status in the public sector. I interviewed Msizi Thabede's father, who worked for the government; we had mutual friends who had gone to school at a prominent Berea high school. Msizi, in his twenties, relayed to me the suspicion within ANC circles of Africans who speak too 'white'. What is needed to obtain government work, he said, is not an accent gained from a formerly white school, but an ANC membership card and 'comrade speak'. Such attitudes are clearly shown in the treatment of Lindiwe Mazibuko. A prominent former leader of the opposition Democratic Alliance, Mazibuko studied at a formerly white private school and faced constant ridicule by members of the ANC for being 'un-African'.[44]

Thus, if states generally have 'a monopoly over legitimate symbolic violence', in South Africa the state is a highly contested institution.[45] On the one hand, many heroes of the liberation struggle place their children in formerly white schools. In contrast to the National Party's successful promotion of Afrikaans, the post-apartheid state has not overseen the rise of African languages in circles of power.

Yet, English-speaking elites have not had everything their own way. Whereas Mandela promoted reconciliation, his successor Thabo Mbeki launched an 'African renaissance'. In turn, Mbeki's perceived elitism and aloofness led to his downfall at the hands of Jacob Zuma. Schooled for only a few years, Zuma struggles at times in English, like the majority of South Africans, but his dances and songs and speeches in isiZulu had, at the peak of his power, an unparalleled ability to sway audiences.

Moreover, parents who might advocate English-medium schooling (especially the verbal benefits) can also be strong advocates of isiZulu (including its written form). Established in 2002, the daily newspaper *Isolezwe* now has nearly 1 million readers. Colloquial and unpretentious in tone, *Isolezwe* stories might cover popular singers and TV personalities or dilemmas such as those regarding the payment of *ilobolo*. Readers also enjoy the cartoons of Qap's Mngadi that hinge on comic parodies of everyday life, especially gender dynamics. In sum, as sociolinguist Rajend Mesthrie warns us, any attempt to map the politics of prestige must resist presenting a 'mono-pyramid model of the prestige language'.[46] We return later to this point.

## Conclusions

In South Africa today, it is repeatedly said that richer parents are able to buy qualifications. And it is indeed the case that at top fee-charging schools almost every learner will not just pass the matriculation exam but will do so at the level required for university access. Yet the education system produces inequalities not only in who attains qualifications. Formerly white schools in particular command prestige because they bestow symbolic power, especially prestigious English. For better-off Bluff residents, the move to traditional Berea schools allows access to social networks in 'Harry Potter' English-medium schools that can enhance work prospects.

While schooling affects a person's work trajectory, I also found that white families have strong social networks anchored in past advantages. Even poorer residents benefit not just from good local schools but also from 'backup plans' that might include working as a contractor or relocating overseas.

For Umlazi residents, schooling plays a vital part in their social trajectory – very often the difference between finding and not finding work. Townships remain physical manifestations of black South Africans' expulsion from the 'white' city and their placement in poorly resourced schools whose teachers might not be fluent in English. Umlazi parents know that multiracial schools have better facilities and higher pass rates, but most will say that their biggest advantage is their native English teachers. Now accessed through cash, the 'white tone' gained from formerly white schools is one reason why these institutions maintain their position at the top of the schooling hierarchy. But schools themselves are active agents in making racial-cultural hierarchies, and it is to this that we now turn.

*Part IV*

# Racialised market – 2000s onwards

# 6    'What can you do for the school?'
The racialised market

---

The first half of the 1990s witnessed apartheid's demise: Nelson Mandela was freed from prison, tense political negotiations followed, and then in 1994 the African National Congress (ANC) emerged victorious from the country's first democratic elections. Public schools built for whites generally cooperated among themselves to slowly admit black students whom they thought had the 'ability to be assimilated'. I used the term *marketised assimilation* to highlight continuities between the 1990s and the preceding two decades, when better-off black learners began to 'fit into' white private schools.

The 1990s ended with Mandela stepping down as president but with the country still facing enormous challenges. The ANC had hoped that its adoption of free-market economic policies would draw in foreign investors, but growth remained sluggish. Matriculation pass rates failed to improve and the Department of Education began to shift blame downwards, reporting exam results at the school level from 1999.

This chapter, which focuses particularly on schools, outlines the development in the 2000s of what I call the *racialised market*. Competition among schools intensified to what one deputy principal called 'dog-eat-dog' levels, but this did not improve equity and academic standards in the education system, nor drive a shift towards nonracialism. Educational resources were diverted from classrooms into marketing and scholarships, and from parents' pockets into the costs of travelling. And it was not sports with a long history of multiracial teams, notably soccer, that attracted scholarships, but 'white sports', including rugby.

Consider, for example, the front-page story in a local newspaper in 2000: 'Rival schools' rugby ruckus!'[1] The event that led to this story was the refusal of Durban High School (DHS), the city's oldest and most prestigious school, to play a scheduled rugby match with Glenwood High School, its old rival and neighbour on the Berea. DHS pulled the plug on the game after taking umbrage at Glenwood's plan to gain an advantage by fielding an older ('post-matric') player. Rugby controversies became regular events in the 2010s: from accusations that aggressive schools 'poached' star players, to charges of complicity when players faked their ages to shine against younger opponents.[2]

Table 6.1 *Public schools' political economy and means of promoting prestige*

|  | Political economy (fees are annual for 2012) | Prestige |
|---|---|---|
| **Formerly white** | Fees range from R5,000 to R30,000, good to excellent infrastructure, middle- to upper-middle-class alumni, location in rich suburbs | **White tone** (demographics and cultural whiteness, e.g. white sports), exam results |
| **Formerly African** | Fees range from R0 to R750, very poor infrastructure, poor alumni, location in poor areas | **Exam results**, discipline, bilingualism |

The generous sports scholarships/bursaries given by boys' schools are one reason why, by 2012, their average fees were 50 per cent higher than those of girls' schools. That some of the beneficiaries can be black players underscores a critical point developed in this chapter: formerly white schools are showing fidelity not simply to white people but to whiteness, or what I call 'white tone'. A second way in which schools promote their white tone is cruder: by actively seeking out students with 'white' phenotypic traits, for instance skin colour and hair texture. Foregrounding these configurations of whiteness adds weight to our study of the labour market that revealed the particular value given to 'white' English.

Focusing primarily on formerly white schools, this chapter also considers growing competition among schools built in Umlazi Township for black Africans. While many Umlazi residents aspire to send their children to 'multiracial' schools (formerly white, Indian, or Coloured schools), some of the township's excellent township schools still achieve 100 per cent pass rates. We consider how they have adopted new selection methods to maintain their prestige.

Thus, taking the system as a whole, we see that the top schools across the system increasingly came to ask parents and learners the following question: 'What can you do for the school?'[3] A positive response, implied or stated, might be boosting a school's fee base, academic results, sports prowess, or 'white tone'.

Table 6.1 introduces economic-symbolic aspects of the schooling market that explain differences between and within groups of schools built for whites and black Africans. It may seem backward-looking to conceptualise schools using apartheid's racial categories. However, I stress how money now flows through the veins of the schooling system in patterns shaped by apartheid's racial and spatial inequalities and in ways that can intensify rather than flatten acts of racialism and racism. I insist that common questions ('Why are black schools continuing to perform so poorly?', or 'Why do white schools sometimes exclude black students?') can best be answered by thinking relationally: that is, by adopting an approach that foregrounds connections and hierarchies within the schooling system. And I insist that we need to consider the racialised, classed, and gendered *processes* at work.

Thus, the table presents two interrelated logics: schools' need to strengthen their financial viability (what I call their *political economy*), and their efforts to gain *prestige* in order to attract desirable students. The school's priority for intervention, discussed later, is in bold. Because the boundaries between semi-private public schools and fully private schools are now blurred, I start with a short discussion of the latter.

## Private schools, old and new

*Little England on the Veld*, the title of Peter Randall's landmark book, captures the character of Natal's first schools, which were established in or near the Midlands farming area in the nineteenth century (as introduced in Chapter 2). In 2013, I stood by the cricket field in one of these schools enjoying the rhythmical sound of leather ball on willow bat. Cricket's ability to meld sport with civility, and propriety with whiteness – 'It's not cricket,' as the saying about unfairness goes – is brilliantly captured by Caribbean scholar C. L. R. James in his book *Beyond a Boundary*.[4]

Where, I wondered, was the school's marketing officer, whom I thought I had arranged to meet at this cricket facility? When I tried his mobile phone, he told me (as if I should have known) that he was waiting for me at one of the other five cricket pitches! After we met up, we drove from game to game, undertaking much of the interview in his golf cart.

Although black students were admitted to private schools from 1976, most students I saw at the school that day were white. Fees at private schools, which can exceed R200,000 a year for boarders (US$18,000), are reflected in excellent facilities, incredible exam results (often using exams set by the Independent Exam Board, which has more status internationally), and access to powerful social networks.[5] One newspaper advert for a private school showcased a young white man and an older white man playing golf together under the headline 'Friends for life'.[6] South Africa's private schools in turn form part of a network of elite schools that criss-cross the former British Empire.[7]

Yet if these genteel traditional private schools have retained their position in the upper echelons of society, two corporations, ADvTECH and Curro, are driving the expansion of private education today. Listed on the stock exchange, these companies are nimble operators who build new schools or take over old ones; they locate schools near potential markets and separate their portfolio into different brands. Curro, for instance, runs lower-end 'Meridian' schools that charge around R1,000 a month and higher-end 'Curro Select' schools that charge R5,000 to R7,000 a month.[8] In line with the growth of these businesses, private schooling grew steadily – if not dramatically – to account for 4 per cent of South African pupils in 2016 from 2 per cent in 2000.[9] It is these new private schools that compete most directly with public schools, which themselves have become semi-private, as we shall see below.

### The marketisation of public schools

The newly elected ANC-led government believed that abolishing fees introduced in rich white schools would be too costly for the state. It also continued the late apartheid state's initiative of devolving powers to parents by giving governing bodies the ability to decide a school's language policy, admissions, and finances – now justified not by the threat of a radical state but the need for 'people's education'.[10] A third significant act, undertaken in a climate of 'fiscal discipline', was that the state offered nearly 17,000 teachers severance packages.[11] Some of these teachers were then re-employed by fee-charging public or fully private schools.

New laws, however, imposed significant new regulations on public schools. The state's initial task was an unenviable one: to consolidate the fragmented apartheid education system that comprised 15 separate departments. The first major piece of legislation – the 1996 South African Schools Act – contained clauses to integrate the system, outlaw discrimination, and protect poor students from exclusion if their guardians were unable to pay fees. All citizens gained the right to free education until the end of high school or grade 12 – the new name for standard 10. At fee-charging schools, an income-based formula came to determine the fee remissions parents could receive.[12] Then, from 2007, the state designated the poorest schools as 'no-fee' schools and gave them additional funding. By 2017, no-fee schools had grown to account for 65 per cent of all students.[13]

These state interventions raise an important conceptual point: when we talk about the marketisation of schooling we need to be clear that the market is formed *in relation* to (rather than simply being restricted by) new schooling regulations. Operating like businesses, public schools are free to take legal action against parents to recoup outstanding fees. But as public institutions they cannot expel children whose parents cannot or will not pay fees. As such, schools charging high fees have a powerful incentive to admit students from middle-class backgrounds; one of a school's worst fears is that it might be burdened with the cost of financing a student's entire education at the school.

The unionisation of teachers also affected the powers of schools. Founded in 1990, the South African Democratic Teachers Union (SADTU) had considerable success in improving the conditions of black teachers, who were paid much less than whites in the apartheid era. However, detractors argue that SADTU developed too close a relationship with the ruling ANC party and therefore the state. They argue that the union facilitates 'cadre deployment' instead of ability-based promotions – which were not, of course, practised under apartheid.[14] SADTU has a considerable number of members in, and therefore influence over, the country's poorest schools.

SADTU has been a vocal critic of formerly white schools; ironically, however, some of its actions have worked to protect these schools from state intervention. Many SADTU members had direct experience of apartheid school inspectors and wanted to permanently end their powers. Thus, the strong culture of regular inspections – albeit one hard to enforce in the 1980s when townships were 'ungovernable' – was never resurrected. Two 'circuit managers' I spoke with (the new name for inspectors) complained about their lack of resources, and one principal referred to them as 'postmen'.

Given the autonomy that formerly white schools enjoy, when I began my research in 2009 I started to develop a basic typology of formerly white schools' different paths.[15] However, over time it became clear that most schools had tried at some stage to follow similar strategies, albeit with those at the top of the schooling hierarchy perfecting their use. Since many of these practices have been recorded in existing research, and I want to leave space for analysis, I list them here without providing many examples. I recognise that this presentation of a kind of archetypal formerly white school can downplay differences among schools (and I specifically consider girls' schools later), but it does allow me to draw out some important themes. The four school strategies I summarise below are: selecting and excluding pupils; maximising revenue from fees; enhancing social networks and alliances; and improving academic results.[16]

### Selecting and excluding pupils

Built to admit children from a local community, formerly white public schools can now spend an enormous amount of time selecting and excluding certain students. The vast majority of schools I visited (over 60 in total) held admissions interviews. In a process that can last up to six months, principals and their deputies – this vital task is rarely delegated further – use interviews to judge parents' social background, assess the language and other skills of potential students, and collect written forms of verification.[17] Schools also ask primary schools and preschools for reports on a learner's performance and character, whether parents paid fees in a timely manner, and about the involvement of the parents in the school. This need for parents and children to build up a good record gives feeder schools considerable power when it comes to collecting fees from parents.

### Collecting fees

It is hard to overstate the importance to formerly white schools of school fees. These ranged from R5,000 to R30,000 a year per learner in 2012 (the latest year for which I have citywide figures; by 2017, some Durban schools charged as much as R50,000). As well as conducting admissions interviews, schools can request that parents 'donate' money to secure a child's place (the language of 'donations' is used because admission payments are contrary to the South African Schools Act).

Also important is the amount of fees a school collects as a proportion of the total fees billed. According to interviews I conducted, this ranged widely from 10 per cent to almost 100 per cent. The different collection rates are determined by parents' capacity to pay fees (affected by their income, etc.), the school's ability to demonstrate value for money, and the level of coercion the school is prepared to use to collect outstanding fees. The latter might involve using debt collection firms or informal measures such as excluding in-debt grade 12 children from the coveted matriculation dance. Indebted parents can even be asked to provide in-kind labour to the school, for example by repairing its buildings.

### Enhancing social networks

Schools can form pacts with other schools to gain advantages in the schooling market. In 2013, three Durban North schools – a preschool, junior primary, and senior primary school – formed a 'memorandum of agreement' or 'three-school alliance' to encourage progression from one to the other.

Formerly white schools also recognise the need to develop new links with black middle-class parents, especially those with influence in government. Doing so protects schools from criticism that they are not implementing the letter and spirit of new laws. Senior teachers in a number of Durban's top schools told me that government officials constantly made requests to have their children admitted (see also Chapter 8). As one principal of a popular girls' school said:

Oh, it's all the time, terrible pressure, and to get their girls in ... we've got some very high-ranking officials' children who are at our school, and in a sense, that situation protects [us] ... I've been forced to take certain people ... but I've just,

I've always insisted that I get that in writing, because any day, the media comes along and exposes you for particular things.

### Improving results and teaching

Almost all formerly white schools have high matriculation pass rates (the average being 91 per cent in Durban in 2014). These are upheld thanks to high fees that allow schools to maintain libraries and computer labs and employ extra 'governing body' teachers (in excess of government-employed teachers). On average, Durban's formerly white schools have 18 state-paid teachers and employ an average of 9.4 governing body teachers; the average number of governing body teachers in formerly Indian, Coloured, and African schools are 1.4, 1.3, and 0.6 respectively. Schools also improve their matriculation results by encouraging weak pupils who are likely to fail the matriculation exam to leave for a lower-ranked school or a further education and training (FET) school (with vocational courses). Weaker students can also be encouraged to take easier subjects: for instance, maths literacy rather than pure maths.

## White tone

In this section I want to move beyond description and argue that insights can be gained by recognising the incentive schools face to brand themselves by promoting their 'white tone'. Of course, there is nothing new about businesses selling whiteness in South Africa. Historian Lynn Thomas shows that skin lighteners were targeted at whites because they 'appealed to white women and some men by playing on a bourgeois and racialised aesthetic that valued skin purged of evidence of outdoor labour and intimacy with dark-skinned "others".' From the 1950s, sophisticated advertising campaigns targeted potential black consumers of skin-lightening products.[18]

But does the concept of 'white tone' overplay the importance of race to the workings of the schooling market? Most of Durban's formerly white schools, after all, now have a majority of black students. If, for the sake of argument, we temporarily downplay race, schools can be positioned as businesses whose primary concern is to admit middle-class fee-paying children. These fees are channelled into improving facilities and employing extra teachers. Formerly white schools employ teachers who are familiar with the culture of the institution, and this explains why the majority have only slowly appointed black teachers. Moreover, it is inevitable that they will ask black children to 'fit in', even if assimilation should perhaps be 'benign' rather than 'aggressive'.[19]

This narrative has many problems, but the central one is that it confuses the growth of a multiracial middle class (an outcome of schooling) with the deployment of race in the production of this class (the process of schooling). It also forecloses an analysis that shows how race–class configurations change over time.

To recognise the salience of race in schools' actions, but also provide points for further comparison, let us return to 1996, when Nadine Dolby conducted ethnographic research at a school in Durban that desegregated early. Two years after the first democratic elections, the school was the only formerly white one in Durban with a majority of black students. Long seen by whites as something of a reject school, Fernwood's falling enrolments had threatened the school's viability in the 1980s.[20] Admitting fee-paying black learners allowed it to recast itself as a 'rainbow' school and fill its empty desks.

However, Dolby found that, as the school became racially mixed, the headmaster more vigorously promoted 'white sports' such as rugby and athletics. The school also rejected 'third-world' standards, for instance by making sure that 'shoes are shined, hair is neat, name badge is properly displayed'.[21] Dolby writes: 'Like sports, the Fernwood uniform operates, for the administration, as a symbolic connection to the whiteness of Durban.'[22]

Dolby's ethnography also shows how race remained significant among students. At one fashion show, white students fought to play techno music that they saw as a sign of 'global whiteness'. The view that black children are outsiders who must assimilate into white schools can underscore racial abuse; one 1999 study by Salim Vally and Yolisa Dalamba found that 60 per cent of surveyed students reported racist incidents in their schools.[23]

But Dolby also shows that popular culture enabled students to cross racial boundaries, for instance when they entered nightclubs from which they would previously have been barred.[24] Schools are also meeting places where young love can dissolve boundaries formulated by apartheid. And Kira Erwin and Kathryn Pillay's recent study of Durban schools shows that black and white students harbour reservations about being asked to identify using apartheid's racial categories, for instance when applying to universities.[25]

These studies show that learners and educators enact and challenge processes of racialism and racism *within schools*. However, below I argue that white schools came to compete more intensely *among* themselves. Especially from the 2000s, a school's 'white tone' signified its strong leadership, ability to attract well-off parents, and capacity to provide benefits in the form of qualifications, cultural dispositions, and social networks. I justify this point by considering two aspects of white tone: schools' valuing of phenotypic traits that signal whiteness; and their investment in 'white' sports as cultural signs of whiteness. I then show how schools widened their catchment areas in the late 1990s and early 2000s.

### White tone and white students: the return of the phenotype

'It's a demographic tightrope that we're walking at the moment and it's wobbling, it's wobbling, because in order for us to attract the right black – and particularly the Indian – parents and kids, I've got to make sure that my white numbers are up,' said one principal, Mr Madden, to me.[26] The logic he refers to goes like this. When a school loses white learners it can gain a reputation as 'going black' – understood here as meaning 'going African'. The right black learners would be those whose parents can afford to pay fees, with preference given to Indian over African students.

In such cases, learners' perceived phenotypic differences, such as skin colour or hair texture, help shape the school's racial image, or its 'demographics'. Apartheid's four racial categories still largely provide a template for these interpretations. Thus, the desegregation of the schooling system did not signal the death knell of the 1950 Population Registration Act but rekindled racial classification through a different logic.

Two further anecdotes illustrate the importance schools place on maintaining a critical mass of children perceived to be white. First, a teacher told me that one of his superiors had seized on a photograph he had taken that captured a large number of white learners in the frame – the deputy principal wanted to use it on the school's web page. Second, even more brazenly, and supported by Nadine Dolby's research, a parent told me that his son was offered a scholarship because, as the school said in so many words, it needed more white learners.[27]

While white learners can signal a school's prestige, the number of white schoolchildren has been dropping in Durban's public schools since at least the 1970s; as we saw in Chapter 4, it was only desegregation that saved some schools from closing. While most white parents still send their children to public schools, white families' relatively high earnings mean that some have turned to expensive private schools. As Figure 6.1 displays, another reason for the relative scarcity of white learners in the public schooling system is that, from 2001 to 2011, Durban's absolute black African population increased by nearly 400,000 and the white population fell by 54,000 (in Cape Town and Johannesburg the black African population also increased significantly; the white population also grew, but at a much slower rate).[28] Reasons for Durban's falling white population include decreasing birth rates, emigration, and relocation to other cities.

Durban's population shifts, together with schooling desegregation, meant that by 1999 formerly white schools had on average 214 white students and 141 black African students; by 2010 the figures were

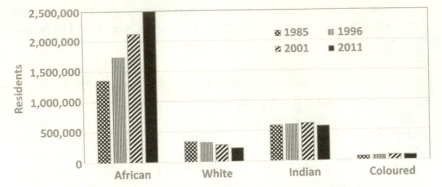

Figure 6.1 eThekwini's residential population by race, 1985–2011.
*Sources*: Doug Hindson and Brian O'Leary, *Durban's Changing Racial
Geography 1985–1996* (Durban: eThekwini Municipality); Posel,
'Micro-data analysis of patterns and trends in eThekwini Municipality'.
Although eThekwini's boundaries changed slightly over time, Hindson
and O'Leary used the city's 2001 boundaries for their report.

155 and 285 respectively (the average numbers of Indian learners were
76 and 124, and Coloured learners were 24 and 36).[29]

What is not captured in average figures, however, is how over time
desegregation became increasingly uneven in formerly white schools:
that is, a small number of schools retained a majority white student
body, and the rest desegregated to a much greater degree. Uneven
desegregation, or what some scholars call 'resegregation', has several
manifestations that are not mutually exclusive. One example is when
Afrikaans-medium schools effectively remain white because their language policy works to favour a group of learners who, in Durban, are
almost all white. Second, uneven schooling desegregation can reflect the
continued racial segregation of the city. In the late apartheid and post-
apartheid periods, 'white flight' saw a pattern of white people moving
from central Durban to the city's outer suburbs (see Chapter 7).

My focus, however, is on uneven desegregation among competing
schools in suburbs that are well-connected by transport infrastructure.
How did these patterns emerge? As I indicate below, it is through
examples of schools 'going black' and 'going white' that many teachers
and parents came to believe that a school needed to retain a white
demographic profile to support a virtuous cycle of high fees and high
standards – and the more people believed this, the more it became reality.

Consider a school I heard discussed by several teachers as an 'idealis-
tic' experiment. The school opened on the premises of a closed-down
Afrikaans school.[30] Its first principal – who had taught at Durban High
School, no less – recalled to me his motivation to make this school into a
kind of multiracial version of the city's oldest school. However, over time

the school failed to attract white students, lost prestige, and collected less in fees. Causality cannot be neatly ascribed in these instances, but the school's dropping revenue prevented it from hiring extra teachers and its matriculation pass rate declined. A somewhat similar case, involving a school in Pretoria that changed its name to 'Diversity High', is noted by Saloshna Vandeyar and Jonathan Jansen.[31]

The opposite of a school 'going black' is when a school 'goes white'. The Berea primary school mentioned at the start of this book went from having predominantly black students to enrolling a majority of white students by the 2000s. The school did not initiate this change by raising its fees or investing in new facilities. Instead, it developed an aggressive policy to persuade white parents to attend the school, and, as this happened, it raised its fees. According to supporters of this controversial Berea principal, he had come into a failing school and had 'turned it around', 'done a good job', and 'improved standards'. My daughter's Berea preschool rented the school's hall on one occasion and sports facilities on another, and black and white parents with whom I spoke were impressed by these facilities and the principal's welcome.

### White tone and white sports: 'You judge a boys' school by the success of its rugby team'

A second way in which schools promote white tone – one anchored less in phenotypic differences – is by intensifying their promotion of 'white sports'. During the twentieth century, rugby became *the* national white sport after it won enthusiastic support from both English and Afrikaans speakers, and because the black rugby tradition was essentially silenced – Nelson Mandela himself had played rugby at a mission school.[32] Of course, success or failure on the sports field is embodied in emotions and physical acts that cannot simply be reduced to race or other social relations; at the same time, neither can they be separated from these dynamics.

Some Durban schools' obsession with winning at rugby reached new heights in the 2000s. One marketing officer at a rugby-centred school told me that his job was created in 2000 and that his duties included travelling as far as Pretoria to 'buy' rugby stars. The professionalisation of rugby at all levels of the game in the 1990s helped infuse schoolboy rugby with money, as seen in 'classic clashes' (matches between old rivals) shown live on television. Schools, in this competitive era, could quickly move from victims to perpetrators: Hilton College declared in 2014 that it would stop playing rugby with the 'professional' Glenwood High School after being thrashed 67–7; then, just two years later, it was censured by three Gauteng schools for poaching their top sports players.[33]

The upshot is that a number of South Africa's boys' schools now invest huge sums of money in scholarships. In one school, a teacher told me that 60 per cent of its students had some kind of scholarship, most aimed at sportsmen. One referee of schoolboy rugby matches, I was told by the referee's brother (a teacher I interviewed), was even on the payroll of a prominent school – he was paid to look out for talent.

Mr Davis, a former teacher of a popular English-medium Durban boys' school, explained to me in 2013 the imperative on schools to foreground sports, especially rugby:

[I]n the past ten years, it's become very professional. I mean schools are throwing huge amounts of money at sport and it's not just here, it's all around the country, and basically if you don't remain competitive on the sports field you are not going to attract the quality kids, and obviously with the quality comes the ... fee-paying people so it's like a catch 22. So a lot of schools are now marketing themselves, especially with first-team rugby ... the girls' schools have got it right – they are not worried about sports ...

The money swirling around schoolboy rugby modifies meanings of whiteness and blackness. In the early 1990s, many white schools desegregated by admitting more Indian and Coloured learners than African students. 'Going black', in other words, was most often signalled by 'going African'. This meaning still exists. However, Mr Davis raised concerns about the implications of schools enrolling too many Indian learners, telling me that 'Indians don't play rugby, unlike the African okes ['blokes' or 'males'] who get stuck into rugby because they are robust chaps'.

Such stereotypes about Indians 'penetrating' white spaces go back generations, as we have seen. Over the course of my research I was told by white teachers and parents that 'Indian' (or 'Muslim') parents were targeting 'their' school. In fact, Durban's large and varied Indian middle class had developed diverse strategies that included enrolling their children in private Islamic schools, private Christian schools, 'traditional' public schools, and the best schools in formerly Indian townships. Moreover, in contrast to stereotypes that 'Indians don't play sports', there is a long history in Indian communities of sports, most notably soccer and cricket.[34]

The positive association between Africanness and rugby, however, indicates that what matters is not simply a narrow counting of racialised bodies but the old saying that 'you judge a boys' school by the success of its rugby team'. Consider the case of Khule Nkosi, recruited by a Durban boys' school from a small town in KwaZulu-Natal on a package worth R100,000 a year, including boarding costs.

Khule grew up in a poor township and pursued his passion for rugby when he joined a regional team. Aware of the opportunities offered by the sport, he used false ID to claim that he was three years younger than his true age. Although he was much larger than his teammates, the Durban secondary school that recruited him never questioned his age. Khule justified his actions by describing the situation of his former schoolmates:

'Starting from zero I had nothing to lose, from time to time I kept telling myself that many boys my age from the township were either washing cars during the day and stealing at night, or they were in prison.'[35]

Khule's 'rags to riches' story, via an elite white school, is not exceptional; indeed, he chose this school because one of his friends had been recruited in a similar way. Grassroots rugby programmes in previously black-designated areas are limited in scale and scope, making the transformation of sports' underlying structures a 'shallow and elite-driven process'.[36] Not surprisingly given the concentration of resources in elite schools, almost all national 'Springbok' players, black and white, studied at a handful of formerly white schools (as is also the case for cricket).[37]

Notably, the upsurge of schoolboy rugby also came at the expense of soccer in formerly white areas. South Durban teams – including Ramblers, Wanderers, Bayview, and Fynnlands – were once symbolic of a working-class counterculture. As late as May 1991, the front page of the *Southlands Sun* led with a story about a huge soccer tournament in the white suburb of Woodlands/Montclair 'involving 18,000 players and watched by 5,000 enthusiastic fans. It was the biggest of its kind in the southern hemisphere.'[38] Soccer, showcased in 2010 when the country hosted the FIFA World Cup, and with a long history of multiracial teams, was in many ways the obvious sport on which to build a nonracial South African sporting culture.[39]

Yet, by the 2000s, fewer white Durbanites kicked soccer balls around. Many of south Durban's white children had moved out of residential areas (some emigrating) or travelled daily to attend schools in Berea or other suburbs. Now, in south Durban's formerly white suburbs, South African soccer can be coded as predominantly black, and weeds cover the soccer field that once hosted the 1991 tournament (although the English Premier League is avidly watched on television). Perhaps not surprisingly, given the money invested in schoolboy rugby, the national rugby team has fared better than the national soccer team in the post-apartheid era.

All of the developments mentioned above involve changes to schooling's geography in the 2000s, and it is to this that we turn now.

## Changing geographies of schooling

Integral to growing competition among formerly white schools is the expansion of their de facto catchment areas. In the 1960s it was taken for granted that most children would attend their local school. By the 1990s schools were advertising available places in local newspapers. Yet by the early 2000s around half of the adverts posted in south Durban's free local newspaper, *Southlands Sun,* were from schools located *outside* the newspaper's distribution area. Some adverts were posted from schools as far away as Pietermaritzburg (80 kilometres from Durban), for example when a boys' school advertised its 'elite sports fixtures'.[40] Berea schools began to advertise in the Bluff's local paper in the 2000s, and Bluff residents also recall seeing posters on lamp posts advertising schools in Berea.[41]

As already noted, in the early period of schooling desegregation few Bluff parents were enthusiastic about driving their children through south Durban's notoriously truck-heavy traffic to alternative Berea schools. Over time, however, Bluff parents came to see Berea's schools as offering more prestige and better access to the world of work. Upper-middle-class schools enabled this change by no longer turning their noses up at 'rough and tough' white areas, instead beginning to see them as a potential source of students who might enhance the prestige and financial viability of the school. Consider, from the perspective of the schooling system, how one parent from the Bluff was encouraged to transfer his energies from a Bluff to a Berea school.

Mr Cosgrave had lived all his life on the Bluff. A manager of a local business, he had been committed to the Bluff's schools – he had attended school locally himself – and after his daughter enrolled in a primary school he became the chair of its governing body. When parents from a competing school handed out advertising flyers at his school's gates, he told them in no uncertain terms to leave. As late as 2012 he oversaw the school's hiring of a consultant to advise them on a strategy to keep Bluff children from leaving the school. The consultant's advice, Mr Cosgrave told me, was to 'increase fees to improve the quality of facilities and encourage better applicants'. But this strategy did not sit well with parents from the working-class/lower-middle-class Bluff.

Over time, Mr Cosgrave became dissatisfied with the school's female principal, whom he said was not proactive enough in promoting the school. 'You know what,' he told me, 'we pay school fees, which pays for salaries. If you are not interested in listening to us, we will find somewhere else where we can go.' In the end, Mr Cosgrave followed the path trodden by an increasing number of Bluff parents and moved his daughter to a Berea school known for its aggressive recruitment of white children.

From the perspective of the Berea school, an energetic and knowledgeable parent like Mr Cosgrave was a potential asset. The Berea school's principal encouraged him to stand for election to the school's governing body, which he did. The principal regularly asked Mr Cosgrave about applicants from the Bluff. 'Do you know who these people are? Are they in fine [financial] standing or not?'

Map 6.1 suggests that, by 2012, Berea secondary schools educated more white students from the Bluff than local Bluff secondary schools. Bluff parents' commitment to local schooling lasted longest for primary schools because they do not have the high-profile pressure of matriculation exams and their relatively small size allowed local parents to remain loyal to one or two. Had our survey been conducted five years later, however, it would have shown that more primary-school children, like the daughter of Mr Cosgrave, are now schooled in Berea.[42]

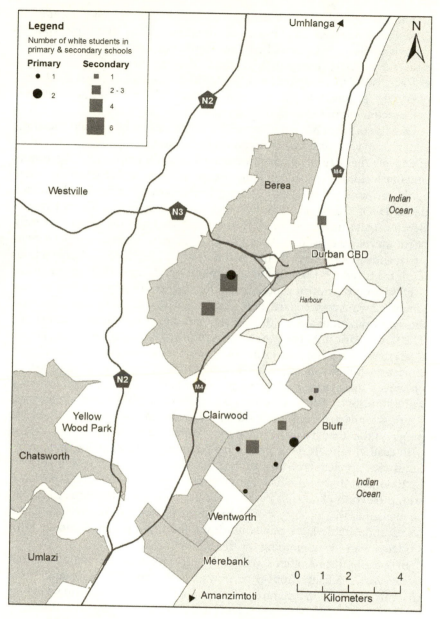

Map 6.1 Schooling location of surveyed white children living on the Bluff, 2012.
*Source:* Data from the Household Survey (see Appendix 1).

The movement of Bluff learners to Berea schools helps accentuate differences between Berea and Bluff schools. The top three public schools in Berea maintained an almost 100 per cent matriculation pass rate and by 2015 charged three times the fees of Bluff schools – on average, R30,000 compared with R10,000. In contrast, the matriculation pass rate at the two Bluff secondary schools that admit boys has fallen below 90 per cent in recent years.

Of course, schools' spatial strategies differ according to their location, history, capacity, and leadership. Some schools, usually the least popular, effectively maintain local catchment areas and fill empty seats by admitting black children travelling long distances; others actively increase their applicant pool, a few using boarding facilities to cater for non-local students. Deals are struck, with far-reaching consequences. When I visited Berea's Afrikaans school in 2013, a teacher told me that he had recently been approached secretly by a group of parents from a south Durban Afrikaans school. They told him that they would defect to the Berea school if it introduced a bus service to transport their children daily into Berea.

How do government regulations affect the geography of schooling? In Chapter 2 we saw that apartheid's obsession with racial divisions prevented the development of a citywide school board that administered admissions. The South African Schools Act gives schools' governing bodies the power to set their own admissions rules but provinces retain overall control over education policy. In effect, a kind of 'soft zoning' was able to satisfy provinces' emphasis on black students not being excluded from formerly white suburbs as well as schools' wish to maintain power over admissions. Thus, schools actively recruit students from far away but accept (at least publicly) that they have an obligation to admit local students.

In reality, schools deter poor local residents from applying and sometimes visit applicants to ensure that their stated local address is correct. In 2006, two Berea schools fought bitterly over which one of them should admit the child of a foster parent – should distance from home to school be measured by car or by foot?[43] From the perspective of the school, the fewer undesirable local pupils it admits the more places it can fill with students who 'do something for the school'.

In July 2012, soon after I arrived for my sabbatical, the issue of school feeder zones became front-page news in Durban. The KwaZulu-Natal government released a memorandum stating that schools should no longer give automatic preference to students from their catchment area. Formerly white schools' location in affluent suburbs, officials said, resulted in them excluding black students who tended to live further away.[44]

The school zoning controversy brings into sharp relief the social forces that shaped schooling in the 2000s. To start with, as I have already outlined, formerly white schools had a selective approach to zoning, enforcing it when it suited them. But as well as indicating the power that schools still wielded, the zoning controversy reveals struggles being fought by fractions of Durban's black and white middle class. An official from the Department of Education whom I interviewed as the controversy raged told me that the pressure to end catchment areas came from middle-class black parents whose children had been refused entry into some of the city's most prestigious schools. This corresponds with my finding that it was usually only black parents with strong social connections (principals, senior government officials, etc.) who succeeded in having their children admitted to prestigious schools that were not near their homes.

In contrast, the voices of poorer black families were inaudible. To have any chance of entering a top school, a child living with their domestic worker mother would invariably have to call heavily on the principles of zoning. Had zoning ended, domestic workers would have been some of the chief losers.

In the end, the Department of Education was unable to propose a viable alternative to zoning and dropped the plan. Of the nine provinces, only Gauteng challenged schools' power to administer admissions. From 2015 onwards, this densely populated province moved to a centralised online applications process for admissions into grades 1 and 8 – in part to assert greater power over predominantly white Afrikaans schools. But what examples are there of teachers and parents themselves opposing trends towards the marketisation of schools? For insights into this question, we turn to girls' schools.

## Girls' schooling and the gendered market

It is evident by now that the schooling market came into being due to specific actors – who could, at times, hold their hands up and say that they were just following rules they could not control. Principals at boys' schools in particular became CEO-like figures whose primary focus was the school's admissions and marketing strategy rather than teaching. This 'cut and thrust' business model challenged past ideals of gentlemanly honour anchored in the British private school model.

Consider the different paths of two 'sibling' schools located close together in an upper-middle-class western suburb. Despite their similar histories, by 2012 the boys' school charged roughly twice the annual fees of the girls' school (R31,000 compared with R17,600). Moreover, the boys' school had twice the proportion of white learners as the girls' school (65 per cent compared with 32 per cent).[45]

Differences like these arise because girls' schools generally do not compete with the same bravado as boys' schools, and less money is invested in poaching students. One female former principal of a girls' school told me that most girls' school principals had informally agreed with one another not to follow boys' schools' aggressive tactics:

Well, for good reason or for bad reason, the governing body made a conscious decision that scholarships are immoral. Well, they are, because if you've got a talented youngster and you go touting him around ... and your school still costs you X amount to run, you've got to divide it amongst the other children ... for me it's a moral, it's a values issue, it's teaching values ...

Among parents there is also concern about schools' aggressive poaching of certain learners. After all, it is the families who have to pay the high fees that are required to finance the buying of sports stars and other expenses. Parents can also lament how schools' competitive approaches undermine their academic missions. One mother with children at a boys' and girls' school noted that 31 learners at her daughter's school got 'full house' matriculation results, whereas only two boys at her son's school achieved this – 'And it doesn't faze them because they have got the top rugby players ...'

Although girls' schools agreed not to overuse scholarships, there are signs that this might be changing. One school principal of a private girls' school in Berea told me how she worried that a competitor girls' private school had recently appointed a male principal who set about aggressively recruiting sporty children. Parents were now seizing the chance to bargain for fee concessions, according to the female principal: 'I think a lot of parents try and sell their children. They try and sell them to the highest bidder; as far as if they are a good swimmer or a good hockey player, whatever, they will be applying for scholarships in any independent school they can get them in to.'

## Umlazi Township's market

Greater competition among white schools unfolded as thousands of black children left Umlazi to enter better-resourced 'multiracial' schools. Map 6.2 shows the schooling location of 155 children who lived in the surveyed neighbourhood of Umlazi Township. It is noticeable that most learners at 'multiracial' schools attend south Durban's formerly Indian and Coloured schools, or institutions in working-class white areas such as the Bluff and lower Berea. Prestigious Berea schools rarely admit Umlazi-based learners because apartheid planners built African townships far away from upper-middle-class suburbs, and these schools prefer black children with a proven ability to pay high fees, or with well-connected parents.

A counterintuitive finding, given the difficulty of moving young children around the city, is the greater movement of primary compared with secondary-school children (on Map 6.2 there are slightly more dots than squares outside the township). There are three main reasons why young learners travel so much for schooling today. First, parents/guardians see an advantage in their children being taught by native English-speaking teachers at an early age. Second, parents correctly see attendance at a multiracial primary school as being necessary if a

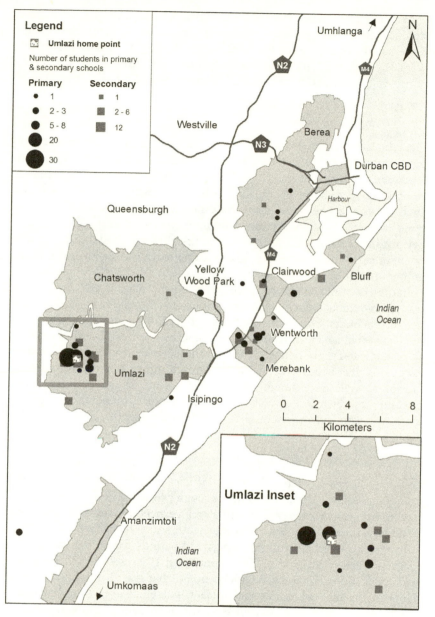

Map 6.2 Schooling location of surveyed children who live in one section of Umlazi Township, 2012.

child is to enter a multiracial secondary school. Third, and considered more below, the continued strong reputation of several secondary schools in Umlazi means that they attract learners from across and beyond the township.

Map 6.2 of Umlazi also shows that secondary-school children travel significantly inside the township itself for schooling (indicated by the dispersal of squares). Secondary schools at the top of Umlazi's schooling hierarchy achieved their success by following three main strategies: improving results; selecting and excluding pupils; and collecting fees.[46]

### Improving results

Over the last decade, average matriculation pass rates at Umlazi's schools have ranged from 40 per cent to 100 per cent. Some schools, such as Zwelibanzi High, continue to achieve very high pass rates and remain celebrated as 'miracle schools'.[47] Other historically excellent schools, such as Vukuzakhe High, have become cast as a '[s]uccessful school gone wrong'.[48] While results fluctuate year by year, the highest-performing schools all follow the long-standing model for success: opening early and closing late, undertaking extra classes in the holidays, and maintaining strict discipline.

In the era of desegregation, excellent township schools can also be contrasted favourably to formerly white schools that are said to produce disrespectful 'coconuts' who can't even speak proper Zulu (I consider these points in more detail later). In turn, teachers' commitment is rewarded with the satisfaction and status that come with a school's good results, as well as work experience that is well received if they seek to move to a different school. However, while government officials and the media can understandably celebrate top township schools as 'miracle schools', this sentiment ignores the way in which these schools pick and choose students.

### Selecting and excluding pupils

In the early apartheid period, black African children tended to exit the schooling system at the end of junior or senior primary school. This 'stepped' pattern occurred because it was difficult for learners who finished one school to find the resources to move into expensive, scarce higher schools.

In the late apartheid and post-apartheid periods, schooling enrolments increased across all grades. Yet, comparing 1995 and 2012, the South African Institute for Race Relations noted that the 'throughput' of students in the highest grades had in fact worsened over time.[49] Today, around half of all South African students drop out of school at the final three grades (grades 10–12, which are not compulsory). This new pattern has emerged, in part, because schools compete based on their publicised pass rates. This is the case across the schooling system. However, rural and township schools' limited resources mean that they are less able to push weaker students over the matriculation line than better-resourced schools, for instance those that were formerly white.

There are three main methods by which Umlazi's four top-performing schools pick and choose students. Illustrating the tendency noted above, two Umlazi schools filter out weaker students before they take the final matriculation exam. One teacher called this a pyramid system, saying that his school admitted 300 pupils in the eighth grade, and this dropped to 80 students by grade 12. In response to such practices, the government announced in 2015 that it would put more pressure on schools to 'progress' (i.e. move up) all students into higher grades.

A second method, implemented by two schools, and contrary to the 1996 South African Schools Act, is the holding of entrance tests (sometimes called 'interviews'), which in effect are exams in maths and English. Admissions tests, as already noted, have been practised for decades in Umlazi. Two Department of Education officials with whom I spoke, and who themselves had taught at Umlazi's 'excellent' schools, were well aware that admissions exams were practised in the township.[50]

A third selection method is the admittance of children who are the appropriate age for the grade. This excludes students who repeat grades when they fail end-of-year exams (as well as students moving into the area, as we shall see).

*Collecting fees*

In Umlazi, 11 out of a total of 84 schools were designated as 'no-fee' schools in 2015.[51] Average fees, however, are only R200 a year. There is extensive pressure on parents to pay these fees, especially if their children attend one of the township's most prestigious schools. Although the South African Schools Act explicitly states that guardians receiving social grants are exempt from paying school fees, schools in Umlazi can argue the reverse: that parents who receive a social grant have money to pay for school fees.

I look later at how school fees deter some students from attending better schools in Umlazi. But we can note that guardians' ability to pay fees is used less as a means of filtering out students in Umlazi than in the formerly white suburbs. Moreover, the relatively low fees do not allow the top schools to plough money into scholarships to poach certain students. Consequently, relationships among schools are less poisoned by competition than between formerly white schools. Rather than opposing another school's admissions tests, a lesser-ranked school is usually willing to accept students excluded from the best schools. Indeed, the allocation of teachers (and the principal's salary) is primarily related to the number of learners enrolled at the school.

## The making of symbolic power: political economy and prestige in the schooling system

Having considered formerly white and black schools, it is now time to draw out some common themes. Schools are, of course, varied and contested institutions. In cities other than Durban, rugby may play a lesser role in signifying whiteness, and Afrikaans-medium schooling may play a greater role. Yet I emphasise here some important principles that cut across South Africa's schooling market. All fee-charging schools in the modern era are subject to a set of pressures: to collect fees; to increase the number of students applying; to enrol smart, well-behaved, and athletic students; and to attain high matriculation marks. To consider this institutional logic at a higher level of abstraction – that is, one that encompasses all schools – I utilise the concepts of *political economy* and *prestige*.

I use the term 'political economy' to emphasise not only the centrality of fees to schools' finances. Formerly white schools have other advantages anchored in the apartheid system: assets, including spacious buildings, computers, swimming pools, and experienced and highly qualified teachers; the capacity to raise money or attain other assistance from businesses, grants, and through old boys (and, to a lesser extent, old girls); and location, with parents living in affluent neighbourhoods being most able to pay high fees and provide other support to a school.

In theory, with enough redistribution of resources, the state could equalise the political economy of schooling. Yet, the state's efforts to equalise education came with the injection of quite modest extra resources. In 2009 in KwaZulu Natal, a quintile 1 school (the poorest category) received only R635 extra state funding per pupil per year compared with a quintile 5 school.[52] Yet the latter might gain an extra R10,000 to R30,000 a year per learner in fees.

Prestige, or the 'name' a school enjoys, represents a school's place in a symbolic hierarchy. Prestige is not clear-cut because parents and students value different things. However, our Household and Schooling Survey showed clear patterns when it asked parents to state the five top local and outside (i.e. outside the suburb) schools. On the Bluff, 56 per cent of white parents favoured just two outside secondary schools. These were a boys' and a girls' school in Berea (chosen schools included Afrikaans and English schools and ranged geographically from those located in areas from Amanzimtoti to Westville). Within Umlazi Township, 60 per cent of respondents chose only three out of the total of 27 Umlazi schools as 'top' township secondary schools. Although there are perceived differences between primary schools, these are a lot narrower.

Efforts by schools to enhance political economy and prestige create competition on two main spatial scales: within a suburb/township and across well-connected parts of the city. Umlazi schools primarily compete with and measure themselves against other Umlazi schools. In turn, formerly white schools compete, at first, with local schools on a suburb-by-suburb basis before competing with schools across the city.

A final point to make is that enhancing a school's political economy can enhance its prestige – and is intended to do just that – and vice versa. This happens when an affluent school invests in sports scholarships to improve a team's performances or employs more teachers to boost academic results. And if a school has prestige, its governing body can set higher fees and it has a greater chance of getting parents to pay the expected fees. As in society as a whole, political economy and prestige must always be thought of as existing in a dialectical (two-way) relationship.

One way of revealing a school's priorities is to ask the following question: what would lead to a school *losing* prestige? Many parents and teachers at formerly white schools would say, or imply, that a school loses prestige if it 'goes black'. For the principals of formerly white schools, keeping a school white in tone, either by attracting white pupils or by achieving good rugby results, or in other ways, leads to higher fees and more resources. Most parents in Umlazi would argue that 'a collapse in matriculation results' would reduce a school's prestige. Attaining good results allows a school to collect more fees, select the township's better students, and impose stricter discipline – another virtuous cycle.

Table 6.1, presented earlier, helps explain why formerly white schools, although divided in new ways, remain at the top of the schooling hierarchy. Their high fees and excellent facilities give them a strong political economy, while their prestige is enhanced by their ability to bestow a 'white tone' on their students. These points must be considered alongside labour market trends, including the value of 'white' English. In fact, the two are mutually constitutive.

These social relations in the schooling system are simultaneously spatial relations. The overall difference in prestige and political economy across the city is apparent in schoolchildren generally moving north and west in Durban. And when students do move, they take with them fees that could have been invested in their local schools. To repeat two vital points: movement generates inequality – the movement of children is a counter-vailing force to state efforts to redistribute resources in the other direction; and learners move to access not just qualifications but also symbolic power.

One question raised by this analysis is where private schools fit in. The oldest ones have excellent grades and offer wonderful sports facilities. They sit comfortably at the top of the schooling system. But the many newer private schools directly target parents disaffected with public schools. Private schools vary from 'low-fee', predominantly black schools, to higher-fee schools located in upper-middle-class areas. They can be found at all points in the system.

Finally, where do 'no-fee' schools fit in? The establishment of such schools has been very successful in increasing poor learners' access to schooling. But they have low prestige, can avoid gateway subjects such as pure maths, and produce the lowest matriculation results and fluency in English. They are generally located at the bottom of the schooling system.

### Conclusions

This chapter has moved from mundane acts like the passing of a rugby ball to abstract terms such as prestige. It does not capture every case: there are no-fee schools with excellent results; some high-fee schools have poor results; in some cities Afrikaans still has considerable prestige; and some girls' schools might compete as much for pupils as boys' schools. I show, however, that schools' actions are underpinned by certain logics whose construction needs to be unpacked. Umlazi's secondary schools compete over exam results in particular. In formerly white areas, competition among schools exists because high fees and 'white tone' are seen to be mutually reinforcing.

Thus, schools' actions are shaped by an imperative to improve their *political economy* and *prestige* within a marketised system. These logics have replaced state-imposed racial segregation as a mode of organisation. The 'pencil test' is no longer used as it was by white schools in the 1950s and 1960s to exclude learners with 'non-white' hair. The boundaries of whiteness are no longer fortified, as they were in the 1970s and 1980s, by a national system of racial segregation.

But this chapter has also shown that schooling desegregation is not a linear process and that it changed significantly in the 2000s. No longer do schools prioritise the admission of a small number of black students with the 'ability to be assimilated', as they did from the 1970s to the early 1990s. Today, Afro-textured hair is not just an affront to assimilation. 'Black hair' can be seen to undermine a school's ability to brand itself with a white tone and charge high fees.

Although a person thought of as phenotypically white has an inherent advantage in a system that values white tone, formerly white schools also value middle-class or rugby-playing black learners. Political freedom has meant that aspects of whiteness are bought and sold and not arbitrarily imposed by the state.

I consider in Chapters 7 and 8 the strategies and actions of parents. We will also return to the ways in which excellent township schools challenge a single hierarchy of prestige headed by formerly white schools. But let us remind ourselves how formerly white schools act in fundamentally different ways today to how they did in the periods of *racial modernism* and *marketised assimilation*. The question they ask is less 'What can I do for the children of my local area?' Nor is it 'How can I admit "nice blacks" to our local school?' In the era of the racialised market, the key questions have become 'What can the learner do for the school?' and 'How can I attract "quality" learners from across the city?' And these logics reconfigure race, class, and gender in new ways – working through prejudice but exceeding the boundaries of the term. We turn now to the ways in which families on the Bluff navigate this schooling market.

# 7    New families on the Bluff
Selling a child in the schooling market

Mrs Jane Mitchell, a thin, grey-haired woman in her fifties, steers me past her four energetic dogs into her living room. She, a housewife, and her husband, a bank worker, moved into this three-bedroom house in the 1980s. Situated on the Bluff's inner ridge, her neighbourhood was 'middle class', she told me. Some young white families like hers had been attracted to the Bluff's affordable family housing; another group had upgraded to the neighbourhood from local 'railway houses'.

In 2012, the following people shared the property with Mr and Mrs Mitchell: the couple's married daughter and her husband and child; their unmarried daughter; Mr Mitchell's father, who lived in a room built in the backyard; and a woman who rented the *kia* or maid's quarters (this woman had been classified as 'black African', whereas the Mitchell family had been classified as 'white').

However, when I returned in 2015, Mrs Mitchell's mother had recently moved in, and her married daughter's family had moved out to a rental flat on the Bluff. In 2016, Mrs Mitchell's daughter separated from her husband, moved back temporarily, and then rented a garden cottage on the Bluff. Mrs Mitchell's son and his wife had just bought a house on the same street. Were this an African or Indian family, a large vocabulary would be readily available to discuss its 'fluid kinship relations' or 'joint family system'. But a major aim of apartheid policy was to promote the white nuclear family.

The Mitchells, however, were not only changing their family structure but stretching their vision of schooling beyond the local suburb. Although Mrs Mitchell had schooled her three children at Bluff schools in the 1990s and early 2000s, she did not want her three-year-old granddaughter, Mary, to attend local schools. Mrs Mitchell told me in 2012 that she and her daughter (Mary's mother) already had their eye on a primary school about 20 minutes' drive away on the Berea ridge. This was recommended by a neighbour because of 'the manners, the discipline, what the children are learning ... and it's not that black'. Certain Berea schools, as we have seen, were well known as accepting – and sometimes even giving financial incentives to attract – desirable Bluff children. Indeed, as the city desegregated, some Berea schools came to see the 'rough and tough' Bluff as a potential pool of white students.

Two years later, anxiety filled the Mitchells' living room. Mrs Mitchell's daughter had put together a strong application for the Berea school. She had highlighted Mary's swimming skills and even solicited a letter from her swimming teacher to testify to her talent at the sport. Yet Mary had not been admitted. The family pointed to a mediocre preschool report, which they blamed on the child's learning disability. However, her daughter was accepted into their second-choice Berea school.

This chapter continues to focus on the 'rough and tough' Bluff and, to a lesser extent, on upper Berea schools. Its first aim is to grasp white Bluff families' changing make-up and how this interacts with different educational strategies. I show that being white and middle class does provide important benefits. As Chapter 6 showed, formerly white schools assign particular value to students with phenotypic traits and cultural practices coded as white. Yet not all white families access their first-choice public schools, which are typically located now in Berea. The most prestigious schools tend to choose out-of-area students who add something to the school, whether a reliable source of fees or an ability to improve a sports team. In particular, lower-income families and single mothers can struggle to access top Berea schools. If, in the past, local schools brought together Bluffites in a system of advantage based on segregation, today schooling is a wedge that can separate white families and penalise children whose parents are unmarried.

A further aim of the chapter is to examine how residential and schooling desegregation interact with each other. We will follow the lives of a new community of shack dwellers who lived within a stone's throw of an excellent Bluff primary school. Yet their children, black and poor, were of little value to local schools and most studied hundreds of kilometres away in rural areas. I also outline in this chapter how two new groups showed commitment to local schooling: black middle-class families who bought or rented accommodation on the Bluff; and domestic workers who placed their children in local schools. I begin, however, by situating the Bluff and Berea in the context of Durban's changing racial geography from the 1980s to the present.

## Durban's changing racial geography

Today, more than 20 years into democracy, the Bluff suburb still offers a relatively affordable and comfortable life for families such as the Mitchells. Between 2012 and 2017, only one of the 27 white families with whom I was in contact left the area. If residents considered moving, it was usually into Durban's affluent western and northern suburbs.

Mr Cosgrave, who, as I noted in Chapter 6, decided to send his daughter to a Berea school, described for me the Bluff's continued attraction: 'I have lived on the Bluff my whole life. I don't think there is anywhere else I could live. It's an awesome community. My church is on the Bluff, my parents, the golf course is on the Bluff ... my tennis club is on the Bluff. We have lovely shopping centres.' In decades gone by, residents complained about the sour smell of the Bluff's whaling station, as well as pollution from south Durban's industries. However, the whaling station closed in the 1970s, and the Merebank and Wentworth townships built for Indian and Coloured residents suffer the brunt of pollution from the adjacent Engen oil refinery.[1]

As such, residents such as Mr Cosgrave and the Mitchells believe that living on the Bluff and sending their children to more prestigious Berea schools give families the best of both worlds – or, at the very least, help prevent the downward social mobility of a family.

We have noted the differences between the 'rough and tough' Bluff and the 'larney' Berea suburbs. How did these areas desegregate as apartheid ended? Based on census data collected in 2001, Schensul and Heller classified the Bluff as a white 'holdout' or 'legacy' area.[2] Black residents settled more slowly on the Bluff than in formerly white suburbs such as Malvern, Escombe, and Hillary that are located further from the beaches and the city centre – that is, closer to the city's largest black townships.

Somewhat surprisingly at first glance, the Berea ridge, home to the city's 'traditional' schools, desegregated faster than the Bluff. More specifically, Berea's distinctive slope shaped the patterns of racial mixing. The lower Berea returned, in many respects, to its pre-apartheid character as a racially mixed lower-middle-class area, whereas the upper Berea trans-formed into a racially mixed upper-middle-class area. Both trends were enabled by the large number of flats for rent and sale on the Berea ridge and the area's close proximity to employment opportunities in the CBD.

The 2011 census data revealed the continuation of this desegregation to the point that it is no longer possible to label the Bluff a 'white legacy' area. Map 7.1 shows that whites are now a minority group in the Berea–Bluff area. However, by subdividing the suburbs further we see that desegregation was spatially uneven, with black residents disproportio-nately concentrated in the lower parts of the Berea, as noted, and at the Bluff's northern and southern extremes – the latter bordered by the formerly Coloured township of Wentworth.[3]

Citywide, the significant pace of desegregation in the Bluff and Berea contrasts with the much whiter western and northern suburbs such as Kloof, Hillcrest, and Umhlanga; it is here that developers built gated communities for 'secure living', 'a bit of paradise', and a 'perfect haven'.[4] These affluent outer suburbs have similarities to what in the US are called 'edge cities'. Yet unlike the latter, they do not plough local taxes into schools to create silos of educational privilege. Educational resources are allocated by the province and through parents' school fees – the latter being independent of a person's place of residence. Moreover, a growing number of black middle-class families are now moving into these areas.[5]

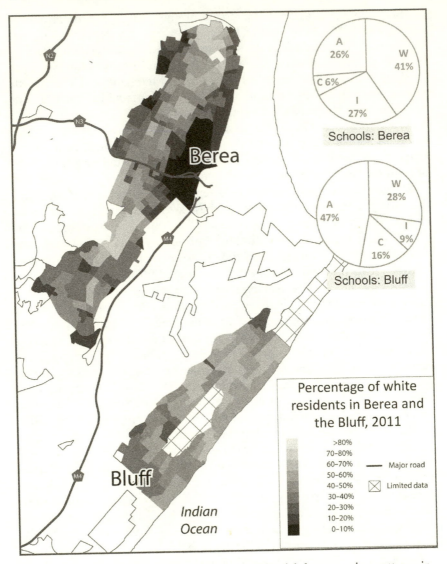

Map 7.1 Contrasting school and residential desegregation patterns in Berea and the Bluff.
*Source:* Census 2011, Department of Education (2012 data).

Map 7.2 covers the whole of the eThekwini municipality and shows these citywide patterns. It also reveals how formerly Indian, Coloured, and African townships have changed little in terms of their dominant racial group.

Residential patterns notwithstanding, what is particularly striking about South African urban areas, and a major theme of this book, is the mobility of schoolchildren (and fees). This creates a mismatch

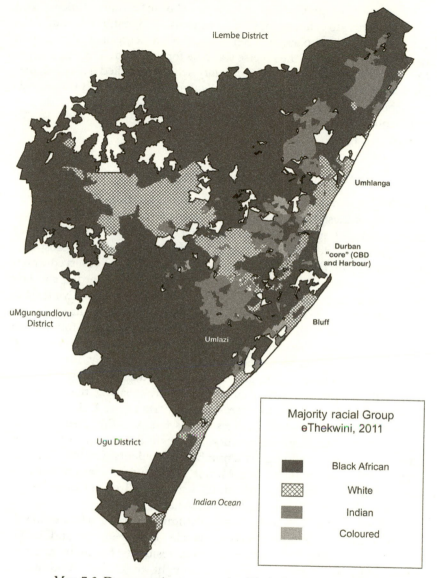

iLembe District

Umhlanga

Durban
"core" (CBD
and Harbour)

uMgungundlovu
District

Bluff

Umlazi

Ugu District

Indian Ocean

Majority racial Group
eThekwini, 2011

Black African

White

Indian

Coloured

Map 7.2 Desegregation patterns in eThekwini. This shows the whiter
areas to the west, north, and south of the city's core.
*Source:* Census 2011.

between schools and their local population. In a musical chairs-like
movement, black learners living in south Durban's townships enrolled
in Bluff schools, and Bluff students moved into Berea schools. Schools
in the western suburbs also desegregated significantly in part through
children's daily travel.

The ability of prestigious schools to choose certain students and white parents to choose desirable schools – dynamics outlined in Chapter 6 – helps explain why Berea's schools desegregated slower than its residences, whereas the reverse was true for the Bluff. The three upper Berea English-medium public secondary schools enrolled a much higher proportion (41 per cent) of white pupils than did the three Bluff secondary schools (28 per cent), even though only 28 per cent of the Berea's population was white compared with around 50 per cent of the Bluff's (see Map 7.1).[6]

## Whiteness and class among Bluffites

Apartheid aimed, largely successfully, to propel working-class whites into middle-class lifestyles: a decent and rising salary, educational advancement, spacious housing, the ownership of a car, and the employment of a maid. Its racial ideology rested partly on the myth that white prosperity was driven by merit and hard work. However, the idea of deserved whites depended not just on portrayals of black people as primordial and lazy but on criticism of a small group of whites who failed to take advantage of opportunities in society. Among English speakers in particular, idle and stupid Afrikaners were the butt of 'van der Merwe jokes'.[7] It follows that when 'middle-class' residents such as Mrs Mitchell talk of 'lower-class' whites, their tone can be somewhat derogatory – to imply, for instance, that a poor family *failed* to upgrade from a rented railway house.

Although a greater proportion of Afrikaans-speaking than English-speaking families still live in lower-income parts of the Bluff, apartheid propelled some Afrikaans speakers into what Mrs Mitchell calls the 'upper class'. The three-class structure she describes – lower, middle, and upper – was mentioned by a number of residents. On the Bluff, the 'upper class' can live on or near Marine Drive, a road that traverses the eastern cliffs and enjoys commanding views of the Indian Ocean and its marine wildlife, including dolphins and whales.

Thus, while the Bluff had a famed community spirit, white solidarity always contained within it certain cracks that went beyond ethnic (Afrikaans–English) affinities. And when residents began to compete for schools, and schools themselves sought to exclude undesirable whites, these cracks deepened and turned into chasms.

Today, a Bluff family's income is an important determinant of whether its schoolchildren attend local or Berea schools. The Household and Schooling Survey conducted in 2012 found that white families with children in schools outside the Bluff had almost double the average income of those attending school on the Bluff: R38,000 per month compared with R20,000 per month. To the school, a high income signifies a family's ability to pay school fees and to navigate the practicalities of travelling to school. In transportation terms, a Berea school might be a 15- to 40-minute drive away from the Bluff, depending on traffic. Although some carpooling takes place and some children use buses, the most flexible transportation method, which allows for after-school activities, is a family member driving a child to school.

Additionally, higher-income parts of the suburb might share 'hot knowledge' about schools' changing reputations.[8] And information can flow through informal networks centred on paid-for children's activities, such as private dance or swimming classes.

In studying class and race among Bluff families over a five-year period, my access to and rapport with interviewees was made easier because I am white and middle class, with my own school-aged child. The research raised some difficult, and sometimes uncomfortable, questions, because many of the dynamics I critically describe are not, of course, restricted to South Africa. In Toronto, where I work, the reality is that 'doing the best for our child' motivates better-off parents, professors included, to live in middle-class areas that are much whiter than the city at large.

During research, I did not begin discussions talking about race, but it hovered around many conversations. I was unable to talk with Afrikaans speakers in their home language, but when we spoke in English they tended to be less guarded in talking about race compared with English informants. For instance, when I asked Mrs Coetzee about sports, she used the country's most insulting racial slur to say in a matter-of-fact way that 'soccer was considered a Kaffir sport'.

What was striking during the interviews with native English speakers, and a point I noted repeatedly in field notes, was a 'look' that I interpreted as a form of race talk. This was fleeting eye contact and a brief pause, inferring that what was said (declining standards, lack of discipline, increase in crime, etc.) had a racial marker. It was a 'you know what I mean' statement. Of course, the 'look' and these pauses reflect the nature of the interview process, whereby informal conversations were mixed with interviews tape-recorded by a university researcher. The 'You know what I mean?' cannot be reduced to a single meaning but it suggests inherent complicity in the research process, 'since you are one of us' (that is, white and middle class).

However, I believe that the pauses also betray the uncertainty of race after it became unmoored from segregation. They imply a 'What do you think?' or perhaps an 'internal conversation'.[9] The anxiety about the 'future of whitey', to recall one letter to a newspaper in 1979, has a long genealogy. If 30 years ago this anxiety could motivate parents to encourage their children to study harder in a local school, navigating the educational market today involves a disorientating new geography and set of dilemmas.

So, in uncertain times, how do white parents make decisions on how they will raise their children and choose schools? Which schools have a 'name' and are 'on the up'? As I have already noted several times, if white parents had prioritised racial separation above all else, the biggest winners would have been Afrikaans-medium schools, which, to this day, admit very few black students. However, these schools fared badly in the 1990s. For parents, what I refer to as a school's 'white tone' crystallises a number of its moving parts: its racial demographics, class character, educational standards, sports achievements, leadership, direction of change, fidelity to 'traditional' uniforms and hairstyles, and so on.

Prestige and whiteness are not synonymous, but when a school 'goes black' it tends to lose prestige, income from fees, and an ability to employ extra teachers and perform well in sports. This can – but does not always – result in a fall in average exam results.

Consider a hypothetical case in which a white child decided in the spirit of nonracialism that they should learn the most common home language in Durban: isiZulu. Or perhaps the case of a child who excels at soccer. These learners would be much less appealing to a Berea school than a child who shines at rugby, hockey, surfing, swimming, or 'drummies' (drum majorettes). Families' efforts to nurture certain activities can be experienced in innocent ways: as 'keeping up with trends' or 'doing the best for our child'. From the perspective of Bluff parents, 'selling' their child to a Berea school might secure a certain 'up-classing' into what one parent called a 'Harry Potter school'.[10] No wonder the Mitchells emphasised Mary's swimming skills.

But white tone exerts a pull and is not an inexorable force. As the example of Mrs Entwistle in Chapter 5 shows, white parents can look at the country's racist past, their minority position in society, and the changing labour market, and conclude that they do not want their children to develop an 'attitude' by entering a school that so crudely promotes whiteness.

Whiteness therefore provides a partial compass, an easy alibi, for parents' and schools' actions, because it is associated with prestige, but what is associated with whiteness is never predetermined, fixed, or unchallenged. Indeed, as the multiracial middle class grows in size, the configuration of practices that historically made up whiteness, such as taste in sports or accent, become considered more in terms of class. Another reason why we cannot draw simple conclusions about families' strategies, however, is that changes are taking place in the very structure of families, a point to which I now turn.

## White extended families

Writing in the 1970s about an unnamed, white working-class Durban suburb, possibly the Bluff, John Argyle challenged the view that all white families were 'nuclear' (in his terminology 'elementary').[11] He found that large family units, aided by the relatively sizeable plots of houses, could contain multiple generations of a family. Yet, Argyle's study still showed that four out of five families were made up of parents and their children.

Although our Household and Schooling Survey was small and not strictly comparable with Argyle's, it indicated that a much higher proportion of white families were not nuclear. Around half (13) of the 27 white families I interviewed and/or surveyed either had elderly parents staying with them (six in total) or children who had finished school/ higher education (ten in total). The national census figures also suggest that the proportion of three-generational white families is on the increase.[12] In contrast, black families moving to the Bluff had often broken away from large extended family units and had more nuclear forms than white families: 47 out of the 55 surveyed Indian, Coloured, and African households were two-generational.

On several occasions, white Bluffites, when talking about the changing family structure, made comments similar to those of Barbara, who was 45 years old. She discussed the advantages of an idealised Indian family (actual changes in family structures among those identifying as 'Indian' are not looked at here):

And I think I said to you last time as well, that more and more families are sticking together for longer. I am seeing that. Like one of my friends just told me on the weekend her parents have just moved in with her and her husband. And it makes sense that you can do it and hold it altogether – why not. The Indians have always been known to do that. And it works and they all go to the park together and there are 100 of them, and it is like one big family and that is how it should be. You know what a funny thing is? That it is the whites that have so much family conflicts. It is not the Africans, and it is not the Indians. It is the whites.

As Barbara noted, it is relatively common for elderly family members to live with their children on the Bluff. I interviewed Stephanie Korte, in her fifties, four times. She was in the process of moving her mother into her refurbished maid's quarters when I interviewed her a second time in 2014. Stephanie remembers a very different situation when she was young. Her retired grandparents used to live in Albert Park, close to Victoria Embankment in town. 'It was lovely ... they never had a car ... So she would go for walks to town shopping.' However, in the 1980s, Albert Park became one of Durban's first suburbs to 'grey' (desegregate illegally), and in the 2010s it became dubbed 'Whoonga Park' (it was a hotspot for the use of the heroin based drug called whoonga).[13] A new breed of gated retirement villages ballooned after apartheid, but one had to be rich, and preferably own a car, to live in them.

When the elderly live with their children, they can help with the labour and costs of their grandchildren's schooling. Take Tina's family, whose father moved to the Bluff to work on the railways. Her mother had to sell the house when he passed away unexpectedly. 'She gets a small pension from my father,' Tina said, 'but it doesn't go very far, because she has still got the debts that she must pay.' When Tina's mother moved in with her daughter, she helped raise Tina's two children. She drove them to school most days and did a lot of the cooking and cleaning in the house.

Thus, 'doing the best for our child' became a sentiment embodied in everyday intimate acts: a father sitting behind one of the many trucks that clog Solomon Mahlangu Drive (formerly Edwin Swales) to take his child to school, and a grandmother making sandwiches for a child in the morning or collecting the child from a sports event in the afternoon. Discussing the moral duty of parents to make sacrifices for their children, Doreen, a white resident in her fifties, told me: 'That's what you have your kids for, to educate them properly. If you are not prepared to dig into your pockets and change your lifestyle for the better, I think you are being selfish.'

## The gendered work of schooling white children

The demand for cold cash in today's school system means that, in the words of one resident, 'You need two salaries for schooling.' We noted that in the post-war period white women increasingly entered the labour force and, in the 1970s and 1980s, a growing number of preschools were established. A 1996 study found that working wives earned significantly less than their husbands. They exited the schooling system earlier, often took breaks from work to care for young children, and sometimes returned to work on a part-time basis.[14]

Today, one way in which white mothers earn money to help pay school fees is by providing child-related services. I interviewed two mothers who ran swimming schools from their homes, a mother who worked as a sports coach, and another who worked as a private tutor. Bluff mothers also undertook part-time work that included administering a cycle club, working in a swimming pool shop, and answering calls for a private ambulance company.

Although mothers took on significant responsibilities as income earners, they continued to play a leading role in the raising of children. In the 1960s and 1970s, women's magazines discussed the pros and cons of marriage and the extent to which men should help with household chores.[15] Yet one 1970s story noted that, for men, 'Taboo jobs are putting the children to bed, and serving and supervising youngsters' meals.'[16] The continued explicit gendering of parenting is apparent in the title of the magazine *Mum's Mail*, which launched in Durban in 2003 to provide advice on parenting and local activities (in 2017, we received copies through our daughter's primary school).

For fathers, the rising cost of school fees can embolden but also threaten masculinities centred on a man's breadwinner role. Mr and

Mrs Steyn, discussed earlier, are parents in an Afrikaans-speaking family who made the tough decision to place their two children in English-medium schools. Mrs Steyn's husband, a fitter and turner, had prioritised his children's education to a point where he had delayed retirement to pay for the cost of a university education. Mrs Steyn told me: 'My husband is 69 years old, and we did plan, but we didn't plan hard enough to make enough money to study one day. So, my husband has to work to let them study. That is what he will do till the day he dies to make sure that those two go to study.'

Moreover, compared with mothers, Bluff fathers generally have greater access to educational loans. Tina, mentioned above and in Chapter 5, was a mother who attained a court order to force her ex-husband to pay child support. However, Tina and their daughter eventually persuaded him to underwrite a large loan so that their daughter could attend a private higher education college in Durban. Although her ex-husband owns a house, Tina and her partner only rent a property on the Bluff.

When deciding who to admit, the most prestigious schools take a strong interest in a learner's family setting. If, in the apartheid period, schools were envisaged as community institutions supporting male-led nuclear families, today a father's presence is interpreted through the lens of the market – two salaries are better than one, and men generally earn more than women. Although most white people marry, divorce rates doubled from 1965 to 1985; recent figures show that 17 per cent of white children are not living with their fathers (the overwhelming majority live with their mothers).[17]

I was told several times by teachers at Berea schools that children of single mothers were looked at particularly unfavourably during admissions, and some schools explicitly require parents to show their marriage certificates. Schools are worried that if a single mother loses her job she might claim the right to fee exemptions. Thus, the schooling market is theoretically neutral to family type – what matters is who can pay fees – but in reality works to promote patriarchal and heteronormative families.

Single mothers themselves recognised the disadvantages they faced. Mrs Spencer told me that her daughter had won regional 'drummies' competitions while at primary school (drum majorettes are rather like cheerleaders). Her success had led to her being offered places at three high schools, including a prestigious school in Berea. Yet none of the girls' schools offered a scholarship, and she ended up studying at a comparatively low-fee school on the Bluff that did not require transportation costs.

Consider another Bluff single mother, Mrs Botha. We talked in the run-down photocopying and printing shop where she worked. She wanted to send her son to a Berea school and said, 'So if you go to an up-market school, you will meet up-market people, and those will create jobs for you one day.' But she could not afford the transportation costs, and her son attended the nearest school on the Bluff.

## White children's obligations to their parents

In the 2010s, the term 'black tax' came to signify the obligation of black wage earners to support family members. Part of the criticism implicit in this term is that white families provide only a downward (i.e. from parents to children) flow of resources – and lots of it. This is largely but not wholly accurate. In addition to elderly parents living with families, my findings suggest that children can live with their parents for years after they finish school, and, if they work, they can share in the expenses of the home.

I spoke with Barbara five times over the course of my research, and we also had several email exchanges. She was in her forties and worked part time for an insurance company. Her deceased father, a railway worker, had bought the house in which they now lived, and the bond or loan was nearly paid off. One afternoon, fresh from interviews that morning in Umlazi, I threw in a question about whether Barbara expected, at any stage, to be looked after by her son – a situation that is common in the township. She looked at me with a mix of confusion and amazement. 'What do you mean, like in the future, for me personally?' When I asked the same question of a Bluff father, he replied in even more frank terms: 'The last thing our children would do is build us a house or buy us a car.'

However, other parts of my conversation revealed that Barbara had in fact considered her future as materially tied to her son's prospects. Barbara had encouraged David to attend a formerly white technical high school in town because he was 'good with his hands and not head'. He had squeezed through his matriculation year with a pass. When I visited the family in 2012, Barbara told me that she had alerted him to a job at the state-owned Transnet (formerly the South African railways), but she wasn't hopeful that he would be successful because of affirmative action policies that favoured black candidates. However, he was hired and began contributing to expenses in the house. He lived in the granny flat (a converted *kia*), whereas Barbara stayed in the house with her boyfriend. In 2013, she told me the following:

My idea, okay, is that eventually David would obviously have his family, and he would take over the house and I would be in the granny flat because I mean I am just one person. So, it would make sense. Cost-wise and security-wise and you know, interaction-wise and that sort of thing, and it would definitely make sense.

I chatted with David on several occasions and he showed little enthusiasm for his job; he preferred to spend his time with friends playing computer games or relaxing on the beach. David's laid-back attitude left

Barbara exasperated. Clearly it would affect both of them. Now that David had secured employment with a parastatal, whose benefits included a thirteenth and fourteenth cheque (i.e. two extra months' pay), Barbara worried that he might be fired because of the frequent days he took off work. 'You know, if he loses his job, I'm up shit creek, excuse the term.'

When I visited Barbara again in 2015, her boyfriend had moved out, and David had moved back into the main house. The granny flat was now being rented to a young white man from out of town who worked 'on the railways'.

However, in 2016 it took longer than normal to arrange to chat with Barbara. When I eventually visited her house, she looked upset and told me that David had moved in with three white co-workers who were older than him. She was worried. Was he wasting his life doing drugs with his friends? Would he keep his job? Was he getting into too much debt? The main wall in the living room looked bare and it took me a while to figure out why: David had taken his flat-screen TV to his new house. Worried about her son's future, Barbara's eyes filled with tears. 'I looked at his friend with his dirty beard,' she told me, pausing as she held back the tears, 'and I thought that could be him in five years.'

## Domestic workers: from live-in to rent-in

In the booming post-war period, an army of live-in domestic workers cleaned Bluff houses and helped raise white children. Yet, today, only two families of the 82 we surveyed and/or interviewed had full-time live-in domestic workers. A common arrangement was for a domestic worker to work part time at several houses and either rent a room on the Bluff or travel daily to the suburb. Indeed, most Bluff families have converted their domestic workers' living quarters (*kia*) into garden cottages. This change is reflected in the growing use of the term 'garden cottages' in advertisements renting out these backyard buildings.[18]

One consequence of the diminishing number of live-in domestic workers was that so-called '*kia* kids' (children of domestic workers) did not pour in to local Bluff schools as opponents of schooling desegregation had feared. Some domestic workers do live with their children on the Bluff and send them to local schools. In other instances, a domestic worker can claim that she lives in the school's catchment area, even when this is not true. Deceiving a school can require the support of an employer, as Mrs Entwistle told me. 'I just say to [the school] she doesn't have a light account [an electricity bill] and a phone. I know it's wrong, but her daughter is in grade 10 now, and she is doing very well in the area ... And then I pay for two of her children's school fees.' One reason why Mrs Entwistle misleads the school is that she saw how well her domestic worker cares for her elderly mother, including undertaking very intimate acts such as bathing her.

As live-in domestic workers decreased in number, what we might call 'rent-in' relationships became more common. Like the Mitchell's house, this arrangement centres on a domestic worker renting a backyard room and 'helping out' in lieu of rent, while also working for other families. Mrs Hlongwa, whom I interviewed three times, told me that domestic workers with experience and strong references can secure part-time work relatively easily:[19]

Ja. No, we are not worried, because if your employers know you, they know you. They can't change you for somebody else. You bond together. They can't live without you. They can't start a new person just because she is with the money. No, most [domestic workers] are very, very honest.

Mrs Hlongwa's own life stretches from the era of live-in to 'rent-in' domestic work. In the 1980s, her mother's employer had allowed the young Mrs Hlongwa to live illegally in a *kia*. In contrast to the dominant pattern today, Mrs Hlongwa travelled daily from the Bluff to attend a school in Umlazi. After leaving school, she found work as a domestic worker in the house of a friend of her mother's employer. When this madam moved, she placed an advert in the paper to help Mrs Hlongwa find another employer, and this was how she became connected to Mrs Brunelda. When I first visited the house, Mrs Hlongwa paid rent (minus a sum for cleaning their house) to Mrs Brunelda while also working for two other employers. She talks of how 'the money is better if you work part time'. All four of Mrs Hlongwa's children lived with her and her husband and went to school on the Bluff.

Mrs Brunelda, a native Afrikaans speaker, had moved to the Bluff in 1971 when her father, a policeman who worked in the harbour, was transferred from Johannesburg. She explained to me (in English) how live-in maids became less common:

[Live-in maids] became very expensive really ... years and years ago, we didn't pay the blacks. Life was much cheaper because I had a maid working for me for R20 a month, and she worked full time, but then things became more expensive, and you couldn't just give her R20.

These conversations capture changes to what have long been complicated and uneven relationships between employers and their domestic workers. In the apartheid era, domestic workers had no choice but to accept inhuman treatment, for instance being fed with 'servants' meat' (a cheaper, low-quality cut) and being forced to use different cutlery, cups, and plates from their employers.[20] Legislation introduced after 1994 gave domestic workers a right to a minimum wage, regular work hours, overtime pay, and annual and sick leave. However, as Mrs Hlongwa's example shows, idioms of 'racial maternalism' endured.

Shireen Ally found that it was mainly when relationships broke down that workers activated their new employment rights (e.g. to challenge unfair dismissal).[21]

These intimate employer–worker relations mean that changes in the health of an employer or where the family lives (as we see later) can have a cascading effect. In 2014, the elderly Mrs Brunelda died. When I spoke with Mrs Hlongwa in 2015, she said of her former employer: 'She was the one who used to help us a lot.' Mrs Hlongwa had a more distant relationship with Mr Brunelda, and he soon asked her to move out so that he could rent out the garden cottage for more money. Mrs Hlongwa and her family moved to a settlement south of the city, and her children began to travel every day to school on the Bluff, at a cost of R650 per month per child. Things took a turn for the worse when Mrs Hlongwa's husband, a carpenter, sustained a work injury. In 2016, she told me by phone that she had stopped working for Mr Brunelda altogether.

In addition to the long-term move away from live-in domestic workers, Bluff families turned to two groups for more casual arrangements: immigrants and shack dwellers (elsewhere in the country, labour brokers became common intermediaries between employers and domestic workers).[22] After 1994, a large number of immigrants from other African countries came to South Africa in search of work. In response to horrific xenophobic violence that peaked in 2008, those with the means gravitated towards perceived safe spaces in the city. I met a number of families from Zimbabwe living in overcrowded accommodation in the cheap parts of the Bluff, notably Fynnlands. Tanaka Bagera had left Zimbabwe when its economy faltered. She had worked as a nurse, and her husband worked as a truck driver, a common occupation for Zimbabwean men in Durban. However, until she could requalify as a nurse in South Africa, she was working as a domestic worker. The second group of domestic workers, shack dwellers (discussed below), work on a casual basis washing clothes or cleaning for as little as R60 a day.

### Live-in domestic workers and their children

The full-time, live-in domestic worker – the dominant model of domestic work in the past – remains a feature mainly of the 'upper-class' areas of the Bluff and Durban's more affluent suburbs. Mrs Dlamini worked for Mr and Mrs Warden for over 25 years at their Marine Drive house. Born in rural KwaZulu-Natal, she raised her three children (Sindy, Samke, and Busi) in a small *kia* situated at the back of a large two-storey house. Sindy, Mrs Dlamini's eldest daughter, was born in 1990, and a few years later Mrs Dlamini sent her to a local preschool that admitted black children.

Mrs Dlamini's white employer, Mrs Warden, who did not have her own children, told me that she came to admire Mrs Dlamini's sacrifices for her children and began to help with the cost of school fees. Perhaps more importantly, especially in the early days of desegregation, the presence of a white woman signalled to the school that the children had an affluent sponsor.

Mrs Warden reflected on her relationship with the children: 'For me the girls [daughters] are my responsibility ... They are part of the family. They really are.' She was aware that her whiteness helped them access good schools. 'I have gone with Mrs. Dlamini. I have done all the talking. I know what I want. We know what we want, and by the time Samke got to that school, we knew exactly what we had to do. We had all the papers and the documents. It does help a lot [me being there].'

However, Mrs Warden is critical of white families who undercut a domestic worker's authority with her children. Mrs Warden and Samke both stated independently that Mrs Warden was careful not to make decisions that undermined Mrs Dlamini – of course, this is an arrangement formed through highly unequal power dynamics. A key boundary (also noted by Romero in her study of a Mexican-American 'maid's daughters') was the child moving to live inside the main house, as Mrs Warden explains:[23]

MRS WARDEN: I think there is a very fine line that people in South Africa must be very careful of. When the whole black–white situation first arose, everybody wanted to have black children and adopted the domestic's child, and the child must be inside and the mom must be outside. That's just not on.

AUTHOR:      Were people doing that then?

MRS WARDEN: It would have been post-1994 because it was the thing to be seen with a little black child. And in the case of my cousin, [his domestic worker's child] lived inside the house, and mommy lived outside. That's not fair. To me, 'They are your children, and I respect that,' and I never want to hurt or let them feel threatened that I am ever going to take the child away. So, it was very much that threat in the beginning.

It is immediately clear from watching Samke and Mrs Warden (whom Samke calls 'auntie') interact that they have great affection for one another. On the mantelpiece in the lounge are school photographs of the three daughters. Samke and Mrs Warden converse easily in English.

Independently, both Samke and Mrs Warden gave me the impression that Mrs Dlamini, Samke's mother, was something of a country bumpkin who spoke little English. Thus, when I interviewed Mrs Dlamini, I started to ask questions in isiZulu. In fact, her English was very good, so we switched back and forth. She told me that the father of her children 'was full of nonsense ... I said to him, take your bag and go.' In reference to her commitment to school, she told me: 'I said to myself, I don't want my children to be like me. *Ngafuna ukuthi bathole* [I wanted them to get] proper education and get the things I didn't get.' She had helped her own mother after finding work. 'When we started working, we send money to home; we build the house for her. I do hope my children do the same to me.'

I got to know Samke fairly well; her access to the internet from home allowed us to keep in touch by email and WhatsApp. She told me that the majority of students at her Bluff girls' school travelled daily from Umlazi, and some had labelled her a 'coconut'. Thus, a term used in Umlazi to criticise any students who schooled outside the area could also be employed to criticise someone seen as acting even more 'white'. Samke told me that her best friends were Indian from the nearby township of Merebank with whom she shared interests such as certain television shows and leisure activities including going to the shopping mall.

When I returned in 2015, however, everything was in flux. The Wardens were in the final stages of selling their Bluff house and intended to move far outside the city.[24] The new owners were not prepared to employ Mrs Dlamini. Recognising the difficulty of the situation, Mr and Mrs Warden gave Mrs Dlamini R50,000 to buy a house. On one occasion, Mrs Dlamini told me that they were looking to rent a place on the Bluff as a temporary solution. However, a week later, Samke told me that they were thinking of moving west of the city to where they had relatives and could buy a small tin house for R35,000.

Suddenly, therefore, the Wardens' move brought into sharp focus apartheid's racial topography: cheaper places that the Dlaminis could afford were predominantly black places. Samke had not identified strongly with rural areas or townships; in fact, when I chatted with her in 2012 about my research in Umlazi, she had talked about the township as a 'ghetto'.

In 2015, I received a WhatsApp message from Samke. She said that instead of buying the small house, they had decided to rent a place in Umlazi Township that was better connected to the city by public transport. In 2016, I gave them a ride home from the government medical clinic on the Bluff, which Mrs Dlamini had visited in preference to Umlazi's clinic. The small, two-room concrete block building in Umlazi that they rented cost them R800 a month. Samke said she was getting used to the area but hadn't even spent time in the local shopping mall because she did not want to get too comfortable. She was thinking of forgoing an honours degree to find work with the goal of buying a house in a cheap, formerly white suburb. She thanked recent 'Fees Must Fall' protests for allowing her to access NSFAS (government) funding for the first time. In 2017, Samke was working as an intern in Cape Town.

## The black middle class on the Bluff

The term 'black middle class' is widely used today in South Africa but I employ it in this section to refer specifically to black families who moved onto the Bluff. In Chapter 2, I discussed Mr Reddy, who was one of the first 'Indian' residents to move to the area in 1994. As we saw, Mr Reddy trained numerous white workers who were then promoted above him. Despite encountering racism his whole life, he slowly climbed the employment ladder. Encouraged by an estate agent, he moved to the lower-class Fynnlands area near the port and railway station. Giant liquid tanks overlook Fynnlands (one resident called it a 'petrol farm'), and it now has a majority black population. The house he purchased was built in the 1940s and sold to a white railway worker at a reduced price in the 1980s.

A five-minute drive away, Mr Reddy's son, a mechanical engineer, stays with his wife and two children on the affluent Marine Drive. They sent their older child to a Berea primary school after jumping through a number of admission hoops, including attending an interview, providing proof of previous fee payments, and giving the school a 'donation'.

Because the Bluff had been a racially mixed area before the Group Areas Act removals of the 1950s and 1960s, desegregation for some black residents represented a homecoming. Close to where Mr Reddy lives, I met Marcus Lottering; he stays in a house bought by his son, who worked as a teacher in the United Kingdom. When he was young, Mr Lottering lived in an area called 'White City' near Wentworth station and he vividly remembers his family being removed to apartheid's Wentworth Township, which was built for Coloureds. He worked for many years in the Bluff's whaling industry.

Most black Bluff families with whom I spoke told me that a major reason for their move into the area was access to better schools. However, over time, as we have seen, Bluff schools lost prestige and funding as better-off local residents moved to Berea's schools. Premila Govender rented and then bought a railway house on the southern side of the Bluff and at first schooled her son locally. After several years, she moved her son to Merebank's top (formerly all-Indian) school because she was concerned about the drop in discipline at the Bluff's English boys' school. This was not an easy decision. Formerly white schools had far better facilities, she said, but Indian schools were cheaper and a few had high academic standards. Compared with other schools in Merebank, the one she chose admits by far the largest proportion of Indian learners and charges the highest fees. This represents a similar pattern to formerly white areas, where one or two schools will retain a reputation as premier institutions.

A few of the black residents I interviewed, like Mr Reddy's son, sent their children to Berea's prestigious public schools or private schools. However, as noted, a black child is less likely to be admitted than a white child. Another option to improve the education of children was private tuition. Mrs Chetty told me: 'If you don't do extra lessons, you are just going to be an average person.'

Compared with Indian and Coloured residents, many of whom had moved from the nearby Merebank and Wentworth Townships, the number of African middle-class families on the Bluff was quite small during the time of my research. In part, this reflects the relatively stagnant industrial and transportation sectors that dominate local employment. In contrast, in Berea and the CBD can be found more professional and white-collar jobs, and a livelier social scene for young people. One black African family who moved to the Bluff, however, was the Cibane family, who accessed their house through Transnet and sent their daughters to school locally. Another couple, Mr and Mrs Khathini, who are both teachers, bought the house at a good price when the bank foreclosed, and they sent their two children to local schools.

## Shack dwellers at King's Rest

I have argued that schooling provides learners access to prestige, and that schools can actively recruit learners who 'do something for the school'. But what happens when groups are economically and symbolically marginalised in society even though they live close to excellent schools? Three decades ago, Bluff schools would have admitted all local students without hesitation, but not today. We consider now a group of shack dwellers who lived for seven years on the Bluff.

In 2002, a shack settlement, dubbed by residents *Emantombazaneni* (Place of Women) to commemorate its first five female settlers, sprang up in the bushes close to the King's Rest train station on the northern side of the Bluff. The weakening and then scrapping of apartheid laws had empowered poor people to move to empty areas like this.

Yet the derogatory language of 'slums' passed seamlessly from apartheid into the democratic era. During apartheid, 'slums' were the enemy of planners who bulldozed tens of thousands of shacks in areas such as Cato Manor and relocated families into new urban townships. Shacks re-emerged in the 1970s, and especially after the scrapping in 1986 of pass laws (which restricted black Africans' movement). After 1994, the state built over 3 million low-cost 'RDP' houses (named after the ANC's flagship Reconstruction and Development Programme). However, reduced household sizes, in part caused by low marriage rates, means that the absolute number of shacks grew from 680,000 to 1.9 million from 1995 to 2006.[25] Frustrated by its inability to stem shack growth, the KwaZulu-Natal government proposed a coercive Slum Elimination Bill that was only halted in court by the social movement *Abahlali baseMjondolo* (people of shacks).[26]

In 2009, I met some of the 200 people who lived in *Emantombazaneni* through a social worker friend. The *imijondolo* (shacks) at this site were constructed from wooden planks, bits of plastic, and reeds, which are all materials obtained for free from the area (Figure 7.1). Shack dwellers earned a small income as casual domestic or factory workers or by collecting and selling scrap metal.

Figure 7.1  A Bluff shack.

Biographies of shack dwellers at *Emantombazaneni* show that many of the oldest residents entered the city in the 1980s, when the state had stopped building houses, formal work was in decline, and influx controls had weakened. Others came later. The widely recognised founder and leader of the Bluff shack settlement was Nomvula, who was 47 years old when I first met her in 2009. She was born in Mount Ayliff on the Eastern Cape some 300 kilometres away, and she had lived previously in Johannesburg and elsewhere in Durban. Nomvula had five children, ranging in age from 12 to 23. Her three school-age children were staying with her sister in Mount Ayliff and attended school in this rural area.

When I began working in the area, I discussed with Nomvula and the social worker possible ways in which my presence might benefit not only my research but also the community. They suggested that I hold a meeting and hand out information in isiZulu about the schooling rights of children. The information I provided stated that local schools could not legally deny entry to a student who could not afford to pay fees. While this intervention was met positively, bigger forces were at work. Of the 30 school-aged children born to the 25 people with whom I spoke (17 women and eight men), only two children were living with family members in the settlement, with five living with relatives elsewhere in Durban. Most residents said that they preferred for their children to be raised in rural areas because of the higher cost of living in the city, the small size of the shacks, the insecurity of tenure, and fears around safety – a canal running along the side of the settlement posed a stark danger to young children.[27]

What was so striking about this settlement, therefore, was that it was located a few hundred metres away from a formerly white primary school, yet not a single parent sent their children to this institution. A few residents had made inquiries, but the school was hostile. A monolingual English-speaking secretary, the first port of call, promulgated the belief that parents must be able to afford fees to access the school. The children of shack dwellers were poor, black, unfamiliar with English, and had little 'value' to schools in the marketised education system.

Map 7.3 displays the locations of school-going children born to parents with whom I spoke. These stretched from KwaZulu-Natal to the Eastern Cape and as far away as Johannesburg.

What happened next to these shack dwellers shows how state policy can create dehumanising cycles of poverty that cut children off from schooling opportunities. One day in late 2009, government officials informed the shack dwellers that their homes would be destroyed to make way for the expansion of Durban's port. They were relocated 15 kilometres south in a 'transit camp' in Isipingo, close to Umlazi Township. City officials promised that they would be given low-cost RDP houses within months. In the democratic era, transit camps were a stubborn presence in cities, being, according to one minister, a temporary path 'for development to take place'.[28]

I stayed in contact with around 30 residents whose life histories I had first recorded in 2009 while they lived on the Bluff. Most were adamant that their lives, precarious as they had been on the Bluff, had worsened after they had been moved to Isipingo transit camp. In the Bluff suburb, many residents had walked from house to house, collecting bits of scrap metal. They then transported the scrap on a shopping trolley by train from King's Rest station to Jacobs station (a trip that costs R3.50) and pushed it to a scrap metal dealer. This gruelling work generated R50 to R80 per day. Casual domestic work on the Bluff was a very important source of additional income for women, and daily wages ranged from R50 to R100.

However, in Isipingo, the tiny income gained from selling scrap metal all but disappeared. Cardboard, the most available scrap, earned residents only R10 a day when it was collected. Domestic work was much harder to find, and wages ranged from R20 to R35 per day. While a few men continued with their employment in Bluff factories, those relying on more casual work in the suburb found that travel costs were not enough to justify commuting for work. The concentration of around 2,000 residents in the bleak transit camp made competition for local opportunities intense.

Inexplicably, the transit camp had been built next to the Isipingo River on a flood plain – the city's own publicly available GIS data revealing this danger.[29] And it was a rainstorm and a terrible flood in October 2013 that

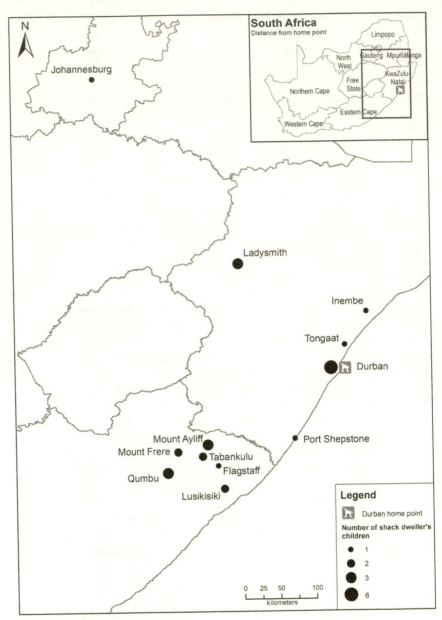

Map 7.3 Location of children with parents living in the Bluff shack settlement.

sparked one of the biggest protests to take place at the camp. After heavy rainfall, water swept into the prefabricated rooms, which were only 6 metres in length and separated by a millimetres-thin wall (Figure 7.2). The deluge left a line of dirt a metre high on the walls that became a

Figure 7.2 Isipingo transit camp. Water marks can be seen on the side
of the structures.

permanent symbol of residents' suffering. At a loss what to do, transit
camp residents used the only power they had: their location next to the
busy M35 road. They burned tyres and blockaded the road.

I continued to visit the transit camp during my research trips.
Residents told how the debilitating tuberculosis germ took hold of
the settlement and diarrhoea became common among young and old.
Children grew up playing alongside illegally connected electric cables
that slithered invitingly along walkways (these are called *izinyokanyoka*,
*inyoka* meaning 'snake'). The permanent limp of one young boy stood as
a tragic warning of the disfigurement that one massive shock unleashed.
Had electricity connections not been made, paraffin and candle fires
would have taken their own noxious toll.

In an immense position of privilege, in 2012 I was asked by former
Bluff residents to help expose the inhuman conditions in the transit
camp. I wrote an op-ed piece for the local newspaper. The eThekwini
mayor, under fire for years from the shack dwellers' movement *Abahlali
baseMjondolo*, came to the settlement the day after the article was published and promised to move residents to an area with better living
conditions.[30] But residents still waited. And waited. And waited. For
housing.

Eventually, by 2016 – a full seven years after being told they would get a house within months – the city had moved the majority of residents from Isipingo into low-cost houses. Busi Mkhize, a resident I got to know quite well, was given a house in 'Cornubia', the state's flagship housing development located north of the city. Busi was 40-something, although her wrinkled face and crooked shoulders betrayed an age at least 20 years older. I visited shortly after her move into a new Cornubia house, a bare, two-storey, two-bedroom structure. It was small, and the stairs were difficult for elderly people to climb, but the settlement was a major improvement on the transit camp. On the floor lay an aluminium can, evidence that Busi had been collecting tins to support herself – although at the isolated Cornubia development it took three days to earn only R40 from this scrap metal.

That day, Busi and her friends were talking about a nearby rally organised by the ANC to drum up support for the local government elections that would be held two weeks later. Rumour had it that two cattle would be slaughtered to feed ANC supporters. I gave Busi and her friends a lift to the gathering. As they hoped, free meat and *ujeqe* (steamed bread) were being served, and loud music created a party-like atmosphere. Although residents such as Busi had been dumped in an inhuman transit camp before being given formal accommodation, the ANC used the rally to emphasise that it had eventually 'delivered' housing and had therefore earned residents' votes. Indeed, when the election results were counted, the ANC had won more than 50 per cent of the national vote, although it lost control of three major cities to opposition parties.

How did this move from the Bluff to Isipingo and then Cornubia affect shack dwellers' children? One day in Isipingo in 2013, Busi told me tearfully that she could not afford to see her three children, who lived with her uncle on the northern fringes of Durban. Her children had moved there after the death of Busi's mother, who had looked after them in the family's rural home. The overcrowded transit camp had sucked health and finances out of Busi. The last time she had seen her children was four or five months earlier.

I offered to take her to where her children stayed, which was an upgraded informal settlement, roughly a 45-minute drive away. As we entered the small house, she hugged her children tightly. Her oldest daughter began to chat at a furious pace, but her younger daughters were quieter. We stayed for several hours. On the way back, wiping tears from her eyes, Busi told me how unhappy she was that she had not been able to bring any gifts or provide support, including for their schooling. She asked, 'Why was my youngest daughter sad? Was she angry because I wouldn't stay the night?' She told me that she was worried that her 17-year-old daughter would find a boyfriend to support her and that she would catch HIV. Tears turned to shivers as she told me about her high blood pressure and other health problems.

Not only sadness accompanied the absence of this mother from her child but a sense of self-blame. In her children and their education lay the possibility of support as she aged, but the bond between them appeared to be weakening. Busi's inability to stay in contact with her children left her with painful feelings of guilt. A Cornubia house obtained several years later had not changed this situation: one child was still enrolled in a school close to her relative, and her other two children had returned to a rural area, where life was cheaper.

In sum, a combination of forces, including high school fees, a bias towards English in schooling admissions, and the dangers to children of living in a shack, prevented shack dwellers from benefiting from the Bluff's local schools. Eventually, after a long stay in a transit camp, their housing improved, but not the prospects of their children. We reflect more on this story when considering the politics of schooling in Chapter 9.

## Conclusions

In the early 1990s, the vast majority of white Bluff parents rejected the Own School Association's racist campaign to keep local schools white. As schools desegregated, many parents maintained a strong commitment to Bluff schools. Yet, over time, parents began to send their children to Berea's schools, first to secondary and boys' schools and then to primary-level and girls' schools. In turn, Berea's schools positioned the 'rough and tough' Bluff as a suburb comprising a pool of white students with prospective fee-paying parents.

While the value given to whiteness in the schooling market generally favours white-identified learners, not all white families benefit equally. Formerly white schools can place value on both white phenotypic traits and white cultural forms such as sports, but they are also businesses that rely on school fees to maintain facilities. Consequently, a white family's income affects its ability to access schools outside its home area and the child's desirability from the perspective of schools. White families also have different abilities to 'sell' their children to schools, for instance by marketing their prowess at certain sports. Schools can see children of single mothers as particularly risky – a job loss away from claiming an exemption from paying fees. To pool resources and provide greater flexibility in the care of children, some white families live in larger-sized households.

Black parents are moving – and in some cases moving back – to the Bluff and enrolling their children in local schools, although sometimes they prefer non-local schools. Children of black domestic workers can now access local schools. Yet we saw that a group of shack dwellers, without the ability to address schools in English and under threat of removal, schooled their children in distant rural areas. Black and poor, their children had little value in the education market. We turn now to consider families living in Umlazi Township.

# 8    Beneath the 'black tax'
## Class, family relations, and schooling in Umlazi

I first met cousins Zodwa Mzala, 15, and Sindisiwe Mzala, 18, in 2012. At that time, they lived in the same house – yet to my surprise they attended schools 20 kilometres apart. In the evenings, they sat down to 'eat from the same pot', to use a common definition of the 'household'. This food pot was paid for, and consumed by, an ever-changing group of people. Along with Zodwa and Sindisiwe, 12 other family members lived in the house; some received social grants, a few a regular salary, many were unemployed. Apartheid townships such as Umlazi are still by far the most common place where urban black South Africans live, and often with many other family members.

Many scholars came to prefer the concept of the 'household' to the 'family' precisely because it emphasises how groups pool money and other resources, sometimes contesting their distribution. Research across the continent shows frequent movements, including of children, in and out of households.[1] But we know much less about why co-resident children might study at very different schools. Zodwa's local Umlazi school charged only R100 fees a year in 2012. Sindisiwe's formerly white school on the Bluff charged R10,000. In fact, if we consider household members old enough to have gone to school after apartheid, their schools ranged from a few hundred metres away to over 20 kilometres away. Matriculation pass rates for the secondary schools they attended ranged from 60 per cent to 95 per cent. The histories of the schools are vastly different: five were formerly African-only, four Indian-only, and one formerly whites-only.

No two children anywhere in the world have the same social trajectory. But as Zodwa and Sindisiwe sit together to eat a regular meal, their prospects for the future are vastly different. Three years after I first met the family, Sindisiwe articulated in a confident 'white' accent her plans to study hotel management, whereas Zodwa, I heard, was unemployed. In 2017, Sindisiwe was working as a clerk and saving up money to attend university; Zodwa was still looking for employment. Key to their different schooling trajectories was their parents' work situation. Zodwa lived with her unemployed father; Sindisiwe's schooling was paid for by her mother, who worked in Johannesburg.

However, if educational access is not an individual but a family matter, so too are its benefits. In the 2010s, the term 'black tax' exploded into media and political circles. The phrase refers to black wage earners' obligations to support family members and implies that whites do not face the same burdens. When I asked Umlazi residents about the concept of a 'black tax', most were adamant that working people do and should support their families. Revealingly, however, the term resonated most strongly with better-off residents who were more likely to be in formal work. Some poorer families had not even heard of the term and were shocked to consider family support as a 'tax'.

That the principle behind the 'black tax' – family support – resonates so strongly in Umlazi shows how capitalism and apartheid simultaneously divided black family members and yet made them interdependent. It questions stereotypes of the 'black middle class' as upwardly mobile individuals hooked on consumption, and the inference that race is now less important in society. It shows, in other words, how race and class remain profoundly entangled and gendered. The focus of this chapter is on these ordinary ways in which schooling mediates such family relations, rather than on the 'black tax' phrase itself.

As we have seen, in the 1970s a tier of better-off Umlazi residents embraced excellent local schools and a few even began to enrol their children in private white schools. From the 1990s, children could, in theory, enter any school regardless of their 'race'. In this chapter I pay particular attention to Umlazi children attending 'multiracial' schools outside Umlazi: that is, formerly white, Indian, or Coloured schools. White schools sit at the top of the hierarchy not just because of their better exam results and facilities but because they impart cultural dispositions such as an English accent, a dynamic I denoted through the term 'white tone'.

The high cost of multiracial schooling means that it stands as a good proxy for families' ability to mobilise educational resources in the schooling market. In 2012, annual fees averaged R200 a year for a township school, R1,000 for a former Indian or Coloured school, and R10,000 for a formerly white school (the highest fees being almost R30,000). Transport costs from Umlazi to a multiracial school might add an extra R6,000 a year.

Not surprisingly, we will see in this chapter how better-off households are the most likely to send a child to a multiracial school. Yet household income does not correlate neatly with a child's schooling trajectory, precisely because very few households are 'nuclear' (i.e. composed of married parents and their children). What matters most to a child accessing a multiracial school is that they have a *wage-earning parent*; this parent might live with their child or might live elsewhere. Untangling these processes requires us to examine subtle gendered educational processes unfolding *within* households and *between* households. These points matter in understanding class formation and ultimately how educational inequalities persist and change over time.

Although multiracial schools are central to the formation of a black middle class, we will also see in this chapter how some Umlazi parents criticise these schools for producing cheeky children who disrespect – perhaps even refuse to support – family members. Consequently, I show that some families, especially their male members, remain heavily invested in Umlazi's long-standing excellent schools. These schools select students ostensibly on the basis of merit, but in reality in a way that penalises poor learners.

Throughout this book I foreground the spatiality of schooling and work, and I want to begin this chapter by showing how the 'friction of distance' particularly affects Umlazi's residents. If you live in Umlazi, climbing the racialised schooling hierarchy requires sending children north towards central Durban, which is some 20 kilometres away. The labour market, too, became more distant when service work grew in relation to south Durban's beleaguered factories. Therefore, I explore briefly in the following section how township dwellers use the local transport system: trains, buses, and taxis.

## Travelling for work and school

Umlazi's primary schools were built in distinct neighbourhoods or 'sections' in the 1960s on the assumption that children would walk to a local school. Work was almost entirely located outside the immediate area: townships were built as dormitory settlements. Trains, and to a lesser extent buses, were the main form of public transport to take working men, the archetypical heads of four-roomed houses, to south Durban's booming factories. In the 1980s, privately operated minibus taxis became popular. However, regardless of the mode of transport, part of the everyday experience of being black in apartheid South Africa was travelling long distances to work.

Yet today, out of Umlazi's recorded population of 400,000 people, only 54,000 men and 43,000 women are employed. More women have entered the labour force than in previous generations, although on average they earn less than men and are less likely to be in waged work.[2] Consequently, public transport is no longer fashioned primarily around male work, and it is increasingly directed towards schooling. How does this operate?

It was 5.45 a.m. and a dark (and, by Durban's standards, cold) winter morning in August 2015 when I set off with my research assistant, Lwandle, and her fiancé/husband, Dumisani, for the train station (this ambiguous marital status is because Dumisani had paid some *ilobolo* or bridewealth for Lwandle). We walk at a rapid pace, as do many schoolchildren that morning; in the afternoons you are more likely to see students sauntering along the pavementless roads, chatting with friends. From their uniforms we deduce that some early starters are attending schools outside the township, and others are walking to the excellent Umlazi secondary schools that open early.

Trains remain the cheapest form of public transport; our single train trip from Umlazi to Merebank station costs R7.[3] Merebank station is located close to Mobeni's factories and roughly halfway to the city centre. We board the crowded 6.10 train and grab the straps attached to the roof. The train jolts forward just as one young man jumps dangerously through the closing door. Some schoolchildren would have travelled later, but the cramped conditions on trains are not generally favoured by young people. Trains have a working-class feel, from the compressed bodies, to the rhythm of songs, to the fruit sellers circulating to fuel early-morning bodies.

Around 60 per cent to 70 per cent of train passengers are women. A large contingent, many wearing *doekies* (headscarves), get off with us at Merebank station; most of this group move to another platform to wait for a train departing for the huge, formerly Indian, township of Chatsworth. Lwandle and Dumisani tell me that they are undertaking domestic work in the township.

Dumisani himself is travelling to fulfil a two-month contract doing *itoho* (casual work) as a clothes packer. Employed through an agency, he earns only R270 a week and has waited two years for this small opportunity. Other men, he says, are travelling just to look for casual work. In Umlazi, *itoho* is an omnipresent word that clearly differentiates temporary from permanent work (people will say that they are not working, just doing *itoho*). In past eras, when employers struggled to fill positions, Durban's workers could prefer '*togt*' (daily) labour to longer-term contracts (the term *itoho* possibly derived from *togt*). However, in line with the global rise in more precarious employment, numerous labour brokers/agencies now supply companies with casual labour.[4] Workers employed on short-term contracts by these intermediaries are paid less than regular workers and denied certain employment rights.

On another day, I take a bus with Lwandle that leaves Umlazi at 6.15 a.m. The signs on the fronts of the buses reveal that more than half are heading to formerly white suburbs – ours is travelling to Fynnlands on the Bluff. I see only two adult men on the bus; the biggest group of passengers by far is schoolchildren. As the bus moves slowly through the township's sections, a young woman in school uniform, maybe 15 years old, sits glued to a book called *Conversations with God*. Others chat or look out of the window. Several miles in, a woman in her forties, perhaps a domestic worker travelling to work on the Bluff, begins a beautiful, slow, and soul-lifting song, '*Enkazimulweni Enkazimulweni. Ngiyathanda*

Figure 8.1 A child sleeps in the back of a *malume* (uncle) taxi. Children today can spend more time travelling to and from school than at school. Photograph: Mark Hunter.

*ukumbona*' ('Glory Glory, I Love You, See Him'). The bus's slow speed, regular stops, and large loop round the township means that it takes one and a half hours to make a journey that takes 30 minutes by car.

Secondary-school children and workers can travel by a third type of public transport: a regular minibus taxi (i.e. open to all passengers). However, to transport young pre- and primary-school children, parents typically use *malume* (uncle) taxis that charge between R400 and R500 a month. These are the only taxis in the township that pick up and drop off passengers at their homes. *Umalume* means 'a mother's brother' or 'male mother' and is reflective of a certain maternal trust that is passed on to these drivers, often by mothers, who play a central role in initiating children's movements.[5] Yet this trust can be destroyed in a tragic flash: in 2017, 20 learners were killed after an overcrowded *malume* taxi crashed and burned near the Mpumalanga–Gauteng border.[6]

In early 2013, I travel by *malume* taxi to Umlazi from a formerly white suburb. The taxi is one of about 60 that pass through the Umlazi neigh-bourhood I study (Lwandle undertook a survey of every *malume* taxi that passed through the section where our research was based). The taxi's first pickup in the morning is at 5 a.m. and Lwandle and I join the *malume* driver at 11 a.m. as he begins his return trip. At midday, we start to collect children, and as we move from school to school, children in the taxi sleep, play, or do homework (Figure 8.1). At around 2 p.m. our taxi enters Umlazi Township crammed with 21 children aged five to nine years old. Suddenly, as we pass the busy V-section intersection, we are jolted back and forth by the minibus's vibrations. The driver slows down, yanks the bare metal handbrake four or five times, and gets out to inspect a flat tyre. Today, the Umlazi children spend longer in the minibus than at school.

It needs to be noted that these transport routes do not capture the many men who live in hostels outside Umlazi or in company compounds, or who work at night in jobs that include private security. Yet they reveal how transport systems that once would have been full of working industrial men are now used heavily by women and schoolchildren. As I am pondering this on the bus, I notice a sticker on the back of a taxi that passes us. 'So many women, so little time,' it says. But, as if in response, another such sign I see a few minutes later states: 'No money, no honey!'

### Getting to class after apartheid: income, housing type, and schooling

If paid work in Umlazi is now scarce and transport costs and times are significant, let's review some basics about who gets to attend what school. The Household and Schooling Survey conducted for this book collected information from one neighbourhood broadly representative of the township as a whole. Of the school-going children, it found that three out of ten (47 out of 155) had travelled outside the township to attend a multiracial school for at least one year, one in ten enrolling in the most expensive formerly white schools. A slightly smaller number, 41 (around one in four), were attending a multiracial school at the time of the survey.

Umlazi's average per capita income of R1,900 a month (around US $140) is low but above that for South Africa as a whole, a consequence principally of the large number of poor rural households.[7] In Umlazi, a family's housing type, itself associated with per capita household income, is an important indicator of who attends multiracial schools and for how long: thus a child's per capita household income and likelihood of attending a multiracial school increase depending on whether the person lives in a shack, a municipal four-roomed house, or a larger house built by private developers (see Appendix 1 for specific figures).

Conceptually, however, we need to understand households not as bounded entities but as *connected*, including through children's schooling. Umlazi is linked not just to the wider Durban city, and other metropolitan areas, but to rural areas in which many relatives live. Between the initial survey conducted in 2012 and a follow-up survey in

2014, six of the 155 children in our study area had moved to stay with relatives in a rural area, mainly for economic reasons.[8]

One such learner who moved to a rural area is Sinethemba, born in 2002. I got to know her mother, Nandi, whose three-roomed shack was located close to a small stream that cut through the township – a physical barrier that had halted the building of four-roomed houses. Beginning in the early 1980s, around 60 shacks had been constructed in this small open space using wood, mud, corrugated steel, and other scrap materials. Early occupants were typically sons and daughters moving from overcrowded township houses, migrants from rural areas, and renters of rooms seeking a more permanent place to live.[9]

Nandi ran a shebeen, or informal drinking establishment. When we walked to interviews in the morning, Lwandle and I often saw her vigorously sweeping the living room and throwing out old bottles. The open space outside her house was also a favourite place for children to throw a plastic bag filled with wet paper in a game called *ushumpu*. After we greeted Nandi, we sometimes exchanged a joke or two with her about the shebeen business. However, one day, the rattle of bottles was not to be heard. She had tired of paying bribes to the police because the establishment was unlicensed. The fall in family income triggered Sinethemba's move to stay with relatives in a rural part of KwaZulu-Natal.

South Africa's geography does not fit neatly into 'rural' and 'urban' classifications. Crops are grown in urban plots, Umlazi itself has expanded into what would once have been called rural areas, and proximity to roads, cities, and other infrastructure greatly affects the experiences of 'rural' households. Difficulties in definitions aside, if we consider former reserve/homeland areas (excluding their generally recognised cities) to be rural, it can generally be said that they have the lowest living expenses. This is because rural households typically grow some food, live rent-free, and access 'no-fee' schools. One in three South Africans, many living in rural areas, now receive means-tested social grants, including the old age pension and child support grant (worth respectively R1,600 and R380 a month in 2017, or US$145 and US$35).[10]

Yet, on average, rural schools have much poorer exam results than urban schools; they are also less likely to impart fluency in English.[11] Consequently, revisits to our 122 surveyed households found that ten children had moved from rural areas into the township, the typical reason being to access educational institutions, especially higher education institutions.[12]

Just north of Umlazi, I came across the starkest example of school-children (and money) moving from rural to urban areas. In the formerly Coloured township of Wentworth, I interviewed Mrs Dove after I saw an advertisement she had placed for boarding accommodation in a school I visited. She rented out 20 bunkbeds squashed into four rooms of her extended house. Most of the parents whose children stayed with her, she told me, were teachers from the Eastern Cape, a predominantly rural province notorious for its poor schooling.

Thus, Umlazi Township is a node in a wide network of people who might change location for educational reasons. Seen as a whole, the trend is for poorer students to concentrate in rural areas, and better-off students to attend township schools. But the prize for many Umlazi families is a learner's attendance at a multiracial school, to which we now turn.

## The road to multiracial schools: work, gender, and location

Umlazi's parents gather information about multiracial school from relatives, neighbours, and *malume* drivers; the latter are sometimes encouraged by schools to recruit students. Parents invariably find at least one school that will admit their children. The logic of the racialised schooling market is that Indian, Coloured, and white students move to higher-prestige schools, and this leaves empty desks that need to be filled.

Tellingly, it is rare to find a teacher who lives and works in Umlazi whose own child studies in the township. Teachers have unparalleled knowledge of the schooling system and relatively high incomes (racially differentiated teaching salaries were equalised after apartheid). A female principal I spoke with works in a lower primary school in Umlazi that teaches grades 1–4 in isiZulu. Explaining why the school has struggled to fill its desks, she said:

Parents take them to Chatsworth [formerly an Indian area very close to the school], Wentworth [formerly a Coloured area], and to those white schools where they can learn to speak English. Because in our schools, we use the mother tongue, which is Zulu ... So we teach all the subjects in Zulu ... Not even one of the 15 teachers [at this school] send their children to an Umlazi school.

Formerly white schools enjoy the most prestige but there is great variation among these schools, as we have seen. South and central Durban's most popular schools, located in the upper Berea, charge the highest fees and are the most selective when it comes to admissions. When Umlazi children did access the top formerly white schools, fathers often played a leading role. For instance, one recent school leaver told me that her father, a senior government official with close ties to the ruling ANC party, had successfully lobbied for her to attend a prestigious Berea school. Consider, too, the case of an Umlazi school principal, Mr Mdletshe, who persuaded the principal of a Berea primary school to admit his son (he and his family live in a formerly Coloured part of the city). He heard from other teachers that the school was an excellent one but that it preferred white learners. Mr Mdletshe's application was rejected at first, but he arranged a meeting with the principal:

MR MDLETSHE: The principal said the policy of the school is that a learner must be close to a school in terms of proximity ... And I said, 'There is no way, Mr Davis, that I cannot request you to take my child. Let me tell you that I am a deputy principal.' At that time I was a deputy principal ... I said to him, 'We will be meeting with you one day as a principal and I will be a principal one day. We will be sharing certain issues.' At that time I had a master's degree. I said, 'I cannot subject my child to a situation which I know very well,' and I spoke to that guy.

AUTHOR: But did you prefer that school partly because it had so many white children?

MR MDLETSHE: Yes, you are quite right. As I said, my elder daughter was the only child in that [another formerly white] particular school, only black child. She's doing very well. And I wanted to see my son and other two girls going to the same area [this refers to 'schooling type' rather than geographical area, since the schools are 20 kilometres away]. If I could find a school with no blacks, I will take my child to that particular school.

AUTHOR: Why would that be better?

MR MDLETSHE: I [want] to see them being competent for a workplace. In terms of being fluent in English, knowing their rights and they have all the equipment. They are going to have quality and the best education. It's what any parent will strive for.

While fathers tend to be more likely than mothers to occupy senior work positions, some mothers are able to use social contacts and spatial knowledge to successfully enrol their children in Durban's top schools. We saw that, on the Bluff, children of domestic workers can access local schools.

Another case of a mother's place of work benefiting her child – and a striking example of the payback of educational support *in educational support* – is the example of Mrs Zondi from Umlazi. Now in her fifties, she worked in the 1990s as a caterer at the formerly white University of Natal (now the University of KwaZulu-Natal). It was through living and working in a formerly white area that she learned about her children's right to access nearby schools. Her first two children attended formerly white schools, and her last three enrolled in formerly Indian schools (two currently attend these schools). To my surprise, I learned that Mrs Zondi's working daughter went on to pay for Mrs Zondi to train to become a nurse. When I visited the family in 2014, Mrs Zondi had just qualified as a nurse and had found work in a hospital.

Privately developed township areas (such as Chappies, considered in Chapter 4) are also important nodes for the exchange of information on schooling. One mother at Chappies with a child in a prestigious Berea school helped a neighbour access the school when she told the principal that the child's education was fully financed by a trust fund from a life insurance policy. Young Chappies residents I interviewed relayed how they saw multiracial schooling as a means to get out of the township. 'My parents upgraded,' one 21-year-old said in a distinctive accent sculpted by formerly white schools. 'We want to do the same.'

## Umlazi's excellent schools in context

While most Umlazi residents say that multiracial schools, especially formerly white schools, are the best schools in the city, some view township schools as prestigious for different reasons. Indeed, Umlazi's residents do not use a single undisputed scale to rank the prestige of Durban's schools. As noted in Chapter 4, in the 1970s and 1980s several excellent secondary schools stood out amid a sea of poorly performing schools. Although their fortunes wax and wane, 100 per cent matriculation pass rates are not uncommon in several schools.

Umlazi's excellent schools, as we have seen, became famous not just for their results but for encouraging English usage. However, they also had a commitment to teaching isiZulu. In the 1980s, a person's ability to speak 'deep' isiZulu signalled a pride in African culture and, more practically, meant that they did not antagonise the Zulu nationalist Inkatha movement, which had considerable power in the township.[13]

Today, multilingualism in township schools retains its importance, but for different reasons. IsiZulu, though no longer so strongly tied to Inkatha/ANC politics, remains the language of Africanness, respect, and amasiko (customs). A formerly white school might bestow a 'white' accent, but it cannot provide the same knowledge of isiZulu.[14]

This brings me to a second difference between township and outside schools: the acceptance of corporal punishment in the former, a practice that many parents support despite it being outlawed by the 1996 Schools Act.

The association between excellent township schools and positive aspects of Zuluness allows them to be contrasted favourably with formerly white schools that are said to produce amaModel C (a somewhat disparaging term for those schooling at formerly white schools). The archetypical model C student, according to critics, is a cheeky 'coconut' out of touch with their African roots; someone who might not give way to an old person in the street or who might fill a taxi with loud English words.[15] Thus, if, a century ago, all schools could be labelled as 'things of the whites', now it is the formerly white schools that are most thought of in this way.

However, codings of whiteness are differentiated and relational. A confident young person might be criticised as arrogant because '*uzenza umlungu'* (they 'make themselves like a white') when in fact they are speaking fluent English after attending a formerly Coloured or Indian school. This is because the benefit received by so-called *amaMulti* learners (those attending multiracial schools) is closely associated with the linguistic power obtained from English-medium teachers.

The high status of some of Umlazi's excellent secondary schools helps explain why primary-school learners tend to travel in greater numbers than older learners to schools outside the township. A common pattern is for children to be sent to learn English at a multiracial primary school, and then return to a cheaper secondary school that has high pass rates.

Umlazi's excellent schools have relatively low fees compared with multiracial schools, but schooling costs can still exclude poorer students. Thabisile Ntombela conducted research with shack dwellers who lived on land close to an excellent Umlazi school that charged around R1,000 a year.[16] She found that guardians living in the settlement were mostly unaware of laws requiring schools to provide fee remissions to poorer students and were deterred by the cost of fees that were at the upper end of those for township schools. Shack dwellers also face other educational disadvantages. Many are migrants to Umlazi and apply late for popular schools or fall foul of age-based admissions criteria aimed to exclude children who repeat a schooling year.[17] Thus, the seemingly meritocratic principles operating in Umlazi's excellent schools, symbolised by admissions exams, disproportionately disadvantage poor and migrant children, a significant number of whom live in shacks.

Moreover, the practice at excellent Umlazi schools is that a learner's attendance is contingent on their behaviour and performance. In the Mzala family, during our first visit in 2012, we learned that Zinhle had passed an entrance exam to enrol in one of Umlazi's best schools. However, when we returned in 2014, we found that Zinhle had failed a grade and had transferred to a worse-performing school. The pressure to do so came not only from teachers but from her own sense of shame. Her sister, Sne, had also attended an excellent township school but failed an exam and enrolled in a school that, she said, would 'take anyone'.

### Steady work: sponsoring a child to attend a multiracial school

The ending of the racial colour bar at work and the implementation of black economic empowerment policies propelled a group of black people into management positions in businesses, and especially in the public sector (the richest of this group have been referred to as 'black diamonds').[18] Consequently, some families have the financial ability to relocate from townships to more affluent suburbs. Ivor Chipkin has noted that, when families move to a formerly white suburb, they can partially insulate themselves from the claims of kin.[19] But there is a large jump in housing prices from townships to suburbs, especially the ones that host the best schools. Moreover, the large number of people who benefit from *ikhaya*, or the family house, means that it can rarely be sold to finance a move. Improved facilities, notably the building of Umlazi's Megacity Mall and KwaMnyandu Mall, also influence families' decision not to leave the township.

For many residents, living in the township and sending a child to an outside school is an affordable path to upward intergenerational social mobility (crossing generations), and, by association, intragenerational social mobility (within a generation): that is, if a child does well for itself, it can support its family.

The Mzala household, introduced earlier, has a higher than average per capita income and household size for an Umlazi dwelling. Mr and Mrs Mzala, who acquired the house in the 1960s, have now died, but Mrs Mzala had placed a great emphasis on schooling, and her children attended some of Umlazi's best schools (these are now the oldest members of the household). Today, the family's schooling reflects a very common dynamic in the township: children attending multiracial schools are funded by a parent who works in a stable job. Two sisters, Nosipho and Philile, and Nosipho's daughter Nqobile all send their children to multiracial schools. Nosipho works in a factory, her sister Philile is a schoolteacher, and Nqobile, educated by Nosipho, also now works in a factory.

Our Household and Schooling Survey showed that most guardians/sponsors sending children to multiracial schools were in formal employment (Table 8.1).[20] Children's sponsors tend to be located in the middle 'cluster of classes' as laid out in Nattrass and Seekings' model of (household) stratification.[21] This group, while not affluent, represents some of the principal beneficiaries of the post-apartheid period: namely, public-sector employees (such as teachers and nurses) and unionised industrial workers. Notable, too, is that sponsors of schooling tend to be in *permanent* (i.e. not casual or *itoho*) work. This is necessary because regular fees and, even more importantly, regular transport costs must be paid; it is possible to get exemptions from the former but certainly not the latter. Secure work provides benefits even after a person's death, when life insurance policies fund a child's schooling.

How do working parents with children at multiracial schools conceive of their lives? Alexander and colleagues found that, in Soweto Township, there is no easy translation for the English concept of the 'middle class', the closest isiZulu term being *phakathi* (in between).[22] Terms such as *uzenza umlungu* ('you make yourself like a white') show how forms of differentiation can take on racial codings: to be white under apartheid was, after all, to be privileged in all walks of life.

Moreover, if middle-class life can be characterised by a sense of security and comfort, many working Umlazi parents who send children

Table 8.1 *Occupation of main sponsors of children attending multiracial schools in surveyed Umlazi households*

| Grandmother (5 children in total) | Mother (19 children) | Father (16 children) |
|---|---|---|
| Domestic worker/informal baker | Teacher (4) | Toyota factory worker (5) |
| Social worker | Nurse (2) | Other factory worker (2) |
| Nurse | Deceased – trust fund (2) | Deceased – trust fund |
| Pensioner | Factory worker (2) | Telkom worker |
| Social worker | Municipal employee | Municipal employee |
|  | Telkom (telecommunications) worker | Teacher |
|  | Grant administrator | Businessman |
|  | Transnet (railway) worker | Delivery driver |
|  | Hospital porter | Private investigator |
|  | Caterer | Baker |
|  | Bank clerk | Department of Education official |
|  | Cleaner |  |
|  | Customs officer |  |

to multiracial schools reject this label and say that they are struggling (*strugglisha* – taken from the English word). They have to support themselves, pay all of the costs for their children, and provide assistance to poorer family members. They can take on high levels of debt.[23] In short, the frequently discussed 'black middle class' is very often an *aspiring* middle class. Their children's future lies in accessing good schools, particularly multiracial schools, and hopefully if a child finds work they won't forget their families.

Indeed, for wage earners in Umlazi, never-ending family obligations – the so-called 'black tax' – are a routine part of everyday life, a burden but one that raises the status of a wage earner. Even if someone lives alone – in a shack, say – it is common for them to have relatives living in Durban and a family node in a rural area that needs support. The majority of the original four-roomed 'family houses' have been extended, with extra rooms or backyard buildings in which multiple family members live. But how, more specifically, does education come together with changing and varied family bonds?

## The intimate politics of the educational market: to *khulisa* and *fundisa* a child

Children in Umlazi have diverse living arrangements that can change gradually or suddenly. In line with national figures, our survey found that, out of the 155 school-attending children, only 19 per cent live with both their mother and father (69 per cent and 29 per cent live with only their mother and father respectively).[24] Of the children's fathers and mothers, 30 per cent and 15 per cent respectively are no longer alive; an HIV/AIDS prevalence rate of 20 per cent contributes to high death rates.[25]

The long history of men's migration to work in mines or factories normalised fathers' separation from their children. In the 1970s, women's migration accelerated, especially as shack settlements re-emerged in cities.[26] One related change in families that cannot be over-stated is the halving of marriage rates from the 1960s; this was linked in complicated ways to women's movement as well as to rising unemployment and the high cost of marrying.[27] Evidence of the low marriage rate can be found in the multigenerational structure of the Mzala home. Eight children are living with their mother and not their father, and two with their father but not their mother. Much more than on the Bluff, schooling trajectories therefore derive from complex inter- and intra-household dynamics.

In a setting of constant change in households, let me introduce here what is special about schooling costs compared with other support provided for children. These differences are indicated in isiZulu by the terms *ukufundisa* (here, to push someone financially through schooling, or literally 'cause to learn') and *ukukhulisa* (to raise someone, or literally 'cause to grow').

As is widely noted, many household members pitch in to provide care and resources to raise/*khulisa* a child. Doing so involves stretching out family relations from the child's household in fluid, centrifugal ways. Thus, to discuss relatedness, Umlazi residents use terms that include *umndeni*, or broadly 'family', which can include not just the 'nuclear' parts of the family but a circle of relatives, and *isihlobo*, which can mean 'blood relation of a distant nature'.[28]

It follows that when children 'eat from the same pot', an array of sources can contribute to the costs: family members in formal work or *itoho*, those receiving social grants, and those who are absent as well as those present. Poverty therefore arises from an absence of certain social relationships rather than simply one's own insufficient earnings. As Alexander and colleagues note in *Class in Soweto*, so important are families in cushioning hard times that those burdened with the least-rewarded work, such as street hawkers, are in a sense 'too poor to be unemployed'.[29]

If children eating from the same pot is an everyday part of families raising (or *khulisa*-ing) multiple children, why does their schooling differ? Here, we need to turn to the concept of *ukufundisa* (sponsoring a child financially) for guidance. *Ukufundisa* exerts a centripetal educational force on a child because the schooling market typically focuses on birth parents to pay the high costs to fund their children's schooling. It follows that parents who support learners, and in turn expect future assistance, figure prominently in narratives of the 'black tax'.

It should be noted that I am using here a relational definition of *ukufundisa*: 'to cause to learn' or to push a child through school. As the causative form of *ukufunda* (to learn), *fundisa* has some similarities with *khulisa*, although it has a stronger inference of sacrifice, including through the provision of financial support for a child's education.

This interpretation of *ukufundisa* differs slightly from the most well-known English translation: 'to teach'. *Umfundisi* means both 'teacher' and 'priest', a connection that results from the fact that it was missionaries who opened the first schools for black South Africans. For generations, scholars have placed emphasis on how these Christian institutions encouraged greater individualism – for instance, by creating new private forms of courting, smaller nuclear families, and reduced obligations from children to their parents.[30] Here, however, I am more concerned with emphasising how schooling creates and mediates social bonds.

If the moral economy of households means that someone cannot eat while a family member goes hungry, schooling expenses do not have to be spent equally on co-resident children. Precisely because wage earners face so many demands for assistance, their spending of money on a child's education is a way to 'earmark' part of their salary. Paying school fees therefore acts as a form of savings that spans decades and can be realised when a child finds work and supports their parents. As noted earlier, for generations mothers took the lead in recognising this special status of schooling.

Thus, the fundamental relational sense of *fundisa* derives from the sacrifices a parent makes, hoping that they will have benefits for all the family. This creates a sense of interdependence among certain kin or prospective kin, something Marshall Sahlins calls a 'mutuality of being'.[31] Although family relationships change over time, this formulation helps us understand the sense of shared fate between children and their mothers, fathers, grandmothers, and perhaps siblings. It is not incorrect to note, as many scholars do, that a parent and a child have a reciprocal relationship (i.e. they help one another with a series of gifts and debts over a lifetime), but this does not quite capture how a mother, in particular, can view her children's future and her own as inherently intertwined, with schooling serving as an important intermediator.

In addition to parent–child relations, a second important family relationship is between siblings. Elderly residents, including Precious Mhlongo whom we met in Chapter 3, often had an elder working sibling who had helped with their schooling. Writing in the 1980s, when women increasingly entered employment, Isak Niehaus compared 'harmonious' sibling relationships to more conflictual marital relations.[32] Particularly strong bonds between sisters mean that children frequently make claims on maternal relatives.[33]

Yet, several factors mediate against a wage earner playing a significant role in sponsoring the attendance of their sibling or sibling's child at a multiracial school: the high cost of schooling, the reduced number of siblings, the commonness of siblings being related through only one parent, and the attention siblings must give to their own children's schooling costs. Central to this is the rapid drop in fertility rates: women moved from having on average six children in 1970 to three in 2001 and 2.3 in 2011.[34]

Twenty-six-year-old Thobile weighed the benefits of paying for the schooling of a sibling's child with the uncertainty about whether such commitments would be fully recognised in the future:

If my sister is struggling, I can take her child to the same school as my child ... [But] after her child gets educated and maybe finishes university, my sister can say that she didn't ask me to send her child to the university. This is the reason people do not like to help someone else's child.

Thobile's comment returns us to how we need to differentiate between the kinds of help siblings provide. Many residents assist a sibling to buy food or clothes, or to pay rent. Very few, however, fundisa a sibling's children in an expensive multiracial school. Moreover, the above comments also speak to how a child's aunt can be seen as undertaking an act of goodwill for her sister rather than necessarily generating a debt with the child themself. This criss-crossing set of obligations helps explain why debts from children to a sponsoring aunt are seen as diluted in comparison with debts from children to their parents.

As Thobile's testimony suggests, conflict can arise because of the expectations created when a person sponsors another's schooling. But education, like work, is precarious for the poor. Hopes can be dashed when a student's need to respond to a family emergency takes precedence over long-term educational aims. Indeed, one reason why large numbers of students drop out of higher education is because government funding can be diverted to support families, for instance in the case of illness.[35]

In other cases, well-paid work does not result from studying. Mrs Dube is one person I know with a family member who had attended higher education. Her four-roomed house had not been extended with extra rooms, unlike most, and her furniture was old and frayed. Mrs Dube told me that one of her sons was in jail after being caught stealing to fund his addiction to whoonga, a heroin-based drug that came to prominence in the township in the 2010s.

However, her son's incarceration was not what brought tears to her eyes that day. She got most upset when talking about her niece,

Thandeka, who had stayed with her like a daughter and, after doing very well in local schools, received a bursary to study at the University of Cape Town. Even though she had found work as a clerk with a major supermarket chain, she was not regularly supporting Mrs Dube's branch of the family. She gave R1,000 when Mrs Dube's other son had died in a car accident, but nothing more.

When I attended a conference in Cape Town in 2015, I tracked down Thandeka. From the way her aunt spoke, I had expected to find a confident, upwardly mobile, service-sector worker. The first indication that this was not the case came when we arranged to meet at a shack settlement called *Imizamo Yethu* ('our efforts') close to the city's picturesque Hout Bay suburb. Thandeka had bought a shack there for R7,000 and was living in the settlement with her three children. She had dropped out of university after becoming pregnant. Her current work, she said, was only temporary – as a junior clerk in the supermarket chain called Checkers. And yet she faced ongoing demands (the 'black tax') from relatives who seemed to think her income was unlimited.

## The schooling market and intimate relations

In Umlazi, we have seen how mothers, from the early history of the township, endeavoured to *fundisa* their children. This was because of the disadvantages women faced in the labour market, at home, and in the legal domain. This became cemented materially in the long history of children finding work and buying their mothers gifts of furniture, paying for additions to their houses, and even buying them whole new houses. However, mother–child bonds do not exist in isolation. They can be mediated by the relationship between a child's mother and father. Moreover, children might be raised by a father's family and develop particular obligations to this node of relatives. These questions require us to look at children's living arrangements.

Only 19 per cent of Umlazi residents aged over 15 are married, according to 2011 census data. Although marriage in the region has long been seen as a 'process' and not an 'event', there is little ambiguity about the fact that *ilobolo* (bridewealth) is necessary for people to become married. Nor is there any real alternative to formal work as a way to pay the significant marriage expenses, perhaps between R20,000 and R80,000. As such, married couples are typically better off than unmarried residents, and this means that they are quite likely to fund a child's attendance at a multiracial school.[36]

A second scenario is where couples cohabit after some marriage payments have been made. I first met 34-year-old Phindile at her shack in 2012.[37] Phindile's mother, Thobeka, whom I met on the same occasion, lived in the adjacent shack. She had grown up on KwaZulu-Natal's south coast and, for much of the 1980s, was employed as a live-in domestic worker in the white suburb of the Bluff.

When Phindile first told me that she was being *lobola*-ed (paid bride-wealth for), I remember thinking that, although uncommon, marriage is still one of the only ways in which a poor woman can transform her life. Phindile sometimes stayed with Nhlanhla, her partner, and at other times resided with her family. By 2014, she had moved in permanently with Nhlanhla.

Her brother, Sakhile, the eldest man in her immediate family, felt that the cash equivalent of two cattle that Nhlanhla gave before the couple moved in together was too low. This payment was described as an *umcelo* gift; *umcelo* comes from *ukucela* (to ask), because it was given as part of the groom's representatives 'asking' for the bride. Sakhile had requested the more common payment of six cattle before the couple officially moved in together, slightly more than half of the typical payment of 11 cattle for *ilobolo*. But he took the two nevertheless.

In July 2015, Lwandle and I visited Phindile in her new house. Nhlanhla was out working as a delivery driver. Located about a 15-minute drive from her previous shack, the site was situated on tribal land (thus under the authority of an *inkosi* or chief); for decades, such land had been eaten away by the formal and informal expansion of Umlazi Township. Nhlanhla had bought the plot for R10,000 from a resident who subdivided his homestead, and he gained the chief's permission to settle because they were a marrying couple (he paid fees of around R4,000 to the chief's assistant, although the receipt I saw was for only R2,500).

A lot of pride had gone into making the house neat, welcoming, and functional. The main room, combining a lounge and kitchen, managed to pack in a three-piece sofa set, a small table decorated with pink plastic flowers, a microwave, a refrigerator, and five pots stacked neatly on a stand. A sense of living beyond the bare minimum of life was given by the room's satellite television, a music system, and nicely framed photographs on the wall.

Phindile told me that Nhlanhla was not considering saving up for further *ilobolo* transfers at this point. Rather, the couple was focusing their disposable income on the financial responsibilities they had. Their older child was due to start primary school the following year, and they had plans to send him to a formerly Coloured school outside Umlazi, which meant budgeting for school fees and transport costs. The loan they had taken out to build the house needed to be paid off within five years. A ceiling was needed to hide the bare corrugated iron roof. The concrete block walls in the bedroom required plastering. She was *ingoduso* (a betrothed woman), Phindile said, and one day they would marry – but marriage was not a priority at this stage of their life.

This is an example of what I have called elsewhere 'legitimate cohabit-ation', where small *ilobolo*-related gifts are given to legitimise a couple living together.[38] Because of these payments, this couple had a higher status than couples who *kipita*-ed (illegitimately cohabited). One reason for the stalling of *ilobolo* payments was that the couple faced other potential expenses, including schooling. In other words, the importance placed on schooling can take resources away from the prized status of being married.

In many instances, however, parents do not marry or legitimately cohabit: that is, they live in separate households or can cohabit, perhaps in a shack, without any *ilobolo* having being paid (*kipita*). The HIV/AIDS epidemic generated a large literature, including my own work, showing how chronic unemployment, rising inequalities, and reduced marriage rates result in a kind of 'provider love', whereby girlfriends can expect gifts from boyfriends, be they money, food, or help paying rent.[39] Money, then, can trickle down through society from better-off men to women.

At the same time, a provider masculinity has long been intertwined with men paying school fees and other costs. Women's potential attrac-tion to a 'provider father' came to light when I interviewed Snikiwe Busane. She told me that her boyfriend was employed and already supporting children from another mother. Yet this was not a negative point in her eyes. It signified that he was a good catch, a potential respectable father.

As noted, our survey and national figures suggest that fewer than one in three black African children live with their fathers (compared with four out of five white children).[40] However, given the high rates of unemploy-ment, the fact that the Umlazi survey found that 55 per cent of children receive some support from their fathers is not insignificant. It helps qualify simple narratives of what can often be called a 'crisis in masculin-ity' and focus attention on understanding how children's schooling is a key arena in which gender and masculinities are being reworked.

For the roughly seven out of ten fathers who do not live with their children, schooling opens up a series of dilemmas and contestations. A father's relationship with a young child is mediated by his relationship with the child's mother. Thobani, a young man of 23, said: 'Fathers argue with the mothers, and then they stop supporting the child.'

However, it is quite common for a child to live with the father's family, in part because marriage has a long association with the passing of rights in children (see below). In these cases, it is very often the paternal grandmother who initiates this move and plays a large role in raising the child. Even if women (mothers, sisters, aunts, and grandmothers) still do much of the daily childcare, however, it is not unusual to find men taking day-to-day responsibility for their children.

Consider Thando, an unmarried 23-year-old man who works in a small spaza (informal) shop and looks after his daughter from a former relationship. His mother, a nurse, works in Durban North, and is one of the few residents I knew who transported a child by car to school. But Thando changes the child's nappies, wakes up with the child at night, and spends a lot of time playing with the child, he told me. Judging from the number of photographs he showed me on his cell phone, he had clearly developed a strong bond with his child. When I asked him what other men said about his caring for his child, he replied: 'Some are saying I am a real man because I managed to pay inhlawulo ['damages' for pregnancy] and also took my child.' This is very different from records of the somewhat distant relations fathers historically had with their children.[41] Although Thando never became umnumzana (head of a household/a gentleman) at the helm of umuzi (homestead/home), his masculine status was boosted when he became a supportive ubaba (father).

In some instances, an unmarried father (sometimes helped by his mother) pays school fees but lives apart from his child's mother. Then, an absent father can form strong paternal bonds even if he does not raise (khulisa) a child on a day-to-day basis. This was seen when Gugu, in her early twenties, discussed in negative terms her father's lack of support, but then in more positive terms the bonds formed when an absent father fundisa-s a child:

GUGU:     If your father left you, then you must forget about him because your
          mother was struggling to raise you. I almost failed my matric
          [secondary-school leaving exam] because my father was not there,
          and I was struggling, and we were living with my mother.
AUTHOR:   What about if your mother didn't fundisa you but you lived with her
          and your father fundisa-ed you?
GUGU:     You have to support both [if you find work].

When fathers are unemployed or in casual work, as many are, they lack amandla (power – namely financial power) to support their children. Additionally, the government's child support grant is supposed to be received by a child's guardian, which is usually the mother. As Gugu suggests, in cases when men provide no support for a child (45 per cent in our survey), this can create intense feelings of resentment in children towards their fathers. This is also seen in daughters' or sons' comments such as 'He does nothing for me' or 'He only brings me chips.' Being cast as isahluleki (a failure) is a crushing reality for many South African men today.

Consider the father of Thembelihle. Thembelihle, who lives in an extended four-room house, attended one of the township's excellent secondary schools and passed her matriculation exam with seven As.

When the television and radio reported her achievements, her father phoned many times to congratulate her, but she refused to answer. He had not supported her in her schooling, and so why should he share in the glory?

So far, I have focused on male–female relations, but, of course, not all people in Umlazi identify as men or women or desire intimate sexual relations with someone of the opposite gender, or, indeed, with anyone at all. The equality clause in South Africa's 1996 constitution bans discrimination on the basis of race, gender, age, disability, and sexual orientation. Legislation made same-sex marriages legal in 2006. However, the 'families of choice' framework that was developed in rich Western countries to challenge heteronormativity is less useful in settings marked by great inequality and poverty.[42]

Ntombi Mthethwa was 20 when I spoke with her. Dressed in blue overalls after a day's employment on a public works programme, she told me that she had mothered a young child with a man who had left the area. She said that she would like to live with her girlfriend and pay *ilobolo* (bridewealth) for her, but that they did not have the resources and worried about the possible stigma they might face. Extreme violence against those with non-normative sexualities is a harsh reality: if historians have now shown the long existence of same-sex relations in the region, the myth remains that such relations are somehow 'un-African'.[43] Thus, Ntombi gave priority to her son's schooling, but she was unable to raise her child with the person she loved.

To further contextualise the fluidity of different intimate arrangements, albeit among male–female couples, the following is a typical course of events when a woman in Umlazi becomes pregnant and her boyfriend has not already made customary payments to the mother-to-be's family. First, the pregnant woman's mother and relatives go to the boyfriend's house to ask for recognition of paternity and *inhlawulo* (a fine or damages, usually the cash equivalent of one cow). A variety of situations, sometimes overlapping and typically unfolding rather than planned, can then occur: a man can deny or accept paternity, he or his family can pay *inhlawulo*, the child's surname can be changed to the father's, the father can provide support, he can give *ilobolo* to marry the woman, and the child can move in with its father's family.

The association between *inhlawulo* and *ilobolo* with fathers' rights over children helps explain why a higher proportion of young African children compared with white children live with their unmarried fathers. Education can justify this move if the father's family has more money to educate the child or if his family lives close to a good school.

Even when parents split up acrimoniously, mothers are often keen to retain links with a child's father. The father of a young woman who has just given birth might oppose his grandchild taking on the name of the boyfriend's family, especially if no *ilobolo* or *inhlawulo* has been given. However, the new mother might see a child taking their father's surname as enhancing links between the child and her boyfriend's family.[44] Mothers' reluctance to sever links with their children's fathers is richly described by both Grace Khunou and Brady G'Sell, and is an important reason why legal claims for child maintenance, supported by changes to the law, are not pursued in many instances.[45]

In addition, a father's links to a child, including through payments of *ilobolo* and *inhlawulo*, are important to appease *amadlozi* (ancestors) and thus ensure the health of the child. Hylton White provides a compelling account of the way in which unemployment wreaks havoc on the ability of individuals to undertake rituals. 'Life cycles and their ritual representations,' he argues, 'are more often out of step than contemporaneous.'[46] Among Umlazi residents, I found that a child's ill-health or an improvement in their health was an important reason for its movement to another house. A child's illness might be said to be the result of *amadlozi* being upset that a child's father did not pay *inhlawulo*; alternatively, *amadlozi* could be upset if children did not stay with their fathers' families. In such discussions, calls on tradition are impossible to separate from modern appeals to act in the best interest of the children. And tradition is also a term that is inherently gendered, as we will see.

### Gender and moralities of schooling choice

There are many examples of fathers funding their children to attend multiracial schools. However, returning to the Mzala family, it is notable how the mothers all strongly advocate multiracial schooling. Nomusa, Philile's 20-year-old daughter, told me that she tried to persuade the father of her child to send their child to a multiracial school, but he argued that 'there is nothing wrong with black schools' and that children attending multiracial schools become cheeky and 'do not respect as much as children who go to black schools'. She continued by emphasising the importance of native English teachers found at multiracial schools.

I want my child to have respect, but I want to give Thandiwe [her daughter] an opportunity in her life. She will be fluent in English when she goes to an interview and can understand everything happening there. If you have good English, you always have a better chance in life.

Although language practices are gendered in complex ways, men's support of isiZulu and women's promotion of English have been noted by Thobekile Dlamini in her study of politeness, language, and gender in *inhlonipho*.[47] *Inhlonipho* (in simple terms, respect) is one of the most powerful concepts in isiZulu. Practices of *inhlonipho* have changed over time, but its essence is that women respect men, and the young respect the old. This can be enacted through certain deferential bodily dispositions and avoidances: for instance, women kneeling when serving men or elders, avoiding certain places in the house, or avoiding certain words in conversation.

The fact that some parents with the means to choose elite schools still choose Umlazi schools shows how schooling decisions are gendered and classed in important ways. School principal Mr Nsimande sent his daughter, Thenjiwe, to a formerly Coloured preschool but then brought her back to the township to attend a primary and high-performing secondary school. Thenjiwe told me that her father had said to her that he saw her cousins leaving the township and losing the ability to speak isiZulu properly and show *inhlonipho* to others.

A parent's own schooling, religion, and income, as well as many other factors, play a part in schooling decisions. However, most residents say that men are more likely than women to portray multiracial schools as undermining *inhlonipho* because they produce cheeky children with a lack of respect for men and elders. In contrast, most mothers with whom I spoke said that multiracial schools posed a threat that can be controlled. IsiZulu is spoken at home, and children can be taught to act with *inhlonipho*.

Mothers can define *inhlonipho* in different ways to fathers. Mothers tend to be less interested in advocating 'traditional' gendered and generational practices and more concerned that a child will retain their sense of *ubuntu*. *Ubuntu*, in this usage, means much more than its common translation in the media as a kind of 'African generosity'. It is fundamentally a relational term referring to humanness, a meaning captured by the phrase *umuntu ngumuntu ngabantu* (a person is a person through other persons).

Indeed, it is this relational meaning of *ubuntu* that is employed to chastise someone as being 'selfish' (often using the English word) or lacking 'Africanness' when they are *fundisa*-ed and then do not support their sponsors. The term used would be *akanabo ubuntu* – the person doesn't have *ubuntu*, or humanness.[48] The 'black tax' in this context has a positive meaning: it represents a moral code that can be contrasted with the perceived selfishness and individualism of white society, or, more specifically, whiteness.

The risk that multiracial schools might break relational ties, including family obligations, is implied by two commonly used terms to rebuke children schooled at formerly white, Coloured, or Indian schools: *uyazitshela* and *uyazifonela* – meaning, respectively, that a person tells themself or phones themself. These insults imply that an individual is becoming disconnected from others.[49] In both cases, the reflexive form of the verb suggests that a person is contravening the relational sense of being *fundisa*-ed: that is, they are forgetting that one's schooling is sponsored by others and for the benefit of more than oneself.

## Conclusions

Umlazi Township was built far from central Durban, some 20 kilometres away. The racial and spatial hierarchies of the past have transmuted into the movements of the present. Almost all children who leave Umlazi for schooling travel north to attend a school in a formerly Indian, Coloured, or white suburb. While a small tier of better-off families left Umlazi to live in these areas, schoolchildren's travel to multiracial schools is both a cause and a consequence of more families not moving out of the township.

Children's schooling interacts in critical ways with changing family dynamics. When children are *khulisa*-ed by multiple people – parents, grandmothers, aunts, siblings, and sometimes uncles – these amount to centrifugal connections that extend out from the child. However, a centripetal force puts the spotlight on parents as the family members with primary responsibility for *fundisa*-ing children: that is, paying their school fees and transport costs. This interweaving of education and social bonds is not new; however, residents can now access a large number of multiracial schools that demand considerable financial resources.

To understand the logic of the 'black tax', we therefore need to begin by revisiting the long history of mothers pushing their children through schools. However, the specific term came to the fore in the 2010s as a relational one disproportionately used by black wage earners who have passed through 'white' spaces – for instance, a formerly white university where they interact with white students whose parents might be providing significant support. The black tax is simultaneously a redundant and politicising term, a sign of familial love and a reminder of racialised structures of inequality. It denotes how black wage earners can straddle different moral and political economies.

It follows that the social backgrounds of children – where and with whom they live, to whom they were born – as well as the practices of schools greatly affect who gets to attend the city's best and worst schools. However, because families are defined as including a wide number of relatives, most Umlazi residents will have a relation who attends or attended a multiracial school. Racial hierarchies that were based on segregation and created a visible enemy – the apartheid state – have transformed into hierarchies reflected in parents 'doing the best' for their children. And most Umlazi residents consider the main attraction of multiracial schools to be not better facilities or higher passer rates but their ability to bestow prestigious cultural dispositions: the geography of forced segregation has transmuted into a geography of the schooling market and of symbolic power. We return to these themes in Chapter 9 to shed further light on the way in which race, class, and gender come together, and the politics this entails.

# 9 Conclusions
## Hegemony on a school bus

Despite the redistribution of state funding to poorer schools, the South African education system remains one of the most unequal in the world. In rural areas, most schools are now 'no-fee' institutions, but they continue to have inadequate facilities and weak connections to formal work. In urban areas, public schools can charge fees anywhere from R100 to R50,000 a year.

I demonstrate in this book how the marketisation of education works as a countervailing force to state redistribution: fees move up the schooling system as scores of learners, black and white, travel daily to attend schools their families perceive as better than local schools.

Governments' attempts around the world to promote 'schooling choice' have attracted considerable attention, albeit with research being largely based in the Global North. *Race for Education* differs from most studies because it emphasises the routine logics and actions of schools and families and therefore challenges the view that schooling marketisation results simply from top-down 'neoliberal' state policy. Moreover, it provides a framework for understanding how gender, race, and families – families here explicitly *not* conceptualised as 'nuclear' – are formative institutions in schooling marketisation.

Drawing on research from Durban, the study recognises the importance of educational qualifications to a person's employability, but it does not stop there. A key argument it makes is that schools today sell powerful symbolic attributes, including language and accent, in the context of an increasingly service-centred economy. Whereas apartheid schooling was based on racial segregation, the schooling market today allows certain groups to buy prestige. Prestige remains associated with configurations of whiteness, and these dynamics help explain why race is not withering away in the schooling system.

The South African case also contributes to what we might call the 'hegemony question' in schooling. Why do subaltern groups not revolt against iniquitous education systems? Published in 1977, Paul Willis's *Learning to Labour* famously studied how working-class 'lads' rebelled against teachers' authority and in doing so consigned themselves to working-class jobs.[1] For Willis, and many other ethnographers of social inequality, a single or several schools became the central institution(s) to be researched. However, in a context when the apartheid state created such huge differences among schools, my method follows the children through Durban's uneven geography. The title of this concluding chapter, 'Hegemony on a school bus', suggests that the movements of children in a marketised system can create a certain amount of social consent. The worse-performing schools have become free and give quantitatively more qualifications to learners. Families with the means can pay for learners to travel to better-performing schools.

This combination of fee-charging quality schools and poor-quality free schools is common in the Global South, and is certainly (if fees are interpreted more widely as costs) the direction of schooling around the world. In South Africa, it provides a prescient window into two key tensions marking the country's transition: the numerical deracialisation, but not fundamental 'de-whitening' of privilege (seen in the classed nature of schooling desegregation and, more widely, in the growth of a multiracial English-speaking (sub)urban middle class); and state efforts to redistribute spending to the poor (seen in the introduction of 'no-fee' schools and in the rise in non-contributory social grants).

I develop these points, first, by summarising South Africa's changing contours of class, race, and gender and by showing how they interact with schooling. I then reflect on the politics of education and, finally, focus on the cultural politics of language, a topic that encapsulates all of these themes and is a prominent one throughout this book.

## Class formation

Apartheid South Africa was an exemplary case of racial capitalism because of its large mining and manufacturing sectors and extreme form of racial segregation. Race and class were one and the same: to be black was to be poor. When growing class divisions emerged among black people from the 1970s onwards, scholars working in the Marxist tradition used labour as a prism through which to view the ways in which race and class 'articulate'. If, after apartheid ended, some on the left raised the spectre of 'class apartheid', David Goldberg's description of 'racial neoliberalism' insists on the formative role of race.[2] However, even this approach does not foreground education, including its interaction with gender and the family.

The most influential study of class formation after apartheid, and for this reason an important point of reference, is Jeremy Seekings and Nicoli Nattrass's *Class, Race, and Inequality in South Africa* (published in 2005 and updated with their 2015 *Policy, Politics, and Poverty in South Africa*).[3] This impressive analysis details rising inequalities from the 1970s and the growth of the black middle class after the end of apartheid.

In conceptualising a 'distributional regime' that derives not only from the labour market but also from social grants, Seekings and Nattrass reveal how state policy blends processes of commodification and decommodification – an analysis that fits well with the schooling system's combination of no-fee public schools (a kind of welfare approach) and high-fee public schools (a market approach).[4]

The most controversial of Seekings and Nattrass's arguments is that there has been a growth in what they label as an 'underclass' (I do not consider controversies surrounding the term 'underclass' itself, just the concept). Seekings and Nattrass argue that households that make up the underclass, almost all of which are 'African', face systematic disadvantages even compared with other poor households, because they have no *wage earner* – that is, no one who can share an income and provide other members with potential assistance to access work. It is not just unemployment that drives inequality, they argue, but a concentration of unemployed people in one household.

A provocative point that Seekings and Nattrass make is that the 'underclass' would particularly benefit from a growth in low-wage employment.[5] Some new labour regulations, they suggest, protect unionised workers at the expense of poorer South Africans – a point hotly contested by scholars who emphasise how wage earners distribute money among poorer family members.[6]

At a general level, my education-focused study supports Seekings and Nattrass's insistence that employment status plays a central role in intergenerational class (im)mobility. I show that educational opportunities are not allocated in a meritocratic way. The quality of education a learner experiences is still largely determined by where they live and by what racial group the school was originally built for. Employment prospects and household income differ across the city and most children living in formerly white suburbs will have at least one parent who is able to finance schooling. It is rarer for children from Umlazi Township to have a parent who is in formal work, although in such instances leaners can travel to access 'multiracial' schools (i.e. formerly Indian, Coloured, and white schools). Thus, at an aggregate level, per capita household income, itself closely related to employment and race, predicts a learner's schooling trajectory.

Yet generalisation obscures a lot of important processes. When I first started research in Umlazi, I was surprised to find a few children emerging from wooden shacks dressed in the uniform of a formerly white, Coloured, or Indian school. Our survey found that three out of ten learners in our survey had studied in these schools for at least one year.

To understand these dynamics, I show the importance of recognising differences *within* and connections *among* households. Seekings and

Nattrass consider links between households through remittances, but in Umlazi we found that educational resources are not shared by families in the same way as items such as food: co-resident children can 'eat from the same pot' but go to very different schools (be *fundisa*-ed differently). No household shares resources equally among members, but we saw that education is earmarked in particular ways. Consequently, when an absent father or mother sends their child to an expensive school, this learner can have vastly improved prospects compared with another learner in the same household. In other words, someone who might later in life become part of the 'underclass' can share a house or shack with someone who might become part of the 'middle class'.

Viewing class formation as comprising *connections* between households complicates a static view of household poverty and its reproduction over generations. I demonstrate that class formation crosses rural–urban areas when, for instance, a rural-based teacher sends a child to live with urban relatives to attend a well-performing school. Moreover, in Umlazi Township, it is not uncommon for children to move from one household to another and/or receive support from outside family members. Although I did not conduct a large survey, I can show reasons for this geography that are common across the country: low marriage rates lead to a situation whereby mothers and fathers live apart, high unemployment means that employment situations vary widely within families, and high migration rates mean that children move considerably within extended families.

As such, considered from the perspective of education, class formation is a fundamentally spatial process. The schooling market propels this movement: it pulls better-off children into urban areas, and it encourages relatives living outside a child's household, especially parents, to earmark resources for their child's schooling. Because the census takes a snapshot of society, it is unable to capture the ways in which schooling connects households in such ways.

We consider later the relationship between families and the politics of schooling, but a further point follows immediately from the above: that gender is much more central to processes of class formation than most accounts (including Seekings and Nattrass's) suggest. I showed in Chapter 3 the long-standing emphasis mothers placed on schooling. Today, in many parts of the country, marriage rates are low and most children do not live with both of their parents. Moreover, learners interact with an education system that is gendered to the core, whether in schools' macho competition or the single-sexed structure of elite schools.

*Race for Education* therefore highlights how a learner's schooling path results from multiple interacting processes that are gendered, raced, and classed, in a society where schools themselves are in flux. The school a person attends can be shaped by the employment patterns of the child's mother and father, connections with outside family members, migration events, the child's own agency, and much more. Indeed, a female member of a household where no one is employed – that is, a person who Seekings and Nattrass would call part of the 'underclass' – might mother a child with a better-off man who then goes on to send the child to a multiracial school (and, later in life, the child might support the mother's household). While mothers are more likely to sponsor a child's schooling, fathers can play an important role, such as when they pay for a child's school fees, when the child moves in with its paternal grandmother, or when a deceased father's life insurance pays for schooling.

The extent to which such patterns of intergenerational class mobility occur (and, of course, the labour market has always enabled a small number of children from poor households to access high-paid work) should not, however, be exaggerated. Partnership patterns do not occur in a random way: for instance, working men and women are disproportionally likely to marry one another. Moreover, a poor female shack dweller is more likely to find a father who can support his children in an urban than a rural area, and this perpetuates rural–urban divides (for Seekings and Nattrass, the underclass is primarily located in rural areas).

## The limits of qualifications

Historically, black people were most excluded from schooling, but we need to remember that, until relatively recently, university education was rare for most whites, especially women and the working class. Today, although children's schooling pathways are somewhat unpredictable, children born to parents with a relatively high income tend to exit the schooling system with the most credentials/qualifications. However, I place a significant emphasis in this book on the basic maths whereby schooling credentials such as 'matric' are devalued the more people have them. This truism often eludes policymakers, or is ignored by them.

Consider Minister Gigaba's announcement in February 2018 that the state would commit resources to fund free higher education for the poor. In stating that 'unemployment is lowest for tertiary graduates' he repeated the commonly held view that a quantitative increase in schooling will reduce the rate of unemployment.[7] Of course, countries with higher-skilled populations tend to be more economically prosperous. But it needs to be noted that the rapid expansion of schooling in South Africa over the last 40 years has done little to promote equality, raise education standards, or increase economic growth. The reality is that employers use qualifications, in part, to screen large pools of applicants, and that this accounts for much of the association between qualifications, work opportunities, and pay.

Decentring credentials in this way leads us to conclude that no-fee (decommodified) schools do not provide an inherent benefit to the poor when it comes to finding work. While a generation ago a matriculation certificate might have secured someone a job, today it probably won't even lead to an interview. I am not, of course, arguing against the expansion of education, and certainly not free education. But I insist that education shapes, and is shaped by, society in ways that still remain poorly understood. Education is fundamentally different from a policy issue such as housing because a housing market does not lessen the benefits of state-provided housing, or at least not in a simple way: a roof is a roof. In contrast, the value of a qualification depends on how many other people have the same qualification.

If accessing qualifications is necessary, but not always sufficient, in finding work, what else matters? It has long been noted that individuals with particular social connections can gain advantages in finding work (Seekings and Nattrass note that someone gains social capital when they live with an employed person). In this book I show the importance of schooling in creating social links. After 1991, 'traditional' white schools were no longer the preserve of the white upper-middle classes. Black and working-class white students – that is, groups previously barred or under-represented – can now become part of this exclusive world. Indeed, the 'up-classing' of working-class whites through schooling is shown in the comment by one family that their son was entering a 'Harry Potter school'.

A related theme in the book is that schools provide cultural dispositions or symbolic power that can advantage certain students. Today, residents of Umlazi Township give a main motivation for sending children to multiracial schools as accessing English through native English teachers. The 7 per cent of public schools that were all-white bestow particularly powerful cultural dispositions, especially a learner's 'white' English accent. Durban also has a large number of English-medium formerly Indian schools where many black Africans study, in part because Indian learners 'move up' into formerly white schools.

Considering the world of work, I gave the example of telephone call centres in Durban – one of the fastest-growing industries in recent years – that require only a basic matriculation pass. Service-sector employers such as call centres see English as vital to communication, and employers in all sectors use English to screen multiple applicants for work.

As already noted, higher-income families living in Umlazi are the most likely group to send their children to schools outside the township. To overcome apartheid's legacy, their fundamental imperative is to promote class mobility, a move signified by accessing previously segregated 'multiracial' and especially 'white' schools. In a society fresh from institutionalised racial domination, intergenerational mobility (that is, the social mobility of children) can propel intragenerational social mobility (the social mobility of parents). The so-called 'black tax' is a glue that bonds the two together. The term became widely used in the early 2010s, just prior to the upsurge of student protests, to highlight the pressure to support families faced by black workers, and to suggest that white people do not have the same burdens. It is an intersectional term, showing that race and class must always be thought of together, but one that also anchors discussions within the family.

If black learners generally travel north and west, white children can either stay in local schools or attend – and sometimes be lured into through scholarships – the country's most expensive and illustrious schools. Yet not all white families are advantaged in the schooling market. Popular schools with the greatest ability to choose learners can view single mothers as a potential liability, a job loss away from claiming fee exemptions. In these cases, however, white learners tend to benefit from family and community networks to operationalise a 'back-up plan'. Moreover, if a significant number of white households have long been made up of three or more generations, such family types are more common today; grandparents also help look after schoolchildren and transport them to school.

We now turn in more detail to how race has been delinked from institutionalised segregation and tied to cultural/symbolic power.

### Race after Mandela

This study of education shows how race is formative of class and vice versa and therefore rejects the common narrative that society simply moved from race to class apartheid. I focus mostly on the politics of race in the schooling system, rather than on racial violence, which remains a reality in South Africa. I use the term *racial modernism* to denote the early apartheid period when many new schools were built in segregated suburbs and townships. The Bluff's white children attended well-funded local schools and moved into protected jobs. Umlazi's learners attended underfunded primary schools in demarcated sections of the township.

From the 1970s, class differentiation among parents and the rising status of English laid the groundwork for what I call *marketised assimilation*. From 1976, a small number of black children with 'the ability to be assimilated' were admitted into private white schools. Some Umlazi learners, we saw, also travelled to attend excellent secondary schools that emphasised the importance of mastering English. Processes of class formation and the cultural grammar of privilege created the conditions for an occurrence that surprised many commentators in the early 1990s: most white parents voted to desegregate public schools. Indeed, in Durban, white parents could easily have chosen to send their children to all-white Afrikaans schools; instead, Afrikaans-speaking learners drifted into English-medium schools.

This loose periodisation allows me to foreground the era of the *racialised market* from the late 1990s. In this period, white, as well as black, learners began to move extensively across the city for schooling. The value schools and parents placed on 'white tone' intensified.

The continued association between prestige and whiteness means that phenotype has not lost its importance in society: schools can openly court white-identified learners because 'demographics' mark a school's fidelity to past standards and privileges. In other words, apartheid's four racial categories are kept alive when a child's perceived phenotypic traits – be they skin colour or hair texture – continue to be used to interpret whether a child is 'white', 'Indian', 'Coloured', or 'African'. Critics of affirmative action policies like to blame the state for continuing to use and thus reify these categories, but I show how they are integral to the workings of the schooling market.

However, racial classification is not as exact as it was at the height of apartheid. A school today can retain a white image if white parents are dominant at the ritual morning drop-off, even if their children might be 'mixed-race'. Apartheid's 'pencil test' is no longer used to exclude non-whites from school on the basis of whether or not their hair is straight – although 'white hair' remains valued in the education market.

Moreover, because whiteness and white people have become increasingly delinked, any learner who is seen as a potential asset to a school might be offered a scholarship or bursary. This includes a star black rugby player who might enhance a school's prestige. It includes a brilliant black student who can help brand the school as retaining 'first-world' academic standards.

It follows from the above that schooling is central to the ways in which class and race are being reformulated. In the early apartheid era, being middle class would have increased the chances of a person being classified as 'white' rather than 'Coloured'. However, today a person's class is no longer simply a means by which they are inserted into the straight-jacket of race. A prestigious school can choose to admit a black student from a high-earning family rather than a white student who lives with a single mother. This situation is gendered in other ways: girls' schools compete less aggressively, now charge lower fees, and have desegregated in a less uneven way.

Specifically, I develop the concept of 'white tone' to make three conceptual moves. First, I use it to show how formerly white schools came to market themselves on the basis of their whiteness. Second, I use it to show how cultural attributes gained at school – for instance, a 'white accent' – can be rewarded (or not) in society. White tone is, at its loosest, a relational term used to capture continuities and changes in cultural prestige – and to emphasise that these are not colour-blind. Third, I use it to reflect the entangled meanings of race and class in colonial societies, where being rich can be partially coded as being white.

White tone is always changing. The fact that black people speak 'white' English at formerly white schools changes the meaning of whiteness and blackness, and much more. The rapid growth of a black middle class works to both uphold and undermine aspects of whiteness.

## The balance of forces

This book does not lay out neat policy recommendations but aims to dissect the power-laden processes that rework the schooling system. Formerly white schools rooted in the British private school model continue to present themselves as neutral custodians of modernity and standards. Although they are quick to criticise government interference, they have largely retained the power to administer admissions they have long enjoyed. The partial exception is in Gauteng Province, where a centralised admissions system has been introduced. Revealingly, however, this intervention was reportedly designed to challenge the power of overwhelmingly white Afrikaans schools rather than English-medium schools. Whereas in the apartheid era Afrikaner nationalists promoted Afrikaans-only schools, the black middle class is heavily invested in English-medium schools.

One important development after apartheid has been the rapid growth of two education corporations, Advtech and Curro, which have driven a significant, though not spectacular, rise in the number of for-profit schools (and, in the case of Advtech, also the rise of labour brokers). These businesses benefit directly from the perceived failures of the public system, failures they and the media are only too happy to publicise. In recent years, the Centre for Development Enterprise has repeatedly made the case that so-called 'low-fee' private schools are viable alternatives to dysfunctional public schools.[8] This book, however, shows that the public education system is already thoroughly marketised, with disastrous consequences for social equality. South African schools' ability to charge fees already sets them apart from public schools around the world that remain publicly funded but compete in a 'quasi-market'.

But does the state have the financial ability and inclination to drive improvements in public education? If inspectors (or circuit managers, as they are now called) have been downgraded to 'postmen', if state entities have been 'captured' by shady forces, does this suggest that the state lacks the capacity to intervene? Some parts of the media put a great deal of blame on the teachers' union SADTU for the government's failures to implement education policy. Supporting this position, several principals of Umlazi's excellent schools told me that SADTU's 'deployment' of favoured people into top education jobs is undermining the tradition of excellent schools. However, it is also true that SADTU, established in 1990, was a latecomer to South Africa's union world.[9] The basic structure of the unequal education system was already in place.

Today, the social movement Equal Education is the most prominent political force fighting for the redistribution of educational resources. It is still a relatively small movement, but it has used the courts and taken to the streets to improve the infrastructure of poor schools and bring attention to the long distances rural learners walk to school, among other issues. However, in the main, there are few groups making the case for the huge injection of funding into poor schools that is necessary to improve infrastructure such as electricity and toilets, facilities including computer labs and libraries, and the quality of teaching. Unless significant funding is provided, children and their school fees will continue to be pulled up the system to richer schools, thus undermining the government's redistribution efforts.

Furthermore, the tendency of children in Durban to move to schools to the north and west shows how schooling hierarchies rest on and reify spatial injustices rooted in apartheid segregation. Countrywide, the poorest schools remain located in rural areas, and the richest schools are to be found in affluent, leafy suburbs. The Education Department's 2012 proposal to end zoning in KwaZulu-Natal was fought against by the middle class; poorer South Africans were largely excluded from these debates.

At the same time, South Africa's social geography contains its own contradictions. Domestic workers, who wash, clothe, and clean for privileged families, can fight for their own children (sometimes with their employers' support) to access good local schools. Moreover, shack settlements can be located near excellent schools to which some residents successfully demand access (although we return below to the case of Isipingo's shack dwellers). At the Kennedy Road settlement, where *Abahlali baseMjondolo* (the shack dwellers' movement) was founded, over time parents fought to access local (formerly Indian) schools for their children.[10]

## Politics and consent

The picture painted above is one of socially dominant groups having a strong stake in the continuation of the country's unequal schooling system. A question that needs to be asked is why more learners and parents have not taken to the streets to demand better schooling. Why do South Africans rank education policy more positively than state policy on electricity, water, sanitation, healthcare, HIV/AIDS, and affordable housing?[11]

For an insight into this question, consider the case of the shack dwellers who were removed from the Bluff and dumped in the dangerous 'transit camp' at Isipingo. The road blockade and other protests carried out by the Isipingo community have likely been added to a database on 'service delivery protests' to boost South Africa's status as the 'protest capital of the world'.[12] Taking to the streets probably did speed up residents' access to formal housing.

However, we saw that this community once lived only a few minutes' walk from a well-resourced Bluff primary school. Had their children attended this school they would have enjoyed small classes, used a well-stocked library, and become fluent in English. Yet, the vast majority of residents left their children with family members in rural parts of the Eastern Cape and KwaZulu-Natal provinces. The nearby formerly white school, afraid of taking in poor black students who might not pay its fees, rebutted the few inquiries from poor parents. Admissions material was printed only in English. These barriers meant that shack dwellers were unable to take advantage of – and, in many cases, were unaware of the existence of – laws requiring that schools give fee exemptions to the poor. A few parents had enrolled their children in local schools in Isipingo, but as the settlement was supposed to be temporary, no new schools were built.

Despite these disadvantages, however, children from this community will still probably be schooled to a higher level than their parents and grandparents. Most, in fact, will attend 'no-fee' schools. For those who remember apartheid schooling, gaining a matriculation pass for free is an improvement – and more than 400,000 people now pass this exam every year. This suggests that, for now, the structure of the education system is redirecting social struggles away from basic education towards disputes over 'service delivery' and higher education (where fees are charged, although financial aid looks set to expand greatly). Whether this will remain the case in the future is difficult to predict.

However, there are other reasons why calls for 'people's education' in the 1980s were allowed to give way, with seemingly few protests directed towards basic education, to a market system shot through with inequalities. In a marketised system, learners themselves or their parents can be blamed if children are not admitted to a desirable school. 'The student didn't work hard enough.' 'They didn't train properly in rugby.' 'The parents have a bad record of paying fees.' 'They live too far away.' Once admitted, the logic extends to 'Why should the school's matriculation pass rates suffer because you don't follow the rules?'

As noted, children raised under the same roof can 'eat from the same pot' but learn at vastly different schools. From the perspective of poor communities, the face of class inequality might not be a rich businessman driving a deluxe car – or even a corrupt councillor protected by armed guards. It might be your brother, sister, or cousin. Even very poor black

South Africans are likely to have a family member, albeit perhaps a distant one, who has been able to access a fee-paying school from which they were barred under apartheid: namely, a formerly white, Indian, or Coloured school.

If jealousies and feelings of resentment are part of everyday family life, family members also see a relative who obtains an elite education as someone who might provide future financial support or help in finding work. It is common for wages from one person who succeeds educationally to help other family members. At certain times this can become politicised as a 'black tax', but in everyday life it is also experienced as a mark of humanity, love, and care.

Yet there is another mechanism legitimising inequalities in society that has been prominent in this book, and that is symbolic power – a mechanism we consider below through language.

## The cultural politics of language

The Negro of the Antilles will be proportionately whiter – that is, he will come closer to being a real human being – in direct ratio to his mastery of the French language.        Frantz Fanon, *Black Skin, White Masks*[13]

When Afrikaner nationalists gained political power in 1948, they implemented policies to raise the status of Afrikaans in relation to English, the socially dominant (and other official) language. Simultaneously, apartheid policy forced black Africans into separate Bantustans where they were taught in one of nine African languages. In demarcating these ethnolinguistic boundaries, officials built on a long colonial history: from the nineteenth century, missionaries had compiled the first African-language dictionaries, and in doing so helped create these languages. Bantu education therefore enforced African languages in schools but devalued them in wider society.

All postcolonial states face the dilemma of whether to promote or downgrade the colonial language. A strategy followed by Indonesia after it gained independence was to promote Indonesian (a standardised form of Malay) in opposition to the colonial language of Dutch. In South Africa, one important early proposal, put forward by Neville Alexander, was to harmonise the nine African languages into two mutually intelligible groups (Sotho and Nguni).[14] However, this initiative and attempts to intellectualise African languages – for instance through developing African-language literature in the way that was done for Afrikaans – received little traction within the government. Afrikaans lost its special status, and English became the 'first among equals'.

In many respects, therefore, South Africa followed the familiar postcolonial path whereby the colonial language retained high prestige in society. This parallels the situation in North African countries such as Morocco and Tunisia, where elites remain heavily invested in French despite an official policy of Arabisation. And it resonates with the large number of English-speaking postcolonies from Zimbabwe to Ghana.

What made South Africa somewhat different is that its mineral wealth attracted a large settler population, and this engendered a particular politics. Since the founding of South Africa's liberation movement in 1912, and especially after the 1976 Soweto Uprising, many within the liberation movement saw English as a means to overcome the state's 'divide and rule' ethnic strategy. Afrikaans, a creole language spoken at home by large groups of black people (and, in the Cape, especially by the Coloured community), could be cast as the language of white Afrikaner oppression. Moreover, from the 1970s onwards, a group of better-off township families began to send their children to the best township and mission schools that promoted English, as well as to private white schools. After apartheid, this path accelerated when white public schools opened their doors to black students. The status of English was further boosted with the shift among Afrikaans-speaking white families towards English-medium schools. In the world of work, the rise of the service economy consolidated English as the language of business, trade, and consumption.

It is important to note, however, that learners in impoverished schools are not simply taught 'incorrect' English; they speak less prestigious English. Learners and teachers creatively adapt English on an ongoing basis, but 'black' English can be read by groups in social power as English littered with 'errors'.[15] What the post-apartheid state's advocacy of multilingualism did, therefore, was to add nine African languages to the two previously official languages, English and Afrikaans, and allow English to become the first among equals – with 'white English' having the most prestige.

In the political realm, the politics of English burst onto the scene in 2015 when students challenged higher education institutions to decolon-ise education. Within the student movement itself, however, divisions emerged between those attending historically white universities and those attending historically black universities – institutions where there are longer traditions of students challenging fee hikes. This was the context in which Melo Magolego wrote (as quoted earlier): 'An accent serves as a visa to opportunity but also a passport boldly asserting your origins. That is to say, a model-C accent is a passport asserting you [are] one of the coconut bourgeoisie.'[16]

Here, Magolego is underlining how the education system allocates unequally not just academic credentials but symbolic attributes. The term 'model C school', which started as a bland administrative concept, came to denote a formerly white middle-class English school. Outwardly colour-blind, the phrase exemplifies how whiteness was delinked from state-backed segregation and tethered to middle-class English cultural forms.

Indeed, even if a learner from a rural area passes the matriculation exam and has a good command of English, they will find it hard to obtain work in a service-oriented economy. When qualifications are devalued, and service work is in the ascendancy, employers see middle-class 'white' English (and, to a lesser extent, Coloured and Indian English) as indexing certain skills and as a way to screen multiple applicants. What we have today, therefore, is a system in which African languages continue to be devalued, and English skills and accent – accessed through money and schools – increasingly play a role in perpetuating inequalities.

However, to say that 'white' English benefits anyone who accesses it is not to say that everyone benefits equally. By the 2010s, some of the 'born free' generation had passed through formerly white schools from pre-school to university. In these institutions, they could be positioned as second-class citizens in the corridors of whiteness. Panashe Chigumadzi writes: 'Coconuts [people who are black on the outside and white on the inside] are of course privileged socio-economically by this very proximity to whiteness. That is the Rainbow Nation that we live in. And yet, it is those experiences of whiteness as a system and as a physical embodiment in our teachers and classmates that cause us pain.'[17] If the black middle class is sewn into the fabric of 'white tone', this group also contains some of its loudest critics.

This book has shown how these changes and contestations over language work themselves out in a schooling system characterised by a *racialised market.* When fees travel up the system to formerly white schools, this places resources in institutions that uphold the power of middle-class 'white' English. Class and race inequalities become fused in mundane, everyday speech. And the lines of prestige remain stubborn when the most prestigious schools connect students to the most influential jobs. However, this book has also shown cracks and challenges to schooling hierarchies, not only from high-profile student protests but in townships and everyday disputes over language.

I turn for insights into cultural struggles to Italian Marxist Antonio Gramsci, who was deeply involved in debates over Russia's and Italy's national languages. Gramsci was born in 1891 in Sardinia, an island marginalised economically and culturally from mainland Italy. He was acutely aware that what became the 'standard' Italian language disadvantaged those who spoke more rural dialects and languages. (The naming of a linguistic variety as a 'dialect' or 'language' is itself loaded.[18]) Language use was a way in which children from privileged backgrounds '"breathe in," as the expression goes, a whole quantity of notions and attitudes which facilitate the educational process properly speaking'.[19]

Gramsci famously used the concept of hegemony to draw attention to the cultural basis of 'specific distributions of power and influence'.[20] However, less well known is that his first significant engagement with the term 'hegemony' was when he trained at university as a linguist, where the word was being used as a synonym for linguistic 'prestige'.[21] This sense must be kept in mind when reading the statement that, without 'prestige', a ruling class 'might be incapable of establishing its hegemony, hence of founding a state'.[22]

Aware that the ruling class used the standardisation of Italian as a means to cement their power, Gramsci encouraged his own children to learn Sardinian.[23] However, he questioned the extent to which local dialects could provide the tools to challenge prestige in society because they had a 'limited and provincial' conception of the world.[24] He was also critical of the use of the artificially created language Esperanto (based on words common to most European languages) to potentially join subaltern groups, because it was created outside people's everyday lives.[25] Peter Ives writes that, for Gramsci, 'The creation of a truly common language requires the interaction and creative engagement among those who speak the diverse dialects, the elements of which will be transformed into a new language and worldview'.[26] Gramsci therefore recognised the national language as a living entity, but he wanted to reflect subaltern groups' – and not just elites' – ways of living and talking.

If we substitute English for Italian, we can see that struggles similar to those Gramsci described are an integral part of South Africa's history. For black South Africans, social and political advancement necessitated the use of the colonial language, but this never happened in a straightforward or uncontested way. In the early twentieth century, all schooling could be cast as a 'thing of the whites'. Today, the term 'coconut' is a derogatory term but one that can be reclaimed, as noted by Panache Chigumadzi in the context of university protests.

These contested dynamics play out in the world of work. 'White' English might secure a person a job at a telephone call centre, a restaurant, or elsewhere in the growing service sector. However, in a context in which English is a second language for most South Africans, the negative connotations of 'white' English can also influence the hiring process. The government is a significant employer in the country, and, as one young person told me, managers might give preference to someone with 'comrade speak'.

Indeed, University of the Witwatersrand linguist Leketi Makalela argues that second-language English accents (L2 accents) are becoming more acceptable in certain spheres, including radio shows, the topic of one of his studies.[27] In turn, Rajend Mesthrie, based at the University of Cape Town, has shown that black African women are leading adopters

of what used to be 'white South African English' and are changing the
dialect along the way.[28]

To overcome language hierarchies, Makalela argues for an approach
he calls '*ubuntu* translanguaging'. The term 'translanguaging' is used in
linguistics to go beyond 'multilingual' approaches that can reiterate the
artificial separation of languages. *Ubuntu* here – a concept that, as noted
earlier, implies interconnected lives – is used to underscore how fixed,
bounded languages are not natural but rooted in colonial domination.[29]
For Makalela, attaining a linguistic democracy requires different Englishes to blend in a less hierarchical fashion and undermine the authority
of British Standard (or 'white') English.[30] And doing this cannot be
separated from efforts to promote African languages.

Thus, this translanguaging framework simultaneously disturbs linguistic essentialism – the policing of boundaries around languages – and
challenges hierarchies among dialects and languages. It recognises the
importance of African languages but argues that subordinate groups will
not benefit by being cut off from English. It is consistent with the view
that the schooling system should provide fluency in English but that this
must go hand in hand with raising the status of the English spoken by
poorer people (i.e. not 'white English') and increasing the prestige of
African languages.

The need to challenge the forces that lead to linguistic essentialism and
hierarchisation are echoed to some extent in the study of race. This book
has shown how schooling has been formative of and formed by the twin
processes of racialism (race-thinking, or organising society into racial
groups) and racism (organising racial groups into hierarchies).
Nonracialism, if understood as challenging the conception of separate
races (racialism), cannot take place without interventions to end racial
hierarchies (anti-racism). How this might happen is not just a philosoph-
ical question but one that must consider the concrete worlds in which
race exists. This book reveals how racial segregation is no longer the
principal force shaping racial hierarchies; the market plays a paramount
role. Like struggles over English, these are contested in multiple realms,
whether organised by social movements such as Equal Education, or in
everyday life.

To date, formerly white institutions have attracted overriding attention
in discussions on the decolonisation of schooling. However, I want to
end this book by returning to Umlazi's 'excellent' schools. These remain
overcrowded institutions that charge fees of only a few hundred rand a
year – 50 times less than formerly white schools. Yet, in Umlazi, the
names of schools that once were great, some of which are still excellent,
are well known to residents: Umlazi Commercial, Menzi, Zwelibanzi,
Vukuzakhe, Velabahleka, Ogwini, and Comtech.

The best Umlazi schools promoted and still promote English alongside isiZulu. Their discipline and attention to the basics of schooling challenge the association between excellence and whiteness. If formerly white schools are now asked to mentor township schools, why does the reverse not take place? Why are more resources not being channelled into creating or maintaining excellent multilingual schools in poor areas? As it stands, poor people are gaining more educational qualifications but remain distant from social and economic worlds of power.

# Appendix 1  A note on quantitative and survey data

### Durban Schooling Data

What I call 'Durban Schooling Data' draws from statistics collected by the Department of Education for each school in Umlazi Education District. This district, one of 12 in the province of KwaZulu-Natal, includes schools from most of the city excluding its western parts. It is thus a divergent district and, because of its urban character, a relatively high-performing one. These data, available for selected years, allow for an analysis of schools' racial breakdown, fees, and matriculation pass rates, among other variables.

Merged with these data is the 2000 School Register of Needs Survey prepared by the Developmental Policy Research Unit, which was accessed through DataFirst at the University of Cape Town. This provides information on a school's racial classification under apartheid and its number of state and 'governing body' teachers (the latter paid from school fees).

Thus, the source I call 'Durban Schooling Data' refers to the 441 schools in Umlazi Educational District, although data were not available for every school, making the actual sample smaller depending on the variable being explored (the biggest gap was for data on fees, which were absent in 29 per cent of schools). The number of schools these data cover, according to the former departments, are: Department of Education and Training – 24; KwaZulu – 177 (these two data sets were merged to comprise 'formerly African schools'; the former were 'black' schools located in 'white' areas, and the latter schools located in the KwaZulu homeland); the formerly white House of Assembly – 75; the formerly Indian House of Delegates – 142; the formerly Coloured House of Representatives – 23. The study excluded 12 'new Education Department' schools, which were a mixed group of renamed schools, merged schools, and newly established schools. Using this data set, key attributes of Durban's public schools are given below (Table A1.1).

Table A1.1 *Key attributes of Durban's schools by former racial classification*

|  | Formerly African | Formerly White | Formerly Indian | Formerly Coloured |
| --- | --- | --- | --- | --- |
| **Number of schools** | 201 | 75 | 142 | 23 |
| **Average annual fees of fee-charging schools, 2012** | R201 | R9,767 | R973 | R854 |
| **Average number of privately paid teachers, 2000** | 0.6 | 9.4 | 1.4 | 1.3 |
| **Average matriculation pass rate, 2014** | 59% | 91% | 70% | 83% |
| **Percentage legacy segregated, 1999/2012 (percentage of learners who are of the 'race' the school was built for)** | 100% / 100% | 47% / 26% | 59% / 38% | 40% / 27% |

## Household and Schooling Survey

What I call the 'Household and Schooling Survey' was specifically designed for this study. This collected information on the composition of households, household income, members' occupation and schooling history, the financing of schooling, and the relationship status of parents, among other variables. It had two aims. First, its data were drawn upon during qualitative interviews, for instance when asking about the schooling of household members. Second, data were analysed statistically and using GIS tools, for instance to show the number and location of children from Umlazi attending 'multiracial' schools outside the township.

The survey comprised 231 households: 122 in Umlazi, 75 on the Bluff, and 37 in the formerly Indian township of Merebank. Because of its relatively small size, I treat the survey results as illustrative only, and always seek to verify findings using interviews and other sources.

The book focuses primarily on families living in an area built for whites (the Bluff) and black Africans (Umlazi Township). Employment rates are much higher on the Bluff and many residents are available only at the weekend or in the evening; I and my research assistant (who lived in the area) primarily used word of mouth and the 'snowball' technique (one interview leading to another) to recruit informants. I interviewed white and black Bluff families but utilise survey data primarily from the latter. This is because black families have generally moved quite recently onto the Bluff; this made it difficult, for instance, to compare the effects of schooling on life paths. White Bluff families constituted only 20 of the surveyed households (although I interviewed an extra seven) and so

Table A1.2 *Summary of Housing and Schooling Survey in Umlazi*

| Type of housing | Number of households sampled in survey | Number of households with children attending school | Number of children attending school | Percentage of schooling time spent in outside school |
|---|---|---|---|---|
| **Four-roomed** | 74 | 39 | 93 | 25 |
| **Private** | 10 | 8 | 21 | 32 |
| **Informal** | 38 | 21 | 41 | 17 |
| **Total** | 122 | 68 | 155 | 24 |

I draw heavily on interviews and correspondence with families that took place over a five-year period.

The Umlazi survey had a higher sample size and a better sample method, and I draw on its findings with more confidence than those from the Bluff. The specific research area, centred on two streets and adjoining settlements, was close to where my research assistant lived. Its boundaries were chosen because it has three common housing types in roughly similar proportions to their presence in the township as a whole: original four-roomed houses, many now extended (74 surveyed); privately built larger houses constructed in the 1980s and 1990s (10 surveyed); and informal housing or shacks that mushroomed in the 1980s and 1990s (38 surveyed). Figures on the number of people living in privately built housing in Umlazi are not available, but in Johannesburg's Soweto Township they accommodate 11 per cent of Sowetans according to Alexander et al.'s *Class in Soweto* (p. 68). According to 2011 census data, 21 per cent of households live in informal settlements in the Umlazi section where the survey was conducted.

Of the 122 surveyed households in Umlazi, 68 contained school-going children; this amounted to 155 children currently attending primary and secondary school, 47 of whom had attended school outside the township (pre-schools are not considered). Of these 47 children, 30 had attended only schools outside Umlazi, whereas 17 had mixed inside and outside schooling; interviews were able to probe why these patterns occurred. Because we conducted extensive interviews, most of the 122 surveyed houses were chosen for interviews. In both areas, a small monetary 'thank you' for participation was given.

A summary of the Umlazi households and their schooling is given below (Table A1.2). 'Percentage of schooling time spent in outside school' is the number of years a student spent in outside schools as a proportion of their total years of schooling; this captures the ability of families to send their children to outside schools for a sustained period of time, rather than, say, for a single year.

### GIS and census data

Geographical information system (GIS) data on the location of schools and boundaries of suburbs were attained from eThekwini Municipality's website. All 2011 census data were accessed through Supercross software, a copy of which was provided by Statistics South Africa. The 2011 census's small area layer (SAL) data were used to map residential desegregation.

# Notes

## Chapter 1

1 Figures taken from 'Durban Schooling Data' outlined in Appendix 1.

2 African National Congress, '1994 national election manifesto', www.anc.org.za/content/1994-national-elections-manifesto (accessed 9 January 2017).

3 'Achille Mbembe on the state of South African political life', *Africa Is a Country*, 19 September 2015, http://africasacountry.com/2015/09/achille-mbembe-on-the-state-of-south-african-politics (accessed 9 January 2017). On Fanon and South African students, see Nigel Gibson, 'The specter of Fanon: the student movements and the rationality of revolt in South Africa', *Social Identities* 23, no. 5 (2017), pp. 579–99.

4 Panashe Chigumadzi, 'Of coconuts, consciousness and Cecil John Rhodes', speech, 14th Annual Ruth First Memorial Lecture, University of the Witwatersrand, Johannesburg, 17 August 2015, www.journalism.co.za/wp-content/uploads/2015/08/Ruth-First-FINAL-Draft-_-Panashe-Chigumadzi .pdf (accessed 9 January 2017).

5 'Racism row over South Africa school's alleged hair policy', *The Guardian*, 29 August 2016, www.theguardian.com/world/2016/aug/29/south-africa-pre toria-high-school-for-girls-afros (accessed 14 September 2016); Ra'eesa Pather, 'Sans Souci Girls' High allowed discrimination, says Western Cape education department', *Mail & Guardian*, 10 January 2017, http://mg.co.za/ article/2017-01-10-sans-souci-girls-high-allowed-discrimination-western-cape-education-department (accessed 14 September 2016).

6 On attempts to theorise race–class connections, see Stuart Hall, 'Race, articulation and societies structured in dominance' in *Sociological Theories: race and colonialism* (London: UNESCO, 1980); Deborah Posel, 'Rethinking the "race–class debate" in South African historiography', *Social Dynamics* 9, no. 1 (1983), pp. 50–66; Harold Wolpe, *Race, Class and the Apartheid State* (Trenton NJ: Africa World Press, 1990 [1988]). Steven Friedman's recent book on Harold Wolpe offers an extensive review of the race–class debate. This includes a discussion of Wolpe's turn to viewing education in the 1990s as a terrain of class–race struggle – influenced by Jonathan Hyslop's work and cut short by Wolpe's death in 1996. See Steven Friedman, *Race, Class and Power: Harold Wolpe and the radical critique of apartheid* (Pietermaritzburg: University of KwaZulu-Natal Press, 2015). Important empirical books on race–class

dynamics in South Africa (educational work will be considered later) include Owen Crankshaw, *Race, Class and the Changing Division of Labour under Apartheid* (London: Routledge, 1997); Jeremy Seekings and Nicoli Nattrass, *Class, Race, and Inequality in South Africa* (New Haven CT: Yale University Press, 2005); Peter Alexander et al., *Class in Soweto* (Pietermaritzburg: University of KwaZulu-Natal Press, 2013); Roger Southall, *The New Black Middle Class in South Africa* (Johannesburg: Jacana Press, 2016).

It was black feminist scholars who pioneered 'intersectionality' approaches that foregrounded gender in addition to race and class. See Patricia Hill Collins, 'Learning from the outsider within: the sociological significance of black feminist thought', *Social Problems* 33, no. 6 (1986), pp. 14–32; Kimberlé Crenshaw, 'Demarginalizing the intersection of race and sex: a black feminist critique of antidiscrimination doctrine, feminist theory, and antiracist politics', *University of Chicago Legal Forum* (1989), pp. 139–67. Shireen Hassim's work on women's organisations in South Africa is an invaluable guide to gender, race, and nationalism in South Africa See Shireen Hassim, *Women's Organizations and Democracy in South Africa: contesting authority* (Madison WI: University of Wisconsin Press, 2006).

7  For a recent overview of the United States' race–class literature, see David Roediger, *Class, Race, and Marxism* (London: Verso, 2017).

8  On class apartheid, see Patrick Bond, 'From racial to class apartheid: South Africa's frustrating decade of freedom', *Monthly Review* 55, no. 10 (2004), pp. 45–59.

9  David Goldberg, *The Threat of Race: reflections on racial neoliberalism* (Oxford: Blackwell, 2009).

10  David Harvey, *A Brief History of Neoliberalism* (Oxford: Oxford University Press, 2007); Wendy Brown, *Undoing the Demos: neoliberalism's stealth revolution* (New York NY: Zone Books, 2015), p. 30. Other scholars, in addition to David Goldberg, place emphasis on how race shapes neoliberalism. See Ruth Wilson Gilmore, 'Fatal couplings of power and difference: notes on racism and geography', *Professional Geographer* 54, no. 1 (2002), pp. 15–24; Joshua Inwood, 'Neoliberal racism: the "Southern Strategy" and the expanding geography of white supremacy', *Social and Cultural Geography* 16, no. 4 (2015), pp. 407–23; David Roberts and Minelle Mahtani, 'Neoliberalizing race, racing neoliberalism: placing "race" in neoliberal discourses', *Antipode* 42, no. 2 (2010), pp. 248–57. A further group of scholars argues that neoliberalism is an amorphous, vague, and incoherent term that raises more questions than it answers. See, for instance, Clive Barnett, 'The consolations of "neoliberalism"', *Geoforum* 36 (2005), pp. 7–12; James Ferguson, 'The uses of neoliberalism', *Antipode* no. 41 (2009), pp. 166–84. Accounts more sympathetic to the term, but seeking to define and clarify its worth, include Helga Leitner, Jamie Peck, and Eric Sheppard, *Contesting Neoliberalism: urban frontiers* (New York NY: Guildford Press, 2007). On schooling's ability to provide a 'meso-level' analysis of neoliberal reforms, see Claudia Hanson Thiem, 'Thinking through education: the geographies of contemporary educational restructuring', *Progress in Human Geography* 33, no. 2 (2009), pp. 154–73.

11  On 'routine and insidious' market making in Indonesia, see Tania Li, *Land's End: capitalist relations on an indigenous frontier* (Durham NC: Duke University Press, 2014), p. 8.

12  Leon Tikly and Thabo Mabogoane, 'Marketisation as a strategy for desegregation and redress: the case of historically white schools in South Africa', *International Review of Education* 43, no. 2/3 (1997), pp. 159–78.

13  Julia de Kadt et al., 'Children's daily travel to school in Johannesburg-Soweto: geography and distance in the birth to twenty cohort', *Children's Geographies* 12, no. 2 (2014), pp. 170–88. For quantitative work, based on time-diary data, on the large amount of time black African learners spend travelling for school (on average 75 minutes a day), see Dorrit Posel and Erofili Graspa, 'Time to learn? Time allocations among children in South Africa', *International Journal of Educational Development* 56 (2017), pp. 1–10. For qualitative studies on schoolchildren's movement, see, for Cape Town, Aslam Fataar, 'Self-formation and the "capacity to aspire": the itinerant "schooled" career of Fuzile Ali across post-apartheid space', *Perspectives in Education* 28, no. 3 (2010), pp. 34–45; for Johannesburg, Jarred Bell and Tracy McKay, 'The rise of "class apartheid" in accessing secondary schools in Sandton, Gauteng', *Southern African Review of Education* 17 (2011), pp. 27–48; for Pietermaritzburg, Anthony Lemon, 'Shifting geographies of social inclusion and exclusion: secondary education in Pietermaritzburg, South Africa', *African Affairs* 104, no. 414 (2005), pp. 69–96.

14  On 'racial modernism', see Belinda Bozzoli, 'Why were the 1980s "millenarian"? Style, repertoire, space and authority in South Africa's black cities', *Journal of Historical Sociology* 13, no. 1 (2000), pp. 78–110.

15  Zimitri Erasmus, *Race Otherwise: forging a new humanism for South Africa* (Johannesburg: Wits University Press, 2017); Kelly Gillespie, 'Reclaiming nonracialism: reading *The Threat of Race* from South Africa', *Patterns of Prejudice* 44, no. 1 (2010), pp. 61–75; Jon Soske 'The impossible concept: settler liberalism, Pan-Africanism, and the language of non-racialism', *African Historical Review* 47, no. 2 (2015), pp. 1–36; Michael MacDonald, *Why Race Matters in South Africa* (Cambridge MA: Harvard University Press, 2012); Victoria Collis-Buthelezi, 'The case for black studies in South Africa', *The Black Scholar* 47, no. 2 (2017), pp. 7–21.

16  Zimitri Erasmus, 'The nation, its populations and their re-calibration: South African affirmative action in a neoliberal age', *Cultural Dynamics* 27, no. 1 (2015), pp. 99–115; Gerhard Maré, *Declassified: moving beyond the dead end of race in South Africa* (Johannesburg: Jacana, 2014).

17  'Minister drives DA to boiling point with "black face" comment', *eNews Channel Africa*, 10 November 2016, www.enca.com/south-africa/minister-drives-da-to-boiling-point-with-black-face-comment (accessed 7 June 2017).

18  Giordano Stolley, 'Penny Sparrow fined R5 000 for racist rant', *IOL News*, 12 September 2016, www.iol.co.za/news/crime-courts/penny-sparrow-fined-r5-000-for-racist-rant-2067166 (accessed 7 June 2017); Jeanette Chabalala, '"I was scared for my life": man who was forced into coffin', *News24*, 16 November 2016, www.news24.com/SouthAfrica/News/i-was-scared-for-my-life-man-who-was-forced-into-coffin-20161116 (accessed 7 June 2017).

19  This is according to the broad, and more appropriate, definition of unemployment that does not exclude persons who are discouraged from looking for work. See Seekings and Nattrass, *Class, Race, and Inequality in South Africa*, p. 45. On human capital theory, see Gary Becker, *Human Capital: a theoretical and empirical analysis, with special reference to education* (Chicago IL: University of Chicago Press, 1993).

20 South African Government, *Diagnostic Overview* (Pretoria: South African Government, National Planning Commission, Department of the Presidency, 2011), p. 13, 14. One revealing account from the poorly performing Eastern Cape Province showed that it was not even possible to calculate how many schools were in existence. Lawrence Wright (ed.), *South Africa's Education Crisis: views from the Eastern Cape* (Grahamstown: NISC (Pty) Ltd, 2012), p. 45.

21 Vijay Reddy, 'The state of mathematics and science education: schools are not equal' in Sakhela Buhlungu, John Daniel, Roger Southall, and Jessica Lutchman (eds), *The State of the Nation South Africa 2005–2006* (Cape Town: HSRC Press, 2006). For a short recent discussion on inequality, see 'FactCheck: is South Africa the most unequal society in the world?', http://theconversation.com/factcheck-is-south-africa-the-most-unequal-society-in-the-world-48334 (accessed 7 June 2017).

22 Frantz Fanon, *The Wretched of the Earth* (New York NY: Grove Press, 1984 [1961]).

23 Seekings and Nattrass, *Class, Race, and Inequality in South Africa*, p. 227.

24 Statistics South Africa, *Youth Employment, Unemployment, Skills and Economic Growth, 1994–2014* (Pretoria: South African Government, 2014), p. 10. For Durban, Lombard and Crankshaw, using data that defined unemployment quite narrowly, found a rate of only 1 per cent among whites compared with 22 per cent among black Africans. See Mighael Lombard and Owen Crankshaw, 'Deindustrialization and racial inequality: social polarisation in eThekwini?', *Cities* 60 (2017), p. 231.

25 For Durban, see Lombard and Crankshaw, 'Deindustrialization and racial inequality'; for the national picture, see Statistics South Africa, *Youth Employment, Unemployment, Skills and Economic Growth, 1994–2014*.

26 South African Institute of Race Relations, *Race Relations Survey 1991/2* (Johannesburg: SAIRR, 1992), p. lxxxv.

27 Edward Fiske and Helen Ladd, *Elusive Equity: education reform in post-apartheid South Africa* (Washington DC: Brookings Institute, 2004); Linda Chisholm (ed.), *Changing Class: education and social change in post-apartheid South Africa* (Cape Town: HSRC Press, 2004). See also Shireen Motala, 'Privatising public schooling in post-apartheid South Africa: equity considerations', *Compare: A Journal of Comparative and International Education* 39, no. 2 (2009), pp. 185–202; Yusuf Sayed and Shireen Motala, 'Equity and "no fee" schools in South Africa: challenges and prospects', *Social Policy and Administration* 46, no. 6 (2012), pp. 672–87. Crain Soudien's book *Realising the Dream* (Cape Town, HSRC Press, 2012) is an important account of race, class, and desegregation, from which I draw. Soudien stresses how assimilation became more strident after 1990, and then from 1994 schools managed assimilation by invoking cosmopolitan identities (I emphasise a shift from what I call marketised assimilation to the racialised market).

28 Calculated from Durban Schooling Data (see Appendix 1) for seven boys' and seven girls' schools. The average fees for girls' and boys' schools were R9,590 and R16,043 (2007 and 2012) and R13,099 and R24,117 (2007 and 2012) respectively.

29 Lombard and Crankshaw, 'Deindustrialization and racial inequality', p. 229; see also Statistics South Africa, *Youth Employment, Unemployment, Skills and Economic Growth, 1994–2014*.

30  Pierre Bourdieu, *The State Nobility: elite schools in the field of power* (Palo Alto CA: Stanford University Press, 1996).

31  Pierre Bourdieu, *Language and Symbolic Power* (Cambridge: Cambridge University Press, 1991); Antonio Gramsci, *Selections from the Prison Notebooks of Antonio Gramsci* (New York NY: International Publishers, 1971).
For a useful discussion of similarities and differences between Bourdieu and Gramsci, see Michael Burawoy and Karl von Holdt, *Conversations with Bourdieu: the Johannesburg moment* (Johannesburg: Wits University Press, 2012).

32  Bourdieu, *Language and Symbolic Power*, p. 130, 164.

33  Ernst G. Malherbe, *Education in South Africa. Vol. 2: 1923–1973* (Cape Town: Juta, 1977), p. 268.

34  Muriel Horrell, *Bantu Education to 1968* (Johannesburg: South African Institute of Race Relations, 1968), p. 52; South African Institute of Race Relations, *Race Relations Survey 1989/90* (Johannesburg: SAIRR, 1990), p. 824. On the rapid expansion of schooling in the Global South, see Caroline H. Bledsoe et al. (eds), *Critical Perspectives on Schooling and Fertility in the Developing World* (Washington DC: National Academy Press, 1999). The United States itself saw a rise from 50 per cent to 80 per cent of young people gaining a high-school diploma from the 1950s to the 1970s. David Baker, *The Schooled Society: the educational transformation of global culture* (Palo Alto CA: Stanford University Press, 2014), p. 224.

35  South African Institute of Race Relations, *South Africa Survey 2016* (Johannesburg: SAIRR, 2016), p. 524.

36  Fred Hirsch, *Social Limits to Growth* (London: Routledge, 1978), pp. 5–6; Max Weber, 'The "specialist" and the "Cultivated Man": certificates and the origin of ideas in science', in Stephen Kalberg (ed.), *Max Weber: readings and commentary on modernity* (Oxford: Blackwell, 2005), p. 138. Sara Berry's study in Nigeria shows how schoolteachers saw 'prestige dwindle as the educational system grew'; Sara Berry, *Fathers Work for Their Sons: accumulation, mobility, and class formation in an extended Yoruba community* (Berkeley CA: University of California Press, 1985), p. 192. For an excellent critique of how the huge 'development' industry is premised on an over simplistic view of education as *inherently* promoting equality and justice, see Craig Jeffrey, Patricia Jeffrey, and Roger Jeffrey, *Degrees without Freedom? Education, masculinities and unemployment in North India* (Palo Alto CA: Stanford University Press, 2007).

37  That employers use qualifications mainly for screening candidates is argued in Randall Collins, *The Credential Society: a historical sociology of education and stratification* (New York NY: Academic Press, 1979), though this is critiqued by David Baker. See Baker, *The Schooled Society*.

38  During the 1980s, a 'multiracial' institution (e.g. a school, hotel, or restaurant) was one that did not uphold strictly apartheid segregation; 'grey areas' was a term used for desegregating suburbs. While the use of 'multiracial' and 'nonracial' can overlap, the former implies that learners are racialised first (for instance as an African) before being admitted into an institution. For a recent historical discussion on the two terms, see Soske, 'The impossible concept.'

39  The figures on white schools in 1995 are taken from Tikly and Mabogoane, 'Marketisation as a strategy for desegregation and redress', p. 161. There were 1,860 white schools out of a total of 25,162, educating 8.5 per cent of the school-going population.

40  The term 'white South African English' (and black/Indian/Coloured South African English) is used by linguists, with qualifications. As Rajend Mesthrie says: 'The use of ethnic descriptors should not be taken as unqualified acceptance of old apartheid labels – though few linguists would dispute that the sociolects described here are very much still in existence'; Rajend Mesthrie, 'Introduction' in Rajend Mesthrie (ed.), *Language in South Africa* (Cambridge: Cambridge University Press, 2004), p. 7.

41  Statistics South Africa, *Community Survey 2016 in Brief* (Pretoria: South African Government, 2016), p. 38.

42  W. E. B. Du Bois, *Black Reconstruction: an essay toward a history of the part which black folks played in the attempt to reconstruct democracy in America, 1860–1880* (New York NY: Russel and Russel, 1935); Frantz Fanon, *Black Skin, White Masks* (London: Pluto Press, 1986 [1952]); Stephen Biko, *I Write What I Like* (San Francisco CA: Harper and Row, 1978).

43  This is, of course, a simplification. In his seminal history of *racial capitalism*, Cedric Robinson challenges the common view that racism's roots lie in the relationship between European and non-European peoples and shows how earlier internal relations within Europe were constituent of racism. Cedric Robinson, *Black Marxism: the making of the black radical tradition* (Chapel Hill NC: University of North Carolina Press, 2000).

44  Goldberg calls these traditions 'naturalism' and 'historicism'. See David Goldberg, *The Racial State* (London: Blackwell, 2002).

45  Goldberg, *The Racial State*, p. 248. See also Ruth Frankenberg, *White Women, Race Matters: the social construction of whiteness* (Minneapolis MN: University of Minnesota Press, 1993); David Roediger, *The Wages of Whiteness: race and the making of the American working class* (London: Verso, 1991). For South Africa, see Melissa Steyn, *Whiteness Just Isn't What It Used to Be: the master's narrative and the new South Africa* (Albany NY: SUNY Press, 2001); Nicky Falkof, *Satanism and Family Murder in Late Apartheid South Africa* (London: Palgrave Macmillan, 2015); Deborah Posel, 'Whiteness and power in the South African civil service: paradoxes of the apartheid state', *Journal of Southern African Studies* 25, no. 1 (1999), pp. 99–110. The classic comparative study of white supremacy in South Africa and the United States is George Fredrickson, *White Supremacy: a comparative study in American and South African history* (Oxford: Oxford University Press, 1981). For a discussion and critiques of the concept of whiteness, see Peter Kolchin, 'The new history of race in America', *Journal of American History* 89, no. 1 (2002), pp. 154–73; Andrew Hartman, 'The rise and fall of whiteness studies', *Race and Class* 46, no. 2 (2004), pp. 22–38.

46  See Raewyn Connell, *Masculinities* (Berkeley CA: University of California Press, 2005), p. 44.

47  Jonathan Hyslop, 'The imperial working class makes itself "white": white labourism in Britain, Australia, and South Africa before the First World War', *Journal of Historical Sociology* 12, no. 4 (1999), pp. 398–421; Marilyn Lake and Henry Reynolds, *Drawing the Global Colour Line: white men's countries and the international challenge of racial equality* (Cambridge: Cambridge University Press, 2008); Roediger, *The Wages of Whiteness*.

48  John Lambert, '"Munition factories … turning out a constant supply of living material": white South African elite boys' schools and the First World War', *South African Historical Journal* 51 (2004), p. 67; Jane Kenway

et al., *Class Choreographies: elite schools and globalization* (London: Palgrave Macmillan, 2017).

49 Biko, *I Write What I Like*, p. 57.

50 Du Bois, *Black Reconstruction*, p. 528. In the area now called Canada, the state encouraged the forced assimilation of indigenous groups through 'residential schools', a policy recognised as 'cultural genocide' by the 2015 Truth and Reconciliation Commission. Truth and Reconciliation Canada, *Honouring the Truth, Reconciling for the Future* (Winnipeg: Truth and Reconciliation Commission of Canada, 2015).

51 Paul Gilroy, *Between Camps: nations, culture and the allure of race* (London: Penguin Books, 2000), p. 33.

52 'Tone' has been used to describe South African schools since at least the 1880s. For instance, when practices to pay teachers in the 1880s by results were hotly debated (and ultimately ended) the Superintendent said that he took into account in his evaluations the tone and general aspect of the school. Ernst G. Malherbe, *Education in South Africa. Vol. 1: 1652–1922* (Cape Town: Juta, 1925), pp. 191–2. Decades later, following the 1899–1902 Anglo-Boer War, Lord Milner's plans to unite whites by anglicising Afrikaners led him to say: 'Language is important, but the tone and spirit [of education] is even more important.' Hermann Giliomee, 'Being Afrikaans in the new (multi-lingual) South Africa', *New Contree* 40 (1996), pp. 59–73, http://dspace .nwu.ac.za/bitstream/handle/10394/5333/No_40(1996)_Giliomee_H(b).pdf? sequence=3 (accessed 29 November 2016). On 'internal' and 'external' school tone, see Peter Randall, *Little England on the Veld: the English private schooling system in South Africa* (Athens OH: Ohio University Press, 1985).

53 The quote, cited by Randall, is from a book by Jonathan Gathorne-Hardy. Randall, *Little England on the Veld*, p. 77.

54 Lawrence Maxim Walrond, *Ratoon: tying the roots of my family name to my parents' lives* (Victoria: Friesen Press, 2015), p. 168.

55 My use of 'tone' has some similarities to Basil Bernstein's term 'expressive order', which is used to capture learners' 'conduct, character and manner'. Basil Bernstein, *Class, Codes and Control. Volume I: theoretical studies towards a sociology of language* (London: Routledge, 1971), p. 183.

56 W. E. B. Du Bois, *The Souls of Black Folk* (Oxford: Oxford University Press, 2007 [1903]), p. 8.

57 Fanon, *The Wretched of the Earth*, p. 16. On the 'ambiguities of dependence' in South Africa, see Shula Marks, *The Ambiguities of Dependence in South Africa: class, nationalism, and the state in twentieth-century Natal* (Baltimore MD: Johns Hopkins University Press, 1986).

58 Norma Wildenboer, 'Fewer Afrikaans schools a worry', *DFA*, 14 July 2017, www.dfa.co.za/news/fewer-afrikaans-schools-a-worry/ (accessed 10 August 2018).

59 Melo Magolego, 'TUT students vs the coconut bourgeoisie', *Mail & Guardian*, 26 October 2015, http://thoughtleader.co.za/melomagolego/2015/10/26/ tut-students-vs-the-coconut-bourgeoisie/ (accessed 29 November 2016).

60 For a critique of Bantu education written at the time of its introduction, see Isaac Tabata, *Education for Barbarism: Bantu (apartheid) education in South Africa* (London: Prometheus, 1959). Key historical overviews of schooling include Peter Kallaway (ed.), *Apartheid and Education: the education of black South Africans* (Johannesburg: Ravan Press, 1984); Peter Kallaway (ed.), *The*

*History of Education under Apartheid 1948–1994* (New York NY: Peter Lang Publishing, 2002). On private schools that admitted black students, see Pam Christie, *Open Schools: racially mixed Catholic schools in South Africa 1976–86* (Johannesburg: Ravan Press, 1990). On schooling, labour, and protest, from a historical-sociological perspective, see Jonathan Hyslop, *The Classroom Struggle: policy and resistance in South Africa 1940–1990* (Pietermaritzburg: University of Natal Press, 1999). For a review of 'liberal' and 'revisionist' education traditions in South Africa, see Michael Cross, 'A historical review of education in South Africa: towards and assessment', *Comparative Education* 22, no. 3 (1986), pp. 185–200.

61 Meghan Healy-Clancy, *A World of Their Own: a history of South African women's education* (Charlottesville VA: University of Virginia Press, 2013); Peter Kallaway and Rebecca Swartz, *Empire and Education in Africa: the shaping of a comparative perspective* (New York NY: Peter Lang, 2016); Daniel Magaziner, *The Art of Life in South Africa* (Athens OH: Ohio University Press, 2016); Robert Morrell, *From Boys to Gentlemen: settler masculinity in colonial Natal, 1880–1920* (Pretoria: UNISA Press, 2001); Goolam Vahed and Thembisa Waetjen, *Schooling Muslims in Natal: identity, state and the Orient Islamic Educational Institute* (Pietermaritzburg: University of KwaZulu-Natal Press, 2015).

62 See, for discussions, Hein Marais, *South Africa: limits to change, the political economy of transformation* (London: Zed Books, 2001); Patrick Bond, *Elite Transition: from apartheid to neoliberalism* (London: Pluto Press, 2000); Gillian Hart, *Rethinking the South African Crisis: nationalism, populism, hegemony* (Athens GA: University of Georgia Press, 2013).

63 Jeremy Seekings and Nicoli Nattrass, *Policy, Politics and Poverty in South Africa* (London: Palgrave Macmillan, 2015).

64 Stuart Woolman and Brahm Fleisch, 'South Africa's unintended experiment in school choice: how the National Education Policy Act, the South Africa Schools Act and the Employment of Educators Act create the enabling conditions for quasi-markets in schools', *Education and the Law* 18, no. 1 (2006), pp. 31–75.

65 David Plank and Gary Sykes, *Choosing Choice: school choice in international perspective* (New York NY: Teachers College, 2003), p. vii.

66 This literature is now huge. It includes Lois André-Bechely, 'Finding space and managing distance: public school choice in an urban California district', *Urban Studies* 44, no. 7 (2007), pp. 1355–76; Michael Apple, *Educating the 'Right' Way: markets, standards, god, and inequality* (London: Routledge, 2006); Stephen Ball, *Class Strategies and the Education Market: the middle classes and social advantage* (London: Routledge, 2003); Stephen Ball, Richard Bowe, and Sharon Gewirtz, 'Circuits of schooling: a sociological exploration of parental choice of school in social class contexts', *Sociological Review* 43, no. 1 (1995), pp. 52–78; Tim Butler and Chris Hamnett, 'The geography of education: introduction', *Urban Studies* 44, no. 7 (2007), pp. 1161–74; Tim Butler and Gary Robson, *London Calling: the middle classes and the remaking of inner London* (London: Berg, 2003); Martin Forsey, Scott Davies, and Geoffrey Walford (eds), *The Globalisation of School Choice?* (Oxford: Symposium Books, 2008); Stephen Gorard, '"Well. That about wraps it up for school choice research": a state of the art review', *School Leadership and Management* 19, no. 1 (1999), pp. 25–47; Pauline Lipman, *The New Political Economy of Urban Education* (London: Taylor and Francis, 2011); Katharyne Mitchell,

'Neoliberal governmentality in the European Union: education, training, and technologies of citizenship', *Environment and Planning D: Society and Space* 24, no. 12 (2006), pp. 389–407; Gary Orfield and Erica Frankenberg, *Educational Delusions? Why choice can deepen inequality and how to make schools fair* (Berkeley CA: University of California Press, 2013); Diane Ravitch, *The Death and Life of the Great American School* (New York NY: Basic Books, 2010); Diane Reay, 'Tony Blair, the promotion of the "active" educational citizen, and middle-class hegemony', *Oxford Review of Education* 34, no. 6 (2008), pp. 639–50. On higher education, see Simon Marginson, 'National and global competition in higher education', *Higher Education* 52, no. 1 (2006), pp. 1–39.

67 'ANC thumbs-down for model C schools', *Natal Mercury*, 21 September 1992.

68 Fiske and Ladd, *Elusive Equity*. Efforts to install a flexible vocational education system also resulted in a decentralised and marketised form of provision. For an incisive critique of post-apartheid vocational policy and the National Qualifications Framework, see Stephanie Allais, *Selling Out Education: national qualifications framework and the neglect of knowledge* (Rotterdam: Sense Publishers, 2014).

69 Francesca Villette, 'Sharp rise in no-fee pupils', *Cape Times – IOL*, 7 June 2016, www.iol.co.za/capetimes/sharp-rise-in-no-fee-school-pupils-2031750 (accessed 14 September 2016).

70 See, for instance, Prachi Srivastava and Geoffrey Walford, 'Non-state actors in education in the Global South', *Oxford Review of Education* 42, no. 5 (2016), pp. 491–4.

71 South African Government, *The State of Education in KwaZulu-Natal: a report for KZN Treasury* (Pietermaritzburg: South African Government, KwaZulu-Natal Department of Education, 2010), p. 54.

72 South African Government, *Education Management Information Systems: 2011 snap survey report for ordinary schools* (Pietermaritzburg: South African Government, KwaZulu-Natal Department of Education, 2012), p. 2.

73 The long distances that children walk to rural schools have been a major campaign area for Equal Education (see https://equaleducation.org.za/). (Note: as the book went to press several leaders of Equal Education were accused of sexual harassment, though I do not consider this here). On 'multiple deprivations' and schooling, see Felix Maringe and Relobohile Moletsane, 'Leading schools in circumstances of multiple deprivation in South Africa: mapping some conceptual, contextual, and research dimensions', *Educational Management, Administration and Leadership* 43, no. 3 (2015), pp. 347–62.

74 Edith Dempster and Vijay Reddy, 'Item readability and science achievement in TIMSS 2003 in South Africa', *Science Education* 91, no. 1 (2007), pp. 36–74.

75 Statistics in this paragraph, as all employment and demographic data unless otherwise stated, are derived from 2011 census data analysed using Super-cross software provided by Statistics South Africa (see Appendix 1).

76 'Wits SRC president Nompendulo Mkhatshwa and Shaeera Kalla address the students at Luthuli House', YouTube video, 19:25, posted by It's Happening, 23 October 2015, https://youtu.be/KrSgJkVRzqM (accessed 14 September 2016).

77 For an influential feminist account arguing that the mother–child bond is produced and not natural, see Micaela Di Leonardo (ed.), *Gender at the Crossroads of Knowledge: feminist anthropology in the postmodern era* (Berkeley

CA: University of California Press, 1991), p. 26. As Patricia Hill Collins notes, black feminist scholars have long studied mother–children relationships within an overall system of interlocking/intersecting oppression; Collins, 'Learning from the outsider within'. For an incisive account of the need to historicise 'matrifocality' in Cape Town, see Rebekah Lee, *African Women and Apartheid: migration and settlement in South Africa* (London: Tauris Academic Studies, 2009). A similar point has been made about the concept of 'motherhood'. See Cherryl Walker, 'Conceptualising motherhood in twentieth century South Africa', *Journal of Southern African Studies* 21, no. 3 (1995), pp. 417–37. For a more recent discussion, see Elena Moore, 'Transmission and change in South African motherhood: black mothers in three-generational Cape Town families', *Journal of Southern African Studies* 39, no. 1 (2013), pp. 151–70.

Specific studies on generational relationships include Ben Carton, *Blood from Your Children: the colonial origins of generational conflict in South Africa* (Charlottesville VA: University of Virginia Press, 2000); Jennifer Cole and Deborah Durham (eds), *Generations and Globalization: youth, age, and family in the new world economy* (Bloomington IN: Indiana University Press, 2007). On schooling, generation, courting, and sexuality, see Laura Ahearn, *Invitations to Love: literacy, love letters and social change in Nepal* (Ann Arbor MI: Michigan University Press, 2001); Lynn Thomas, *The Politics of the Womb: women, reproduction, and the state in Kenya* (Berkeley CA: University of California Press, 2003).

Further important anthropological accounts that embed schooling in families and communities include Amy Stambach, *Lessons from Mount Kilimanjaro: schooling, community, and gender in East Africa* (New York NY: Routledge, 2000); Caroline Bledsoe, 'The cultural transformation of Western education in Sierra Leone', *Africa* 62, no. 2 (1992), pp. 182–202; Zolani Ngwane, '"Real men reawaken their fathers' homesteads, the educated leave them in ruins": the politics of domestic reproduction in post-apartheid rural South Africa', *Journal of Religion in Africa* 31, no. 4 (2001), pp. 402–26; Jessica Leinaweaver, *The Circulation of Children: kinship, adoption, and morality in Andean Peru* (Durham NC: Duke University Press, 2008). In the Global North, some scholars have argued that the family is not a 'monolithic [nuclear] unit'. Will Atkinson, 'From sociological fictions to social fictions: some Bourdieusian reflections on the concepts of "institutional habitus" and "family habitus"', *British Journal of Sociology of Education* 32, no. 3 (2011), pp. 331–47. Particularly relevant is work noting the emphasis mothers place on their children's education. See Diane Reay, 'Cultural reproduction: mothers involvement in their children's primary schooling' in Michael Grenfell and David James (eds), *Bourdieu and Education: acts of practical theory* (London: Routledge, 1998).

78 There are notable exceptions, of course. Book-length studies giving attention to race and schooling include Kalervo Gulson, *Education Policy, Space and the City: markets and the (in) visibility of race* (London: Routledge, 2011); Lipman, *The New Political Economy of Urban Education*; Orfield and Frankenberg, *Educational Delusions?*

79 At times I use the terms 'family', 'household', and 'kinship' somewhat similarly, while at other times I differentiate among them. Anthropologists working on kinship and families have embraced the more flexible language

of 'relatedness', which I also draw on. Janet Carsten, *Cultures of Relatedness: new approaches to the study of kinship* (New York NY: Cambridge University Press, 2004). I draw later on the rich South African literature on families/households, but for a general overview of 'domestic fluidity' in South Africa, see Andrew Spiegel, 'Migration, urbanisation and domestic fluidity', *African Anthropology* II, no. 2 (1995), pp. 90–113.

80 Laurine Platzky and Cherryl Walker for the Surplus People Project, *The Surplus People: forced removals in South Africa* (Johannesburg: Ravan Press, 1985).

81 South African Institute of Race Relations, *First Steps to Healing the South African Family* (Johannesburg: SAIRR, 2011), p. 2.

82 Jare Struwig, Benjamin Roberts, Steven Gordon, and Yul Derek Davids, *Local Matters: results from the Electoral Commission of South Africa's Voter Participation Survey (VPS) 2015/16*. Report prepared for the Electoral Commission of South Africa (Pretoria: Human Sciences Research Council, 2016).

83 After 1994, the state implemented an ambitious new curriculum that promoted 'outcomes-based education' (OBE). In contrast to apartheid's coercive education strategy, OBE aimed to institute a 'child-centred' curriculum that recognised flexible schooling outcomes. In turn, a less hierarchical definition of skills would feed into a training and accreditation policy that 'recognised prior learning' for those denied formal qualifications. As many have noted, the National Qualifications Framework has been plagued with problems, and OBE was abandoned in 2010 amid criticism that only richer schools had facilities and class sizes that could cope with a goals-based approach. On the qualifications frameworks after apartheid, see Allais, *Selling Out Education*.

84 On the concept of racialism, see Chapter 1 in Goldberg, *The Threat of Race*.

85 Gilmore, 'Fatal couplings'.

86 Erasmus, *Race Otherwise*, p. 112.

87 Figures in this paragraph are taken from Dorrit Posel, 'Micro-data analysis of patterns and trends in eThekwini Municipality' (unpublished report for eThekwini Municipality, January 2015).

88 On the 'invention' of British cities in Africa, including through schooling, see Vivian Bickford-Smith, *The Emergence of the South African Metropolis: cities and identities in the twentieth century* (Cambridge: Cambridge University Press, 2016), p. 25.

89 Chris Taylor, *Geography of the 'New' Education Market: secondary schooling choice in England and Wales* (Aldershot: Ashgate, 2002).

90 See Owen Crankshaw, 'Race, space and the post-Fordist spatial order of Johannesburg', *Urban Studies* 45, no.8 (2008), pp. 1692–711.

91 Sharad Chari has undertaken long-term ethnographical research in Merebank and Wentworth and has written detailed accounts of the history and politics of these two areas. See, for instance, Sharad Chari, 'State racism and bio-political struggle: the evasive commons in twentieth-century Durban, South Africa', *Radical History Review* no. 108 (2010), pp. 73–90; Sharad Chari, 'An "Indian commons" in Durban? Limits to mutuality, or the city to come', *Anthropology Southern Africa* 37, no. 3–4 (2014), pp. 149–59.

92 By concentrating on families and schools located primarily in Umlazi and on the Bluff, my research has affinities with what Gillian Hart calls a 'relational comparison'. A simple comparison between two areas would shed important

light on the vastly unequal education system. But a relational approach brings to light the connections, including through the movement of children, that produce the education system. This relational approach disturbs, if never overcomes, the reification of apartheid's spatial differences in research and writing. See Gillian Hart, *Disabling Globalization: places of power in post-apartheid South Africa* (Berkeley CA: University of California Press, 2006). On overcoming apartheid's racial-spatial legacy in research, see Sarah Nuttall and Achille Mbembe (eds), *Johannesburg: the elusive metropolis* (Durham NC: Duke University Press, 2008); Jennifer Robinson, *Ordinary Cities: between modernity and development* (London: Routledge, 2005). More generally on the 'relational' understanding of space adopted in this study, see Doreen Massey, *Space, Place and Gender* (Cambridge: Polity Press, 1994).

## Chapter 2

1 Describing the use of 'larney' in working-class Indian communities, Thomas Bloom Hansen notes that *'laanie'* is an Afrikaans term for 'fancy', with possible roots in French and Swahili. Thomas Bloom Hansen, *Melancholia of Freedom: social life in an Indian township in South Africa* (Princeton NJ: Princeton University Press, 2012), p. 306.
2 'History of famous school to be written', *Daily News*, 19 August 1958.
3 Rob Donkin, *A Bluff Scruff Miracle* (Wandsbeck: Reach Publishers, 2010), Kindle edition, p. 63.
4 Malherbe, *Education in South Africa. Vol. 2*, p. 155.
5 On white poverty as 'anomalous and unacceptable', see Saul Dubow, *Scientific Racism in Modern South Africa* (Johannesburg: Witwatersrand University Press, 1995), p. 171. On schooling, 'poor whites', and the Carnegie inquiry (1929–32), see Pam Christie and Adele Gordon, 'Politics, poverty and education in rural South Africa', *British Journal of Sociology of Education* 13, no. 4 (1992), pp. 399–418.
6 Figures taken from Hansard records in 1958 as cited in Brij Maharaj, 'Apartheid, urban segregation, and the local state: Durban and the Group Areas Act in South Africa', *Urban Geography* 18, no. 2 (1997), p. 144. For population figures in 1951, see Leo Kuper, Hilstan Watts, and Ronald Davies, *Durban: a study in racial ecology* (London: Jonathan Cape, 1958), p. 51.
7 The 19 per cent of the national population classified as white compares with 68 per cent classified as black Africans, 9 per cent Coloured, and 3 per cent Indians. T. J. D. Fair and N. Manfred Shaffer, 'Population patterns and policies in South Africa', *Economic Geography* 40, no. 3 (1964), pp. 261–74.
8 'S.A. has never had it so good', *Natal Mercury*, 4 March 1964. This front-page newspaper story was reporting on a speech by the Minister of Economic Affairs. Funding for white students increased between 1950 and 1970 from R13.40 to R33.90; in contrast, per capita funding for African students rose only from R0.87 to R1.20. See Malherbe, *Education in South Africa. Vol. 2*, p. 572.
9 'Durban fishing village houses demolished', *Natal Mercury*, 4 March 1961. See also Dianne Scott, 'Communal space construction: the rise and fall of Clairwood and district', PhD thesis, Department of Geographical and Environmental Sciences, University of Natal, Durban, 1994.

10 University of Natal, *The Durban Housing Survey: a study of housing in a multi-racial community* (Pietermaritzburg: University of Natal Press, 1952), p. 363.

11 Scott, 'Communal space construction'; 'Indians again plead: "Do not zone Clairwood"', *Natal Mercury*, 25 March 1965.

12 'Bluff school news', *The Bluff Newsletter*, 2 November 1965.

13 'Tragedy of Natal's "no race" children', *Natal Mercury*, 28 February 1962. Most racial reclassifications were from Coloureds to whites or vice versa. Compared with the Cape in particular, Natal Province had a relatively small Coloured population (45,000 Coloureds lived in Natal in 1960 compared with 1.3 million in the Cape). Figures taken from Muriel Horrell, *The Education of the Coloured Community in South Africa 1652 to 1970* (Johannesburg: South African Institute of Race Relations, 1970), p. 177.

14 Eleanor Preston-Whyte, 'Between two worlds: a study of the working life, social ties and inter-personal relationships of African women migrants in domestic service in Durban', PhD thesis, University of Natal, Durban, 1969, p. 69.

15 On anti-Indian sentiment and 'pegging' laws, see Brij Maharaj, 'Apartheid, urban segregation, and the local state', pp. 135–54.

16 Hilstan Watts et al., 'Group areas and the "Grey Street" complex, Durban', (Durban: Centre for Applied Social Sciences, University of Natal, 1971), p. 3.

17 On this educational complex and Orient Islamic School's establishment, see Goolam Vahed and Thembisa Waetjen, *Schooling Muslims in Natal*. As Vahed and Waetjen detail, Orient School was built in the lower Berea after the city halted plans by the Orient Islamic Educational Institute to build the school on land it owned on the 'white' Bluff. Sastri College, named after the first Agent-General of the government of India in South Africa, was built with the help of the Indian business community and, according to Pravindra Thakur, sought to emulate English boys' grammar schools. This, in part, resulted from the belief that if Indians conformed to Western standards, it would help end the constant threat of repatriation, which only ended in 1961. Pravindra Thakur, 'Education for upliftment: a history of Sastri College 1927–1981', unpublished master's thesis, Department of History, University of Natal, Durban, 1992. Despite the survival of the educational complex, many Indian schools were destroyed by the Group Areas Act. Kuper, Watts, and Davies, put this number at 22 schools, which accounts for one-quarter of the school-going population in Durban. Kuper, Watts, and Davies, *Durban: a study in racial ecology*, p. 200.

18 See, for instance, David Goldberg, *Racist Culture: philosophy and the politics of meaning* (Oxford: Blackwell, 1993), p. 80.

19 See, for instance, Saul Dubow, *A Commonwealth of Knowledge: science, sensibility, and white South Africa 1820–2000* (Oxford: Oxford University Press, 2006).

20 'Tragedy of Natal's "no race" children', *Natal Mercury*.

21 Deborah Posel, 'Race as common sense: racial classification in twentieth-century South Africa', *African Studies Review* 44, no. 2 (2001), p. 103; Keith Breckenridge, 'The book of life: the South African population register and the invention of racial descent, 1950–1980', *Kronos* 40 (2005), pp. 225–40.

22 Indeed eugenics – the most prominent scientific approach to race in the interwar years – had limited influence on race-thinking during the apartheid

period. Dubow writes that 'the implications of eugenic theories became distinctly unpalatable once the fitness of whites in general came under scrutiny'. Dubow, *Scientific Racism in Modern South Africa*, p. 166.

23  Posel, 'Race as common sense', p. 106.

24  Posel, 'Race as common sense'. For schools' ability to judge a learner's 'race' in the period just prior to apartheid, see Annika Teppo, *The Making of a Good White: a historical ethnography of the rehabilitation of poor whites in a suburb of Cape Town* (Helsinki: Helsinki University Press, 2004).

25  'Bluff's "lost tribe" may get home of their own', *Daily News*, 13 May 1957. On the Zanzibaris, see also Scott, 'Communal space construction'; Goolam Vahed, 'The Zanzibaris' in Ashwin Desai and Goolam Vahed (eds), *Chatsworth: the making of a South African township* (Pietermaritzburg: University of KwaZulu-Natal Press, 2013); Preben Kaarsholm, 'Zanzibaris or Amakhuwa? Sufi networks in South Africa, Mozambique, and the Indian Ocean', *Journal of African History* 55 (2014), pp. 191–210. On the role of Durban's Juma (Grey Street) Mosque in assisting the Zanzibaris, see Osman Andool and Rahim Sema, 'The Juma Mosque' local history project, lecturer Mr R. Morrell, History III, Documentation Centre, University of Durban-Westville, Accession no. 903/13.

26  The number of schools is taken from Monica Jacobs, *A Statistical Overview of Education in KwaZulu Natal* (Johannesburg: The Education Foundation, 1992).

27  Edward-John Bottomley, 'Transnational governmentality and the "poor white" in early twentieth century South Africa', *Journal of Historical Geography* 54 (2016), p. 81.

28  Watts et al., 'Group areas and the "Grey Street" complex, Durban', memorandum 1.

29  'From Nobel prize-winners to Springbok cricketers …', *Natal Mercury*, 17 May 1991.

30  Breckenridge, 'The book of life', p. 225, 232.

31  Breckenridge, 'The book of life'.

32  Cited in Gavin Maasdorp and A. S. B. Humphreys, *From Shantytown to Township: an economic study of African poverty and rehousing in a South African city* (Cape Town: Juta, 1975), p. 127.

33  For the history of this term, see Jochen Arndt, 'What's in a word? Historicising the term "Caffre" in European discourses about Southern Africa between 1500 and 1800', *Journal of Southern African Studies* 44 (2018), pp. 59–75.

34  Anthony Trollope, *South Africa. Vol. 1* (London: Chapman and Hall, 1878), p. 275; see also Bickford-Smith, *The Emergence of the South African Metropolis*.

35  Trollope, *South Africa*, p. 276.

36  Kuper, Watts, and Davies' s *Durban: a study of racial ecology*, published in 1958, discusses and quantifies how, as you climb up the Berea ridge from the CBD to Ridge Road, house prices and the proportion of white residents rise quickly.

37  Preston-Whyte, 'Between two worlds', p. 74, 102.

38  Peter Hawthorne and Barry Bristow, *Historic Schools of South Africa: an ethos of excellence* (Cape Town: Pachyderm Press, 1993).

39  Randall, *Little England on the Veld*, p. 11.

40  Randall, *Little England on the Veld*, p. 3.

41 Hendrik van der Merwe et al., *White South African Elites* (Cape Town: Juta, 1974). Private schools distinguished themselves by their richer parents and because Christianity was usually foundational to the institutions (rather than a taken-for-granted feature of the school) – four of the top five private schools were established by the Anglican church and one by the Methodist church.

42 See Morrell, *From Boys to Gentlemen.*

43 Morrell, *From Boys to Gentlemen,* p. 91.

44 Durban Area Transport Survey Memorandum for Executive Committee, 18 October 1966, Box NDE 690, File 102/10 Transport Survey, Natal Education Department Records, Pietermaritzburg Archives Repository, Pietermaritzburg.

45 They pointed out old boys' significant financial support of the schools. Letter from Chairman, Berea High School Old Boys Association and Chairman DOS Old Boys' Association to the Administrator in Executive, Pietermaritzburg, undated (but from surrounding records sent in 1961), Box NDE 364, File P/14 School Zoning, Natal Education Department Records, Pietermaritzburg Archives Repository. Similar language was used to (successfully) oppose attempts at around the same time to abolish school fees in seven elite public schools (including Glenwood and Durban High School). 'Committee of Enquiry into the Question of the Abolishing Fee-Paying Schools', File 48/30, Natal Education Department Records, Pietermaritzburg Archives Repository.

46 This reached a head with the passing of the 1967 National Education Policy Act. See 'School Bill Blitz by Raw', *Natal Mercury,* 11 March 1967.

47 'Memoirs – W. A. Doble', Bluff Memoirs (Brighton Beach) 1874–1965, Brighton Beach Women's Institute, File 22084, Killie Campbell Africana Library.

48 Teppo, *The Making of a Good White.* Susan Parnell, 'Public housing as a device for white residential segregation in Johannesburg', *Urban Geography* 9, no. 6 (1988), pp. 584–602. For details on housing in Durban, see University of Natal, *The Durban Housing Survey.*

49 The early apartheid government sought to cut white immigration, but, in the 1960s, strong economic growth justified generous incentives for immigrants, many being artisans who moved to south Durban, especially from England. On changing immigration policy, see Sally Peberdy, *Selecting Immigrants: national identity and South Africa's immigration policies, 1910–2005* (Johannesburg: Wits University Press, 2009).

50 Jan Van Tonder, *Stargazer* (Cape Town: Human and Rousseau, 2006), p. 148.

51 Kuper, Watts, and Davies, *Durban: a study in racial ecology,* p. 124.

52 Grosvenor Boys' School, *Annual Report: Grosvenor Boys' High School 1966.*

53 Especially from the 1980s, the South African Defence Force came to play an increasingly prominent role in running cadet programmes that primed boys for national military service. 'Military presence grows: the SADF infiltration into S.A. education grows daily', *NEWSA, Newsletter of the National Education Union of South Africa,* February/March 1983.

54 Grosvenor Boys' School, *Annual Report: Grosvenor Boys' High School 1972,* p. 8.

55 Address by Mr Denis Osborne, *Grosvenor Boys' High School Magazine 1967,* p. 7.

56 'New non-academic course for Natal schools announced', *Daily News*, 4 December 1957.

57 Grosvenor Boys' School, *Annual Report: Grosvenor Boys' High School 1966*, p. 6.

58 Haw, *Taking Stock*, p. 73, 78.

59 Grosvenor Boys' School, *Grosvenor Boys' High School Magazine 1987*, p. 41.

60 For example, in 1962, a multiracial soccer team called Coastals with white, Indian, and African members, was formed in Durban, and Special Branch detectives warned the four regular white members that they would be in trouble if they continued to play on the team. Muriel Horrell, *A Survey of Race Relations in South Africa 1962* (Johannesburg: South African Institute of Race Relations, 1963), p. 218. On the history of soccer in South Africa up to the contemporary period, see Peter Alegi, *Laduma! Soccer, politics, and society in South Africa* (Pietermaritzburg: University of KwaZulu-Natal Press, 2004).

61 Durban figures taken from the 1951 census cited in Kuper, Watts, and Davies, *Durban: a study in racial ecology*, p. 85; 1960 national census figures quoted in van der Merwe et al., *White South African Elites*, p. 26.

62 For an account that situates Afrikaans–English divisions within schooling policy from the 1920s to the 1940s, see Brahm Fleisch, 'Social scientists as policy makers: E. G. Malherbe and the National Bureau for Educational and Social Research, 1929–1943', *Journal of Southern African Studies* 21, no. 5 (1995), pp. 349–72.

63 The dramatic exposure of the Broederbond and its members came in 1978 with the publication of Ivor Wilkins and Hans Strydom, *The Super Afrikaners: inside the Afrikaner Broederbond* (Cape Town: Jonathan Ball, 1978). Hermann Giliomee has argued that the influence of the Broederbond, while significant, has been exaggerated in South African history. Hermann Giliomee, *The Afrikaners: biography of a people* (Charlottesville VA: University of Virginia Press, 2003).

64 Giliomee, *The Afrikaners*, p. 53.

65 Haw, *Taking Stock*, p. 45

66 Malherbe, *Education in South Africa. Vol. 2*, p. 204.

67 See Dan O'Meara, *Volkskapitalisme: class, capital and ideology in the development of Afrikaner nationalism, 1934–1948* (Cambridge: Cambridge University Press, 1983).

68 Albert Grundlingh, 'Are we Afrikaners getting too rich? Cornucopia and change in Afrikanerdom in the 1960s', *Journal of Historical Sociology* 21, no. 2/3 (2008), pp. 143–65.

69 Albert Grundlingh, 'Playing for power? Rugby, Afrikaner nationalism and masculinity in South Africa, c. 1900–70', *International Journal of the History of Sport* 11, no. 3 (1994), p. 414.

70 Hendrik Verwoerd, 'Speech Delivered to the Senate, June 7, 1954' in Brian Rose and Raymond Tunmer (eds), *Documents in South African Education* (Johannesburg: A. D. Donker, 1975), p. 266.

71 May Katzen, *Industry in Greater Durban* (Pietermaritzburg: Town and Regional Planning Commission, 1961), p. 9.

72 Bill Freund, *Insiders and Outsiders: the Indian working class of Durban, 1910–1990* (Portsmouth NH: Heinemann, 1995).

73 Charles Feinstein, *An Economic History of South Africa: conquest, discrimination and development* (Cambridge: Cambridge University Press, 2005), p. 126.

74 Personal communication, Professor Vishnu Padayachee, 26 June 2016 (Professor Padayachee is a long-standing friend and colleague and agreed to be quoted).

75 For early history of Indian schools in south Durban, see Scott, 'Communal space construction', Chapter 7.

76 G. C. Oosthuizen, *Challenge to a South African University: the University of Durban-Westville* (Cape Town: Oxford University Press, 1981), p. 24.

77 Rajend Mesthrie, 'Language change, survival, decline: Indian languages in South Africa' in Rajend Mesthrie, *Language in South Africa*.

78 'Differentiated Secondary Education: The report of the Overseas Mission', *Journal of Secondary Education*, June (1956), pp. 32–5; see also Haw, *Taking Stock*, p. 73.

79 'New horizons for Clairwood High', *Fiat Lux*, 4 March 1978.

80 'Mr. P. R. T. Nel', *The Olympian*, 1964, p. 83.

81 Morrell, *From Boys to Gentlemen*.

82 'The education of a girl. Address to the Johannesburg High School Old Girls' Club, D. E. Langley', *Journal of Secondary Education*, September (1954), p. 6.

83 Elaine Unterhalter, 'The impact of apartheid on women's education in South Africa', *Review of African Political Economy* 48 (1990), pp. 66–75.

84 'Much more use of female labour vital', *Daily News*, 20 February 1964.

85 Unterhalter, 'The impact of apartheid', p. 70.

86 Van der Merwe et al., *White South African Elites*.

87 '43 p.c. varsity pass for DGHS', *Daily News*, 11 December 1968.

88 'Our Bluff high schools, Bluff Girls' High School', *The Bluff Newsletter*, February 1965, p. 3.

89 On the feminisation of domestic work, see Deborah Gaitskell, Judy Kimble, Moira Maconachie, and Elaine Unterhalter, 'Class, race and gender: domestic workers in South Africa', *Review of African Political Economy* 10, no. 27–8 (1983), pp. 86–108.

90 Letter from Mrs Fuller to Director of Education, 29 January 1963, General Enquiries Re. Schools Vol. 3, Box 10/P/13, Natal Education Department Records, Pietermaritzburg Archives Repository.

91 Letter from Mr Riddle to Director of Education, 14 May 1964, General Enquiries Re. Schools Vol. 3, Box 10/P/13, Natal Education Department Records, Pietermaritzburg Archives Repository.

92 Letter from IRATEPAYER, *The Bluff Ratepayer*, May 1977, p. 6.

93 Stephen Sparks, 'Civil society, pollution and the Wentworth oil refinery', *Historia* 51, no. 1 (2006), pp. 201–33. Sparks also notes that the second refinery (Sapref), proposed for the northern tip of the Bluff in the late 1950s, was, after opposition, built in Reunion, and thus close to the Indian and Coloured areas.

94 'Bluff drive-in', *Natal Mercury*, 4 June 1962.

95 Allan Pred, *Even In Sweden: racisms, racialized spaces and the popular geographical imagination* (Berkeley CA: University of California Press, 2000), p. 98.

### Chapter 3

1 Maasdorp and Humphreys, *From Shantytown to Township*, p. 71. According to Maasdorp and Humphreys, township officials estimated that the true

population figure in Umlazi was 50 per cent higher than the official one (p. 70). Prior to the building of the modern Umlazi Township, a small municipal-built housing settlement (called Umlazi Glebe) housed around 150 families on the site. University of Natal, *The Durban Housing Survey*, p. 476.

2 For opposition to girls' schooling in colonial Zimbabwe and Zambia, see Elizabeth Schmidt, *Peasants, Traders, and Wives: Shona women in the history of Zimbabwe, 1870–1939* (Portsmouth NH: Heinemann, 1992), p. 136; Anthony Simpson, *'Half-London in Zambia': contested identities in a Catholic mission school* (Edinburgh: Edinburgh University Press for International African Institute), pp. 26–7.

3 On precolonial and early colonial Zulu society, see especially Jeff Guy, *The Destruction of the Zulu Kingdom: the civil war in Zululand 1879–1884* (Pietermaritzburg: University of Natal Press, 1977).

4 Charles Van Onselen, *Studies in the Social and Economic History of the Witwatersrand, 1886–1914. 2 vols.* (Johannesburg: Ravan Press, 1982); Dunbar Moodie, *Going for Gold: men, mines and migration* (Berkeley CA: University of California Press, 1994).

5 Norman Etherington, 'Kingdoms of this world and the next: Christian beginnings among Zulu and Swazi' in Richard Elphick and Rodney Davenport (eds), *Christianity in South Africa: a political, social and cultural history* (Berkeley CA: University of California Press, 1997), p. 97.

6 Jean Comaroff and John Comaroff, *Christianity, Colonialism, and Consciousness in South Africa. Vol. 1: Of revelation and revolution* (Chicago IL: University of Chicago Press, 1991).

7 On Shepstone, see Jeff Guy, *Theophilus Shepstone and the Forging of Natal* (Pietermaritzburg: University of KwaZulu-Natal Press, 2013); Thomas McClendon, *White Chiefs, Black Lords: Shepstone and the colonial state in Natal, South Africa – 1845–1878* (New York NY: University of Rochester Press, 2010).

8 Martin Chanock, *The Making of South African Legal Culture 1902–1935: fear, favour, and prejudice* (Cambridge: Cambridge University Press, 2004).

9 See, for instance, Oyeronke Oyewumi, *The Invention of Women: making an African sense of Western gender discourses* (Minneapolis MN: University of Minnesota Press, 1997).

10 Mervyn Jeffreys, 'Lobolo is child-price', *African Studies* 10, no. 4 (1951), pp. 145–84. Those writing in the Marxist tradition, including Jeff Guy, stress the centrality of childbirth to agrarian labour, see Guy, *Theophilus Shepstone*. For the 'wealth-in-people' framework, see Jane Guyer, 'Wealth in people, wealth in things – introduction', *Journal of African History* 36, no. 1 (1995), pp. 83–90.

11 Jeff Guy, 'An accommodation of the patriarchs: Theophilus Shepstone and the foundations of the system of Native administration in Natal'. Paper presented at the Conference on Masculinities in Southern Africa, University of Natal, Durban, 2–4 July 1997.

12 Shula Marks, 'Patriotism, patriarchy and purity: Natal and the politics of Zulu ethnic consciousness' in Leroy Vail (ed.), *The Creation of Tribalism in Southern Africa* (Berkeley CA: University of California Press, 1991), pp. 215–40.

13 For an important account of how stories of Shaka's legendary power were forged in intricate interactions between the coloniser and colonised, see

Carolyn Hamilton, *Terrific Majesty: the power of Shaka Zulu and the limits of historical invention* (Cambridge MA: Harvard University Press, 1998). As Nafisa Sheik shows, not just 'African' and 'white' but also 'Indian' institutions were relationally constructed, though I cannot do justice to these links here. Nafisa Essop Sheik, 'Entangled patriarchies: sex, gender and relationality in the forging of Natal: a paper presented in critical tribute to Jeff Guy', *South African Historical Journal* 68, no. 3 (2016), pp. 304–17.

14 Moodie, *Going for Gold*; Mark Hunter, *Love in the Time of AIDS: inequality, gender, and rights in South Africa* (Bloomington IN: University of Indiana Press, 2010). Capitalists justified low male wages on the basis that men's families farmed and raised children in rural areas. See Harold Wolpe, 'Capitalism and cheap labour-power in South Africa: from segregation to apartheid', *Economy and Society* 1, no. 4 (1972), pp. 425–56.

15 John Colenso's 1861 dictionary defines *isifebe* (singular of *izifebe*) as 'fornicator; harlot'. John Colenso, *Zulu-English Dictionary* (Pietermaritzburg: P. Davis, 1861), p. 120.

16 Because there were few women in Umlazi old enough (in their eighties or older) to remember the 1920s and 1930s, I rely for this point also on dozens of oral histories I conducted in the early 2000s in Mandeni, 100 kilometres north of Durban, in preparation for my first book.

17 In an important challenge to binary depictions of African society, Leslie Bank has shown ongoing changes to the 'Red' (*abantu ababomvu*) and 'School' (*abantu basesikolweni*) cultural forms famously identified by Philip and Ioana Mayer in 1960s East London. Leslie Bank, 'Men with cookers: transformations in migrant culture, domesticity and identity in Duncan Village, East London', *Journal of Southern African Studies* 25, no. 3 (1999), pp. 392–416; Leslie Bank, *Home Spaces, Street Styles: contesting power and identity in a South African city* (London: Pluto Press, 2011). Philip Mayer, *Townsmen or Tribesmen: conservatism and the process of urbanization in a South African city. With contributions by Iona Mayer* (Cape Town: Oxford University Press, 1971). As well as the Mayers, Absolom Vilakazi in his detailed ethnography of 'Zulu transformations' stressed divisions between educated Christians and uneducated heathens. Absolom Vilakazi, *Zulu Transformations: a study of the dynamics of social change* (Pietermaritzburg: University of Natal Press, 1962).

18 Unterhalter, 'The impact of apartheid', pp. 70–1.

19 Maasdorp and Humphreys, *From Shantytown to Township*, p. 10.

20 Preston-Whyte's study found the following reasons for women coming to the city: death or illness of fathers or husbands (34 per cent); desertion of husband (17 per cent); birth of an illegitimate child (13 per cent); searching for husbands and lovers in towns (17 per cent). Preston-Whyte, 'Between two worlds', pp. 48–50.

21 Preston-Whyte discusses 'frequent home visits' among Durban's domestic workers. Preston-Whyte, 'Between two worlds', p. 130.

22 Mphiwa Mbatha, 'Migrant labour and its effects on tribal and family life among the Nyuswa of Botha's Hill', master's thesis, Department of Bantu Studies, University of Natal, 1960, p. 209.

23 Tom Moultrie and Ian Timæus, 'Fertility and living arrangements in South Africa', *Journal of Southern African Studies* 27, no. 2 (2001), pp. 207–23. That this rapid fall dates back to the 1960s is relevant because it predates the state's massive efforts to introduce family planning in the 1970s. See Barbara Brown,

'Facing the "black peril": the politics of population control in South Africa', *Journal of Southern African Studies* 13, no. 2 (1987), pp. 256–73.

Of course, fertility declines arose from a complex array of interacting issues, including the lesser importance of labour to the rural economy, and the heterogeneity of relationships in urban areas. John Caldwell's well-known argument is that schooling endowed children with a sense of individualism that eroded their 'vertical' support of parents, creating a disincentive for parents to have large families. John Caldwell, *Demographic Transition Theory* (Amsterdam: Springer, 2006). However, Caldwell later stressed how educated children retained an obligation towards their parents, acting as a form of 'insurance'. John Caldwell, 'On net intergenerational wealth flows: an update', *Population and Development Review* 31, no. 4 (2005), pp. 721–40. Writing specifically on South Africa, Caldwell discussed other reasons for the country's fertility decline, including the lowering of child mortality rates. John Caldwell and Pat Caldwell, 'The South African fertility decline', *Population and Development Review*, 19, no. 2 (1993), pp. 225–62. Moultrie and Timæus showed that unmarried and urban women had fewer children than those living in rural areas, in 'Fertility and living arrangements in South Africa'. Relevant, too, is that the old-age pension was extended to Africans in 1944, affecting wealth flows, although it was a small sum. Andreas Sagner, 'Ageing and social policy in South Africa: historical perspectives with particular reference to the Eastern Cape', *Journal of Southern African Studies* 26, no. 3 (2000), pp. 523–53.

24 'Extract from a report of the inter-departmental committee of inquiry in connection with the disturbances and rioting at Cato Manor, Durban on 24 January 1960', KCM 55204, Bourquin Papers, Killie Campbell Africana Library. Maasdorp and Humphreys estimate Cato Manor's population to be 80,000. Maasdorp and Humphreys, *From Shantytown to Township*, p. 25.

25 Figures on the number of domestic workers in Durban in 1966 are taken from Preston-Whyte, 'Between two worlds', p. 217.

26 On conflicting approaches to urban policy, see Deborah Posel, *The Making of Apartheid: conflict and compromise* (Oxford: Oxford University Press, 1991). On the one hand, apartheid's architects envisaged Africans as a 'tribal' people whose future lay in rural areas. Thus, the 1950 Group Areas Act led to the 'repatriation' of Africans without urban rights to 'reserves', the 1951 Bantu Authorities Act gave more power to 'tribal' institutions, and the 1952 Abolition of Passes and Co-ordination of Documents Act strengthened pass laws and extended them to women. However, the uneven way in which laws were implemented and circumvented makes any consideration of influx controls more than simply a matter of listing legislation. At first, tighter pass laws also incentivised those already living in urban areas to reduce their comings and goings from rural homes in order to accrue what was called in Durban 'Durban native' status (the term used in Durban for Section 10 rights that granted permanent residence to those who either were born in the city or had worked there for ten years for one employer or 15 years for several). See Mbatha, 'Migrant labour and its effects'. Moreover, as Evans says, 'A basic tension ... built into the structure of urban administration' was that actual administration of urban Africans was undertaken (until 1972) by cities themselves, and these were invariably run by the more 'liberal' United Party.

Ivan Evans, *Bureaucracy and Race: native administration in South Africa* (Berkeley CA: University of California Press, 1997), p. 35.

Furthermore, townships were administered differently depending on whether they were located in 'reserves' (later 'Bantustans' or 'homelands') or 'white' South Africa. The former provided greater security of tenure and an impetus for schooling, but this point should not be exaggerated because in reality structures of government overlapped. In Durban, on the face of it Umlazi was built on reserve land and administered by the Department of Bantu Administration and Development, and then from the 1970s by the KwaZulu homeland. KwaMashu was built in a 'white' area by Durban City (or Durban Corporation as it was called). In fact, Durban City undertook the planning and construction of both Umlazi and KwaMashu townships. In the 1970s, both Umlazi and KwaMashu were incorporated into the KwaZulu 'homeland', with KwaMashu having a brief period under the control of the Port Natal Administration Board. These administration boards were established by the national state to wrest control of townships from city governance – revealingly, however, Sighart Bourquin moved from heading Bantu administration in Durban to heading the Port Natal Administration Board. In both townships, Bantu education was administered by the national state, although in reality it worked through provincial structures.

27  Pauline Morris, *A History of Black Housing in South Africa* (Johannesburg: South Africa Foundation, 1981), p. 50.

28  Letter from City Engineers Department to Town Clerk, 30 August, 1960, 3/DBN, Box 4/1/5/1432, Durban Archives Repository, Durban. On 51/9 and 51/6 houses, see D. M. Calderwood, 'Native housing in South Africa', PhD thesis, Architecture, University of the Witwatersrand, Johannesburg, 1955.

29  For reference to swimming pools, see 'Umlazi officially opens', *Bantu*, September 1965, p. 342.

30  Paulus Zulu, 'Durban hostels and political violence: case studies in KwaMashu and Umlazi', *Transformation* 21 (1993), pp. 1–23.

31  Memorandum from Department of Native Affairs to All Local Authorities in the Union of South Africa, Regional Directors of Bantu Education, Inspectors of Bantu Education, Bantu School Boards and Urban Areas Commissioners, Box 1860, File 20/1171/12, Department of Bantu Administration and Development, National Archive Repository, Pretoria.

32  Freda Troup, *Forbidden Pastures: education under apartheid* (London: International Defence and Aid Fund, 1977), p. 28.

33  On pupil–teacher ratios, and a wealth of other comparative historical data on schooling, see Johannes Fedderke, Raphael de Kadt, and John Luiz, 'Uneducating South Africa: the failure to address the 1910–1993 legacy', *International Review of Education*, 46 (2000), pp. 257–81.

34  Menzi Senior Secondary School, Inspection and Inspections Report (1967–1985), KwaZulu Government Services, Education and Culture, File BB01346, KwaZulu-Natal Archives Repository, Ulundi.

35  See Owen Crankshaw, 'Class, race and residence in black Johannesburg, 1923–1970', *Journal of Historical Sociology* 18, no 4 (2005), pp. 353–93.

36  Leo Kuper, *An African Bourgeoisie: race, class, and politics in South Africa* (New Haven CT: Yale University Press, 1965).

37  On the size of plots, see 'Umlazi officially opens', *Bantu*, September 1965, p. 342. On vehicular access, see Meeting held at Pretoria on the 19th

February 1954 in the conference room Native Affairs Building in regard to the urbanization of Umlazi, NTS Box 3362, File 2169/307(A), National Archives Repository, Pretoria.

38 These employers attended a meeting in 1971 in Umlazi to discuss training requirements. 'Preliminary Report of an Informal Survey to Establish the Needs of Natal Industries with respect to Trained Semi-skilled Bantu Labour (Signed by Principal Umlazi Vocational Training School, 8 November 1971)', File A02237, KwaZulu-Natal Archives Repository, Ulundi. See also Feinstein, *An Economic History of South Africa*.

39 Deborah Posel's pioneering study *The Making of Apartheid* showed the centrality of gender to apartheid's urban policy. For KwaZulu-Natal, see also Hunter, *Love in the Time of AIDS*; Jason Hickel, *Democracy as Death: the moral order of anti-liberal politics in South Africa* (Berkeley CA: University of California Press, 2015).

40 'African housing campaign costs Durban R100m', *Natal Mercury*, 26 June 1964.

41 Accounts from Johannesburg and Cape Town suggest that women in these cities might have faced more hostile state controls on housing and influx measures than those in Durban, although East London also seems to have had a somewhat lenient policy towards women accessing township houses. For Cape Town, see Lee, *African Women and Apartheid*; for Johannesburg, Deborah Posel, 'Marriage at the drop of a hat: housing and partnership in South Africa's urban African townships, 1920s–1960s', *History Workshop Journal* 61, no. 1 (2006), pp. 57–76; for East London, see Berthold Pauw, *The Second Generation: a study of the family among urbanized Bantu in East London* (Cape Town: Oxford University Press, 1963). Eleanor Preston-Whyte notes that during her research with domestic workers in Durban (1962–6) there was no compulsory registration of African women, but by 1969 she found that regulations had tightened. Preston-Whyte, 'Between two worlds'. Similarly, Doug Hindson and Deborah Posel argue that although passes were officially extended to women in 1952, local authorities were relatively lenient to women until the 1960s. Doug Hindson, *Pass Controls and the Urban African Proletariat in South Africa* (Johannesburg: Ravan Press, 1987); Posel, *The Making of Apartheid*; Deborah Posel, 'Curbing African urbanization' in Mark Swilling, Richard Humphries, and Khehla Shubane (eds), *Apartheid City in Transition* (Oxford: Oxford University Press, 1991), pp. 19–32.

42 South African Government, *Natal Code of Native Law* (Johannesburg: University of Witwatersrand Press, 1945), p. 11. For Natal women's particular legal 'disabilities', see Jack Simons, *African Women: their legal status in South Africa* (London: C. Hurst, 1968).

43 South African Government, *Natal Code of Native Law*, p. 11.

44 I stumbled across these uncatalogued emancipation cases in the Durban Archives Repository (I was granted permission to peruse the strongrooms under supervision). I estimate that around half of the approximately 500 Bantu Affairs Commissioner's Court cases that I found (covering 1966–7) are emancipation cases.

45 Most emancipation claims were filed by African and Indian lawyers based in the Indian business district. Names and addresses of the lawyers that worked on court cases include: Bhengu, Gcabashe & Co. attorneys, 118 Grey Street;

R. A. V. Ngcobo, 120 Grey Street; A. V. B. Nyembezi, 118 Grey Street; Mr T. N. Makiwane 82 Victoria Street; Don Kali & Company, 118 Grey Street. Racially mixed downtown areas in Durban therefore played a critical role in enabling African women to access information and legal institutions. See also Marijke Du Toit, '"Anginayo ngisho indibilishi!" (I don't have a penny!): the gender politics of "native welfare" in Durban, 1930–1939', *South African Historical Journal* 66, no. 2 (2014), pp. 291–319.

46 Bantu Commissioner's Court, 383/66, *Nesta Msomi v Ex Parte*, Durban Archives Repository.

47 Bantu Commissioner's Court, 327/66, *Winnifred Mhlongo v Fabian Mhlongo*, Durban Archives Repository.

48 I make this estimate based on interviews with Umlazi residents and records of township houses being sold off to renters (many are stored in the National Archives Repository, Pretoria, as a consequence of Umlazi's administration by the Department of Bantu Administration and Development before the township fell under the KwaZulu homeland).

49 Durban city pioneered the 'Durban system': a monopoly on brewing and selling traditional beer to fund segregated 'native' administration. See Maynard Swanson, '"The Durban system": roots of urban apartheid in colonial Natal', *African Studies* 35, no. 3–4 (1976), pp. 159–76.

50 Letter from Department of Bantu Administration to the Town Clerk, Durban, 16 March 1959, KCM 55174, Bourquin Papers, Killie Campbell Africana Library.

51 Posel, 'Marriage at the drop of a hat'. Iain Edwards' study of Cato Manor suggests that officials, keen to clear the area, awarded Section 10 rights relatively freely. Iain Edwards, 'Mkhumbane our home: African shantytown society in Cato Manor Farm, 1946–1960', PhD thesis, University of Natal, Durban, 1989, p. 232.

52 Muriel Horrell, *The African Reserves of South Africa* (Johannesburg: South African Institute of Race Relations, 1969), pp. 92–4; Morris, *A History of Black Housing in South Africa*, p. 74.

53 Letter S. Bourquin to Mrs. Knight, 27 September 1968, Port Natal Administration Board microfilm KCF66, Killie Campbell Africana Library.

54 Case number 47, 27 November 1973, Biziwe Boqo, Black Sash File 367, KCM 39275, Killie Campbell Africana Library.

55 Clement Doke et al., *English/Zulu Zulu/English Dictionary* (Johannesburg: Witwatersrand University Press, 1958), p. 385. As well as the greater security that followed the falling away of influx controls (these being completely removed in 1986), another factor amplifying the claims women made on family houses is that they often outlived their (older) husbands who had been granted the houses. In addition, the state's selling of houses necessitated a relatively simple change from rental agreements to purchase agreements. Thus, the names of lawful occupants of rented houses were transferred to grant deeds (because Umlazi was located on reserve land, residents were given grant deeds, not full title deeds). Crucially, when the original grantee passed away, occupants whose names were on the deed used these to argue that the house must continue to be *used* by multiple family members.

56 Hyslop, *The Classroom Struggle*.

57 Muriel Horrell, *A Decade of Bantu Education* (Johannesburg: South African Institute of Race Relations, 1964), p. 89.

58 Margaret Wong, 'Mass education in Africa', *African Affairs* 43, no. 172 (1944), pp. 105–11.
59 Charles Loram and Thomas McIlwraith, *The North American Indian Today. University of Toronto–Yale University seminar conference, Toronto, September 4–16, 1939* (Toronto: University of Toronto Press, 1943). On Loram, see Sue Krige, '"Trustees and agents of the state"? Missions and the formation of policy towards African education, 1910–1920', *South African Historical Journal* 40, no. 1 (2011), pp. 74–94; Richard Glotzer, 'Charles Templeman Loram: education and race relations in South Africa and North America' in Kallaway and Swartz, *Empire and Education in Africa*, pp. 155–75.
60 Charles Loram, *The Education of the South African Native* (London: Longmans, Green and Co., 1917). Daniel Magaziner shows how Bantu education's emphasis on crafts was taken up by art teachers and learners at Indaleni government school. Magaziner, *The Art of Life in South Africa*.
61 On 'adaptive education' elsewhere in British colonies, see Stephen Ball, 'Imperialism, social control and the colonial curriculum in Africa', *Journal of Curriculum Studies* 15, no. 3 (1983), pp. 237–63.
62 Saul Dubow, *Racial Segregation and the Origins of Apartheid in South Africa, 1919–36* (Basingstoke: Macmillan, 1989).
63 Cynthia Kros, *The Seeds of Separate Development: origins of Bantu education* (Pretoria: UNISA Press, 2010).
64 On Bronislaw Malinowski and his approach to segregation, including through education, see Isak Niehaus, 'Anthropology at the dawn of apartheid: Radcliffe-Brown and Malinowski's South African engagements, 1919–1934', *Focaal: Journal of Global and Historical Anthropology* 76, no. 3 (2017), pp. 1–24.
65 Judith Irvine, 'Subjected words: African linguistics and the colonial encounter', *Language and Communication* 28 (2008), p. 338. Irvine emphasises the importance that most (but not all) missionaries gave to communicating in African languages to enable religious conversion, as well as a sense of the competition among missionaries, variation across the continent, and the way in which standardisation drew from technologies of the time (especially printing presses).
66 Apartheid's language policy was aided by government ethnologist N. Van Warmelo's classification of Bantu speakers into ten 'tribes' based on a 'language map'. On the entangled history of linguists, ethnologists, and race in South Africa, see Chapter 3 in Dubow, *Scientific Racism in Modern South Africa*.
67 Meghan Healy-Clancy, 'Mass education and the gendered politics of "development" in apartheid South Africa and late colonial British Africa' in Kallaway and Swartz, *Empire and Education in Africa*.
68 Union of South Africa, 'Report of the Native Education Commission, 1949–1951', cited in Rose and Tunmer, *Documents in South African Education*, p. 245.
69 Chapter 5 in Hyslop, *The Classroom Struggle*.
70 Eiselen, quoted in Troup, *Forbidden Pastures*, p. 21.
71 Werner Eiselen, 'The standard of English and Afrikaans in our Bantu schools', *Bantu Education Journal* 17, no. 5 (1971), p. 6. On the decline of standards in English, see also Troup, *Forbidden Pastures*.
72 Tabata, *Education for Barbarism*.

73 For a critical discussion of the UNESCO report and detailed empirical study of second language acquisition in Morocco, see Chapter 8 in Daniel Wagner, *Literacy, Culture, and Development: becoming literate in Morocco* (Cambridge: Cambridge University Press, 1993).

74 At this time, schooling was divided along the following lines: lower primary to standard 2 (grade 4); higher primary standards 3–6 (grades 5–8); junior secondary school for Forms 1-III (grades 8 to 10), after which a Junior Secondary Certificate or JC was taken; and high school with Forms IV and V (grades 11 and 12), ending with a Senior Certificate exam.

75 Jacob Dlamini, *Native Nostalgia* (Cape Town: Jacana, 2010), p. 92.

76 City officials viewed respectable Christian couples as the most likely candidates for housing in Lamontville, the city's first township, which was opened in 1934. See Louise Torr, 'Lamontville – Durban's "model village": the realities of township life, 1934–1960', *Journal of Natal and Zulu History*, 10 (1987), pp. 103–17.

77 Monica Wilson and Archie Mafeje, *Langa: a study of social groups in an African township* (Cape Town: Oxford University Press, 1963), p. 26; Kuper, *An African Bourgeoisie*.

78 Alf Gwebu and Joe Motsiri, 'They break up marriages', *Bona*, February (1965), p. 25.

79 Unterhalter, 'The impact of apartheid', p. 71.

80 Cited in Troup, *Forbidden Pastures*, p. 40.

81 Meghan Healy-Clancy showed in her study of Inanda Seminary that the state gave girls' mission schools particular leeway because educated women were deemed to be less threatening than educated men. Healy-Clancy, *A World of Their Own*.

82 Mission schools costs taken from 'Africans pay more than whites for education', *Natal Mercury*, 11 February 1964. Public school costs taken from 'Education – Africans must pay', *Star*, 29 October 1965. This was based on costs in Soweto Township.

83 That schooling costs rose by grade was noted in surveys undertaken in both Umlazi Township and KwaMashu Township in Durban. See Valerie Moller et al., 'A black township in Durban: a study of needs and problems', unpublished report, Durban: Centre for Applied Social Sciences, University of Natal, 1978; Julian May, *A Study of Income and Expenditure and Other Socio-Economic Structures in Rural KwaZulu. Volume 7: Umlazi* (Durban: KwaZulu Finance and Investment Corporation, 1986). In 1967, the Umlazi District School Board controlled 50 schools and funded 38 posts; this was to be 'a very heavy financial task'. 'Annual report for 1967 of the Umlazi District School Board', *Bantu Education Journal* March (1968), pp. 33–4. On the funding of schools in urban areas through a school levy and school boards, see 'Memo: Maintenance of Schools in Urban Bantu Residential Areas', Box 1860, File A20/1171/12, National Archives Repository, Pretoria.

84 On the gendering of school subjects, in the context of violence in schools, see Robert Morrell and Relebohile Moletsane, 'Inequality and fear: learning and working inside Bantu education schools' in Peter Kallaway (ed.), *The History of Education under Apartheid* (Cape Town: Pearson, 2002).

85 James Ferguson, 'The bovine mystique: power, property and livestock in rural Lesotho', *Man* 20, no. 4 (1985), pp. 647–74.

86 Mbatha, 'Migrant labour and its effects', p. 278.

87  Preston-Whyte, 'Between two worlds', p. 381.

88  Jacklyn Cock, *Maids and Madams: a study in the politics of exploitation* (Johannesburg: Ravan Press, 1980), p. 18.

89  May, *A Study of Income. Volume 7: Umlazi*, p. 49.

90  Jonathan Hyslop, 'State education policy and the social reproduction of the urban African working class: the case of the Southern Transvaal 1955–1976', *Journal of Southern African Studies* 14, no. 3 (1988), p. 461.

91  On racial paternalism, see Charles Van Onselen, 'The social and economic underpinning of paternalism and violence on the maize farms of the south-western Transvaal, 1900–1950', *Journal of Historical Sociology* 5, no. 2 (1992), pp. 127–60.

92  On racial maternalism, see Shireen Ally, *From Servants to Workers: South African domestic workers and the democratic state* (Ithaca NY: Cornell University Press, 2009).

93  Preston-Whyte, 'Between two worlds', p. 142. According to Eleanor Preston-Whyte, who conducted PhD research in the 1960s, these close relationships were especially a feature of working-class areas of Durban. In the more upper-middle-class Morningside, she found that '[t]his tolerance of the employers in allowing children on the premises seldom occurred' (p. 142). For a vivid study of the interlinked worlds of black and white women, including through the mediation of education, see Shula Marks, *Not Either an Experimental Doll: the separate worlds of three South African women* (Bloomington IN: Indiana University Press, 1988).

## Chapter 4

1  'Parents' thinking is way ahead of official policy', *Sunday Tribune*, 2 December 1990.

2  Sibusisiwe Nombuso Dlamini, *Youth and Identity Politics in South Africa, 1990–94* (Toronto: University of Toronto Press, 2005), pp. 66–68.

3  'Delene Ltd', *Homelife* 2, no. 10 (1987), p. 4. Chappies is a pseudonym. I chose it because it is the colloquial name of a similar area in Sundumbili Township, Mandeni, which is the site of my first major research project. Chappies was the name of the building company that built the houses, as was the case of the real name of this privately developed Umlazi area.

4  As Pirie notes: 'Poor whites have worked as railway labourers in South Africa for practically the entire history of train transport in the country.' Gordon Pirie, 'White rail labour in South Africa 1873–1924' in Robert Morrell (ed.), *White but Poor: essays on the history of poor whites in Southern Africa 1880–1940* (Pretoria: University of South Africa Press, 1992), p. 101.

5  Evans, *Bureaucracy and Race*, p. 64.

6  Tikly and Mabogoane, 'Marketisation as a strategy for desegregation and redress'.

7  For a recent review of the Durban strikes and Soweto Uprising, see Julian Brown, *The Road to Soweto: resistance and the uprising of 16 June 1976* (Johannesburg: Jacana, 2016).

8  This is in sharp contrast to the growth of real GDP per capita at 2.2 per cent per annum from 1950 to 1973. Feinstein, *An Economic History of South Africa*, p. 145.

9 Marais, *South Africa: limits to change*, p. 141.

10 From 1960 to 1978, the number of registered black nurses and midwives increased from 5,000 to 52,000. Shula Marks, *Divided Sisterhood: race, class and gender in the South African nursing profession* (London: Palgrave Macmillan, 1994), p. 170. In offices, white women still dominated more prestigious front-of-house jobs such as secretaries and receptionists, but by the early 1970s African people made up almost half the salespeople employed by one nationwide chain of furniture stores. Crankshaw, *Race, Class and the Changing Division of Labour*, p. 76.

11 See Hunter, *Love in the Time of AIDS*, p. 75.

12 After the ending of influx controls in 1986, shack settlements mushroomed at an accelerated pace in Durban, and by 1987 the informally housed African population comprised 50 per cent of the total African population, up from 37 per cent in 1980. At this time, scholars increasingly noted divisions between poorer informal settlement dwellers and better-off township dwellers. For these Durban figures (quoting a study by May and Stavrou) and the connection between spatial differentiation and political violence in the 1980s, see Doug Hindson, Mark Byerley, and Mike Morris, 'From violence to reconstruction: the making, disintegration and remaking of an apartheid city', CSDS Working Paper 10 (Durban: Centre for Social and Development Studies, University of Natal, 1993). For the argument that shack settlements became central to social differentiation in Johannesburg, see Chapter 7 in Crankshaw, *Race, Class and the Changing Division of Labour*.

13 Sifiso Mzobe, *Young Blood* (Kwela: Cape Town, 2010), p. 14

14 See Chapter 7 of Bonginkosi 'Blade' Nzimande, 'The corporate guerrillas: class formation and the African corporate petty bourgeoisie in post-1973 South Africa', PhD dissertation, University of Natal, 1991.

15 For a discussion of the Department of Bantu Education's ending of its fixed funding contribution to Bantu education in 1972, see Hyslop, *The Classroom Struggle*, pp. 141–5.

16 May, *A Study of Income. Volume 7: Umlazi*, p. 17.

17 Umlazi Township Council, 'Minutes of the Special Meeting of the Umlazi Township Council held at the Council Chamber on 1.6.78', File ZM8/13/3/20, KwaZulu-Natal Archives Repository, Ulundi.

18 A small number of black schools located in 'white' Natal (for instance, those in Lamontville Township, close to Umlazi, which was never incorporated into KwaZulu) remained outside KwaZulu and under the control of the national Department of Education and Training (DET). However, by 1980 there were eight times as many standard 10 children in KwaZulu than in DET schools (7,340 compared with 908). Buthelezi Commission, *The Buthelezi Commission: the requirements for stability and development in KwaZulu and Natal. Volume II* (Durban: H + H Publications, 1982), pp. 288–9.

19 Doug Tilton, 'Creating an "educated workforce": Inkatha, big business, and educational reform in KwaZulu', *Journal of Southern African Studies* 18, no. 1 (1992), pp. 166–89.

20 Untitled document, KwaZulu Cabinet, Agenda and Minutes 1982, p. 3, KwaZulu-Natal Archives Repository, Ulundi.

21 Fedderke, de Kadt, and Luiz, 'Uneducating South Africa', p. 267.

22 Untitled document, KwaZulu Cabinet, Agenda and Minutes 1982, p. 6, KwaZulu-Natal Archives Repository.

23 For example, on drinking, see inspection reports for Menzi High. 'Teacher Report(s), Menzi High, 1973', File BB01346, KwaZulu-Natal Archives Repository.

24 '20 schools with highest pass rates', *Focus on Education* 6, no. 2 (1991), p. 6.

25 'General Inspection Report on Post-Primary Schools, Zwelibanzi Senior Secondary School, September 2 and 3, 1981, Department of Bantu Education' [note: other reports are titled 'KwaZulu Government Service', so this appears to have been a KwaZulu official using old DBE stationary], File BB02391, KwaZulu-Natal Archives Repository.

26 'Menzi High School, 11–12 April 1984', File BB01346, KwaZulu-Natal Archives Repository.

27 KwaZulu Government Service, 'Memorandum to the Cabinet from Department of Economic Affairs, Movable Assets as Part of the Umlazi Comprehensive Technical High School – Loan Offer, 18 January 1990', File 5/1/3/4/80, KwaZulu-Natal Archives Repository. The government gave Comtech, Umlazi Commercial, and Ogwini extra resources to promote technical and commercial skills, and this helped blur the hierarchies between academic and technical learning.

28 Es'kia Mphahlele, *Es'Kia: education, African humanism and culture, social consciousness, literary appreciation* (Johannesburg: Kwela Books, 2002), p. 68.

29 Bernard Magubane, *Bernard Magubane: my life and times* (Pietermaritzburg: University of KwaZulu Natal Press, 2010), p. 50.

30 Jonathan Hyslop shows that, in the 1950s, the moderate 'professional' union ATASA became the dominant organisation of the teaching profession and remained so for the next two decades, its Natal affiliate being NATU. See Jonathan Hyslop, 'Teachers and trade unions', *South African Labour Bulletin* 11, no. 6 (1986), pp. 90–7.

31 Daniel Magaziner, *The Law and the Prophets: black consciousness in South Africa, 1968–1977* (Athens OH: Ohio University Press, 2010).

32 See the recollection by former student Cyril Gamede, who went on to become the chief executive of Umgeni Water. 'Successful school gone wrong', *Sunday Independent – IOL*, 25 June 2014, www.iol.co.za/sundayindependent/success ful-school-gone-wrong-1708766 (accessed 25 October 2016).

33 In 1982, the interracial Buthelezi Commission debated what it called 'The eternal choice: selective or universal education?' It came down in favour of the need to 'foster and develop leadership qualities … even if this means a selective system'. Buthelezi Commission, *The Buthelezi Commission. Vol. II*, p. 271. On KwaZulu as a liberal 'laboratory' for reforming apartheid, see Daryl Glaser, 'Behind the Indaba: the making of the KwaNatal option', *Transformation* 2 (1986), pp. 4–30.

34 Blade Nzimande and Sandile Thusi, *Children of War: the impact of political violence on schooling* (Durban: Education Policy Unit, University of Natal, 1996), p. 37.

35 Neville Alexander, *Language Policy and National Unity in South Africa/Azania* (Cape Town: Buchu Books, 1989).

36 On English in Transkei and Bophuthatswana, see Jeffrey Butler, Robert Rotberg, and John Adams, *The Black Homelands of South Africa: the political and economic development of Bophuthatswana and KwaZulu* (Berkeley CA: University of California Press, 1977), p. 32, 111; for KwaZulu, see Buthelezi Commission, *The Buthelezi Commission. Vol. I*, p. 73.

37 'Editorial: private schools', *Bantu Education Journal* (September 1973), p. 2.

38 Isaac Kubeka, 'A preliminary survey of Zulu dialects in Natal and Zululand', master's thesis, University of Natal, Durban, 1979.

39 Heather Hughes, *The First President: a life of John L. Dube, founding president of the ANC* (Auckland Park: Jacana, 2011).

40 Tim Gibbs shows the strong schooling connections between homeland elites and ANC-aligned leaders. Timothy Gibbs, *Mandela's Kinsmen: nationalist elites and apartheid's first Bantustans* (Woodbridge: James Currey, 2014).

41 On the extent that employers' demands for 'skills' involved training to improve 'attitude', see Linda Chisholm, 'Redefining skills: black education in South Africa in the 1980s', *Comparative Education* 19, no. 3 (1983), pp. 357–71.

42 See Nzimande and Thusi, *Children of War*, p. 12.

43 Untitled document, KwaZulu Cabinet, Agenda and Minutes 1982, p. 13, KwaZulu-Natal Archives Repository, Ulundi.

44 Inkatha–ANC relations worsened when Buthelezi's authority was challenged by the launch of the ANC-supporting United Democratic Front in 1983 and the formation of the COSATU union federation in 1985. Hostilities peaked in the early 1990s after the release of Nelson Mandela and uncertainty about the transition. See Debby Bonnin, 'Claiming spaces, changing places: political violence and women's protests in KwaZulu-Natal', *Journal of Southern African Studies* 26, no. 2 (2000), pp. 301–16; Dlamini, *Youth and Identity Politics in South Africa, 1990–94*; Gerhard Maré and Georgina Hamilton, *An Appetite for Power: Buthelezi's Inkatha and the politics of 'loyal resistance'* (Johannesburg: Ravan Press, 1987); Thembisa Waetjen, *Workers and Warriors: masculinity and the struggle for nation in South Africa* (Urbana-Champaign IL: University of Illinois Press, 2004).

45 For studies on resistance to apartheid in the 1980s, see Colin Bundy, 'Street sociology and pavement politics: aspects of youth and student resistance in Cape Town', *Journal of Southern African Studies* 13, no. 3 (1987), pp. 303–30; Monique Marks, *Young Warriors: youth politics, identity and violence in South Africa* (Johannesburg: Witwatersrand University Press, 2001); Jeremy Seekings, *A History of the United Democratic Front in South Africa, 1983–1991* (Athens OH: Ohio University Press, 2000).

46 On urban bias in homeland education, see H. Jacklin and J. Graaff, 'Rural education in South Africa: a report on schooling systems in the Bantustans', unpublished report prepared for the National Education Coordinating Committee's National Education Policy Investigation, 1992.

47 The principals I spoke with who led schools at these times talked about 'walking a tightrope' so as not to be seen as antagonising ANC-aligned groups or Inkatha (residents were more likely to note that principals leaned towards Inkatha).

48 Praisley Mdluli, 'Ubuntu-Botho: Inkatha's "people's education"', *Transformation* 5 (1987), pp. 60–77.

49 Clive Glaser, 'Soweto's islands of learning: Morris Isaacson and Orlando high schools under Bantu Education, 1958–1975', *Journal of Southern African Studies* 41, no. 1 (2015), pp. 159–71.

50 Elizabeth de Villiers, *Walking the Tightrope: recollections of a schoolteacher in Soweto* (Johannesburg: Jonathan Ball Publishers, 1990).

51  National Education Crisis Committee, 'People's Education: creating a democratic future' (undated), 15, Box A1984 C16.2, Cullen Archives, National Education Union of South Africa (NEUSA) Papers, University of Witwatersrand, Johannesburg.

52  Siyabonga Maphumulo, 'Leading by example, for 50 years', City of Durban, April 2009, www.durban.gov.za/Documents/City_Government/Media_Publications/Metrobeat/2009/Metrobeat%20April%202009%20Page%2022.pdf.

53  'The 1961 Educational Panel, education and the South African economy' cited in Rose and Tunmer, *Documents in South African Education*, p. 272.

54  Vincent Crapanzano, *Waiting: the whites of South Africa* (New York NY: Random Books, 1985).

55  Falkof, *Satanism and Family Murder in Late Apartheid South Africa*.

56  'Juniors have a hard time finding jobs', *Natal Mercury*, 17 January 1979; see also Crankshaw, *Race, Class and the Changing Division of Labour*, p. 76.

57  'What's the plan for Whitey?', *Natal Mercury*, 10 January 1979.

58  'Schools concerned about job prospects', *Southlands Sun*, 23 January 1987.

59  John Dreijmanis, *The Role of the South African Government in Tertiary Education* (Johannesburg: South African Institute of Race Relations, 1988), p. 27, 47.

60  Jonathan Hyslop, 'Why did apartheid's supporters capitulate? "Whiteness", class and consumption in urban South Africa, 1985–1995', *Society in Transition* 31, no. 1 (2000), p. 40. On reforms to apartheid in the 1970s and 1980s, see also Saul Dubow, *Apartheid: 1948–1994* (Oxford: Oxford University Press, 2014).

61  Preschools charged fees but could apply for a state subsidy. 'Memorandum for Executive Committee', box marked NED European Nursery School Policy, Vol. 2., File NED 50/4, 1/P/1, Pietermaritzburg Archives Depository.

62  Haw, *Taking Stock*, pp. 106–7.

63  Letter from Subject-Inspectress: Infant Teaching and Farm Schools, 10 March 1969, box marked NED European Nursery School Policy, Vol. 2., File NED 50/4, 1/P/1, Pietermaritzburg Archives Depository.

64  See Crankshaw, *Race, Class and the Changing Division of Labour*, p. 159

65  See, for instance, 'Women who cope on their own', *Femina*, November 1982, p. 28.

66  'A so-called privileged white states his case', *Natal Mercury*, 22 February 1980.

67  For instance, 'Letters of application', *Careers for You* 1, no. 1, April 1984.

68  The slogan appears on the front page of *The Child*, summer issue, October–December 1987.

69  'Education: who should carry the can?', *The Child*, autumn issue, January–March 1987, p. 8.

70  Fedderke, de Kadt, and Luiz, 'Uneducating South Africa', p. 266.

71  To reduce the influence of young children in the statistics, I take the number of residents with standard 6 and above as the denominator for calculations of highest educational level. Census reports used here and below are as follows: Population Census 1970, Metropolitan Area Durban (02–05–17); Population Census 1980, Durban/Pinetown/Inanda (02–80-17); Population Census 1991, Durban/Pinetown/Inanda/Chatsworth (03–01–14). I refer hereafter to Census 1970, Census 1980, and Census 1991. Education data are calculated from Census 1970 (Table A5) and Census 1991 (Table 4.1). Population by

age data are calculated from Census 1970 (Table A4), Census 1980 (Table 1), and Census 1991 (Table 1.1). I use the (undifferentiated) statistical area of the Bluff for the 1970 data and for the latter years combine the Brighton Beach, Fynnlands, Grosvenor, Ocean View, Van Riebeeck Park, and Wentworth enumeration areas; for the upper Berea I use Berea North for 1970 and Musgrave for the latter years.

72 Calculated from Census 1970 (Table A9).

73 Education sources cited above. Income statistics calculated from Census 1991 (Table 6.1).

74 The proportion of children under the age of five on the Bluff and in Berea for 1960, 1970, and 1991 was, respectively, 10, 8, and 4 per cent (Bluff), and 8, 4, and 3 per cent (Berea). Sources cited above.

75 Natal Education Department, 'Report on Durban Survey – 1977', NED Box 367, File 10/P/19, Pietermaritzburg Archives Repository.

76 City of Durban, 'City Engineer's Report on the Planning of the Bluff', June 1967, p. 36.

77 Quote from 'Education: new bill will hit fat cats', *Sunday Tribune*, 14 February 1982.

78 'Day of nostalgia for Mansfield High School', *Daily News*, 21 June 1988.

79 Home language data are taken from Census 1970 (Table A6), Census 1980 (Table 2), and Census 1991 (Table 2.1).

80 'Another Natal Afrikaans medium school to close', *Natal Witness*, 11 December 1990.

81 See Hyslop, 'Why did apartheid's supporters capitulate?'

82 Christie, *Open Schools*, pp. 23–4.

83 Natal Education Department table in File 10/P/2, 'Admission of non-Whites to White schools', Natal Education Department Records, Pietermaritzburg Archives Repository.

84 Letter from principal, Holy Childhood Convent School, to Director of Education, Natal Education Department, 26 January 1978, File 10/P/2, Natal Education Department Records, Pietermaritzburg Archives Repository; see also 'First-day nerves for Israel', *Daily News*, 30 January 1978.

85 Christie, *Open Schools*, p. 113; Nzimande, 'The corporate guerrillas', p. 272.

86 Healy-Clancy, *A World of Their Own*.

87 The NED records do not give a specific breakdown by gender of black students admitted into white schools. However, most private schools are single-sex institutions and figures from these show that 78 black girls and 15 black boys were present in white private schools in 1979. Natal Education Department table in File 10/P/2, Natal Education Department Records, Pietermaritzburg Archives Repository.

88 This comment is taken from a letter written in 1978 by St Mary's Anglican girls' school, located near Durban, to the Natal Education Department requesting that it admit a Coloured girl. Letter from St Mary's Diocesan School for Girls, Kloof, to Director of Education, Natal Education Department, 18 May 1978, File 10/P/2, Natal Education Department Records, Pietermaritzburg Archives Repository. The Director of Education stated in correspondence that he was 'technically breaking the law' by agreeing to admit black students and asked the schools to avoid press statements. Letter from G. Hosking, Director of Education, Natal Education Department, to the principal, Convent High School, undated but from other records 1978,

File 10/P/2, Natal Education Department Records, Pietermaritzburg Archives Repository.

89 Letter from principal, Convent School of Our Lady of Natal to Director of Education, Natal Education Department, 3 December 1979, PAR, File 10/P/2, Natal Education Department Records, Pietermaritzburg Archives Repository. Nursery schools relied on private funding, and this quote also suggests that Coloured schools admitted black African students in the 1970s.

90 Letter from principal, Holy Childhood Convent School, to Director of Education, Natal Education Department, 26 January 1978, PAR, File 10/P/2, Natal Education Department Records, Pietermaritzburg Archives Repository.

91 Letter from principal, Maris Stella Convent to Director of Education, Natal Education Department, 24 December 1977, PAR, File 10/P/2, Natal Education Department Records, Pietermaritzburg Archives Repository.

92 Headmaster of St Barnabas College, Johannesburg, cited in Randall, *Little England on the Veld*, p. 6.

93 Nazir Carrim, *Desegregation in Coloured and Indian Schooling* (Johannesburg: Education Policy Unit, University of the Witwatersrand, 1992).

94 Anthony Lemon, 'Desegregation and privatisation in white South African schools: 1990–1992', *Journal of Contemporary African Studies* 12, no. 2 (1994), pp. 200–21.

95 L Chisholm, 'A brief history of NEUSA', Box A2294/A, Cullen Archives, University of the Witwatersrand. I am not exploring in detail the positions of teachers, but the theme of the 1987 conference of the Teachers Association of South Africa (TASA) – 'Education in post-apartheid society' – shows a clear mood for change. 'Conference '87. Theme ... education in a post-apartheid society', *TASA News* XVIII, no. 5 (1987), p. 1.

96 When President de Klerk held a landmark referendum in 1992 to determine whether reforms to apartheid should be continued, a higher proportion of Durbanites voted in favour than in any other major city. In Durban, 85 per cent of white South Africans voted in the 1992 referendum to continue the reform process. 'Durban records highest "yes" vote majority in SA', *Natal Mercury*, 19 March 1992. The national average was a 69 per cent 'yes' vote.

97 Lemon, 'Desegregation and privatisation in white South African schools', p. 206.

98 The phrase is from a governing body chair in a working-class Durban school studied by Nadine Dolby, *Constructing Race: youth, identity, and popular culture in South Africa* (New York NY: SUNY Press, 2001), p. 33.

99 'Black pupils make history', *Berea Mail*, 18 January 1991; 'New era opens for Natal's "white" schools', *Natal Mercury*, 14 January 1991.

100 'Parent body wants white status quo', *Southlands Sun*, 1 February 1991.

101 'Association against schools' decision to opt for model B', *Southlands Sun*, 8 March 1991. *Kia* is a common misspelling of the term *ikhaya*, which means home.

102 'Whites bombarded with propaganda', *Bluff Ratepayer*, 11 March 1987.

103 'Closed book', *Southlands Sun*, 25 January 1991.

104 'Parents to vote soon', *Southlands Sun*, 8 March 1991; 'Yes to model B', *Southlands Sun*, 28 March 1991.

105 'Du Bois for Grosvenor', *Southlands Sun*, 2 August 1991. It is worth noting that even during this 'swing to the right', only 30 per cent of the electorate actually voted.

106 'The model C money-muncher', *Natal Mercury*, 8 April 1992; 'Schools "mean business"', *Natal Mercury*, 23 June 1992.

107 '"White" schools take hard line on collection of fees', *Natal Mercury*, 26 August 1992.

108 'Dilemma in C', *Natal Mercury*, 28 August 1992.

109 'Quo vadis model C?', *Natal Mercury*, 23 January 1993.

110 'School stands firm', *Southlands Sun*, 23 February 1996.

111 Grundlingh, 'Are we Afrikaners getting too rich?'; Hyslop, 'Why did apartheid's supporters capitulate?'

112 Malherbe, *Education in South Africa. Vol. 2*, p. 526.

113 South African Institute of Race Relations, *Race Relations Survey 1991/2*, p. 208.

114 'The matric conundrum', *Natal Mercury*, 2 January 1993.

115 South African Institute of Race Relations, *Race Relations Survey 1991/2*, p. 208. On Indian schools, see particularly C. Kuppusami and M. Pillay, *Pioneer Footprints: growth of Indian education in South Africa, 1860–1977* (Johannesburg: Nasou, 1978).

116 That is: 'Schools will continue to serve the residents of their geographical areas, which will only change gradually.' 'Will our children have a better education?', KwaZulu Natal Indaba advert, *Southlands Sun*, 24 April 1987.

117 Brij Maharaj and Jabulani Mpungose, 'The erosion of residential segregation in South Africa: the "greying" of Albert Park in Durban', *Geoforum* 25, no. 1 (1994), pp. 19–32.

118 Ethan Chang, 'The ethical limitations of South Africa's education market', Independent Study Project (ISP) Collection, paper 704 (Redlands CA: University of Redlands, 2009).

119 'Association against schools' decision to opt for model B', *Southlands Sun*, 8 March 1991.

120 Pam Christie, 'Transition tricks?: policy models for school desegregation in South Africa, 1990–94', *Journal of Education Policy* 10, no. 1 (1995), p. 49.

121 'Glenardle zoning does not include Umlazi', *Southlands Sun*, 31 May 1991.

122 Broome Commission [Natal] 1937, cited in Rose and Tunmer, *Documents in South African Education*, p. 186.

123 As noted later, interviews suggest that realtors at first tried to push black residents into buying houses in working-class areas such as Fynnlands, though this was not sustainable over time.

## Chapter 5

1 Rajend Mesthrie, '"Death of the mother tongue" – is English a glottophagic language in South Africa?, *English Today* 24, no. 2 (2008), pp. 13–19.

2 For analysis of these changes in Johannesburg and Durban, see Crankshaw, 'Race, space and the post-Fordist spatial order of Johannesburg'; Lombard and Crankshaw, 'Deindustrialization and racial inequality'.

3 Lombard and Crankshaw, 'Deindustrialization and racial inequality'. The authors note that deindustrialisation happened later in Durban than in Johannesburg and Cape Town (the largest and second largest cities).

4 Chris Benner, Charley Lewis, and Rahmat Omar, 'The South African call centre industry: a study of strategy, human resource practices and performance', Global Call Centre Industry Project (University Park PA: Sociology of Work Unit, Pennsylvania State University, 2013). Census data from 2011 show that only 3 per cent of 20–29-year-olds earn more than R6,400 a month in Umlazi Township.

5 Benner, Lewis, and Omar, 'The South African call centre industry', p. 18.

6 Fanon, *The Wretched of the Earth*, p. 67.

7 Mary Gilmartin, 'Language, education and the new South Africa', *Tijdschrift Voor Economische en Sociale Geografie* 95 (2004), pp. 405–18.

8 Bourdieu, *Language and Symbolic Power*. Of the many writings on Bourdieu's work, some criticisms I find useful include those by Raewyn Connell and Andrew Sayer. For Connell, the model is ahistorical, and does not emphasise contestation and change. For Sayer, the model neglects dilemmas or 'internal conversations' among people. Raewyn (Robert) Connell, *Which Way Is Up: essays on sex, class and culture* (London: Allen and Unwin, 1983); Andrew Sayer, *The Moral Significance of Class* (Cambridge: Cambridge University Press, 2005). For a critical application of Bourdieu in South Africa, see Burawoy and von Holdt, *Conversations with Bourdieu*.

9 Bourdieu, *Language and Symbolic Power*, p. 49.

10 Statistics South Africa, *Youth Employment, Unemployment, Skills and Economic Growth, 1994–2014*, p. 11.

11 Statistics South Africa, *Youth Employment, Unemployment, Skills and Economic Growth, 1994–2014*, p. 11.

12 Jeffrey, Jeffery, and Jeffery, *Degrees without Freedom?*

13 As we shall see, the top schools actively select 'quality' students who, we can assume, would have done well in other schools. Also, any attempt to use surveys runs up against a number of difficulties: what timeline should be used (do we, for instance, measure the effects of schooling after five or 25 years?), and how do we account for 'variables' that cannot be measured, such as sexism and racism? Finally, clearly an important comparison group in a future study would be black and white learners who live in the same location. Here, however, I do not consider black Bluff residents because most moved onto the Bluff fairly recently and few had left Bluff schools when our survey was undertaken.

14 See 'Inquiry into "fitness" deaths', eNews Channel Africa, 23 April 2013, www.enca.com/south-africa/inquiry-fitness-deaths (accessed 14 August 2014). Richard Pithouse documents this tragedy in his penetrating collection of essays on post-apartheid society. See Richard Pithouse, *Writing the Decline* (Johannesburg: Jacana, 2016).

15 Of the 12 people in this group, only three were unemployed, two of whom had dropped out of or been expelled from school. Six were studying further (two at universities outside Durban, one at Durban University of Technology, one at Mangosuthu Technikon, one at a FET College, and one on a nursing programme). Work undertaken included professional dancer (man), retail (woman), and fruit and vegetable sales (woman).

16 It needs to be noted that this group attended school before the widespread shift among white Bluff families from Bluff to Berea schools, noted in Chapters 6 and 7. Because it was harder to recruit informants on the Bluff, the sample of 20 people is smaller than that in Umlazi.

17 Lombard and Crankshaw, 'Deindustrialization and racial inequality', p. 229. Of course, whites leaving the city would affect these figures. However, national figures also support the view that white people have moved into higher-skilled work in recent years. See Statistics South Africa, *Youth Employment, Unemployment, Skills and Economic Growth, 1994–2014.*

18 Durban Schooling Data for 2014.

19 South African Government, *Commission for Employment Equity: annual report 2014–2015* (Pretoria: South African Government, Department of Labour, 2015), p. 22. See also Amy Kracker Selzer and Patrick Heller, 'The spatial dynamics of middle-class formation in postapartheid South Africa: enclavization and fragmentation in Johannesburg' in Julian Go (ed.), *Political Power and Social Theory. Volume 21* (Bingley: Emerald Publishing, 2010), pp. 171–208.

20 Southall, *The New Black Middle Class.*

21 Tariq Rahman, 'Language ideology, identity and the commodification of language in the call centers of Pakistan', *Language in Society* 38 (2009), pp. 233–58.

22 The relocation of thousands of call centres to the Global South has been called a 'second global shift', the first having been manufacturing's move to the Global South from the 1970s. In 2006, 409,000 people were employed in India's English-medium industry. See Phil Taylor and Peter Bain, 'United by a common language? Trade union responses in the UK and India to call centre offshoring', *Antipode* 40, no. 1 (2008), pp. 131–54.

23 According to Benner, Lewis, and Omar, 'White women seem to be particularly over represented at team leader and management levels in the industry, with white women comprising nearly 40% of all managers.' See Benner, Lewis, and Omar, 'The South African call centre industry', p. 18.

24 There are around 80,000 call centre workers in South Africa and one survey found that 27 per cent of call centre agents were African (compared with 79 per cent of the population), 35 per cent Coloured (mainly in Cape Town, although there was a possible oversample of this group), 26 per cent white, and 11 per cent Indian. Benner, Lewis, and Omar, 'The South African call centre industry', p. 11, 17.

25 Specifically, between June and August 2010, I interviewed 29 people who had worked or still worked in a call centre, mostly at their homes in Umlazi Township, although sometimes several people gathered in a single home or met in a public place. Interviewees' average age was 24 and we talked with 24 women and five men. This bias towards women is due to the fact that this service industry employs more women than men, and my research assistant was female. In recruiting people to interview, the research assistant (who had herself worked in a call centre) asked friends to introduce us to a network of three or four workers with whom they were well acquainted; a second friend to another three or four workers, and so on. This meant that present at all times with the interviewee was someone they knew well and a research assistant, both of whom were from the area; this familiarity allowed a

generally relaxed and open conversation. Interviews were conducted in isi-Zulu or a mixture of isiZulu and English. Interviewing workers or former workers in Umlazi probably had several advantages over meeting workers at the premises of a firm. It allowed for more time to chat with informants, for us to observe their place of residence, and for us to observe and communicate with other household members. Additionally, it also facilitated a more candid interview than would have been possible had the researchers been associated with the interviewees' place of employment, and thus with their employer.

26  Zodwa said (in 2010) that the company paid its generally young workforce well by Durban's standards (a starting salary of R30 (US$4) an hour for a permanent worker, although, because she worked through an agency, she earned only R22 per hour).

27  See also Dieketseng Motseke, 'Call centre agents and class identity: a Johannesburg case study', master's thesis, Industrial Sociology, Faculty of Humanities, University of Johannesburg, 2009.

28  On the move of English from second to first language among Indians, see Rajend Mesthrie, 'From second language to first language: Indian South African English' in Mesthrie, *Language in South Africa*, pp. 339–55.

29  Fataar, 'Self-formation and the "capacity to aspire"'.

30  Cited in Idowu Omoyele, 'Post-colonial universities are trapped by their past', *Mail & Guardian*, 31 August 2017.

31  Southall, *The New Black Middle Class*, p. 42.

32  See Southall, *The New Black Middle Class*, especially pp. 70–2.

33  Ziyanda Ngcobo, 'Commission probing KZN political killings hears Zuma may be linked to violence', Eyewitness News, 17 July 2017, http://ewn.co.za/2017/07/17/commission-probing-kzn-political-killings-hears-zuma-may-be-linked-to-violence (accessed 30 August 2017).

34  On local patronage politics, see Laurence Piper and Fiona Anciano, 'Party over outsiders, centre over branch: how ANC dominance works at the community level in South Africa', *Transformation* 87 (2015), pp. 72–94.

35  The distributive economy is a term taken from James Ferguson, *Give a Man a Fish: reflections on the new politics of distribution* (Durham NC: Duke University Press, 2015).

36  Cited in Southall, *The New Black Middle Class*, p. 165.

37  Crapanzano, *Waiting*, p. 205.

38  The UK and other Western countries, for instance, have actively 'poached' nurses from South Africa, most of whom are black. See 'Specialist to discuss "poaching" of teachers', IOL News, 18 February 2001, www.iol.co.za/news/south-africa/specialist-to-discuss-poaching-of-teachers-61324 (accessed 26 August 2018).

39  In 2013, of the 468 (almost exclusively white) members of the Bluff Reunited Facebook group who gave their current location, 9 per cent lived in Australia, 7 per cent lived in the UK, 4 per cent lived in New Zealand, 3 per cent lived in the United States, 1 per cent lived in Canada, and 1 per cent lived in Ireland. A total of 57 per cent lived in Durban and 18 per cent lived elsewhere in South Africa. This analysis was undertaken by my research assistant, who accessed open Facebook profiles in what is an open group (i.e. one does not have to be a person's 'friend' to view their stated location, nor be a member of the Bluff Facebook site in order to access basic details about its members).

40  In the post-apartheid period, the University of Natal, after merging with the former Indian UDW, became the University of KwaZulu-Natal (UKZN). Under the leadership of Vice-Chancellor Professor Makgoba, UKZN sought to position itself as the most racially transformed African university (his supporters positioned him as a leader fighting intransigent white academics, his critics as someone intolerant of debate). I do not have space here to develop a model of universities and (racial) marketisation akin to the one I develop for public schools, but it is worth noting that, among the Bluff's white residents, the public universities that have perhaps gained the most status in recent years include the former Afrikaans-medium universities of Stellenbosch and Pretoria (which have both moved towards English-medium education). Private and formerly Afrikaans institutions, along with the University of Cape Town, are often compared favourably with the local UKZN, which today can be coded as 'black'.

41  Goldberg, *The Threat of Race*, p. 337; David Goldberg, *Are We All Postracial Yet?* (Malden MA: Polity Press, 2015).

42  Diane Reay, Gill Crozier, and David James, *White Middle-Class Identities and Urban Schooling* (London: Palgrave, 2011).

43  Reay, Crozier, and James, *White Middle-Class Identities and Urban Schooling*, p. 100.

44  Rajend Mesthrie, 'Towards a distributed sociolinguistics of postcolonial multilingual society: the case of South Africa' in Dick Smakman and Patrick Heinrich (eds), *Globalising Sociolinguistics: challenging and expanding theory* (London: Routledge, 2015), p. 85.

45  Pierre Bourdieu, 'What makes a social class? On the theoretical and practical existence of groups', *Berkeley Journal of Sociology* 32, no. 1 (1987), p. 13.

46  Mesthrie, 'Towards a distributed sociolinguistics of postcolonial multilingual society', p. 85.


## Chapter 6

1  'Rival schools' rugby ruckus!', *Berea Mail*, 9 June 2000.

2  On the falsifying of rugby players' ages, see 'School rugby scandal', *Independent on Saturday*, 26 May 2012. On 'poaching', see Prega Govender, 'How money moves rugby schoolboys', *Sunday Times*, 17 November 2013; Kevin Lancaster, 'Sports row at top Durban schools', IOL News, 21 January 2013, www.iol.co.za/news/south-africa/kwazulu-natal/sports-row-at-top-durban-schools-1455625 (accessed 22 April 2017). On disputes between two Johannesburg schools, see 'Elite rugby school clash over player poaching', eNews Channel Africa, 21 January 2016, www.enca.com/south-africa/elite-rugby-schools-odds-over-player-poaching (accessed 23 April 2017).

3  As Stephen Ball said about schools in the United Kingdom, 'They are in the position, in one way or another, of choosing students, not the other way round.' Stephen Ball, 'Education markets, choice and social class: the market as a class strategy in the UK and the USA', *British Journal of Sociology of Education* 14, no.1 (1993), p. 11. A similar observation has been made about the thousands of new charter schools (publicly funded, privately run) established in the US, which are said to avoid undesirable children such as those

with learning disabilities. See, for instance, Lipman, *The New Political Economy of Urban Education*.

4  Cyril (C. L. R.) James, *Beyond a Boundary* (Durham NC: Duke University Press, 2013 [1963]).

5  The top 20 private schools all charge over R150,000 a year. See 'Most expensive schools in South Africa in 2015', BusinessTech, 13 January 2015, http://businesstech.co.za/news/general/77123/most-expensive-schools-in-south-africa-in-2015/ (accessed 9 September 2016).

6  'Friends for life', KZN Education Supplement, *Southlands Sun*, September 2001.

7  Kenway et al., *Class Choreographies*.

8  'Model Curro schools', Curro Group, www.curro.co.za/educational/model-curro-schools/ (accessed 21 November 2016). See also CDE, *Hidden Assets: South Africa's low-fee private schools* (Johannesburg: Centre for Development and Enterprise (CDE), 2010). There are important regional patterns to private schooling. The Durban region has a smaller number of low-fee private schools than Johannesburg; possible reasons for this include the smaller middle-class and the large number of fee-charging Coloured and especially Indian schools. A notable growing sector in KwaZulu-Natal is Islamic private schools. Goolam Vahed and Thembisa Waetjen chart how, in 1996, the Orient Islamic School opted to move from state-aided to private status, becoming one of the now 20 independent Muslim schools in KwaZulu-Natal alone. See Vahed and Waetjen, *Schooling Muslims in Natal*.

9  South African Institute of Race Relations, *South Africa Survey 2016*, p. 466. Two striking aspects of new private schools' geography need to be noted. First, almost all new schools are established in cities. If you walk around any central business district you will see large signs advertising low-fee private schools. Second, higher-fee private schools are typically established in affluent suburbs where they compete directly with formerly white public schools. The deputy principal of one relatively new upper-middle-class private school in north Durban shared data with me showing that 75 per cent of students' families live in nearby suburbs (including Durban North, Umhlanga, Mount Edgecombe, La Lucia, and Glen Ashley). Fees at this school are slightly higher than they are at formerly white public schools, ranging from R30,000 to R80,000 a year depending on the learner's grade. He told me that the school advertises itself as a modern alternative to Durban's 'traditional' schools; it has excellent resources and co-educational learning, and encourages students to wear 'multiforms' rather than uniforms.

10  As Crain Soudien argues, decentralisation became recast as a means to promote democratic participation in schools, although it 'is constructed in racial, and indeed also class, tension'. Soudien, *Realising the Dream*, p. 121.

11  Andy Duffy, '17 000 teachers take retrenchment option', *Mail & Guardian*, 25 October 1996 (accessed 9 November 2016).

12  Parents qualify for full fee exemption if their combined annual gross income is less than ten times the annual school fees per learner. Partial exemptions are available for those whose income is more than ten times but less than 30 times the annual fees.

13  On the growth of no-fee schools, see Francesca Villette, 'Sharp rise in no-fee pupils', *Cape Times – IOL*, 7 June 2016, www.iol.co.za/capetimes/sharp-rise-in-no-fee-school-pupils-2031750 (accessed 14 September 2016).

14  Thulani Zengele, 'The unionization of the teaching profession and its effects on the South African education system: teacher unionism in South Africa', *Journal of Social Sciences* 35, no. 3 (2013), pp. 231–9.

15  Mark Hunter, 'Racial desegregation and schooling in South Africa: contested geographies of class formation', *Environment and Planning A* 42 (2010), pp. 2640–57.

16  On the strategies of formerly white schools, see Bell and McKay, 'The rise of "class apartheid" in accessing secondary schools'; Christie, 'Transition tricks?'; Fiske and Ladd, *Elusive Equality*; Lemon, 'Shifting geographies of social inclusion and exclusion', pp. 69–96; Simon Maile, 'School choice in South Africa', *Education and Urban Society* 37, no. 1 (2004), pp. 94–116; Soudien, *Realising the Dream*; Tikly and Mabogoane, 'Marketisation as a strategy for desegregation and redress'; Woolman and Fleisch, 'South Africa's unintended experiment'.

17  Although the 1996 South African Schools Act expressly forbids admissions tests, one Berea primary-school principal gave me a copy of an 'assignment' he asked children to undertake during the interview (this involved writing and drawing tasks).

18  Lynn Thomas, 'Skin lighteners, black consumers and Jewish entrepreneurs in South Africa', *History Workshop Journal* 73, no. 1 (2012), p. 263. Moreover, the marketing of white 'civilisation' opened a space for the commodification of African ethnicities, for example at the Shakaland Cultural Village that was established for tourists of Zulu tradition. See Jean Comaroff and John Comaroff, *Ethnicity, Inc.* (Chicago IL: University of Chicago Press, 2009).

19  Crain Soudien develops a typology of aggressive assimilationism, assimilationism by stealth, and benign assimilationism. Soudien, *Realising the Dream*.

20  'Fernwood' is a pseudonym.

21  Nadine Dolby, 'Making white: constructing race in a South African high school', *Curriculum Inquiry* 32, no. 1 (2002), pp. 19–20; Dolby, *Constructing Race*.

22  Dolby, 'Making white', p. 19.

23  This study was of 1,729 learners, black and white. The report shows how racism is also gendered, with particularly virulent attacks directed towards black women. Salim Vally and Yolisa Dalamba, *Racism, 'Racial Integration' and Desegregation in South African Public Secondary Schools: a report on a study by the South African Human Rights Commission (SAHRC)* (Johannesburg: SAHRC, 1999).

24  Nadine Dolby, 'Youth and the global popular: the politics and practices of race in South Africa', *European Journal of Cultural Studies* 2, no. 3 (1999), pp. 291–309; Dolby, *Constructing Race*.

25  Kira Erwin and Kathryn Pillay, 'The power of dreams: young people's imaginings of non-racialism, racialism and racism in South Africa', unpublished paper, 2016; see also Maré, *Declassified*.

26  This interview was with the principal of a private school. However, because this school is located in a fast desegregating area of Berea, he articulates the dilemmas faced by all formerly white schools.

27  Dolby, 'Making white', p. 12.

28  Whites dropped from 8.9 per cent of eThekwini's population to 6.5 per cent. See Posel, 'Micro-data analysis of patterns and trends in eThekwini Municipality', p. 9.

29  See Appendix 1.

30 This was a model D school. In the early 1990s, a handful of white schools opted for the model D option (introduced subsequent to models A, B, and C), which completely removed racial quotas. See Christie, 'Transition tricks?'.

31 Saloshna Vandeyar and Jonathan Jansen, *Diversity High: class, culture, and character in a South African School* (Washington DC: University Press of America, 2008).

32 David Black and John Nauright, *Rugby and the South African Nation* (Manchester: Manchester University Press, 1988).

33 Tim Whitfield, 'School rugby: stop the money rot', *The Mercury*, 28 August 2014; Prega Govender, 'Hilton, stop poaching our sports stars', *Mail & Guardian*, 10 February 2017.

34 On the history of black cricket, see Ashwin Desai, Vishnu Padayachee, Krish Reddy, and Goolam Vahed, *Blacks in Whites: a century of cricket struggles in KwaZulu-Natal* (Pietermaritzburg: University of KwaZulu-Natal Press, 2002).

35 This interview was conducted via Facebook chat by a research assistant who knew Khule Nkosi (a pseudonym).

36 Black and Nauright, *Rugby and the South African Nation*, p. 113. On the government's failure to transform sports at the grassroots level, see particularly Ashwin Desai (ed.), *The Race to Transform Sport in Post-Apartheid South Africa* (Cape Town: HSRC Press, 2010); on cricket, see Ashwin Desai, *Reverse Sweep: a story of South African cricket since apartheid* (Johannesburg: Jacana, 2016).

37 Liz McGregor documents how 40 per cent of Springboks capped since 1992 come from just 21 schools. Liz McGregor, *Springbok Factory: what it takes to be a Bok* (Johannesburg: Jonathan Ball, 2013). Ashwin Desai's powerful analysis of cricket argues that 'class privilege . . . has seen resources shift upwards to an elite group of players and reinforces and exacerbates a division between professional and amateur levels of the game'. Desai, *Reverse Sweep*, p. 215.

38 'Record for Ramblers', *Southlands Sun*, 17 May 1991.

39 If Mandela's support for the Springbok rugby team's victory in the 1995 World Cup rugby final literally became the stuff of movies (the film *Invictus*), it is hard to argue that the state gave more symbolic credence and material support to rugby compared with soccer. Mandela donned the Bafana Bafana shirt when South Africa won the 1996 African Nations Cup and the country successfully hosted the 2010 soccer World Cup. State support for grassroots rugby and soccer was, in fact, equally bad.

40 See, for example, KZN Education Supplement, *Southlands Sun*, September 2001. On schools' use of the white press for advertising, see Tikly and Mabogoane, 'Marketisation as a strategy for desegregation and redress'.

41 Another strategy schools can use to deepen (rather than enlarge) their catchment area is to change their admissions policy to move from a single-sex to a co-educational institute. One south Durban boys' secondary school became co-educational and remained predominantly white; its sister girls' school quickly became predominantly black.

42 Note: while this survey has a small sample, these findings are supported by many interviews with parents and teachers as well as by school-based statistics.

43 'Foster mum in no-go zone', *Berea Mail*, 6 October 2006.

44 'Integration at schools to be "forced"', *Natal Mercury*, 13 July 2012.

45 In 1998, the annual fees of these girls' and boys' schools were R4,500 and R5,000 respectively; by 2012 they charged R17,600 and R31,000 respectively. Figures calculated from Durban Schooling Data.

46 There is a smaller literature on recent changes in formerly black schools compared with formerly white schools. However, see Ursula Hoadley, 'School choice in a South African working class context' in Linda Chisholm, Shireen Motala, and Salim Vally (eds), *Critical Perspectives in South African Education: reconstituting the educational realm* (Cape Town: Juta, 2003), pp. 28–44; Thabisile Ntombela, 'Investigating factors which influence parental school choice in post-apartheid South Africa: a case study of Umlazi Township', unpublished master's thesis, School of Development Studies, University of KwaZulu-Natal, 2013; Vuyisile Msila, 'School choice and intra-township migration: black parents scrambling for quality education in South Africa', *Journal of Education* 46 (2010), pp. 81–98.

47 Jonathan Jansen, 'A day in SA's miracle school', *Times Live*, 8 September 2011, www.ufs.ac.za/docs/default-source/all-documents/times—a-day-in-sas-miracle-school-656-eng.pdf?sfvrsn=0 (accessed 8 November 2016).

48 'Successful school gone wrong', *Sunday Independent – IOL*, 24 June 2014, www.iol.co.za/news/successful-school-gone-wrong-1708766 (accessed 8 November 2016).

49 South African Institute of Race Relations, *South Africa Survey 2016*, p. 500. Fiske and Ladd argue that, from 1995 to 1999, the probability of students making it to grade 12 fell over time, suggesting that this might be because 'schools responded to the new pressure to demonstrate higher pass rates'. Fiske and Ladd, *Elusive Equity*, p. 179. Of the cohort who took the final matriculation exam in 2013, 479,300 learners were lost between grades 10 and 12, representing a 45 per cent dropout rate. See Equal Education, 'Equal Education (EE) statement on the 2013 matric results: higher pass rate but drop outs, poor quality passes and inequality persist', https://equaleducation.org.za/2014/01/06/equal-education-ee-statement-on-the-2013-matric-resultshigher-pass-rate-but-drop-outs-poor-quality-passes-and-inequality-persist/ (accessed 11 November 2016).

50 When one school faced criticism from unions for admission tests, Ntombela reports that parents of admitted students pressured the school not to end them. Ntombela, 'Investigating factors which influence parental school choice in post-apartheid South Africa'.

51 South African Government, 'Kwa-Zulu Natal no-fee schools, 2015' (Pretoria: South African Government, Department of Education, 2015), www.education.gov.za/Portals/0/Documents/Publications/KZN%20No%20Fee%20Schools%202015%20list.pdf?ver=2015-07-21-135945-233 (accessed 11 November 2016).

52 See South African Governement, *The State of Education in KwaZulu-Natal*, p. 54.


## Chapter 7

1 The South Durban Community Environmental Alliance (SDCEA) is a prominent environmental justice organisation based in south Durban. See www.sdcea.co.za (accessed 3 May 2017).

2 Daniel Schensul and Patrick Heller, 'Legacies, change and transformation in the post-apartheid city: towards an urban sociological cartography', *International Journal of Urban and Regional Research* 35, no. 1 (2011), pp. 78–109.

3 The map of residential desegregation is based on analysis of small area layer (SAL) data from the 2011 census. When these small areas are combined to approximate the boundaries of suburbs, this shows that the Berea population was 28 per cent white, 40 per cent black African, 26 per cent Indian, and 5 per cent Coloured. In contrast, the formerly white parts of the Bluff had a population that was 49 per cent white, 22 per cent black African, 13 per cent Indian, and 16 per cent Coloured.

4 'We have the selection – the choice is yours ...', Moreland advert, *Berea Mail*, 18 November 1998.

5 In addition to black families moving into upper-middle-class areas, some black students can travel to attend schools in these areas, and children of live-in domestic workers can also be admitted to local schools. Thus, by 2012, two high schools that serve the western suburbs had only a relatively small majority (57 per cent) of white students. Figures provided by the Department of Education for Pinetown District (western parts of Durban fall outside the Durban Schooling Data). On Johannesburg's racially mixed edge city areas compared with US edge cities, see Crankshaw, 'Race, space and the post-Fordist spatial order in Johannesburg', pp. 1692–711.

6 The differences were less marked in primary schools because competition among these schools took longer to develop than in secondary schools (see Chapter 6). However, as already noted, several primary schools in Berea also had a large proportion of white students. It should also be noted that quite a lot of variation exists among Berea's three English-medium secondary schools referred to here, with one school having nearly two-thirds white students, and two having boarding institutions. One of the Bluff's secondary schools was a formerly Afrikaans-medium school and still retains a small (overwhelmingly white) Afrikaans stream.

7 The jokes rest on the ridiculous actions of a fictitious character called van der Merwe (a common Afrikaner surname). See Posel, 'Whiteness and power in the South African civil service'.

8 Stephen Ball and Carol Vincent, '"I heard it on the grapevine": "hot" knowledge and school choice', *British Journal of Sociology of Education* 19, no. 3 (1998), pp. 377–400.

9 Sayer, *The Moral Significance of Class.*

10 This emphasis on parents preparing children for competitive admissions processes differs from what Annette Lareau describes as parents' 'concerted cultivation' to give their children a sense of entitlement that advantages them *within a school*. See Annette Lareau, *Unequal Childhoods: class, race, and family life* (Berkeley CA: University of California Press, 2011).

11 John Argyle, 'The myth of the elementary family: a comparative account of variations in family household structure amongst a group of South African whites', *African Studies* 36, no. 2 (1977), pp. 105–18.

12 Between 1996 and 2001, the proportion of three-generational South African white families rose from 6.5 per cent to 9.5 per cent (the figure for rural African families was 39 per cent in 2001). Acheampong Yaw Amoateng, Tim B. Heaton and Ishmael Kalule-Sabiti, 'Living arrangements in South Africa'

in Acheampong Yaw Amoateng and Tim Heaton (eds), *Families and House-holds in Post-Apartheid South Africa* (Cape Town: HSRC Press, 2007), p. 52.

13 Maharaj and Mpungose, 'The erosion of residential segregation in South Africa'.

14 See Chapter 5 in Moira Maconachie, *Alliance and Agreement: marriage among white South Africans* (Cape Town: HSRC Press, 1996).

15 In line with similar discussions in women's magazines elsewhere in the world, an article in the South African magazine *Femina* in 1970 told the reader: 'A successful marriage is rather like a business … Know yourself, your needs – then sum up his. If they're not going to balance, now is the time to make a quick escape.' 'Love is a bargain', *Femina*, 3 September 1970.

16 'Men and marriage', *Femina*, 17 September 1970.

17 Maconachie, *Alliance and Agreement*, p. 24; South African Institute of Race Relations, *First Steps to Healing the South African Family*, p. 2.

18 I looked at classified adverts in the *Natal Mercury* for one month, January, in the years 1960, 1970, 1980, and 1988 (the last year held at the Killie Camp-bell Africana Library). In the 1960s and 1970s the adverts section did not mention garden cottages/garden flats. By 1988, two out of 40 adverts in the 'flats to let' section were for garden flats. Yet, I recall that when I was a master's degree student in Durban in 1997, the paper was full of adverts for garden cottages, and I stayed in two on the Berea. Today, the *Natal Mercury* has a large separate section advertising 'garden cottages' for between R2,000 and R3,500 a month. Moreover, writing about Johannesburg, Nicky Falkof notes the rise of rented garden cottages around the same time period. Nicky Falkof, 'Out the back: race and reinvention in Johannesburg's garden cot-tages', *International Journal of Cultural Studies* 19, no. 6 (2016), pp. 627–42.

19 The interviews took place inside her employer's house (rather than in her own place of residence, which was a more common practice). While we were given privacy, explicit criticism of her employer would have been difficult.

20 On domestic workers' poor working conditions, see Cock, *Maids and Madams*; Rebecca Ginsburg, *At Home with Apartheid: the hidden landscape of domestic service in Johannesburg* (Charlottesville VA: University of Virginia Press, 2011); Ally, *From Servants to Workers*.

21 On domestic workers' ambiguous approach to new rights, see Ally, *From Servants to Workers*. Writing about employer–domestic worker relationships, Rebecca Ginsburg notes: 'This, then, is the great ambiguity: White children grew extremely close to their African caretakers, for a while; their nannies returned the love, up to a point; the women's own children longed for them, until they didn't; and the women working in the city never stopped worrying about the children who had, in many cases, sent them to the city in the first place.' Ginsburg, *At Home with Apartheid*, p. 101.

22 On labour broking, Du Toit notes: '[C]lients no longer have to support their domestic workers financially or give their second-hand clothes and used household appliances to the domestic workers, or provide Christmas or birthday gifts for the domestic workers and their families.' David du Toit, 'From "Cinderella cleaners" to "maids from heaven": clients' and domestic workers' perceptions of housecleaning services in Stellenbosch', *South African Journal of Labour Relations* 37, no. 1 (2013), p. 111.

23 Mary Romero, *The Maid's Daughter: living inside and outside the American dream* (New York NY: NYU Press, 2011).

24 In her study of domestic workers' children being raised in white households, Alice Morrison notes assimilation through 'language, accent, mannerisms' and the disruption that occurred when a child moved out of its mother's employer's house. Alice Morrison, '"In-between": a study of domestic workers' children who have been informally fostered by their mothers' employers', master's thesis, School of Built Environment and Development Studies, University of KwaZulu-Natal, 2015.

25 For data comparing 1995 and 2006, see Mark Hunter and Dorrit Posel, 'Here to work: the socioeconomic characteristics of informal dwellers in post-apartheid South Africa', *Environment and Urbanization* 24, no. 1 (2012), pp. 285–304 (Dorrit Posel undertook the quantitative analysis). In isiZulu, the word *imijondolo* (perhaps taken from *umjendevu*, widow) seemed to come into existence in the 1970s and 1980s to describe both 'backyard shack' structures and shacks in informal settlements – it implies the poverty of living in a non-formal, temporary place of residence. See Hunter, *Love in the Time of AIDS*.

26 After a legal challenge by *Abahlali baseMjondolo*, the KwaZulu-Natal Elimination and Prevention of Re-emergence of Slums Act was found to be unconstitutional. For more on this (and on many other matters relating to shack dwellers), see www.abahlali.org. For an excellent review of the history of shack settlements in Durban, see Richard Pithouse, *Business as Usual? Housing rights and slum eradication in Durban, South Africa* (Geneva: Centre on Housing Rights and Evictions (COHRE), 2008). Other important sources on shacks in South Africa include Richard Ballard, 'Middle class neighbourhoods or "African Kraals"? The impact of informal settlements and vagrants on post-apartheid white identity', *Urban Forum* 15, no. 1 (2004), pp. 48–73; Sarah Charlton and Caroline Kihato, 'Reaching the poor? An analysis of the influences of the evolution of South Africa's housing programme' in Udesh Pillay, Richard Tomlinson, and Jacques du Toit (eds), *Democracy and Delivery: urban policy in South Africa* (Cape Town: HSRC Press, 2006), pp. 252–82; Owen Crankshaw, 'Squatting, apartheid and urbanization on the southern Witwatersrand', *African Affairs* 92, no. 366 (1993), pp. 31–51; Marie Huchzemeyer and Aly Karam (eds), *Informal Settlements: a perpetual challenge* (Cape Town: UCT Press, 2006).

27 On shack residents' raising of children in rural areas because of the possibility of shack fires in their East London settlement, see Bank, *Home Spaces, Street Styles*, p. 108.

28 Mike Mabuyakhulu, 'Meeting people's housing rights', *Natal Mercury*, 9 February 2009. Mabuyakhulu was responding to a letter two colleagues and I wrote to criticise the passing of a 'slum removal' bill in KwaZulu-Natal. In response, KwaZulu-Natal's Economic Development Minister portrayed us as naîve do-gooders who wanted poor people to live in shacks. The original article (written with Marie Huchzermeyer and Kerry Chance) and response by Mike Mabuyakhulu are reproduced here: Kerry Chance, Marie Huchzermeyer, and Mark Hunter, 'Forced removals', *Natal Mercury*, 29 January 2009, http://abahlali.org/node/4768/; Mike Mabuyakhulu, 'Meeting people's housing rights', *Natal Mercury*, 9 February 2009, http://abahlali.org/node/4782/. On transit camps, see Kerry Chance, 'Transitory citizens: contentious housing practices in contemporary South Africa', *Social Analysis* 59, no. 3 (2015), pp. 62–84.

29 Downloadable from eThekwini's own GIS site, 'eThekwini Municipality GIS', at http://gis.durban.gov.za/gis_Website/intranetsite/#about (accessed 6 December 2016).

30 'Temporary camps that become prisons', *Natal Mercury*, 8 October 2012. It needs to be noted that the mayor's visit to the site the next day was primarily a response to years of pressure exerted by *Abahlali baseMjondolo* activists and activists at Isipingo (some of whom were members of *Abahlali*).

## Chapter 8

1 On the household, see especially Jane Guyer, 'Household and community in African studies', *African Studies Review* 24, no. 2/3 (1981), pp. 87–137 and Jane Guyer and Pauline Peters, 'Conceptualizing the household: issues of theory and policy in Africa', *Development and Change* 18, no. 2 (1987), pp. 197–214. On industrial restructuring and household cooperation and conflict in KwaZulu-Natal, see Sarah Mosoetsa, *Eating from One Pot: the dynamics of survival in poor South African households* (Johannesburg: Wits University Press, 2011). On changing urban household in South Africa, see especially Bank, *Home Spaces, Street Styles*. The common 'eating from the same pot' definition does not take into account *absent* household members or connections among households. While a national census requires individuals to be a member of only one household, other studies do not. For a discussion of the approach taken by one demographic surveillance area in KwaZulu-Natal, see Vicky Hosegood and Ian Timaeus, 'Household composition and dynamics in KwaZulu Natal, South Africa: mirroring social reality in longitudinal data collection' in *African Households: an exploration of census data* (Armonk NY: M. E. Sharpe, 2006), pp. 58–77. On women's increased movement, see Dorrit Posel 'Moving on: patterns of labour migration in post-apartheid South Africa' in Marta Tienda, Sally Findley, and Stephen Tollman (eds), *Africa on the Move: African migration and urbanisation in comparative perspective* (Johannesburg: Witwatersrand University Press, 2006), pp. 217–31. On children's high rates of movement (especially among young children), see Rachel Bennett et al., 'An approach to measuring dispersed families with a particular focus on children "left behind" by migrant parents: findings from rural South Africa', *Population, Space, and Place* no. 21 (2015), pp. 332–4; Sangeetha Madhavan, Paul Mee, and Mark Collinson, 'Kinship in practice: spatial distribution of children's kin networks', *Journal of Southern African Studies* 40, no. 2 (2014), pp. 401–18.

2 Umlazi figures are calculated from the 2011 census data. For an overview of employment and unemployment trends, see Chapter 5 and South African Government, *Diagnostic Overview*; South African Government, *The Status of Women in the South African Economy* (Pretoria: South African Government, Department of Women, 2015).

3 In 2015, the cost of two taxis to the Bluff (roughly twice as far as Merebank) was R25 combined, and a single bus ticket was R13.50, although a weekly ticket is cheaper.

4 On *togt* labour in Durban, see Ralph Callebert, 'Working class action and informal trade on the Durban docks, 1930s–1950s', *Journal of Southern African Studies*, 38, no. 4 (2012), pp. 847–61. On labour market casualisation,

see Caroline Skinner and Imraan Valodia, 'Labour market policy, flexibility, and the future of labour relations: the case of KwaZulu-Natal clothing industry', *Transformation* 50 (2002), pp. 56–76; Karl von Holdt and Edward Webster, 'Work restructuring and the crisis of reproduction: a southern perspective' in Karl von Holdt and Edward Webster (eds), *Beyond the Apartheid Workplace: studies in transition* (Pietermaritzburg: University of KwaZulu-Natal Press, 2005), pp. 3–40; Bridget Kenny and Edward Webster, 'Eroding the core: flexibility and the resegmentation of the South African labour market', *Critical Sociology* 24, no. 3 (1998), pp. 216–43; Franco Barchiesi, *Precarious Liberation: workers, the state, and contested social citizenship in post-apartheid South Africa* (New York NY: Suny Press, 2011). On the worldwide precariat, see Guy Standing, *The Precariat: the new dangerous class* (London: Bloomsbury Academic, 2011). As scholars of social mobility in the United Kingdom have argued, widening income inequalities *within* occupational categories makes occupation a less accurate proxy for class relations than in the past. See Philip Brown, 'Education, opportunity and the prospects for social mobility', *British Journal of Sociology of Education* 34, no. 5–6 (2013), pp. 678–700.

5 The 'male mother' is a term used by Radcliffe-Brown, who contrasts the indulgence and tenderness of *malume* to the instructor role of the father, who scolds and punishes his children. Alfred Radcliffe-Brown, *Structure and Function in Primitive Society* (New York NY: Free Press, 1952), p. 20. See also Absolom Vilikazi, *Zulu Transformations: a study of the dynamics of social change* (Pietermaritzburg: University of Natal Press, 1962), p. 45.

6 'South Africa: parliament extends condolences to families of pupils killed in horror taxi crash', News24Wire, 22 April 2017, https://allafrica.com/stories/201704220237.html (accessed 11 September 2018).

7 This estimation of per capita income was derived from 2011 census statistics. One analysis of the 'literal middle group' referred to households with per capita income of between R380 and R1,140 per month (an interval of 50 per cent to 150 per cent of the median per capita income per month in 2008). See Justin Visagie, 'Who are the middle class in South Africa? Does it matter for policy', Econ 3x3, May 2013, www.econ3x3.org/sites/default/files/articles/Visagie%202013%20Middle%20class%20FINAL_0.pdf. For a more detailed discussion of ways to measure and understand the middle class in South Africa, see Southall, *The New Black Middle Class*; Seekings and Nattrass, *Class, Race, and Inequality in South Africa*.

8 The original survey was undertaken in 2012, and the first round of interviews was conducted in 2012 and 2013. We undertook follow-up interviews annually in certain houses up to 2017, and my research assistant, Lwandle, revisited all of the houses in 2014 to record changes in schooling and family structure.

9 Many shack residents in Umlazi have some tenure security. The first shack residents occupied the land for free, whereas others then bought shacks (for between R4,000 and R8,000, and without gaining titles to the property), and a third group rented shacks. This stands in stark contrast to shack dwellers on the Bluff, considered in Chapter 7, who were removed by the state.

10 Social grants have expanded considerably in recent years in value and scope. See Stephan Klasen and Ingrid Woolard, 'Surviving unemployment without state support: unemployment and household formation in South Africa',

*Journal of African Economies*, 18, no. 1 (2009), pp. 1–51. The article shows that the state became the main source of income for more than a third of households in the former homelands in 2009, up from just over a quarter in 2002. Thus, overall, rural areas have been the main beneficiaries of the government's expansion of social grants in recent decades.

11 See, for instance, 'Matric maths scrapped at 300 schools', *Mail & Guardian*, 1–7 August 2014. In KwaZulu-Natal, for instance, there are six times as many no-fee schools in the rural district of Ugu than in the more urban Umlazi district, and children are half as likely to attain bachelor's matriculation passes that enable them to apply to universities. Of course, there are some exceptional rural schools. I interviewed two sisters who lived in the shack settlement who had grown up in a rural area but who spoke fluent English. This was because of the commitment of their teachers and their own hard work (including using English-language media to improve their English).

12 Madhaven and colleagues have shown for rural KwaZulu how better-off rural dwellers develop the most dispersed geographical strategies, including when moving their children to urban areas to attend higher-performing schools that promote English. Madhavan, Mee, and Collinson, 'Kinship in practice', pp. 401–18.

13 See Chapter 7 in Dlamini, *Youth and Identity Politics in South Africa, 1990–94*.

14 For a detailed review of legal cases on language in schools, see Stu Woolman and Brahm Fleisch, 'The problem of the "other" language', *Constitutional Court Review* 5 (2014), pp. 135–72.

15 Stephanie Rudwick, '"Coconuts" and "Oreos": English-speaking Zulu people in a South African township', *World Englishes* 27, no. 1 (2008), pp. 101–16.

16 Ntombela, 'Investigating factors which influence parental school choice in post-apartheid South Africa'.

17 Hoadley, 'School choice in a South African working class context'.

18 For a literary insight into 'black diamonds', see the novel by Zakes Mda: *Black Diamond* (Johannesburg: Penguin, 2011).

19 Ivor Chipkin, 'Middle classing in Roodepoort: capitalism and social change in South Africa PARI long essays 2' (Johannesburg: Public Affairs Research Institute, 2012).

20 I used interviews and surveys to ascertain the child's main financial sponsor for multiracial schools, and the source of this person's income. I could determine this information reasonably confidently for 40 of the 47 cases of children attending multiracial schools.

21 Seekings and Nattrass, *Class, Race, and Inequality in South Africa*, p. 337.

22 Alexander et al., *Class in Soweto*, p. 203.

23 Deborah James, *Money from Nothing: indebtedness and aspiration in South Africa* (Palo Alto CA: Stanford University Press, 2014).

24 For national figures, see South African Institute of Race Relations, *First Steps to Healing the South African Family*.

25 See Patricia Henderson, *AIDS, Intimacy and Care in Rural Kwazulu-Natal: a kinship of bones* (Amsterdam: Amsterdam University Press, 2011); Hunter, *Love in the Time of AIDS*.

26 Hunter, *Love in the Time of AIDS*, chapter 5.

27 I summarised gendered changes in migration, work, and intimacy as the 'changing political economy and geography of intimacy' in Hunter, *Love in the Time of AIDS*.

28 Alfred T. Bryant, *A Zulu–English Dictionary with Notes on Pronunciation* (Marianhill: Marianhill Mission Press, 1905), p. 410, 251.

29 Alexander et al., *Class in Soweto*.

30 For an earlier anthropological perspective on schooling in KwaZulu-Natal, see Vilakazi, *Zulu Transformations*.

31 Marshall Sahlins, *What Kinship Is – And Is Not* (Chicago IL: University of Chicago Press, 2013).

32 Isak Niehaus, 'Disharmonious spouses and harmonious siblings: conceptualising household formation among urban residents in Qwaqwa', *African Studies* 53, no. 1 (1994), pp. 115–35.

33 For a quantitative study showing strong maternal links, see Sarah Harper and Jeremy Seekings, 'Claims on and obligations to kin in Cape Town, South Africa', Working Paper 272 (Cape Town: Centre for Social Science Research, 2010).

34 See Deborah Potts and Shula Marks, 'Fertility in Southern Africa: the quiet revolution', *Journal of Southern African Studies* 27, no. 2 (2001), pp. 189–205; Chapter 2 in National Planning Commission, South African Government, *The National Development Plan* (Pretoria: South African Government, 2011).

35 Examples of how National Student Financial Aid Scheme (NSFAS) money is channelled into families have been collected by Christopher Webb for his PhD thesis currently being completed at the University of Toronto.

36 I developed a rough typology of family types from which children were sent to multiracial schools in Mark Hunter, 'Parental choice without parents: families, education and class in a South African township', *Compare: A Journal of Comparative and International Education* 47, no. 1 (2017), pp. 2–16.

37 This example is adapted from Mark Hunter, 'Is it enough to talk of marriage as a process? Legitimate co-habitation in Umlazi, South Africa', *Anthropology Southern Africa* 39, no. 4 (2016), pp. 281–96.

38 Hunter, 'Is it enough to talk of marriage as a process?'

39 For example, Hunter, *Love in the Time of AIDS*.

40 South African Institute of Race Relations, *First Steps to Healing the South African Family*, p. 2.

41 Thobekile Luthuli, 'Assessing politeness, language and gender in Hlonipha', unpublished master's thesis, Department of Linguistics, University of KwaZulu-Natal, Durban, 2007, p. 43.

42 Kath Weston, *Families We Choose: lesbians, gays, kinship* (New York NY: Columbia University Press, 1997).

43 Marc Epprecht, *Hungochani: the history of a dissident sexuality in Southern Africa* (Montreal and Kingston: McGill-Queen's University Press, 2004).

44 Hunter, *Love in the Time of AIDS*.

45 Grace Khunou, 'Money and gender relations in the South African maintenance system', *South African Review of Sociology* 43, no.1 (2012), pp. 4–22; Brady G'Sell, 'The "maintenance" of family: mediating relationships in the South African maintenance court', *Africa Today* 62, no. 3 (2016), pp. 3–27. On fathers' continued links to children, see also Nolwazi Mkhwanazi and Ellen Block, 'Paternity matters: premarital childbearing and belonging in Nyanga East and Mokhotlong', *Social Dynamics* 42, no. 2 (2016), pp. 273–88.

46 Hylton White, 'Tempora et mores: family values and the possessions of a post-apartheid countryside', *Journal of Religion in Africa* XXXI, no. 4 (2001), p. 464.

47 Luthuli, 'Assessing politeness, language and gender in Hlonipha'; for a fascinating discussion of *inhlonipho* in Umlazi, see Chapter 7 in Dlamini, *Youth and Identity Politics in South Africa, 1990–94.*

48 For a recent discussion of *ubuntu*, see Colin Chasi, 'Ubuntu and freedom of expression', *Ethics and Behavior* 24, no. 6 (2014), pp. 495–509.

49 See Dlamini, *Youth and Identity Politics in South Africa, 1990–94*, p. 127.


## Chapter 9

1 Paul Willis, *Learning to Labour: how working class kids get working class jobs* (New York NY: Columbia University Press, 1981 [1977]).

2 Goldberg, *The Threat of Race.*

3 Seekings and Nattrass, *Class, Race, and Inequality in South Africa*; Seekings and Nattrass, *Policy, Politics and Poverty in South Africa.* Seekings and Nattrass acknowledge some of the limitations of their study discussed here, for instance saying: 'We have little to say about inequalities within households, for example, including those of gender. These are clearly important, but we rely primarily on data about households that provide few clues as to what is happening within them.' Seekings and Nattrass, *Class, Race, and Inequality*, p. 48.

4 Seekings and Nattrass, *Policy, Politics and Poverty in South Africa.*

5 For a short version of this argument, see Jeremy Seekings and Nicoli Nattrass, 'Class, distribution and redistribution in post-apartheid South Africa', *Transformation* 50 (2002), pp. 1–30.

6 Alexander et al., *Class in Soweto*; Ralph Callebert, 'Transcending dual economies: reflections on "Popular economies in South Africa"', *Africa* 84, no. 1 (2014), pp. 119–34; for a response, see Jeremy Seekings, 'Taking disadvantage seriously: the "underclass" in post-apartheid South Africa', *Africa* 84, no. 1 (2014), pp. 135–41.

7 Thabo Mokone, 'R570-billion for free tertiary education', *Sunday Times*, 21 February 2018, www.timeslive.co.za/sunday-times/business/2018-02-21-r57-billion-for-free-tertiary-education/ (accessed 1 March 2018).

8 CDE, *Hidden Assets.*

9 See Logan Govender, 'Teacher unions' participation in policy making: a South African case study', *Compare* 45, no.2 (2015), pp. 184–205.

10 Saren Stiegel, 'What is the price of education? A look at the inefficacy of school fee policy on Kennedy Road', unpublished report (2006) available at http://abahlali.org/node/917/.

11 Jare Struwig et al., *Local Matters.*

12 'It's official: SA is the world capital of protest', *The Times*, 14 June 2016. Protests surged particularly from the 2000s. See Peter Alexander, 'Rebellion of the poor: South Africa's service delivery protests – a preliminary analysis', *Review of African Political Economy* 37, no. 123 (2010), pp. 25–40; Hart, *Rethinking the South African Crisis.*

13 Fanon, *Black Skin, White Masks*, p. 8.

14 Neville Alexander, 'The political economy of the harmonisation of the Nguni and the Sotho languages', *Lexikos* 8 (1998), pp. 269–75.

15 Leketi Makalela, 'Making sense of BSAE for linguistic democracy', *World Englishes* 23, no. 23 (2004), pp. 355–66.

16 Magolego, 'TUT students vs the coconut bourgeoisie'.

17 Chigumadzi, 'Of coconuts, consciousness and Cecil John Rhodes.'

18 Peter Ives, *Language and Hegemony in Gramsci* (London: Pluto Press, 2004), p. 36. The Gramsci literature is huge, but for a recent account by geographers that pays attention to Gramsci's linguistics, see Michael Ekers, Gillian Hart, Stefan Kipfer, and Alex Loftus (eds), *Gramsci: space, nature, politics* (Chichester: Wiley-Blackwell, 2013). See also Craig Brandist, *The Dimensions of Hegemony: language, culture and politics in revolutionary Russia* (Leiden: Brill, 2015).

19 Gramsci, *Selections from the Prison Notebooks*, p. 31.

20 Raymond Williams, *Marxism and Literature* (New York NY: Oxford University Press, 1977), p. 108.

21 See Franco Lo Piparo, 'The linguistic roots of Gramsci's non-Marxism' in Peter Ives and Rocco Lacorte (eds), *Gramsci, Language, and Translation* (Lanham MD: Lexington Books, 2010), pp. 19–49. See also Ives, *Language and Hegemony in Gramsci*.

22 Gramsci, *Selections from the Prison Notebooks*, p. 269.

23 Gramsci also had what, at the outset, looks like an essentially conservative approach to curriculum and teaching methods. In *Antonio Gramsci: conservative schooling for radical politics* (London: Routledge, 1979, p. 24), Harold Entwistle argues that 'he is committed to the notion of an active teacher, a didactic pedagogy, a hardworking desk-bound pupil and a traditional view of academic standards and the function of examinations'.

24 Ives, *Language and Hegemony in Gramsci*, p. 83.

25 Ives, *Language and Hegemony in Gramsci*, p. 59.

26 Marcus Green and Peter Ives, 'Subalternity and language: overcoming the fragmentation of common sense' in Ives and Lacorte (eds), *Gramsci, Language, and Translation*, p. 302.

27 Leketi Makalela, 'Black South African English on the radio', *World Englishes* 32, no.1 (2013), pp. 93–107.

28 Rajend Mesthrie, 'Class, gender, and substrate erasure in sociolinguistic change: a sociophonetic study of Schwa in deracializing South African English', *Language* 93, no. 2 (2017), pp. 314–46.

29 Leketi Makalela, 'Ubuntu translanguaging: an alternative framework for complex multilingual encounters', *Southern African Linguistics and Applied Language Studies* 34, no. 3 (2016), pp. 187–96.

30 Makalela, 'Making sense of BSAE for linguistic democracy'.

# Bibliography

Ahearn, Laura. *Invitations to Love: literacy, love letters and social change in Nepal.* Ann Arbor MI: Michigan University Press, 2001.

Alegi, Peter. *Laduma! Soccer, Politics, and Society in South Africa.* Pietermaritzburg: University of KwaZulu-Natal Press, 2004.

Alexander, Neville. 'The political economy of the harmonisation of the Nguni and the Sotho Languages', *Lexikos* 8 (1998): 269–75.

*Language Policy and National Unity in South Africa/Azania.* Cape Town: Buchu Books, 1989.

Alexander, Peter. 'Rebellion of the poor: South Africa's service delivery protests – a preliminary analysis', *Review of African Political Economy* 37, no. 123 (2010): 25–40.

Alexander, Peter, Claire Ceruti, Keke Motseke, Mosa Phadi, and Kim Wale. *Class in Soweto.* Pietermaritzburg: University of KwaZulu-Natal Press, 2013.

Allais, Stephanie. *Selling Out Education: national qualifications framework and the neglect of knowledge.* Rotterdam: Sense Publishers, 2014.

Ally, Shireen. *From Servants to Workers: South African domestic workers and the democratic state.* Ithaca NY: Cornell University Press, 2009.

Amoateng, Acheampong Ya, Tim B. Heaton, and Ishmael Kalule-Sabiti. 'Living arrangements in South Africa' in Acheampong Yaw Amoateng and Tim Heaton (eds), *Families and Households in Post-Apartheid South Africa.* Cape Town: HSRC Press, 2007.

André-Bechely, Lois. 'Finding space and managing distance: public school choice in an urban California district', *Urban Studies* 44, no. 7 (2007): 1355–76.

Apple, Michael. *Educating the 'Right' Way: markets, standards, god, and inequality.* London: Routledge, 2006.

Argyle, John. 'The myth of the elementary family: a comparative account of variations in family household structure amongst a group of South African whites', *African Studies* 36, no. 2 (1977): 105–18.

Arndt, Jochen. 'What's in a word? Historicising the term "Caffre" in European discourses about Southern Africa between 1500 and 1800', *Journal of Southern African Studies* 44 (2018): 59–75.

Atkinson, Will. 'From sociological fictions to social fictions: some Bourdieusian reflections on the concepts of "institutional habitus" and "family habitus"', *British Journal of Sociology of Education* 32, no. 3 (2011): 331–47.

Baker, David. *The Schooled Society: the educational transformation of global culture.* Palo Alto CA: Stanford University Press, 2014.

Ball, Stephen. *Class Strategies and the Education Market: the middle classes and social advantage*. London: Routledge, 2003.

'Education markets, choice and social class: the market as a class strategy in the UK and the USA', *British Journal of Sociology of Education* 14, no. 1 (1993): 3–19.

'Imperialism, social control and the colonial curriculum in Africa', *Journal of Curriculum Studies* 15, no. 3 (1983): 237–63.

Ball, Stephen and Carol Vincent. '"I heard it on the grapevine": "hot" knowledge and school choice', *British Journal of Sociology of Education* 19, no. 3 (1998): 377–400.

Ball, Stephen, Richard Bowe, and Sharon Gewirtz. 'Circuits of schooling: a sociological exploration of parental choice of school in social class contexts', *Sociological Review* 43, no. 1 (1995): 52–78.

Ballard, Richard. 'Middle class neighbourhoods or "African Kraals"? The impact of informal settlements and vagrants on post-apartheid white identity', *Urban Forum* 15, no. 1 (2004): 48–73.

Bank, Leslie. *Home Spaces, Street Styles: contesting power and identity in a South African city*. London: Pluto Press, 2011.

'Men with cookers: transformations in migrant culture, domesticity and identity in Duncan Village, East London', *Journal of Southern African Studies* 25, no. 3 (1999): 392–416.

*Bantu Education Journal*. 'Editorial: private schools', *Bantu Education Journal*, September 1973.

'Annual report for 1967 of the Umlazi District School Board', *Bantu Education Journal*, March 1968.

Barchiesi, Franco. *Precarious Liberation: workers, the state, and contested social citizenship in postapartheid South Africa*. New York NY: SUNY Press, 2011.

Barnett, Clive. 'The consolations of "neoliberalism"', *Geoforum* 36 (2005): 7–12.

Becker, Gary. *Human Capital: a theoretical and empirical analysis, with special reference to education* (Chicago IL: University of Chicago Press, 1993).

Bell, Jarred and Tracy McKay. 'The rise of "class apartheid" in accessing secondary schools in Sandton, Gauteng', *Southern African Review of Education* 17 (2011): 27–48.

Benner, Chris, Charley Lewis, and Rahmat Omar. 'The South African call centre industry: a study of strategy, human resource practices and performance'. Global Call Centre Industry Project. University Park PA: Sociology of Work Unit, Pennsylvania State University, 2013.

Bennett, Rachel, Victoria Hosegood, Marie-Louise Newell, and Nuala McGrath, 'An approach to measuring dispersed families with a particular focus on children "left behind" by migrant parents: findings from rural South Africa', *Population, Space, and Place* 21 (2015): 332–4.

Bernstein, Basil. *Class, Codes and Control. Volume I: theoretical studies towards a sociology of language*. London: Routledge, 1971.

Berry, Sara. *Fathers Work for Their Sons: accumulation, mobility, and class formation in an extended Yoruba community*. Berkeley CA: University of California Press, 1985.

Bickford-Smith, Vivian. *The Emergence of the South African Metropolis: cities and identities in the twentieth century*. Cambridge: Cambridge University Press, 2016.

Biko, Stephen. *I Write What I Like*. San Francisco CA: Harper & Row, 1978.

Black, David and John Nauright. *Rugby and the South African Nation*. Manchester: Manchester University Press, 1988.

Bledsoe, Caroline. 'The cultural transformation of Western education in Sierra Leone', *Africa* 62, no. 2 (1992): 182–202.

Bledsoe, Caroline H., John B. Casterline, Jennifer A. Johnson-Kuhn, and John G. Haaga (eds). *Critical Perspectives on Schooling and Fertility in the Developing World*. Washington DC: National Academy Press, 1999.

Bond, Patrick. 'From racial to class apartheid: South Africa's frustrating decade of freedom', *Monthly Review* 55, no. 10 (2004): 45–59.

*Elite Transition: from apartheid to neoliberalism*. London: Pluto Press, 2000.

Bonnin, Debby. 'Claiming spaces, changing places: political violence and women's protests in KwaZulu-Natal', *Journal of Southern African Studies* 26, no. 2 (2000): 301–16.

Bottomley, Edward-John. 'Transnational governmentality and the "poor white" in early twentieth century South Africa', *Journal of Historical Geography* 54 (2016): 76–86.

Bourdieu, Pierre. *The State Nobility: elite schools in the field of power*. Palo Alto CA: Stanford University Press, 1996.

*Language and Symbolic Power*. Cambridge: Cambridge University Press, 1991.

*The Logic of Practice*. Cambridge: Polity Press, 1990.

'What makes a social class? On the theoretical and practical existence of groups', *Berkeley Journal of Sociology* 32, no. 1 (1987): 1–17.

Bozzoli, Belinda. 'Why were the 1980s "millenarian"? Style, repertoire, space and authority in South Africa's black cities', *Journal of Historical Sociology* 13, no. 1 (2000): 78–110.

Brandist, Craig. *The Dimensions of Hegemony: language, culture and politics in revolutionary Russia*. Leiden: Brill, 2015.

Breckenridge, Keith. 'The book of life: the South African population register and the invention of racial descent, 1950–1980', *Kronos* 40 (2005): 225–40.

Brown, Barbara. 'Facing the "black peril": the politics of population control in South Africa', *Journal of Southern African Studies* 13, no. 2 (1987): 256–73.

Brown, Julian. *The Road to Soweto: resistance and the uprising of 16 June 1976*. London: James Currey, 2016.

Brown, Philip. 'Education, opportunity and the prospects for social mobility', *British Journal of Sociology of Education* 34, no. 5–6 (2013): 678–700.

Brown, Wendy. *Undoing the Demos: neoliberalism's stealth revolution*. New York NY: Zone Books, 2015.

Bryant, Alfred T. *A Zulu–English Dictionary with Notes on Pronunciation*. Marianhill: Marianhill Mission Press, 1905.

Bundy, Colin. 'Street sociology and pavement politics: aspects of youth and student resistance in Cape Town', *Journal of Southern African Studies* 13, no. 3 (1987): 303–30.

Burawoy, Michael and Karl von Holdt. *Conversations with Bourdieu: the Johannesburg moment*. Johannesburg: Wits University Press, 2012.

Buthelezi Commission. *The Buthelezi Commission: the requirements for stability and development in KwaZulu and Natal. Volume I and II*. Durban: H + H Publications, 1982.

Butler, Jeffrey, Robert Rotberg, and John Adams. *The Black Homelands of South Africa: the political and economic development of Bophuthatswana and KwaZulu*. Berkeley CA: University of California Press, 1977.

Butler, Tim and Chris Hamnett. 'The geography of education: introduction', *Urban Studies* 44, no. 7 (2007): 1161–74.

Butler, Tim and Gary Robson. *London Calling: the middle classes and the remaking of inner London*. London: Berg, 2003.

Calderwood, D. M. 'Native housing in South Africa'. PhD thesis, Department of Architecture, University of the Witwatersrand, Johannesburg, 1955.

Caldwell, John. *Demographic Transition Theory*. Amsterdam: Springer, 2006.
'On net intergenerational wealth flows: an update', *Population and Development Review* 31, no. 4 (2005): 721–40.

Caldwell, John and Pat Caldwell. 'The South African fertility decline', *Population and Development Review* 19, no. 2 (1993): 225–62.

Callebert, Ralph. 'Working class action and informal trade on the Durban Docks, 1930s–1950s', *Journal of Southern African Studies* 38, no. 4 (2012): 847–61.

*Careers for You*. 'Letters of application', *Careers for You* 1, no. 1, April 1984.

Carrim, Nazir. *Desegregation in Coloured and Indian Schooling*. Johannesburg: Education Policy Unit, University of the Witwatersrand, 1992.

Carsten, Janet. *After Kinship: new departures in anthropology*. Cambridge: Cambridge University Press, 2004.

Carton, Ben. *Blood from Your Children: the colonial origins of generational conflict in South Africa*. Charlottesville VA: University of Virginia Press, 2000.

CDE. *Hidden Assets: South Africa's low-fee private schools*. Johannesburg: Centre for Development and Enterprise (CDE), 2010.

Chance, Kerry. 'Transitory citizens: contentious housing practices in contemporary South Africa', *Social Analysis* 59, no. 3 (2015): 62–84.

Chanock, Martin. *The Making of South African Legal Culture 1902–1935: fear, favour, and prejudice*. Cambridge: Cambridge University Press, 2004.

Chari, Sharad. 'An "Indian commons" in Durban? Limits to mutuality, or the city to come', *Anthropology Southern Africa* 37, no. 3–4 (2014): 149–59.
'State racism and biopolitical struggle: the evasive commons in twentieth-century Durban, South Africa', *Radical History Review* 108 (2010): 73–90.

Charlton, Sarah and Caroline Kihato. 'Reaching the poor? An analysis of the influences of the evolution of South Africa's housing programme' in Udesh Pillay, Richard Tomlinson, and Jacques du Toit (eds), *Democracy and Delivery: urban policy in South Africa*. Cape Town: HSRC Press, 2006.

Chasi, Colin. 'Ubuntu and freedom of expression', *Ethics and Behavior* 24, no. 6 (2014): 495–509.

Chigumadzi, Panashe. 'Of coconuts, consciousness and Cecil John Rhodes'. Fourteenth Annual Ruth First Memorial Lecture, University of the Witwatersrand, Johannesburg, 17 August 2015. Available at www.journalism.co.za/wp-content/uploads/2015/08/Ruth-First-FINAL-Draft-_-Panashe-Chigumadzi.pdf (accessed 9 January 2017).

*The Child*, summer issue, October–December 1987.
'Education: who should carry the can?', autumn issue, January–March 1987.

Chipkin, Ivor. 'Middle classing in Roodepoort: capitalism and social change in South Africa'. PARI Long Essays 2. Johannesburg: Public Affairs Research Institute (PARI), University of the Witwatersrand, 2012.

Chisholm, Linda (ed.). *Changing Class: education and social change in post-apartheid South Africa*. Cape Town: HSRC Press, 2004.

Chisholm, Linda 'Redefining skills: black education in South Africa in the 1980s', *Comparative Education* 19, no. 3 (1983): 357–71.

Christie, Pam. 'Transition tricks? Policy models for school desegregation in South Africa, 1990–94', *Journal of Education Policy* 10, no. 1 (1995): 45–55.

*Open Schools: racially mixed catholic schools in South Africa 1976–86.* Johannesburg: Ravan Press, 1990.

Christie, Pam and Adele Gordon. 'Politics, poverty and education in rural South Africa', *British Journal of Sociology of Education* 13, no. 4 (1992): 399–418.

City of Durban. 'City engineer's report on the planning of the Bluff'. Durban: City Engineer's Department, 1967.

Cock, Jacklyn. *Maids and Madams: a study in the politics of exploitation.* Johannesburg: Ravan Press, 1980.

Cole, Jennifer and Deborah Durham (eds). *Generations and Globalization: youth, age, and family in the new world economy.* Bloomington IN: Indiana University Press, 2007.

Colenso, John. *Zulu–English Dictionary.* Pietermaritzburg: P. Davis, 1861.

Collins, Patricia Hill. 'Learning from the outsider within: the sociological significance of black feminist thought', *Social Problems* 33, no. 6 (1986): 14–32.

Collins, Randall. *Credential Society: a historical sociology of education and stratification.* New York NY: Academic Press, 1979.

Collis-Buthelezi, Victoria. 'The case for black studies in South Africa', *The Black Scholar* 47, no. 2 (2017): 7–21.

Comaroff, Jean and John Comaroff. *Ethnicity, Inc.* Chicago IL: Chicago University Press, 2009.

*Christianity, Colonialism, and Consciousness in South Africa. Vol. 1: Of revelation and revolution.* Chicago IL: University of Chicago Press, 1991.

Connell, Raewyn. *Masculinities.* Berkeley CA: University of California Press, 2005.

*Which Way Is Up: essays on sex, class and culture.* London: Allen & Unwin, 1983.

Crankshaw, Owen. 'Race, space and the post-Fordist spatial order of Johannesburg', *Urban Studies* 45 (2008): 1692–711.

'Class, race and residence in black Johannesburg, 1923–1970', *Journal of Historical Sociology* 18, no 4 (2005): 353–93.

*Race, Class and the Changing Division of Labour under Apartheid.* London: Routledge, 1997.

'Squatting, apartheid and urbanization on the southern Witwatersrand', *African Affairs* 92, no. 366 (1993): 31–51.

Crapanzano, Vincent. *Waiting: the whites of South Africa.* London: Random House, 1985.

Crenshaw, Kimberlé. 'Demarginalizing the intersection of race and sex: a black feminist critique of antidiscrimination doctrine, feminist theory, and anti-racist politics', *University of Chicago Legal Forum* (1989): 139–67.

Cross, Michael. 'A historical review of education in South Africa: towards and assessment', *Comparative Education* 22, no. 3 (1986): 185–200.

De Kadt, Julia, Shane A. Norris, Brahm Fleisch, Linda Richter, and Seraphim Alvanides. 'Children's daily travel to school in Johannesburg-Soweto: geography and distance in the birth to twenty cohort', *Children's Geographies* 12, no. 2 (2014): 170–88.

De Villiers, Elizabeth. *Walking the Tightrope: recollections of a schoolteacher in Soweto.* Johannesburg: Jonathan Ball Publishers, 1990.

Dempster, Edith and Vijay Reddy. 'Item readability and science achievement in TIMSS 2003 in South Africa', *Science Education* 91, no. 1 (2007): 36–74.

Desai, Ashwin. *Reverse Sweep: a story of South African cricket since apartheid.* Johannesburg: Jacana, 2016.

(ed.). *The Race to Transform Sport in Post-apartheid South Africa.* Cape Town: HSRC Press, 2010.

Desai, Ashwin, Vishnu Padayachee, Krish Reddy, and Goolam Vahed. *Blacks in Whites: a century of cricket struggles in KwaZulu-Natal.* Pietermaritzburg: University of KwaZulu-Natal Press, 2002.

Di Leonardo, Micaela (ed.). *Gender at the Crossroads of Knowledge: feminist anthropology in the postmodern era.* Berkeley CA: University of California Press, 1991.

Dlamini, Jacob. *Native Nostalgia.* Cape Town: Jacana, 2010.

Dlamini, Sibusisiwe Nombuso. *Youth and Identity Politics in South Africa, 1990–94.* Toronto: University of Toronto Press, 2005.

Doke, Clement, Benedict Vilakazi, D. Malcolm, and J. Sikakana. *English/Zulu Zulu/English Dictionary.* Johannesburg: Witwatersrand University Press, 1990.

Dolby, Nadine. 'Making white: constructing race in a South African high school', *Curriculum Inquiry* 32, no. 1 (2002): 7–29.

*Constructing Race: youth, identity, and popular culture in South Africa.* New York NY: SUNY Press, 2001.

'Youth and the global popular: the politics and practices of race in South Africa', *European Journal of Cultural Studies* 2, no. 3. (1999): 291–309.

Donkin, Rob. *A Bluff Scruff Miracle.* Wandsbeck: Reach Publishers, 2010.

Dreijmanis, John. *The Role of the South African Government in Tertiary Education.* Johannesburg: South African Institute of Race Relations, 1988.

Du Bois, W. E. B. *Black Reconstruction: an essay toward a history of the part which black folks played in the attempt to reconstruct democracy in America, 1860–1880.* New York NY: Russel & Russel, 1935.

*The Souls of Black Folk.* Oxford: Oxford University Press, 2007 [1903].

Dubow, Saul. *Apartheid: 1948–1994.* Oxford: Oxford University Press, 2014.

*A Commonwealth of Knowledge: science, sensibility, and white South Africa 1820–2000.* Oxford: Oxford University Press, 2006.

*Scientific Racism in Modern South Africa.* Johannesburg: Witwatersrand University Press, 1995.

*Racial Segregation and the Origins of Apartheid in South Africa, 1919–1935.* New York NY: St Martin's Press, 1989.

Du Toit, David. 'From "Cinderella cleaners" to "maids from heaven": clients' and domestic workers' perceptions of housecleaning services in Stellenbosch', *South African Journal of Labour Relations* 37, no. 1 (2013): 97–114.

Du Toit, Marijke. '"Anginayo ngisho indibilishi!" (I don't have a penny!): The gender politics of "native welfare" in Durban, 1930–1939', *South African Historical Journal* 66, no. 2 (2014): 291–319.

Edwards, Iain. 'Mkhumbane our home: African shantytown society in Cato Manor Farm, 1946–1960'. PhD thesis, University of Natal, Durban, 1989.

Eiselen, Werner. 'The standard of English and Afrikaans in our Bantu schools', *Bantu Education Journal* 17, no. 5 (1971): 4–7.

Ekers, Michael, Gillian Hart, Stefan Kipfer, and Alex Loftus (eds). *Gramsci: space, nature, politics.* Chichester: Wiley-Blackwell, 2013.

Entwistle, Harold. *Antonio Gramsci: conservative schooling for radical politics.* London: Routledge, 1979.

Epprecht, Marc. *Hungochani: the history of a dissident sexuality in Southern Africa.* Montreal and Kingston: McGill-Queen's University Press, 2004.

Erasmus, Zimitri. *Race Otherwise: forging a new humanism for South Africa.* Johannesburg: Wits University Press, 2017.

'The nation, its populations and their re-calibration: South African affirmative action in a neoliberal age', *Cultural Dynamics* 27, no. 1 (2015): 99–115.

Erwin, Kira and Kathryn Pillay. 'The power of dreams: young people's imaginings of non-racialism, racialism and racism in South Africa'. Unpublished paper, Durban, 2016.

Etherington, Norman. 'Kingdoms of this world and the next: Christian beginnings among Zulu and Swazi' in Rick Elphick and Rodney Davenport (eds), Christianity in South Africa: a political, social and cultural history. Berkeley CA: University of California Press, 1997.

Evans, Ivan. *Bureaucracy and Race: native administration in South Africa.* Berkeley CA: University of California Press, 1997.

Fair, T. J. D. and N. Manfred Shaffer. 'Population patterns and policies in South Africa', *Economic Geography* 40, no. 3 (1964): 261–74.

Falkof, Nicky. 'Out the back: race and reinvention in Johannesburg's garden cottages', *International Journal of Cultural Studies* 19, no. 6 (2016): 627–42.

*Satanism and Family Murder in Late Apartheid South Africa.* London: Palgrave, 2015.

Fanon, Frantz. *Black Skin, White Masks.* London: Pluto Press, 1986 [1952].

*The Wretched of the Earth.* New York NY: Grove Press, 1984 [1961].

Fataar, Aslam. 'Self-formation and the "capacity to aspire": the itinerant "schooled" career of Fuzile Ali across post-apartheid space', *Perspectives in Education* 28, no. 3 (2010): 34–45.

Fedderke, Johannes, Raphael de Kadt, and John Luiz. 'Uneducating South Africa: the failure to address the 1910–1993 legacy', *International Review of Education* 46, no. 3–4 (2000): 257–81.

Feinstein, Charles. *An Economic History of South Africa: conquest, discrimination and development.* Cambridge: Cambridge University Press, 2005.

*Femina*, 'Women who cope on their own', November 1982.

'Love is a bargain', 3 September 1970.

Ferguson, James. *Give a Man a Fish: reflections on the new politics of distribution.* Durham NC: Duke University Press, 2015.

'The uses of neoliberalism', *Antipode* no. 41 (2009): 166–84.

'The bovine mystique: power, property and livestock in rural Lesotho', *Man* 20, no. 4 (1985): 647–74.

Fiske, Edward and Helen Ladd. *Elusive Equity: education reform in post-apartheid South Africa.* Washington DC: Brookings Institute, 2004.

Fleisch, Brahm. 'Social scientists as policy makers: E. G. Malherbe and the National Bureau for Educational and Social Research, 1929–1943', *Journal of Southern African Studies* 21, no. 3 (1995): 349–72.

'State formation and the origins of Bantu education' in Peter Kallaway (ed.), *The History of Education under Apartheid 1948–1994.* New York NY: Peter Lang, 2002.

*Focus on Education.* '20 schools with highest pass rates', *Focus on Education* 6, no. 2, February 1991.

Forsey, Martin, Scott Davies, and Geoffrey Walford (eds). *The Globalisation of School Choice?* Oxford: Symposium Books, 2008.

Frankenberg, Ruth. *White Women, Race Matters: the social construction of whiteness.* Minneapolis MN: University of Minnesota Press, 1993.

Fredrickson, George. *White Supremacy: a comparative study in American and South African history.* Oxford: Oxford University Press, 1981.

Freund, Bill. *Insiders and Outsiders: the Indian working class of Durban, 1910–1990.* Portsmouth NH: Heinemann, 1995.

Friedman, Steven. *Race, Class and Power: Harold Wolpe and the radical critique of apartheid.* Pietermaritzburg: University of KwaZulu-Natal Press, 2015.

Gaitskell, Deborah, Judy Kimble, Moira Maconachie, and Elaine Unterhalter. 'Class, race and gender: domestic workers in South Africa', *Review of African Political Economy* 10, no. 27–8 (1983): 86–108.

Gibbs, Timothy. *Mandela's Kinsmen: nationalist elites and apartheid's first Bantustans.* Woodbridge: James Currey, 2014.

Gibson, Nigel. 'The specter of Fanon: the student movements and the rationality of revolt in South Africa', *Social Identities* 23, no. 5 (2017): 579–99.

Giliomee, Hermann. *The Afrikaners: biography of a people.* Charlottesville VA: University of Virginia Press, 2003.
    'Being Afrikaans in the new (multilingual) South Africa', *New Contree* 40 (1996): 59–73.

Gillespie, Kelly. 'Reclaiming nonracialism: reading *The Threat of Race* from South Africa', *Patterns of Prejudice* 44, no. 1 (2010): 61–75.

Gilmartin, Mary. 'Language, education and the new South Africa', *Tijdschrift Voor Economische en Sociale Geografie* 95 (2004): 405–18.

Gilmore, Ruth Wilson. *Golden Gulag: prisons, surplus, crisis, and opposition in globalizing California.* Berkeley CA: University of California Press, 2007.
    'Fatal couplings of power and difference: notes on racism and geography', *The Professional Geographer* 54, no. 1 (2002): 15–24.

Gilroy, Paul. *Between Camps: nations, cultures and the allure of Race.* London: Routledge, 2004.

Ginsburg, Rebecca. *At Home with Apartheid: the hidden landscape of domestic service in Johannesburg.* Charlottesville VA: University of Virginia Press, 2011.

Glaser, Clive. 'Soweto's islands of learning: Morris Isaacson and Orlando high schools under Bantu education, 1958–1975', *Journal of Southern African Studies* 41, no. 1 (2015): 159–71.

Glaser, Daryl. 'Behind the Indaba: the making of the KwaNatal option', *Transformation* 2 (1986): 4–30.

Glotzer, Richard. 'Charles Templeman Loram: education and race relations in South Africa and North America' in Peter Kallaway and Rebecca Swartz (eds), *Empire and Education in Africa.* New York NY: Peter Lang, 2016.

Goldberg, David. *Are We All Postracial Yet?* Malden MA: Polity Press, 2015.
    *The Threat of Race: reflections on racial neoliberalism.* Oxford: Blackwell, 2009.
    *The Racial State.* London: Blackwell, 2002.
    *Racist Culture: philosophy and the politics of meaning.* Oxford: Blackwell, 1993.

Gorard, Stephen. '"Well. That about wraps it up for school choice research": a state of the art review', *School Leadership and Management* 19, no. 1 (1999): 25–47.

Govender, Logan. 'Teacher unions' participation in policy making: a South African case study', *Compare* 45, no. 2 (2015): 184–205.

Gramsci, Antonio. *Selections from the Prison Notebooks of Antonio Gramsci*. New York NY: International Publishers, 1971.

Green, Marcus and Peter Ives. 'Subalternity and language: overcoming the fragmentation of common sense' in Peter Ives and Rocco Lacorte (eds), *Gramsci, Language, and Translation*. Lanham MD: Lexington Books, 2010.

Grundlingh, Albert. 'Are we Afrikaners getting too rich? Cornucopia and change in Afrikanerdom in the 1960s', *Journal of Historical Sociology* 21, no. 2–3 (2008): 143–65.

'Playing for power? Rugby, Afrikaner nationalism and masculinity in South Africa, c.1900–70', *International Journal of the History of Sport* 11, no. 3 (1994): 408–30.

G'Sell, Brady. 'The "maintenance" of family: mediating relationships in the South African maintenance court', *Africa Today* 62, no. 3 (2016): 3–27.

Gulson, Kalervo. *Education Policy, Space, and the City: markets and the (in)visibility of race*. London: Routledge, 2011.

Guy, Jeff. *Theophilus Shepstone and the Forging of Natal*. Pietermaritzburg: University of KwaZulu-Natal Press, 2013.

'An accommodation of the patriarchs: Theophilus Shepstone and the foundations of the system of native administration in Natal'. Paper presented at the Conference on Masculinities in Southern Africa, University of Natal, Durban, 2–4 July 1997.

*The Destruction of the Zulu Kingdom: the civil war in Zululand 1879–1884*. Pietermaritzburg: University of Natal Press, 1977.

Guyer, Jane. 'Wealth in people, wealth in things: introduction', *Journal of African History* 36, no. 1 (1995): 83–90.

'Household and community in African studies', *African Studies Review* 24, no. 2–3 (1981): 87–137.

Guyer, Jane and Pauline Peters. 'Conceptualizing the household: issues of theory and policy in Africa', *Development and Change* 18, no. 2 (1987): 197–214.

Gwebu, Alf and Joe Motsiri. 'They break up marriages', *Bona*, February 1965.

Hall, Stuart. 'Race, articulation and societies structured in dominance' in *Sociological Theories: race and colonialism*. London: UNESCO, 1980.

Hamilton, Carolyn. *Terrific Majesty: the power of Shaka Zulu and the limits of historical invention*. Cambridge MA: Harvard University Press, 1998.

Hansen, Thomas Bloom. *Melancholia of Freedom: social life in an Indian township in South Africa*. Princeton NJ: Princeton University Press, 2012.

Hart, Gillian. *Rethinking the South African Crisis: nationalism, populism, Hegemony*. Athens GA: University of Georgia Press, 2014.

*Disabling Globalization: places of power in post-apartheid South Africa*. Berkeley CA: University of California Press, 2002.

Hartman, Andrew. 'The rise and fall of whiteness studies', *Race and Class* 46, no. 2 (2004): 22–38.

Harvey, David. *A Brief History of Neoliberalism*. Oxford: Oxford University Press, 2007.

Hassim, Shireen. *Women's Organizations and Democracy in South Africa: contesting authority*. Madison WI: University of Wisconsin Press, 2006.

Haw, Simon. *Taking Stock: the Natal Education Department looks back*. Pietermaritzburg: Natal Education Department, 1995.

Hawthorne, Peter and Barry Bristow. *Historic Schools of South Africa: an ethos of excellence*. Cape Town: Pachyderm Press, 1993.

Healy-Clancy, Meghan. 'Mass education and the gendered politics of "development"' in Peter Kallaway and Rebecca Swartz (eds), *Empire and Education in Africa*. New York NY: Peter Lang, 2016.

*A World of Their Own: a history of South African women's education*. Charlottesville VA: University of Virginia Press, 2013.

Henderson, Patricia. *AIDS, Intimacy and Care in Rural KwaZulu-Natal: a kinship of bones*. Amsterdam: Amsterdam University Press, 2011.

Hindson, Doug. *Pass Controls and the Urban African Proletariat in South Africa*. Johannesburg: Ravan Press, 1987.

Hindson, Doug and Brian O'Leary. *Durban's Changing Racial Geography 1985–1996*. Durban: eThekwini Municipality.

Hindson, Doug, Mark Byerley, and Mike Morris. 'From violence to reconstruction: the making, disintegration and remaking of an apartheid city'. CSDS Working Paper 10. Durban: Centre for Social and Development Studies (CSDS), University of Natal, 1993.

Hirsch, Fred. *Social Limits to Growth*. London: Routledge, 1978.

Hoadley, Ursula. 'School choice in a South African working class context' in Linda Chisholm, Shireen Motala, and Salim Vally (eds), *Critical Perspectives in South African Education: reconstituting the educational realm*. Cape Town: Juta, 2003.

*Homelife Natal*. 'Delene Ltd', *Homelife Natal* 2, no. 10, March 1987.

Horrell, Muriel. *A Survey of Race Relations in South Africa*. Johannesburg: South African Institute of Race Relations, 1970.

*The Education of the Coloured Community in South Africa 1652 to 1970*. Johannesburg: South African Institute of Race Relations, 1970.

*The African Reserves of South Africa*. Johannesburg: South African Institute of Race Relations, 1969.

*Bantu Education to 1968*. Johannesburg: South African Institute of Race Relations, 1968.

*A Decade of Bantu Education*. Johannesburg: South African Institute of Race Relations, 1964.

Hosegood, Vicky and Ian Timaeus. 'Household composition and dynamics in KwaZulu Natal, South Africa: mirroring social reality in longitudinal data collection' in Etienne Van de Walle (ed.), *African Households: an exploration of census data*. Armonk NY: M. E. Sharpe, 2006.

Huchzemeyer, Marie and Aly Karam (eds). *Informal Settlements: a perpetual challenge*. Cape Town: UCT Press, 2006.

Hughes, Heather. *The First President: a life of John L. Dube, founding president of the ANC*. Auckland Park: Jacana, 2011.

Hunter, Mark. 'Parental choice without parents: families, education and class in a South African township', *Compare: A Journal of Comparative and International Education* 47, no. 1 (2016): 2–16.

'Is it enough to talk of marriage as a process? Legitimate co-habitation in Umlazi, South Africa', *Anthropology Southern Africa* 39, no. 4 (2016): 281–96.

'The bond of education: gender, the value of children, and the making of Umlazi Township in 1960s South Africa', *Journal of African History* 55, no. 3 (2014): 467–90.

*Love in the Time of AIDS: inequality, gender, and rights in South Africa*. Bloomington IN: Indiana University Press, 2010.

'Racial desegregation and schooling in South Africa: contested geographies of class formation', *Environment and Planning A* 42, no. 11 (2010): 2640–57.

Hunter, Mark and Dorrit Posel. 'Here to work: the socioeconomic characteristics of informal dwellers in post-apartheid South Africa', *Environment and Urbanization* 24, no. 1 (2012): 285–304.

Hyslop, Jonathan. 'Why did apartheid's supporters capitulate? "Whiteness", class and consumption in urban South Africa, 1985–1995', *Society in Transition* 31, no. 1 (2000): 36–44.

*The Classroom Struggle: policy and resistance in South Africa 1940–1990.* Pietermaritzburg: University of Natal Press, 1999.

'The imperial working class makes itself "white": white labourism in Britain, Australia, and South Africa before the First World War', *Journal of Historical Sociology* 12, no. 4 (1999): 398–421.

'State education policy and the social reproduction of the urban African working class: the case of the Southern Transvaal 1955–1976', *Journal of Southern African Studies* 14, no. 3 (1988): 446–76.

'Teachers and trade unions', *South African Labour Bulletin* 11, no. 6 (1986): 90–7.

Inwood, Joshua. 'Neoliberal racism: the "southern strategy" and the expanding geography of white supremacy', *Social and Cultural Geography* 16, no. 4 (2015): 407–23.

Irvine, Judith. 'Subjected words: African linguistics and the colonial encounter', *Language and Communication* 28 (2008): 323–43.

Ives, Peter. *Language and Hegemony in Gramsci.* London: Pluto Press, 2004.

Jacklin, Heather and J. Graaff. 'Rural education in South Africa: a report on schooling systems in the Bantustans'. Report prepared for the National Education Policy Investigation. Johannesburg: National Education Coordinating Committee, 1992.

Jacobs, Monica. *A Statistical Overview of Education in KwaZulu Natal.* Johannesburg: The Education Foundation, 1992.

James, Cyril (C. L. R.) *Beyond a Boundary.* Durham NC: Duke University Press, 2013 [1963].

James, Deborah. *Money from Nothing: indebtedness and aspiration in South Africa.* Palo Alto CA: Stanford University Press, 2014.

Jeffrey, Craig, Patricia Jeffery, and Roger Jeffery. *Degrees without Freedom?: education, masculinities, and unemployment in north India.* Palo Alto CA: Stanford University Press, 2007.

Jeffreys, Mervyn. 'Lobolo is child-price', *African Studies* 10, no. 4 (1951): 145–84.

*Journal of Secondary Education.* 'Differentiated secondary education: the report of the overseas mission', *Journal of Secondary Education,* June (1956): 32–5.

'The education of a girl: address to the Johannesburg High School Old Girls' Club, D. E. Langley', *Journal of Secondary Education,* September 1954.

Kaarsholm, Preben. 'Zanzibaris or Amakhuwa? Sufi networks in South Africa, Mozambique, and the Indian Ocean', *Journal of African History* 55 (2014): 191–210.

Kallaway, Peter (ed.). *The History of Education under Apartheid 1948–1994.* New York NY: Peter Lang Publishing, 2002.

(ed.). *Apartheid and Education: the education of black South Africans.* Johannesburg: Ravan Press, 1984.

Kallaway, Peter and Rebecca Swartz (eds). *Empire and Education in Africa*. New York NY: Peter Lang, 2016.

Katzen, May. *Industry in Greater Durban*. Pietermaritzburg: Town and Regional Planning Commission, 1961.

Kenny, Bridget and Edward Webster. 'Eroding the core: flexibility and the resegmentation of the South African labour market', *Critical Sociology* 24, no. 3 (1998): 216–43.

Kenway, Jane, Johannah Fahey, Debbie Epstein, Aaron Koh, Cameron McCarthy, and Fazal Rizvi. *Class Choreographies: elite schools and globalization*. London: Palgrave Macmillan, 2017.

Khunou, Grace. 'Money and gender relations in the South African maintenance system', *South African Review of Sociology* 43, no. 1 (2012): 4–22.

Klasen, Stephan and Ingrid Woolard. 'Surviving unemployment without state support: unemployment and household formation in South Africa', *Journal of African Economies* 18, no. 1 (2009): 1–51.

Kolchin, Peter. 'The new history of race in America', *Journal of American History* 89, no. 1 (2002): 154–73.

Krige, Sue. '"Trustees and agents of the state"? Missions and the formation of policy towards African education, 1910–1920', *South African Historical Journal* 40, no. 1 (2011): 74–94.

Kros, Cynthia. *The Seeds of Separate Development: origins of Bantu education*. Pretoria: UNISA Press, 2010.

Kubeka, Isaac. 'A preliminary survey of Zulu dialects in Natal and Zululand'. Master's thesis, University of Natal, Durban, 1979.

Kuper, Leo. *An African Bourgeoisie: race, class, and politics in South Africa*. New Haven CT: Yale University Press, 1965.

Kuper, Leo, Hilstan Watts, and Ronald Davies. *Durban: a study in racial ecology*. London: Jonathan Cape, 1958.

Kuppusami, C. and M. Pillay. *Pioneer Footprints: growth of Indian education in South Africa, 1860–1977*. Johannesburg: Nasou, 1978.

Lake, Marilyn and Henry Reynolds. *Drawing the Global Colour Line: white men's countries and the international challenge of racial equality*. Cambridge: Cambridge University Press, 2008.

Lambert, John. '"Munition factories … turning out a constant supply of living material": white South African elite boys' schools and the First World War', *South African Historical Journal* 51 (2004): 67–86.

Lareau, Annette. *Unequal Childhoods: class, race, and family life*. Berkeley CA: University of California Press, 2011.

Lee, Rebekah. *African Women and Apartheid: migration and settlement in South Africa*. London: Tauris Academic Studies, 2009.

Leinaweaver, Jessaca. *The Circulation of Children: kinship, adoption, and morality in Andean Peru*. Durham NC: Duke University Press, 2008.

Leitner, Helga, Jamie Peck, and Eric Sheppard. *Contesting Neoliberalism: urban frontiers*. New York NY: Guildford Press, 2007.

Lemon, Anthony. 'Shifting geographies of social inclusion and exclusion: secondary education in Pietermaritzburg, South Africa', *African Affairs* 104, no. 414 (2005): 69–96.

'Desegregation and privatisation in white South African schools: 1990–1992', *Journal of Contemporary African Studies* 12, no. 2 (1994): 200–21.

Li, Tania. *Land's End: capitalist relations on an indigenous frontier*. Durham NC: Duke University Press, 2014.

Lipman, Pauline. *The New Political Economy of Urban Education*. London: Taylor and Francis, 2011.

Lo Piparo, Franco. 'The linguistic roots of Gramsci's non-Marxism' in Peter Ives and Rocco Lacorte (eds), *Gramsci, Language, and Translation*. Lanham MD: Lexington Books, 2010.

Lombard, Mighael and Owen Crankshaw. 'Deindustrialization and racial inequality: social polarisation in eThekwini?', *Cities* 60 (2017): 221–33.

Loram, Charles. *The Education of the South African Native*. London: Longmans, Green and Co., 1917.

Loram, Charles and Thomas McIlwraith. *The North American Indian Today*. Toronto: University of Toronto Press, 1943.

Luthuli, Thobekile. '*Assessing politeness, language and gender in Hlonipha*'. Master's thesis, Department of Linguistics, University of KwaZulu-Natal, Durban, 2007.

Maasdorp, Gavin and A. S. B. Humphreys. *From Shantytown to Township: an economic study of African poverty and rehousing in a South African city*. Cape Town: Juta, 1975.

Macdonald, Michael. *Why Race Matters in South Africa*. Cambridge MA: Harvard University Press, 2012.

Maconachie, Moira. *Alliance and Agreement: marriage among white South Africans*. Cape Town: HSRC Press, 1996.

Madhavan, Sangeetha, Paul Mee, and Mark Collinson. 'Kinship in practice: spatial distribution of children's kin networks', *Journal of Southern African Studies* 40, no. 2 (2014): 401–18.

Magaziner, Daniel. *The Art of Life in South Africa*. Athens OH: Ohio University Press, 2016.

*The Law and the Prophets: black consciousness in South Africa, 1968–1977*. Athens OH: Ohio University Press, 2010.

Magubane, Bernard. *Bernard Magubane: my life and times*. Pietermaritzburg: University of KwaZulu Natal Press, 2010.

Maharaj, Brij. 'Apartheid, urban segregation, and the local state: Durban and the Group Areas Act in South Africa', *Urban Geography* 18, no. 2 (1997): 135–54.

Maharaj, Brij and Jabulani Mpungose. 'The erosion of residential segregation in South Africa: the "greying" of Albert Park in Durban', *Geoforum* 25, no. 1 (1994): 19–32.

Maile, Simon. 'School choice in South Africa', *Education and Urban Society* 37, no. 1 (2004): 94–116.

Makalela, Leketi. 'Ubuntu translanguaging: an alternative framework for complex multilingual encounters', *Southern African Linguistics and Applied Language Studies* 34, no. 3 (2016): 187–96.

'Black South African English on the radio', *World Englishes* 32, no. 1 (2013): 93–107.

'Making sense of BSAE for linguistic democracy', *World Englishes* 23 (2004): 355–66.

Malherbe, Ernst G. *Education in South Africa. Vol. 2: 1923–1973*. Cape Town: Juta, 1977.

*Education in South Africa. Vol. 1: 1652–1922*. Cape Town: Juta, 1925.

Marais, Hein. *South Africa: limits to change, the political economy of transformation*. London: Zed, 2001.

Maré, Gerhard. *Declassified: moving beyond the dead end of race in South Africa*. Johannesburg: Jacana, 2014.

Maré, Gerhard and Georgina Hamilton. *An Appetite for Power: Buthelezi's Inkatha and the politics of 'loyal resistance'*. Johannesburg: Ravan Press, 1987.

Marginson, Simon. 'National and global competition in higher education', *Higher Education* 52, no. 1 (2006): 1–39.

Maringe, Felix and Relobohile Moletsane. 'Leading schools in circumstances of multiple deprivation in South Africa: mapping some conceptual, contextual, and research dimensions', *Educational Management, Administration and Leadership* 43, no. 3 (2015): 347–62.

Marks, Monique. *Young Warriors: youth politics, identity and violence in South Africa*. Johannesburg: Witwatersrand University Press, 2001.

Marks, Shula. *Divided Sisterhood: race, class and gender in the South African nursing profession*. Johannesburg: Witwatersrand University Press, 1994.

'Patriotism, patriarchy and purity: Natal and the politics of Zulu ethnic consciousness' in Leroy Vail (ed.), *The Creation of Tribalism in Southern Africa*. Berkeley CA: University of California Press, 1991.

*Not Either an Experimental Doll: the separate worlds of three South African women*. Bloomington IN: Indiana University Press, 1988.

*The Ambiguities of Dependence in South Africa: class, nationalism, and the state in twentieth-century Natal*. Baltimore MD: Johns Hopkins University Press, 1986.

May, Julian. 'A study of income and expenditure and other socio-economic structures in rural KwaZulu'. Volume 7. Durban: KwaZulu Finance and Investment Corporation, 1986.

Mayer, Philip. *Townsmen or Tribesmen: conservatism and the process of urbanization in a South African city. With contributions by Iona Mayer*. Cape Town: Oxford University Press, 1971.

Mbatha, Mphiwa. 'Migrant labour and its effects on tribal and family life among the Nyuswa of Botha's Hill'. Master's thesis, Department of Bantu Studies, University of Natal, Durban, 1960.

McClendon, Thomas. *White Chiefs, Black Lords: Shepstone and the colonial state in Natal, South Africa – 1845–1878*. New York NY: University of Rochester Press, 2010.

McGregor, Liz. *Springbok Factory: what it takes to be a Bok*. Johannesburg: Jonathan Ball, 2013.

Mda, Zakes. *Black Diamond*. Johannesburg: Penguin, 2011.

Mdluli, Praisley. 'Ubuntu-Botho: Inkatha's "people's education"', *Transformation* 5 (1987): 60–77.

Mesthrie, Rajend. 'Class, gender, and substrate erasure in sociolinguistic change: a sociophonetic study of Schwa in deracializing South African English', *Language* 93, no. 2 (2017): 314–46.

'Towards a distributed sociolinguistics of postcolonial multilingual society: the case of South Africa' in Dick Smakman and Patrick Heinrich (eds), *Globalising Sociolinguistics: challenging and expanding theory*. London: Routledge, 2015.

'From second language to first language: Indian South African English' in Rajend Mesthrie (ed.), *Language in South Africa*. Cambridge: Cambridge University Press, 2012.

'"Death of the mother tongue": is English a glottophagic language in South Africa?', *English Today* 24, no. 2 (2008): 13–19.

'Introduction' in Rajend Mesthrie (ed.), *Language in South Africa*. Cambridge: Cambridge University Press, 2004.

'Language change, survival, decline: Indian languages in South Africa' in Rajend Mesthrie (ed.), *Language in South Africa*. Cambridge: Cambridge University Press, 2002.

Mitchell, Katharyne. 'Neoliberal governmentality in the European Union: education, training, and technologies of citizenship', *Environment and Planning D: Society and Space* 24, no. 12 (2006): 389–407.

Mkhwanazi, Nolwazi and Ellen Block. 'Paternity matters: premarital childbearing and belonging in Nyanga East and Mokhotlong', *Social Dynamics* 42, no. 2 (2016): 273–88.

Moller, Valerie, Lawrence Schlemmer, Judson Kuzwayo, and Beata Mbanda. 'A black township in Durban: a study of needs and problems'. Durban: Centre for Applied Social Sciences, University of Natal, 1978.

Moodie, Dunbar. *Going for Gold: men, mines and migration*. Berkeley CA: University of California Press, 1994.

Moore, Elena. 'Transmission and change in South African motherhood: black mothers in three-generational Cape Town families', *Journal of Southern African Studies* 39, no. 1 (2013): 151–70.

Morrell, Robert. *From Boys to Gentlemen: settler masculinity in colonial Natal, 1880–1920*. Pretoria: UNISA Press, 2001.

Morrell, Robert and Relebohile Moletsane. 'Inequality and fear: learning and working inside Bantu education schools' in Peter Kallaway (ed.), *The History of Education under Apartheid*. Cape Town: Pearson, 2002.

Morris, Pauline. *A History of Black Housing in South Africa*. Johannesburg: South African Foundation, 1981.

Morrison, Alice. '"In-between": a study of domestic worker's children who have been informally fostered by their mother's employers'. Master's thesis, School of Built Environment and Development Studies, University of KwaZulu-Natal, Durban, 2015.

Mosoetsa, Sarah. *Eating from One Pot: the dynamics of survival in poor South African households*. Johannesburg: Wits University Press, 2011.

Motala, Shireen. 'Privatising public schooling in post-apartheid South Africa: equity considerations', *Compare: A Journal of Comparative and International Education* 39, no. 2 (2009): 185–202.

Motseke, Dieketseng. 'Call centre agents and class identity: a Johannesburg case study'. Master's thesis, Industrial Sociology, Faculty of Humanities, University of Johannesburg, Johannesburg, 2009.

Moultrie, Tom and Ian Timæus. 'Fertility and living arrangements in South Africa', *Journal of Southern African Studies* 27, no. 2 (2001): 207–23.

Mphahlele, Es'kia. *Es'Kia: education, African humanism and culture, social consciousness, literary appreciation*. Johannesburg: Kwela Books, 2002.

Msila, Vuyisile. 'School choice and intra-township migration: black parents scrambling for quality education in South Africa', *Journal of Education* 46 (2010): 81–98.

Mzobe, Sifiso. *Young Blood*. Kwela: Cape Town, 2010.

Ngwane, Zolani. '"Real men reawaken their fathers' homesteads, the educated leave them in ruins": the politics of domestic reproduction in post-apartheid rural South Africa', *Journal of Religion in Africa* 31, no. 4 (2001): 402–26.

Niehaus, Isak. 'Anthropology at the dawn of apartheid: Radcliffe-Brown and Malinowski's South African engagements, 1919–1934', *Focaal: Journal of Global and Historical Anthropology* 76, no. 3 (2017): 1–24.

'Disharmonious spouses and harmonious siblings: conceptualising household formation among urban residents in Qwaqwa', *African Studies* 53, no. 1 (1994): 115–35.

Ntombela, Thabisile. 'Investigating factors which influence parental school choice in post-apartheid South Africa: a case study of Umlazi Township'. Master's thesis, School of Development Studies, University of KwaZulu-Natal, 2013.

Nuttall, Sarah and Achille Mbembe (eds). *Johannesburg: the elusive metropolis*. Durham NC: Duke University Press, 2008.

Nzimande, Blade and Sandile Thusi. 'Children of war: the impact of political violence on schooling'. Durban: Education Policy Unit, University of Natal, 1996.

Nzimande, Bonginkosi [Blade]. 'The corporate guerillas: class formation and the African corporate petty bourgeoisie in post-1973 South Africa'. PhD thesis, University of Natal, Durban, 1991.

*The Olympian*. 'Mr. P. R. T. Nel', *The Olympian*, 1964.

O'Meara, Dan. *Volkskapitalisme: class, capital and ideology in the development of Afrikaner nationalism, 1934–1948*. Cambridge: Cambridge University Press, 1983.

Oosthuizen, Gerhardus. *Challenge to a South African University: the University of Durban-Westville*. Cape Town: Oxford University Press, 1981.

Orfield, Gary and Erica Frankenberg. *Educational Delusions? Why choice can deepen inequality and how to make schools fair*. Berkeley CA: University of California Press, 2013.

Oyewumi, Oyeronke. *The Invention of Women: making an African sense of Western gender discourses*. Minneapolis MN: University of Minnesota Press, 1997.

Parnell, Susan. 'Public housing as a device for white residential segregation in Johannesburg', *Urban Geography* 9, no. 6 (1988): 584–602.

Pauw, Berthold. *The Second Generation: a study of the family among urbanized Bantu in East London*. Cape Town: Oxford University Press, 1963.

Peberdy, Sally. *Selecting Immigrants: national identity and South Africa's immigration policies, 1910–2005*. Johannesburg: Wits University Press, 2009.

Piper, Laurence and Fiona Anciano. 'Party over outsiders, centre over branch: how ANC dominance works at the community level in South Africa', *Transformation* 87 (2015): 72–94.

Pirie, Gordon. 'White rail labour in South Africa 1873–1924' in Robert Morrell (ed.), *White but Poor: essays on the history of poor whites in Southern Africa 1880–1940*. Pretoria: University of South Africa Press, 1992.

Pithouse, Richard. *Writing the Decline: on the struggle for South Africa's democracy*. Cape Town: Jacana, 2016.

*Business as Usual? Housing rights and slum eradication in Durban, South Africa*. Geneva: Centre on Housing Rights and Evictions (COHRE), 2008.

Plank, David and Gary Sykes. *Choosing Choice: school choice in international perspective*. New York NY: Teachers College, 2003.

Platzky, Laurine and Cherryl Walker for the Surplus People Project. *The Surplus People: forced removals in South Africa*. Johannesburg: Ravan Press, 1985.

Posel, Deborah. 'Marriage at the drop of a hat: housing and partnership in South Africa's urban African townships, 1920s–1960s', *History Workshop Journal* 61, no. 1 (2006): 57–76.

'Race as common sense: racial classification in twentieth-century South Africa', *African Studies Review* 44, no. 2 (2001): 87–113.

'Whiteness and power in the South African civil service: paradoxes of the apartheid state', *Journal of Southern African Studies* 25, no. 1 (1999): 99–119.

*The Making of Apartheid: conflict and compromise.* Oxford: Oxford University Press, 1991.

'Curbing African urbanization' in Mark Swilling, Richard Humphries, and Khehla Shubane (eds), *Apartheid City in Transition.* Oxford: Oxford University Press, 1991.

'Rethinking the "race–class debate" in South African historiography', *Social Dynamics* 9, no. 1 (1983): 50–66.

Posel, Dorrit. 'Micro-data analysis of patterns and trends in eThekwini Municipality'. Report for eThekwini Municipality, January 2015.

'Moving on: patterns of labour migration in post-apartheid South Africa' in Marta Tienda, Sally Findley, and Stephen Tollman (eds), *Africa on the Move: African migration and urbanisation in comparative perspective.* Johannesburg: Witwatersrand University Press, 2006.

Posel, Dorrit and Erofili Graspa. 'Time to learn? Time allocations among children in South Africa', *International Journal of Educational Development* 56 (2017): 1–10.

Potts, Deborah and Shula Marks. 'Fertility in Southern Africa: the quiet revolution', *Journal of Southern African Studies* 27, no. 2 (2001): 189–205.

Pred, Allan. *Even in Sweden: racisms, racialized spaces and the popular geographical imagination.* Berkeley CA: University of California Press, 2000.

Preston-Whyte, Eleanor. 'Between two worlds: a study of the working life, social ties and inter-personal relationships of African women migrants in domestic service in Durban'. PhD thesis, University of Natal, Durban, 1969.

Radcliffe-Brown, Alfred. *Structure and Function in Primitive Society.* New York NY: Free Press, 1952.

Rahman, Tariq. 'Language ideology, identity and the commodification of language in the call centers of Pakistan', *Language in Society* 38 (2009): 233–58.

Randall, Peter. *Little England on the Veld: the English private schooling system in South Africa.* Athens OH: Ohio University Press, 1985.

Ravitch, Diane. *The Death and Life of the Great American School.* New York NY: Basic Books, 2010.

Reay, Diane. 'Tony Blair, the promotion of the "active" educational citizen, and middle-class hegemony', *Oxford Review of Education* 34, no. 6 (2008): 639–50.

'Cultural reproduction: mothers' involvement in their children's primary schooling' in Grenfell Michael and David James (eds), *Bourdieu and Education: acts of practical theory.* London: Routledge, 1998.

Reay, Diane, Gill Crozier, and David James. *White Middle-class Identities and Urban Schooling.* London: Palgrave, 2011.

Reddy, Vijay. 'The state of mathematics and science education: schools are not equal' in Sakhela Buhlungu, John Daniel, Roger Southall, and Jessica Lutchman (eds), *The State of the Nation: South Africa, 2005–2006.* Cape Town: HSRC Press, 2006.

Roberts, David and Minelle Mahtani. 'Neoliberalizing race, racing neoliberalism: placing "race" in neoliberal discourses', *Antipode* 42, no. 2 (2010): 248–57.

Robinson, Cedric. *Black Marxism: the making of the black radical tradition*. Chapel Hill NC: University of North Carolina Press, 2000.

Robinson, Jennifer. *Ordinary Cities: between modernity and development*. London: Routledge, 2005.

Roediger, David. *Class, Race, and Marxism*. London: Verso, 2017.

   *The Wages of Whiteness: race and the making of the American working class*. London: Verso, 1991.

Romero, Mary. *The Maid's Daughter: living inside and outside the American dream*. New York NY: NYU Press, 2011.

Rose, Brian and Raymond Tunmer. *Documents in South African Education*. Johannesburg: A. D. Donker, 2001.

Rose, Nikolas. *Powers of Freedom*. Cambridge: Cambridge University Press, 1999.

Rudwick, Stephanie. '"Coconuts" and "Oreos": English-speaking Zulu people in a South African township', *World Englishes* 27, no. 1 (2008): 101–16.

Sagner, Andreas. 'Ageing and social policy in South Africa: historical perspectives with particular reference to the Eastern Cape', *Journal of Southern African Studies* 26, no. 3 (2000): 523–53.

Sahlins, Marshall. *What Kinship Is – And Is Not*. Chicago IL: University of Chicago Press, 2013.

Sayed, Yusuf and Shireen Motala. 'Equity and "no fee" schools in South Africa: challenges and prospects', *Social Policy and Administration* 46, no. 6 (2012): 672–87.

Sayer, Andrew. *The Moral Significance of Class*. Cambridge: Cambridge University Press, 2005.

Schensul, Daniel and Patrick Heller. 'Legacies, change and transformation in the post-apartheid city: towards an urban sociological cartography', *International Journal of Urban and Regional Research* 35, no. 1 (2011): 78–109.

Schmidt, Elizabeth. *Peasants, Traders, and Wives: Shona women in the history of Zimbabwe, 1870–1939*. Portsmouth NH: Heinemann, 1992.

Scott, Dianne. 'Communal space construction: the rise and fall of Clairwood and district'. PhD thesis, Department of Geographical and Environmental Sciences, University of Natal, Durban, 1994.

Seekings, Jeremy. 'Taking disadvantage seriously: the "underclass" in post-apartheid South Africa', *Africa* 84, no. 1 (2014): 135–41.

   *A History of the United Democratic Front in South Africa, 1983–1991*. Athens OH: Ohio University Press, 2000.

Seekings, Jeremy and Nicoli Nattrass, *Policy, Politics and Poverty in South Africa*. London: Palgrave Macmillan, 2015.

   *Class, Race, and Inequality in South Africa*. New Haven CT: Yale University Press, 2005.

   'Class, distribution and redistribution in post-apartheid South Africa', *Transformation* 50 (2002): 1–30.

Selzer, Amy Kracker and Patrick Heller. 'The spatial dynamics of middle-class formation in postapartheid South Africa: enclavization and fragmentation in Johannesburg' in Julian Go (ed.), *Political Power and Social Theory. Volume 21*. Bingley: Emerald Publishing, 2010.

Sema, Osman and Andool Rahim. 'The Juma Mosque'. Local history project, lecturer Mr R. Morrell, History III, Documentation Centre, University of

Durban-Westville, Accession no. 903/13. Available at http://scnc.ukzn.ac.za/
doc/ThesisMini/Sema_OAR_juma_mosque_1881_onwards_Grey_Street_
Mosque.pdf (accessed 11 September 2018).

Sheik, Nafisa Essop 'Entangled patriarchies: sex, gender and relationality in the
forging of Natal: a paper presented in critical tribute to Jeff Guy', *South
African Historical Journal* 68, no. 3 (2016): 304–17.

Simons, Jack. *African Women: their legal status in South Africa*. London: C. Hurst,
1968.

Simpson, Anthony. *'Half-London in Zambia': contested identities in a Catholic
mission school*. London: Edinburgh University Press for the International
African Institute.

Skinner, Caroline and Imraan Valodia. 'Labour market policy, flexibility, and the
future of labour relations: the case of KwaZulu-Natal clothing industry',
*Transformation* 50 (2002): 56–76.

Soske, Jon. 'The impossible concept: settler liberalism, pan-Africanism, and
the language of non-racialism', *African Historical Review* 47, no. 2 (2015):
1–36.

Soudien, Crain. *Realising the Dream: unlearning the logic of race in the South African
school*. Cape Town: HSRC Press, 2012.

South African Government. 'Kwa-Zulu Natal no-fee schools, 2015'. Pretoria:
South African Government, Department of Education, 2015. Available at
www.education.gov.za/Portals/0/Documents/Publications/KZN%20No%
20Fee%20Schools%202015%20list.pdf?ver=2015-07-21-135945-233.

*Commission for Employment Equity: annual report 2014–2015*. Pretoria: South
African Government, Department of Labour, 2015.

*The Status of Women in the South African Economy*. Pretoria: South African
Government, Department of Women, 2015.

*NEIMS Standards Reports October 2014*. Pretoria: South African Government,
Department of Education, 2014.

*Provincial Budgets and Expenditure Review 2010/11 – 2016/17*. Pretoria: South
African Government, National Treasury, 2014.

*Education Management Information Systems: 2011 snap survey report for ordinary
schools*. Pietermaritzburg: South African Government, KwaZulu-Natal
Department of Education, 2012.

*General Household Survey (GHS) 2011: focus on schooling*. Pretoria: South
African Government, Department of Education, 2011.

*Diagnostic Overview*. Pretoria: South African Government, National Planning
Commission, Department of the Presidency, 2011. Available at
www.education.gov.za/Portals/0/Documents/Publications/National%20
Planning%20Commission%20Diagnostics%20Overview%20of%20the%
20country.pdf?ver=2015-03-19-134928-000.

*The State of Education in KwaZulu-Natal: a report for KZN Treasury*. Pietermaritzburg: South African Government, KwaZulu-Natal Department of
Education, 2010.

*Natal Code of Native Law*. Johannesburg: University of Witwatersrand Press,
1945.

South African Institute of Race Relations. *South Africa Survey 2016*. Johannesburg: South African Institute of Race Relations (SAIRR), 2016.

*First Steps to Healing the South African Family*. Johannesburg: South African
Institute of Race Relations (SAIRR), 2011.

*Race Relations Survey 1992/3*. Johannesburg: South African Institute of Race Relations (SAIRR), 1993.

*Race Relations Survey 1991/2*. Johannesburg: South African Institute of Race Relations (SAIRR), 1992.

*Race Relations Survey 1989/90*. Johannesburg: South African Institute of Race Relations (SAIRR), 1990.

Southall, Roger. *The New Black Middle Class in South Africa*. Johannesburg: Jacana Press , 2016.

Sparks, Stephen. 'Civil society, pollution and the Wentworth oil refinery', *Historia* 51, no. 1 (2006): 201–33.

Spaull, Nic. 'Poverty and privilege: primary school inequality in South Africa'. Working Papers 13/12. Stellenbosch: Department of Economics, Stellenbosch University, 2012.

Spiegel, Andrew. 'Migration, urbanisation and domestic fluidity'. *African Anthropology* II, no. 2 (1995): 90–113.

Srivastava, Prachi and Geoffrey Walford. 'Non-state actors in education in the Global South', *Oxford Review of Education* 42, no. 5 (2016): 491–4.

Stambach, Amy. *Lessons from Mount Kilimanjaro: schooling, community, and gender in East Africa*. New York NY: Routledge, 2000.

Standing, Guy. *The Precariat: the new dangerous class*. London: Bloomsbury Academic, 2011.

Statistics South Africa. *Community Survey 2016 in Brief*. Pretoria: South African Government, 2016.

*Youth Employment, Unemployment, Skills and Economic Growth, 1994–2014*. Pretoria: South African Government, 2014.

*Gender Statistics in South Africa, 2011*. Pretoria: South African Government, 2012.

'Population census 1991: Durban/Pinetown/Inanda/Chatsworth (03–01–14)'. Pretoria: South African Government, 1991.

'Population census 1980: Durban/Pinetown/Inanda (02–80–17)'. Pretoria: South African Government, 1985.

'Population census 1970: Metropolitan Area Durban (02–05–17)'. Pretoria: South African Government, 1977.

Steyn, Melissa. *Whiteness Just Isn't What It Used to Be: the master's narrative and the new South Africa*. Albany NY: SUNY Press, 2001.

Stiegel, Saren. 'What is the price of education? a look at the inefficacy of school fee policy on Kennedy Road', Abahlali baseMjondolo [online], 2006. Available at http://abahlali.org/node/917/

Struwig, Jare, Benjamin Roberts, Steven Gordon, and Yul Derek Davids. *Local Matters: results from the Electoral Commission of South Africa's Voter Participation Survey (VPS) 2015/16. Report prepared for the Electoral Commission of South Africa*. Pretoria: Human Sciences Research Council, 2016.

Swanson, Maynard. '"The Durban system": roots of urban apartheid in colonial Natal', *African Studies* 35, no. 3–4 (1976): 159–76.

Tabata, Isaac. *Education for Barbarism: Bantu (apartheid) education in South Africa*. London: Prometheus, 1959.

Taylor, Chris. *Geography of the 'New' Education Market: secondary schooling choice in England and Wales*. Aldershot: Ashgate, 2002.

Taylor, Phil and Peter Bain. 'United by a common language? Trade union responses in the UK and India to call centre offshoring', *Antipode* 40, no. 1 (2008): 131–54.

Teppo, Annika. *The Making of a Good White: a historical ethnography of the rehabilitation of poor whites in a suburb of Cape Town.* Helsinki: Helsinki University Press, 2004.

Thakur, Pravindra. 'Education for upliftment: a history of Sastri College 1927–1981'. Master's thesis, Department of History, University of Natal, Durban, 1992.

Thiem, Claudia Hanson. 'Thinking through education: the geographies of contemporary educational restructuring', *Progress in Human Geography* 33, no. 2 (2009): 154–73.

Thomas, Lynn. 'Skin lighteners, black consumers and Jewish entrepreneurs in South Africa', *History Workshop Journal* 73, no. 1 (2012): 259–83.

*Politics of the Womb: women, reproduction, and the state in Kenya.* Berkeley CA: University of California Press, 2003.

Tikly, Leon and Thabo Mabogoane. 'Marketisation as a strategy for desegregation and redress: the case of historically white schools in South Africa', *International Review of Education* 43, no. 2–3 (1997): 159–78.

Tilton, Doug. 'Creating an "educated workforce": Inkatha, big business, and educational reform in KwaZulu', *Journal of Southern African Studies* 18, no. 1 (1992): 166–89.

*The Torch.* 'Editorial', *The Torch* 7 (1966).

Torr, Louise. 'Lamontville – Durban's "model village": the realities of township life, 1934–1960', *Journal of Natal and Zulu History* 10 (1987): 103–17.

Trollope, Anthony. *South Africa. Vol. 1.* London: Chapman and Hall, 1878.

Troup, Freda. *Forbidden Pastures: education under apartheid.* London: International Defence and Aid Fund, 1977.

Truth and Reconciliation Canada, *Honouring the Truth, Reconciling for the Future.* Winnipeg: Truth and Reconciliation Commission of Canada, 2015.

University of Natal, Department of Economics. *The Durban Housing Survey: a study of housing in a multi-racial community.* Pietermaritzburg: University of Natal Press, 1952.

Unterhalter, Elaine. 'The impact of apartheid on women's education in South Africa', *Review of African Political Economy* 48 (1990): 66–75.

Vahed, Goolam. 'The Zanzibaris' in Ashwin Desai and Goolam Vahed (eds), *Chatsworth: the making of a South African township.* Pietermaritzburg: University of KwaZulu-Natal Press, 2013.

Vahed, Goolam and Thembisa Waetjen. *Schooling Muslims in Natal: identity, state, and the Orient Islamic Educational Institute.* Pietermaritzburg: University of KwaZulu-Natal Press, 2015.

Vally, Salim and Yolisa Dalamba. *Racism, 'Racial Integration' and Desegregation in South African Public Secondary Schools: a report on a study by the South African Human Rights Commission (SAHRC).* Johannesburg: South African Human Rights Commission, 1999.

Van der Merwe, Hendrick. *White South African Elites.* Cape Town: Juta, 1974.

Vandeyar, Saloshna and Jonathan Jansen. *Diversity High: class, culture, and character in a South African School.* Washington DC: University Press of America, 2008.

Van Onselen, Charles. 'The social and economic underpinning of paternalism and violence on the maize farms of the south-western Transvaal, 1900–1950', *Journal of Historical Sociology* 5, no. 2 (1992): 127–60.

*Studies in the Social and Economic History of the Witwatersrand, 1886–1914.* Johannesburg: Ravan Press, 1982.

Van Tonder, Jan. *Stargazer*. Cape Town: Human and Rousseau, 2006.

Vilikazi, Absolom. *Zulu Transformations: a study of the dynamics of social change*. Pietermaritzburg: University of Natal Press, 1962.

Von Holdt, Karl and Edward Webster. 'Work restructuring and the crisis of reproduction: a southern perspective' in Karl von Holdt and Edward Webster (eds), *Beyond the Apartheid Workplace: studies in transition*. Pietermaritzburg: University of KwaZulu-Natal Press, 2005.

Waetjen, Thembisa. *Workers and Warriors: masculinity and the struggle for nation in South Africa*. Urbana-Champaign IL: University of Illinois Press, 2004.

Wagner, Daniel. *Literacy, Culture, and Development: becoming literate in Morocco*. Cambridge: Cambridge University Press, 1993.

Walker, Cherryl. 'Conceptualising motherhood in twentieth-century South Africa', *Journal of Southern African Studies* 21, no. 3 (1995): 417–37.

Walrond, Lawrence Maxim. *Ratoon: tying the roots of my family name to my parents' lives*. Victoria: Friesen Press, 2015.

Waters, Johanna. 'Geographies of cultural capital: education, international migration and family strategies between Hong Kong and Canada', *Transactions of the Institute of British Geographers* 31 (2006): 179–92.

Watts, Hilstan, R. J. Davies, L. T. Croft, G. L. Trotter, G. G. Maasdcrp, P. N. Pillay, and L. Schlemmer. 'Group areas and the "Grey Street" complex, Durban'. Durban: Centre for Applied Social Sciences, University of Natal, 1971.

Weber, Max. 'The "specialist" and the "cultivated man": certificates and the origin of ideas in science' in Stephen Kalberg (ed.), *Max Weber: readings and commentary on modernity*. Oxford: Blackwell, 2005.

Webster, Edward. *Cast in a Racial Mould: labour process and trade unionism in the foundries*. Johannesburg: Ravan Press, 1985.

Weston, Kath. *Families We Choose: lesbians, gays, kinship*. New York NY: Columbia University Press, 1997.

White, Hylton. 'Tempora et mores: Family values and the possessions of a post-apartheid countryside', *Journal of Religion in Africa* XXXI, no. 4 (2001): 457–479.

Wilkins, Ivor and Hans Strydom. *The Super Afrikaners: inside the Afrikaner Broederbond*. Cape Town: Jonathan Ball, 1978.

Williams, Raymond. *Marxism and Literature*. New York NY: Oxford University Press, 1977.

Willis, Paul. *Learning to Labour: how working class kids get working class jobs*. New York NY: Columbia University Press, 1981 [1977].

Wilson, Monica and Archie Mafeje. *Langa: a study of social groups in an African township*. Cape Town: Oxford University Press, 1963.

Wolpe, Harold. *Race, Class and the Apartheid State*. London: James Currey, 1988.
'Capitalism and cheap labour power in South Africa: from segregation to apartheid', *Economy and Society* 1, no. 4 (1972): 425–56.

Wong, Margaret. 'Mass education in Africa', *African Affairs* 43, no. 172 (1944): 105–11.

Woolman, Stuart and Brahm Fleisch. 'South Africa's unintended experiment in school choice: how the National Education Policy Act, the South Africa Schools Act and the Employment of Educators Act create the enabling conditions for quasi-markets in schools', *Education and the Law* 18, no. 1 (2006): 31–75.

Wright, Lawrence (ed.). *South Africa's Education Crisis: views from the Eastern Cape*. Grahamstown: NISC (Pty) Ltd., 2012.

Zengele, Thulani. 'The unionization of the teaching profession and its effects on the South African education system: teacher unionism in South Africa', *Journal of Social Sciences* 35, no. 3 (2013): 231–9.

Zulu, Paulus. 'Durban hostels and political violence: case studies in KwaMashu and Umlazi', *Transformation* 21 (1993): 1–23.

## Archival sources

### Cullen Archives, University of the Witwatersrand, Johannesburg
National Education Union of South Africa (NEUSA) papers

### Durban Archives Repository, Durban
Bantu Affairs Commissioner's court records (uncatalogued and therefore accessed directly from the strong room)

### KwaZulu-Natal Archives Repository, Ulundi (all records are uncatalogued and therefore accessed directly from the strong room)
KwaZulu Government Services' school inspections reports
KwaZulu Cabinet minutes
Umlazi Township council meeting minutes

### Killie Campbell Africana Library, Durban
Bourquin papers
Port Natal Administration Board microfilm
*Natal Mercury*

### Pietermaritzburg Archives Repository, Pietermaritzburg
Natal Education Department records (uncatalogued and therefore accessed directly from the strong room)

### National Archive Repository, Pretoria
Various Umlazi Township records

# Index

Titles in the series

CPSIA information can be obtained
at www.ICGtesting.com
Printed in the USA
LVHW092112160420
653665LV00001B/27

9 781108 727631